INTRODUCTORY READINGS IN

ANTHROPOLOGY

INTRODUCTORY READINGS IN

ANTHROPOLOGY

Edited by

Hilary Callan, Brian Street and Simon Underdown

berghahn
NEW YORK · OXFORD
www.berghahnbooks.com

Royal Anthropological Institute

Published in 2013 by
Berghahn Books in association with the Royal Anthropological Institute
www.berghahnbooks.com

Library of Congress Cataloging-in-Publication Data

Introductory readings in anthropology / edited by Hilary Callan, Brian
Street and Simon Underdown.
    p. cm.
  Includes bibliographical references and index.
  ISBN 978-0-85745-968-8 (hardback) -- ISBN 978-0-85745-440-9
(hardback) -- ISBN 978-0-85745-969-5 (pbk.) -- ISBN 978-0-85745-995-4
(pbk.) 1. Anthropology--Textbooks. I. Callan, Hilary. II. Street, Brian. III.
Underdown, Simon.
  GN25.I58 2012

                                                              301--dc23

British Library Cataloguing in Publication Data

A catalogue record for this book is available from the British Library

Printed on acid-free paper

ISBN 978-0-85745-968-8 (hardback)
ISBN 978-0-85745-969-5 (paperback)
ISBN 978-0-85745-440-9 (ebook)

The Royal Anthropological Institute runs a comprehensive education
programme which includes information, events and resources for
people interested in anthropology. For more information visit
www.discoveranthropology.org.uk

Contents

III.1   Anthropological Approaches to the Movement of Peoples, Patterns and Processes

Approaches from Biological Anthropology and Archaeology: Adaptation, Dispersal and Diversity, Migration, Disease

Approaches from Social Anthropology: Globalization

III. 2   Local and Global Processes: Ethnographic Perspectives

SECTION IV. PRACTISING ANTHROPOLOGY
METHODS AND INVESTIGATIONS

SECTION V. ANTHROPOLOGY IN THE WORLD

Acknowledgements

The editors and the publisher would like to thank the following for granting permission for the reproduction of material under copyright.

1. 'What Is Natural Selection?' extract from *Principles of Human Evolution* © 1998, R. Lewin and R. Foley. Reproduced with permission by Blackwell Publishers.

2. 'Explaining the Very Improbable', extract from *The Blind Watchmaker* © 1988, Richard Dawkins. Reproduced with permission by Richard Dawkins and Penguin Books.

3. 'What Is Sexual Selection?', extract from *Principles of Human Evolution* © 1998, R. Lewin and R. Foley. Reproduced with permission by Blackwell Publishers.

6. *An Evolving Tale*, © 2007, Simon Underdown, originally published in *The Guardian*.

7. *Race Against Time*, © 2007, Simon Underdown. Originally published in *The Guardian*.

8. *Dem Bones*, © 2007, Simon Underdown. Originally published in *The Guardian*.

9. 'Representations of Non-European Society in Popular Fiction', extract from *The Savage in Literature: Representations of 'Primitive' Society in English Fiction, 1858–1920* © 1975, Brian Street. Reproduced with permission by Routledge Publishing.

10. 'Unravelling 'Race' For The Twenty-first Century', extract from J. MacClancy (ed.), *Exotic No More: Anthropology on the Front Line.* © 2002, Faye V. Harrison. Reproduced with permission by Chicago University Press.

11. 'The Body: Subjugated and Unsexed', taken from 'Privileged, Schooled and Finished: Boarding Education for Girls', extract from S. Ardener (ed.), *Defining Females: The Nature of Women in Society.* © 1978, Judith Okely. Reproduced with permission by Croom Helm Publishers, an imprint of Bloomsbury Publishing.

12. 'How Humans Are Different', taken from 'Why are Humans not just Great Apes?' extract from C. Pasternak (ed.), *What Makes Us Human?* © 2007, Robin Dunbar. Reproduced with permission by OneWorld Books.

13. 'Technical Difficulties and Hopeful Monsters', extract from *The Symbolic Species: The Co-evolution of Language and the Human Brain* © 1997, Terrence Deacon. Reproduced with permission by WW Norton.

14. Extract from *The Savage Mind* © 1966, Claude Lévi-Strauss. Reproduced with permission by W&N Publishers.

15. 'Witchcraft Beliefs', extract from *Social Anthropology* © 1966, Estate of Godfrey Lienhardt. Reproduced with permission by Dr Ahmed Al-Shahi.

16. 'The Ethnographic Study of Language and Communication', extract from *Ethnography: Approaches to Language and Literacy* © 2008, Shirley Heath and Brian Street. Reproduced with permission by NCRLL/Centage.

17. Extract from *Language in Late Modernity* © 2006, Ben Rampton. Reproduced with permission by Cambridge University Press.

18. 'Everyday Literacies In Africa', extract from *Everyday Literacies in Africa: Ethnographic Studies of Literacy and Numeracy in Ethiopia* © 2009, A.H. Gebre, A. Rogers, Brian Street and G. Openjuru. Reproduced with permission by Fountain Publishers.

19. Extract from *Multimodal Discourse: The Modes and Media of Contemporary Communication.* © 2001, G. Kress and T. van Leeuwen. Reproduced with permission by Arnold Publishing, an imprint of Bloomsbury Publishing Plc.

20. 'The Semantics of Biology', extract from *Defining Females: the Nature of Women in Society*, edited by S Ardener © 1978, Kirsten Hastrup. Reproduced with permission by Bloomsbury Academic, an imprint of Bloomsbury Publishing Plc.

21. '"Ladies" behind Bars', John M. Coggeshall, extract from '"Ladies" behind Bars: A Liminal Gender as Cultural Mirror', published in *Anthropology Today*; reprinted in J. Benthall (ed.), *The Best of Anthropology Today* (London: Routledge, 2002) © 1988, Royal Anthropological Institute.

22. Social Views of the Environment, extract from *An Introduction to Social Anthropology: Sharing Our Worlds*, 2nd edn. © 2008, Joy Hendry. Reproduced with permission by Palgrave Macmillan.

23. 'Badger Culling in North Pembrokeshire', Pat Caplan, extract from 'Death on the Farm: Culling Badgers in North Pembrokeshire', published in *Anthropology Today* © 2010, Royal Anthropological Institute.

24. 'The Whaling War', Adrian Peace, extract from 'The Whaling War: Conflicting Cultural Perspectives', published in *Anthropology Today* © 2010, Royal Anthropological Institute.

25. 'Ducks out of Water: Nature Conservation as Boundary Maintenance', in J. Knight (ed.), *Natural Enemies: People–Wildlife Conflict in Anthropological Perspective.* © 2000, Kay Milton. Reproduced with permission by Routledge.

26. 'Feminine Power at Sea', Silvia Rodgers, extract from 'Feminine Power at Sea', published in *RAIN (Royal Anthropological Institute News)*; reprinted in J. Benthall (ed.), *The Best of Anthropology Today* (London: Routledge, 2002) © 1984, Royal Anthropological Institute.

27. 'Why Clothing Is Not Superficial', extract from *Stuff* © 2010, Daniel Miller. Reproduced with permission by Polity Press.

28. 'The Social Character of Humanity', extract from *Small Places, Large Issues: An Introduction to Social and Cultural Anthropology*, 2nd edn. © 2001, T.H. Eriksen. Reproduced with permission by Pluto Press.

29. Extract from *Anthropology of the Self: The Individual in Cultural Perspective* © 1994, Brian Morris. Reproduced with permission by Pluto Press.

30. 'Rites of Passage', extract from *An Introduction to Social Anthropology: Sharing Our Worlds, 2nd edn.* © 2008, Joy Hendry. Reproduced with permission by Palgrave Macmillan.

33. 'Gypsy Women: Models in Conflict', in S. Ardener (ed.), *Perceiving Women* © 1996, Judith Okely. Reproduced with permission by Routledge Publishing.

34. Extract from *The Ritual Process*. ©1966, Victor Turner and Aldine Publishers. Reprinted by permission of AldineTransaction, a division of Transaction Publishers.

39. 'Globalization', extract from *Globalization: The Key Concepts* © 2007, T.H. Eriksen. Reproduced with permission by Berg Publishers, an imprint of Bloomsbury Publishing.

40. 'Looking "The Gift" in the Mouth', extract from "Looking 'The Gift' in the mouth: Russia as donor", published in *Anthropology Today* © 2011, RAI. Reproduced with permission by the Royal Anthropological Institute.

41. 'Anthropology, the Environment and Development', extract from *Bush base: forest farm* © 1992, E. Croll and D. Parkin. Reproduced with permission by Routledge.

42. 'Anthropology at the Bottom of the Pyramid', extract from 'Anthropology at the bottom of the pyramid', published in *Anthropology Today* © 2009, RAI. Reproduced with permission by the Royal Anthropological Institute.

43. 'Japanese Hip-Hop and the Globalization of Popular Culture', extract from *Urban Life: Readings in the Anthropology of the City* (4th edn) © 2008, I. Condry. Reproduced with permission by Pearson.

44. 'Helping or Hindering? Controversies around the International Second-hand Clothing Trade', extract from 'Helping or hindering?: Controversies around the international second-hand clothing trade' published in *Anthropology Today* © 2004, RAI. Reproduced with permission by the Royal Anthropological Institute.

45. 'The Kayapo Resistance', extract from 'The Role of Indigenous Peoples in the Environmental Crisis: The Example of the Kayapo of the Brazilian Amazon' published in *Perspectives in Biology and Medicine* © 2008, T. Turner. Reproduced with permission by Pearson.

46. 'Tourism', extract from *Globalization: The Key Concepts* © 2007, T. H. Eriksen. Reproduced with permission by Berg Publishers, an imprint of Bloomsbury Publishing.

47. 'Foreword' to *Thinking through Tourism*, extract from *Thinking Through Tourism* © 2010, M. E. Kenna. Reproduced with permission by Berg Publishers, an imprint of Bloomsbury Publishing.

48. 'The Road to Refugee Resettlement', extract from *Conformity and Conflict* (11th edn) © 2008, D. Shandy. Reproduced with permission by author.

49. 'Cults: The Persistence of Religious Movements', extract from *An Introduction to Social Anthropology: Sharing Our Worlds* (2nd edn) © 2008, J. Hendry. Reproduced with permission by Palgrave.

50. 'The Power of Mary in Papua New Guinea', extract from 'The power of Mary in Papua New Guinea' published in *Anthropology Today* © 2007, RAI. Reproduced with permission by the Royal Anthropological Institute.

51. 'Arsenal in Bugamba: The Rise of English Premier League Football in Uganda', extract from 'Arsenal in Bugamba: the rise of English Premier League football in Uganda' published in *Anthropology Today* © 2010, RAI. Reproduced with permission by the Royal Anthropological Institute.

52. 'Journeys through Ethnography', extract from *Journeys through Ethnography; realistic accounts of fieldwork* © 1996, A. Lareau and J. Schultz. Reproduced with permission by Westview Press.

53. 'Fieldwork Styles: Bohannan, Barley and Gardner', extract from *Popularizing Anthropology* © 1996, J. MacClancy. Reproduced with permission by Routledge.

54. 'The 'Problem' of Women', extract from *Perceiving Women* © 1989, E. Ardener. Reproduced with permission by Basil Blackwell.

55. 'Notes on (Field) Notes', extract from *Fieldnotes: the making of anthropology* © 1990, J. Clifford. Reproduced with permission by Cornell University Press.

56. 'Interpretation and Analysis', extract from *Reading Ethnography* © 1990, D. Jacobson. Reproduced with permission by State University of New York Press.

57. 'Ethnography as Democratic', extract from *Ethnography, Linguistics, Narrative Inequality: towards an understanding of voice* © 1996, D. Hymes. Reproduced with permission by Taylor & Francis.

58. 'The Turtle and the Fish' Extract from: http://www.beyondthenet.net/dhamma/nibbanaTurtle.htm © Mrs Yuri Siriname. Reproduced with permission.

59. 'My Kind of Anthropology', extract from *Social Anthropology* © 1982, E. Leach. Reproduced with permission by HarperCollins.

60. 'Writing Ourselves: The Mass-Observation Project', extract from *Writing Ourselves: Mass-Observation and Literacy Practices* © 2000, D. Sheridan, B. Street and D. Bloome. Reproduced with permission by Hampton Press.

61. 'Extracts from the Code of Ethics of the American Association of Physical Anthropologists' © American Physical Anthropology Association. Reproduced with permission.

62. 'The Story of Seventeen Tasmanians', extract from 'The Story of Seventeen Tasmanians and the Question of Repatriation', published in the *Newcastle Law Review* © 2009, *Newcastle Law Review*. Reproduced with permission by the *Newcastle Law Review*.

63. 'Extracts from the Ethical Guidelines of the Association of Social Anthropologists of the UK and the Commonwealth' © Association of Social Anthropologists of the UK and the Commonwealth. Reproduced with permission.

64. 'The House of Difference', extract from *The House of Difference: cultural politics and national identity in Canada* © 2002, E. Mackey. Reproduced with permission by Taylor & Francis.

65. 'Fool's Gold', extract from *Fool's Gold: how unrestrained greed corrupted a dream, shattered global markets and unleashed a catastrophe* © 2010, G. Tett. Reproduced with permission by Little, Brown Ltd and Curtis Brown/ICM.

66. 'Organ Donation, Genetics, Race and Culture', extract from 'Organ donation, genetics, race and culture: The making of a medical problem' published in *Anthropology Today* © RAI, 2011. Reproduced with permission by the Royal Anthropological Institute.

67. 'The Anthropology of Science', extract from *Exotic No More: anthropology on the front lines* © 2002, S. Franklin. Reproduced with permission by Chicago University Press.

68. 'The Second Nuclear Age', extract from 'Ethnography in/of the World System: the Emergence of Multi-sited Ethnography', published in *Annual Review of Anthropology* © 2007, H. Gusterson. Reproduced with permission by Berg Publishers, an imprint of Bloomsbury Publishing.

69. 'W(h)ither Anthropology?' extract from 'W(h)ither anthropology? Opening up or closing down' published in *Anthropology Today* © RAI, 2010. Reproduced with permission by the Royal Anthropological Institute.

70. 'Why Anthropology Matters', extract from *Engaging Anthropology: The case for a public presence* © 2006, T. H. Eriksen. Reproduced with permission by Berg Publishers, an imprint of Bloomsbury Publishing.

Cover Art Credits: filmstill from *Going for the Kill. A Very English Village* by Luke Holland (RAI Film Festival 2007); filmstill from *The Seeker* by Philippe Cornet (RAI Film Festival 2007); filmstill from *Dancing Kathmandu* by Sangita Shresthova (RAI Film Festival 2007); *Braveness and the Gaze of Others* by Henrik Hvenegaard (RAI Photo Contest 2010); *Kula Ring Sailing Canoe* by Klaus Eiberle (RAI Photo Contest 2010); filmstill from *Bunong's Birth Practice* by Tommi Mendel (RAI Film Festival

2011); *The Joy of Belonging* by Kabir Orlowski (RAI Photo Contest 2011); filmstill from *Duka's Dilemma* by Jean Lydall (Winner of RAI Film Festival 2003).

The editors and publisher wish to record grateful thanks to the Director of the Royal Anthropological Institute, David Shankland; to the Institute's staff, especially Amanda Vinson, Nafisa Fera and Susanne Hammacher; and to the members of the RAI's Education Committee, especially David Bennett, Peggy Froerer, Joy Hendry and Judith Okely, for their help in selecting and preparing the content of the Reader.

A Note on Original Sources

While some of the content has been written specially for the Reader, most of the material included here has been extracted from longer original sources, and selectively edited in order to illustrate the chosen themes. Many internal references and footnotes have been omitted to render the texts as self-contained and coherent as possible. A full reference to the passage(s) included is given at the end of each extract, together with the references to other works that have been retained in the edited versions. Readers are encouraged to pursue their interests by following up the full versions of the books and articles extracted here.

General Introduction

Hilary Callan, Brian Street and Simon Underdown

Anthropology has often been called 'the most humanistic of the sciences, and the most scientific of the humanities'. If you are encountering the subject for the first time, whether as a student or out of general interest and curiosity, you will quickly discover two things about it. The first is that the broad term 'anthropology' embraces an enormous range of topics and approaches, whose common factor is that they all relate to how we think about living as a human being in society. The second is that at the root of all this diversity and detail, anthropology asks some fundamental general questions: what is it to be human? How do we come to be as we are? What do we have in common as human beings? And in what ways do we differ from one place, time or cultural setting to another?

This Reader aims to provide a sample of original writings drawn from different areas of anthropology and different periods of time to illustrate the enormous scope and range of the discipline. In selecting and presenting the content, the editors have had two purposes equally in view. The first is to make original writings available in an easily accessible form to support teachers and students of anthropology at pre-university level. The design therefore follows the broad format of a General Certificate of Education Advanced Level (pre-university) course now being taught in the U.K. The second is to bring together extracts from original work chosen to appeal to all readers, including those who may be new to anthropology and want to find out more about it.

The material is organised around themes that follow the broad structure of the A Level course. Each section of the reader corresponds to a unit of the A Level course. In Section I 'Being Human: Unity and Diversity', we look at the body and how it is interpreted in anthropology; at ways of thinking and communicating; at how social relations are organised; and at ways of engaging with nature, the environment and human-made objects. Section II, 'Becoming a Person: Identity and Belonging', illustrates anthropologists' ideas about personhood as socially constituted, and ways of defining social boundaries and groups. Sections III and IV of the Reader correspond to the third and fourth units of the course and include material on the themes of globalisation (local and global processes); the practice of anthropology; and anthropological ethics, methods and investigations. A specially written book, *Anthropology: A Beginners' Guide* (Hendry and Underdown, 2012) also follows the broad structure of the anthropology A level course, and is a valuable resource for students and others.

If you approach the Reader by skimming the titles and contents of the extracts, your first reaction will probably be one of bewilderment at the sheer diversity of the topics we touch on – from nature conservation campaigns to witchcraft beliefs, from human evolution to fashion and style, and from the repatriation of indigenous human remains to research on literacy. This eclecticism is deliberate. Like any contemporary discipline, anthropology has roots in the history of ideas, but there is no single 'story of anthropology'. Anthropology as now understood and practised has its origins in a number of intellectual traditions. These reach back to the ancient Greeks, and continue through the European Enlightenment of the eighteenth century and the nineteenth-century debates over evolution, 'man's place in nature', and the impacts of colonial expansion. In recent years, views about human life that come from outside the Western tradition of thought have asserted themselves within anthropology, which is in consequence becoming more like a set of dialogues between world traditions. You can read more about this intellectual history in a number of good books, such as T.H. Eriksen's *A History of Anthropology* (Eriksen 2001). Further information about the scope of anthropology can be found on the dedicated website of the Royal Anthropological Institute's educational outreach programme (www.discoveranthropology.org.uk).

One result of these many influences on the development of anthropology has been the emergence of specialisms and divisions within the discipline, of which the most important has been that between biological anthropology (broadly, the study of human evolution and physical variation) and social and cultural anthropology (broadly, the comparative, in-depth study of contemporary societies and cultures). For much of the twentieth century – and more so in the U.K. and continental Europe than in the U.S. where a more integrated approach prevailed – there was a tendency for these main branches of anthropology to go their separate ways, and intellectual communication across the biological-cultural divide tended to be limited. In recent years, and especially since the beginning of this century, we are seeing more sharing of ideas and findings among anthropologists across the divisions, and as a result new insights are beginning to emerge in answer to the fundamental anthropological question: what is it to be human?

In reading some of the extracts we have included, you will notice signs of these differences of approach. Again this is deliberate. The intention is to show, through the writings included here, that there is no single 'voice of anthropology' to answer all the questions the subject throws up. Rather, we suggest you think of a series of conversations – sometimes of debates – between different anthropological interpretations of the themes we touch on.

We hope that, in using the Reader, you do not take the themes we have selected as rigidly circumscribed or self-contained. There are many connections between them, as you will quickly find. To give just two examples: we include material on ways of thinking about race and ethnicity which bears on all our themes – and many others we could have chosen. We include passages from different writers in these fields and we also include a selection from a book that deals more with the literary representations of such themes in popular fiction that might raise echoes for many readers today. Similarly, the passages by Judith Okely on a girls' boarding school in 1950s England, and by Daniel Miller on how to wear a sari, powerfully illuminate both the ways in which social forces discipline the body, and how dress is used to express social and spiritual meanings and distinctions. If you are following a formal course of study in anthropology, you will find it valuable to return time and again to material included in the Reader as your knowledge deepens of the themes and their interconnections.

One further thing you will notice in the Reader is that anthropology is concerned both with events and processes in the distant evolutionary past that have shaped our humanity, and with the realities of human life in the here and now. Many people, if you ask them what they think anthropologists study, will answer in terms of either bones and fossils, or exotic customs among supposedly 'primitive' peoples remote from the Western mainstream. This impression is reinforced by a great deal of what you will see in the media and in films and on television. It is of course true that anthropologists are interested in the physical evidence of human origins. And a rapidly developing specialism – forensic anthropology – can tell us much about more recent remains, including those of victims of present-day crimes and genocides. Equally, social anthropologists have created a rich record based on the in-depth study of small-scale, sometimes pre-literate societies across the world. Many of these societies were under colonial rule at the time that now classic studies were carried out. But it is quite wrong to assume, as the Victorians routinely did, that these small-scale societies are 'relics' of earlier periods of human development. Indeed, the best of the classic studies (some examples of which are included here) have yielded insights that are of universal relevance to understanding the human condition. Equally, contemporary anthropologists are interested in the social dynamics of the present-day industrial and post-industrial world – including the cyber-world of online networks and relationships. The Reader as a whole should convince you that anthropology is a thoroughly up-to-date subject with much to tell us about all the worlds we live in. As the extracts show, an anthropological approach can shed as much light on (for example) attitudes to 'nature' as revealed in topical controversies over Japanese whaling, species conservation and badger-culling in Wales, as on the equally significant (to the community concerned) traditional ritual practices of an African people such as the Ndembu.

The Reader is divided into four sections, each of which is prefaced with brief signposts to help you navigate through the material. Other 'landmarks' will be found in the linking passages that introduce each extract.

A final word to the user: we are very aware that our themes and selections do not by any means cover the whole of anthropology. Indeed, we realise that huge areas of anthropological enquiry are not covered or even mentioned throughout the Reader. Rather, we hope in these selections to offer you just a glimpse of the subject, and give some hints to help you venture more deeply into the field. We hope that through these selected extracts we have succeeded in awakening your interest, and that as a result you might want to follow up other directions for yourself.

References
Eriksen, T.H. *A History of Anthropology* (London: Pluto Press, 2001).

Hendry, J. and S. Underdown. *Anthropology: A Beginners' Guide* (Oxford: Oneworld Books, 2011).

SECTION I

BEING HUMAN
UNITY AND DIVERSITY

Introduction to Section I

Hilary Callan, Brian Street and Simon Underdown

This first section of the Reader illustrates some key ongoing themes in contemporary anthropology that address our understanding of our common humanity, set alongside the particularities of culture, history and environment that are equally constitutive of the human condition.

I.1 Evolutionary Process and Human Origins

The body form we share as biological humans is the product of a long and complex process of evolution. The passages included here from writings by Lewin and Foley and Dawkins briefly introduce the principles of natural and sexual selection, as first outlined in the nineteenth century by Charles Darwin and elaborated (in some cases corrected) by later scientists. At various points in the Reader, we will look at views of 'nature' and of humanity's relationship to natural events and processes. At this point, it is worth reflecting on what our scientific knowledge of evolution means for our understanding of ourselves. What do you think an understanding of evolutionary processes can or cannot tell us about our experience as human beings? Can the theory of sexual selection, for example, shed light on male and female relations in the present day – and how would we decide this? In more general terms, as Darwin realised, the theory of natural selection shows how essentially random processes can give rise to an appearance of 'design' in the living world. As such, the theory provides an alternative explanation to one of the classical arguments for the existence of a cosmic designer (this is known in the Western philosophical tradition as the 'argument from design'). Anthropologists and other scholars have, however, long recognised the richness and variety of beliefs about the cosmos, across the world and over time. Do you think that there are ways of looking at religious and spiritual experience that do not conflict with a Darwinian scientific understanding? Anthropologists are interested in all these questions, which most of us will also recognise as among the most pressing and urgent of our time.

In the next passage, Simon Underdown, an evolutionary anthropologist, takes up the story of human evolution, emphasising how fluid, patchy and changeable our understanding currently is compared to what seemed a relatively clear picture only a few years ago. Underdown mentions the relationship between modern humans and Neanderthals, and this is elaborated in our next extract, written for the Reader by Chris Stringer. Stringer takes us back in time to this fascinating, mysterious species, long held to be genetically distinct from the modern humans who emerged from Africa in the last 100,000 years and gradually replaced them in Europe and Asia. He shows that according to the latest genomic evidence, the 'human species boundary' may be rather less clear-cut than was previously thought, and that certain present-day human populations may retain some Neanderthal ancestry. Underdown's next passage ('An Evolving Tale') makes an intriguing connection between our current concerns over global climate change, and the role climate change itself probably played in the remote past in shaping the course of human evolution. In the long perspective of evolutionary time, what we may think of as a contemporary crisis – albeit one that is scientifically well-grounded – actually has a very long history indeed.

I.2 The Body

Our next group of extracts have been chosen to illustrate some of the contrasting ways in which anthropologists and other scholars have approached ideas of race and ethnicity. The topic of 'race' is always a sensitive one, not least within anthropology. It cannot, however, be ignored, partly because the long struggles to combat crude racial ideas – and their use as a justification for discrimination, exploitation and oppression – are themselves part of the story of anthropology, as they are part of the broader historical movements for social justice that the past couple of centuries have seen. In his article 'Race Against Time', Simon Underdown demonstrates that crude stereotypes based on the idea of separate and circumscribed 'races' are not supported by science. As anyone can see, and as Underdown points out, modern human physical variation is real; but it is genetically superficial and relatively recent in evolutionary time. Underdown's next passage, 'Dem Bones', shows how the racial ideas of Europeans in the eighteenth and nineteenth centuries informed both the virtual extermination of many peoples and cultures, and the collection of human remains which now constitute, in many cases, our only evidence of the human physical diversity that prevailed until quite recent times. Underdown points to a dilemma that comes up again and again, both in anthropology and in public policy: how to reconcile surviving indigenous peoples' claims to the remains of their ancestors held in scientific collections with the unique knowledge that scientific analysis of ancestral remains can often yield and make available to the world – including their descendants. What do you think about this dilemma? Who should have 'rights' in the artefacts and physical remains of human populations?

From these questions about the relationship between ideas of 'race' and what science can tell us, we turn to two very different passages. Anthropologists have often found in literary works, and other forms of fiction, a good guide to popular thinking about unfamiliar peoples and cultures. Brian Street is a social anthropologist whose work on language and literacy we will meet later in the Reader. The next extract, taken from his book *The Savage in Literature*, summarises how many well-known nineteenth-century novelists called upon theories of 'race' in explaining cultural diversity amongst the people they describe, fictional accounts being often based closely on the author's personal experiences in foreign parts. Consider whether such ideas may still be found in contemporary literary works, or other forms of fiction (think of films such as *Avatar*, for example).

Our next extract is taken from an article by Faye V. Harrison, an African-American anthropologist who grew up with racial discrimination as a daily reality.

This early experience – and challenging it – contributed to her decision to become an anthropologist; and the extracts from her article show how, in the globalising world of this century, ideas of race are interacting with distinctions of class, nationality, wealth and gender to create more complex and shifting forms of inequality than those based on crude, pseudo-scientific racial stereotyping alone.

One conclusion we can draw from these contrasting passages is that the concept of human 'races' is not constant. Rather, it has its own history, in which it has undergone multiple shifts and twists according to particular circumstances. Reflect on how the idea plays out in your own experience. To what extent, if at all, does the concept of 'race' have a consistent application in social policy and practice as it affects our lives today?

Our earlier extracts focused on the body as a physical entity. Consideration of 'race', however, shows that the human body is never 'just' a physical object. It always has social meanings and values mapped onto it – in the case of 'race', for example, those attached to differences of skin pigmentation, facial features, hair type and so forth. A particular focus for recent anthropologists has been precisely on ways in which the body is represented as a social, as well as a physical, entity. Consider the endless ways in which the body is displayed, judged, valued, controlled and modified in response to social expectations. Shifts in fashion, norms of sexual attractiveness, attitudes to age, body modifications such as dieting, body building, tattooing and cosmetic surgery, are obvious examples. You can probably think of many other, sometimes less obvious, ways in which aspects of the body are socially judged as more, or less, acceptable and desirable. Here we include an extract from an article by Judith Okely, in which she applies an anthropological analysis to her own memories of being a pupil at an English girls' boarding school in the 1950s. Okely shows in fine detail how forcefully the values and discipline of the school succeeded in controlling all aspects of the girls' bodily expression through requirements of dress, 'deportment' and acceptable manner. If you are a student in a school or college today, this may seem to you an utterly alien world. But do you think there are any social rules in your own contemporary experience – official or unspoken – about how you present yourself and manage your body?

I.3 Ways of Thinking and Communicating

Human thought and communication are unique among species. While non-human animals can communicate in a variety of ways, human language is deeply different from animal signalling. It also seems to be hard-wired into the human makeup. Children born into different language communities learn their own language very easily at a particular stage of development; no normal child ever fails to acquire a language. The evolutionary origins of true language have long been debated in anthropology, and the debates continue. In the next of our extracts, two evolutionary anthropologists consider the origins of the human capacity for true language. Robin Dunbar looks at the differences between humans and our nearest relatives, the great apes, and concludes that the fundamental difference between us and them lies in the human capacity, through language, to step back from immediate experience and create imagined worlds. We humans, he argues, can not only imagine worlds that are not present to us, but can talk to one another about them, thus opening the way to the emergence of uniquely human attributes such as the capacity for self-awareness, literature and religion. Terrence Deacon argues, in parallel, that human language is not just a more developed or 'evolved' version of animal communication, but is something fundamentally different in kind: unique to the human line.

With language goes the capacity to classify – that is, to place things, people and ideas into groups and categories according to some system of similarity and difference. We humans do this all the time, as a moment's thought will show. But however obvious and 'natural' our own systems of classification may appear to us, they are in fact highly variable from one society to another. To take a single example, the English language groups some of a person's relatives together under the terms 'uncle', 'aunt' and 'cousin'. Speakers of English (and many other languages) think of these as relatives of the same kind. Yet it is extremely common in other societies to make a distinction between relatives on one's father's and those on one's mother's side, calling them by different names, and relating to them in sharply differing ways. In the kinship classification of such societies, one's mother's sister and father's sister are entirely different kinds of relative, whereas in the English system they are both one's 'aunts'. The English system, again, lumps together first cousins on the father's and mother's sides. But in other systems, not only are these kinds of 'cousin' sharply differentiated, but you might be expected to marry someone on one side and forbidden from marrying anyone on the other. Our extract, taken from a classic work of anthropology by the French scholar Claude Lévi-Strauss, illustrates the subtlety and intellectual sophistication of systems of classification far removed from those familiar to – and often taken for granted by – Westerners.

Organising the world within systems of classification goes hand in hand with the universal human need to find explanations. As has been famously said, 'stuff happens' – and much of what happens in life is not to anyone's liking: misfortune, illness, bad harvests, natural or man-made calamities, death itself. In the West we tend to assume that such events have rational causes amenable to scientific explanation. But we still seem to need a concept of chance, accident or randomness, to explain how misfortune strikes in particular instances. We know from medical and epidemiological research that if you smoke you increase your chances of getting lung cancer; and from earth science that some zones are earthquake-prone. But when cancer strikes one heavy smoker and not another, or the earthquake buries one family and not their neighbours, there is still the tendency to ask 'why did it happen to this individual at this moment?' and to answer in terms of fate, chance, blame or (perhaps) religious belief. This phenomenon – sometimes called the 'particularity of misfortune', or more colloquially the 'why me? question' – is a universal human conundrum, and societies have devised different logical systems to understand and cope with it. One of the best known of these is that of the Azande, a Sudanese people studied by the anthropologist E.E. Evans-Pritchard in the late 1920s. Here we include an extract from Godfrey Lienhardt's account of Evans-Pritchard's analysis of Azande ways of explaining misfortune. This shows that the Azande are as practical as anyone else in dealing with the world. But their beliefs and practices relating to witchcraft provide both a logically watertight system for explaining particular bad events, and a powerful formula for dealing with them, for confronting tensions, and for restoring social relationships.

Think about the different ways we have in the West of accounting for misfortune in particular cases. Are our explanations always logical and consistent? For example, under what circumstances do we hold people responsible for their poverty, homelessness or obesity, or their addiction to alcohol, drugs, shopping or gambling – and how far do politics and self-interest enter into such judgments?

From the evolution of language, classification, and systems of logic for dealing with the world, we move to ways in which contemporary anthropologists approach the study of language itself. The extracts that follow also introduce insights into how anthropologists enter the field, the kinds of questions they take with them, and how these questions come to be continually rethought and refined as research progresses. Shirley Heath and Brian Street are social anthropologists who have both specialised in the study of language and literacy, and the complex skills these demand. The passages reproduced here from their book *Ethnography: Approaches to Language and Literacy* illustrate graphically the importance of looking at people's speaking, writing and communication not as 'things' in isolation but as existing within the total context and fabric of their lives. This openness to context is fundamental to anthropology. Reflect on your own experience of the ways language is used, especially in education. Are you conscious of using different language and literacy practices in different settings (classroom, home, street, etc.) and are there pressures to use spoken and written language in particular ways in each situation? Issues of language and power become central, then, to the understanding of forms of communication, whether spoken, written or visual.

The next three extracts look in depth at such anthropological approaches to language, ethnicity, literacy and education. In the passage from Rampton's *Language in Late Modernity*, we see anthropologists coming to recognise that varieties of language are not rigidly tied to particular social or ethnic groups. Rather, people use language in very fluid and creative ways to achieve their ends in contexts that shift and are often ambiguous. The importance of this approach, in practical and policy terms, is illustrated in the extract that follows from Gebre, Rogers, Street and Openjuru's book on adult literacy programmes in Ethiopia, describing how literacy and numeracy programmes need to take account of the complex ways in which apparently 'illiterate' people use public signs, scripts and symbols in conducting their everyday lives. An ethnographic perspective, they suggest, may help teachers to access the literacy practices that their students already engage in, and to build on this in extending their literacy practices, rather than, as in much education, treating them as 'illiterates' or as 'empty vessels' to be filled with the particular knowledge and literacy brought by outsiders. In the extracts from Kress and van Leeuwen's book *Multimodal Discourse*, the authors look at spoken and written language as one of a number of 'modes' – such as gesture, artistic representation or the organisation of living space – in which people are able to communicate, express themselves and convey meaning. They offer two examples: one relating to a well-known Renaissance painting (Titian's *Noli Me Tangere*) and the other drawn from the practice in 1970s England and Australia of knocking down the interior walls of houses in order to express finely articulated nuances of class and income. Again you might apply these ideas to your own situation. For example, think about your own home and the living space you may control, such as your bedroom. What kinds of social meanings are conveyed in the arrangement and use of space? And what other ways of expressing oneself in social situations can you think of, besides speaking and writing? For example, how do we use objects and possessions – and technology – to say things to others about ourselves? Looking at classroom layout may provide a concrete example close to home for many students and their teachers of how the layout, design and use of visual images and so forth are integral to the ordering of social interaction – a theme to which we now turn.

1.4 Organising Social Relations: Kinship and Gender

Anthropologists studying human communities have described an enormous range of ways in which people organise their activities and relationships. Kinship, for example, has already been mentioned. In many societies, this provides a key principle and set of rules governing not only the personal feelings people are expected to have towards one another, but the wholesale organisation of political, economic and religious practices and relationships. In the Western world we tend to think of the family as an intimate and private space, somewhat secluded from the public world of the market and formal social institutions. Yet even here, kinship determined much of the political order until recently (think of European monarchies and the historic power of aristocracies) and is still influential in more subtle ways (think of contemporary political dynasties, or the advantages conferred by wealth inherited within families). What other examples can you think of in our contemporary world, in which a person's place in society can be strongly influenced by whom they are related to?

In this part of the Reader we concentrate on an even more pervasive organising principle of social relations: that of gender. Gender, as understood by anthropologists and other social scientists, refers to the social roles, identities and distinctions that may make use, metaphorically and in other ways, of the biological differentiation between the sexes. The distinction between biologically given *sex* and socially constituted *gender*, as well as the significance of kinship as an organising principle of social life, is clearly set out in the extract we reproduce here from Kirsten Hastrup's article 'The Semantics of Biology: Virginity'. We looked briefly at the theory of sexual selection at the beginning of the Reader, and huge debates have raged around the extent to which, if at all, the biology of sex difference determines the organisation of gender roles in society. Many feminist scholars have convincingly documented the ways in which the doctrine that 'biology is destiny' has been consistently used to justify sex discrimination in all its forms. One way in which anthropology can contribute to these debates is to show just how individual, and elaborate, ideas of gender can be in specific social contexts. Our next extract, from John Coggeshall's article '"Ladies" behind Bars', gives us a glimpse into an all-male U.S. prison environment in which gender identities and performances are played upon at many levels, within a setting based on power and control.

Reflect on your own experience of identifying yourself, and being identified, as a person of a particular gender. Few of us will ever experience the brutally coercive gender performances described in Coggeshall's article. But how much influence do you think culturally transmitted images based on gender – for example, conveyed through education or the media – have in determining how we see ourselves and the choices we make in life?

I.5 Engaging with Nature

Earlier, we looked at the organisation of social relations based on the cultural elaboration of 'natural' facts, using sex and gender as our example. The idea of 'nature' can itself be understood in a number of ways. We saw earlier that the human species, as a product of evolutionary processes, is intimately tied to the natural world; and we share many features with our non-human relatives, although of course we also have characteristics that set us decisively apart from them. A great deal of work has been done by biological anthropologists seeking to reconstruct the environments and ecological systems in which critical stages of human evolution took place; and the dietary and other conditions that determined the success and spread of early populations. There have been fierce debates in recent years over whether particular aspects of human behaviour, such as aggressiveness or a tendency to form groups that exclude outsiders, are a part of our 'nature' or are an arbitrary invention of culture. The answer is probably more complex than has been so far realised, as new insights from both the natural and social sciences shed increasing light on human flexibility, and on the differing ways we humans can build on and sometimes modify the expression of our genetic potential. Through technology, medicine and the like, humans have also gained some control over external natural forces, although every now and again we are reminded of the limits of this control. These arguments aside, there is an irreducible sense in which human life is a part of nature.

But there is another sense of 'nature' in common use, in which nature is seen as standing outside the human sphere. The idea of a 'natural world' external to, and contrasting with, human society, has taken a number of forms within the Western tradition, and the tendency among those who have grown up within that tradition is to take this image for granted. (Think, for example, of phrases such as 'back to nature' or 'natural foods', and how they are used in marketing to exploit a nostalgia for supposedly purer or more authentic ways of living.) The notion of a natural world 'out there' is not common to all world-views, some of which (the Buddhist, for example) see what Westerners might term the human and natural domains as intrinsically continuous and integrated. The case is very similar with regard to ideas about the environment and its relation to human society. There is great variation in the ways in which societies conceptualise and view both 'nature' and 'the environment'; and the relation of these to human activities.

In the first of the two extracts we include here from Joy Hendry's book *An Introduction to Social Anthropology*, the author gives examples of very different views taken by societies towards both nature and the environment, and how these views intersect with the economic and political organisation of the societies in question. The extract that follows, from an article by Pat Caplan entitled 'Death on the Farm: Culling Badgers in North Pembrokeshire', shows in rich detail how, in a very specific local Welsh context, ideas about (and reverence towards) 'nature' are interwoven with conflicts involving science, literary tradition, national identity, language politics and the economics of farming and tourism, in a complex battle over badger culling.

Both nature and the environment are often seen as threatened by human activity. There is of course strong scientific support for this perception (think of man-made climate change, for example, species extinction, and the industrial destruction of rainforests in Amazonia and Asia). But views of the vulnerability of nature and the environment – and human responsibility for protection and conservation – are complex and variable across cultures. Once again, anthropology can help lay open some of this complexity. This is well illustrated in an article by Adrian Peace, 'The Whaling War: Conflicting Cultural Perspectives', part of which we include here. Peace focuses on the conflict over whaling between public opinion and national policy in Australia and Japan. He draws out the contradictory meanings attached to whales by Australians and Japanese, and links these meanings to broader historical, political and economic factors in both countries. In the extract which follows, from her article 'Ducks Out of Water: Nature Conservation as Boundary Maintenance', Kay Milton looks with an anthropologist's eye at international movements for nature conservation. Using the case of the campaign by conservationists to halt the spread of North American ruddy ducks in Europe at the expense of native species, she interprets the culture of conservation as, in part, concerned with the maintenance of boundaries: between biological species, between 'native' and 'alien' populations, and between 'natural' and 'man-made' processes.

Note that anthropologists, in general, do not take a position on the scientific aspects of issues such as culling, whaling or nature conservation, although as private individuals they may hold strong views. Where they can shed light on such controversies is in showing how attitudes to nature and the environment are intimately entwined with broader cultural, national, economic, political and sometimes global concerns.

I.6 The Humanity of Things

The use of objects to convey social messages has already been mentioned. Material culture, or the creation and use of things, is an important area of study within anthropology. Many anthropologists specialise in museum work; and the most enlightened museums nowadays strive to display objects not as isolated exhibits or 'curiosities' but in the context of their meaning and use by the people who created them. Like the human body and the environment, things made and used by people throughout the world have a multitude of meanings and values mapped onto them – so much so that they can often be said to have a 'social life' of their own. This is illustrated in contrasting ways in the next two extracts. In the first, taken from an article by Silvia Rodgers entitled 'Feminine Power at Sea', the author discusses the rituals which at that time accompanied the launch of Royal Navy ships. She describes the many ways in which ships are thought of as female, and she links these ideas to broader notions of femininity, and to beliefs and taboos surrounding actual women at sea. Although many of these practices and beliefs have since disappeared with the advent of mixed-sex ships' crews, the article shows how vividly material creations such as ships are drawn into the meanings and symbols of a human social world. The second extract is taken from Daniel Miller's book *Stuff*. Drawing on his studies of fashion and style in Trinidad, India and London, Miller argues that the clothes we wear are far from being a mere superficial add-on to our innermost selves. Rather, they are an intrinsic component of the self: they 'wear' us as much as we wear them.

I.1   Evolutionary Processes and Human Origins

1   What Is Natural Selection?
R. Lewin and R. Foley

The process of evolution has formed the human species over the course of nearly 7 million years. During this time selective pressures have shaped and shifted the direction in which we have evolved. Despite our self-regarding superiority over other species, humans are in fact no 'more' evolved than their close cousins the chimpanzees or even cockroaches! All are well adapted to their own environment. Darwin's book 'On the Origin of Species' is justly famous and his idea of evolution by natural selection has been described as the best idea to ever occur to a human, but what is natural selection? How does it work and why is it such a great idea? In this extract from their book The Principles of Human Evolution, *the authors offer a brilliantly succinct explanation of how natural selection works and discuss why Darwin's idea is still so strong over 150 years later.*

Darwinism is a theory of how evolutionary change occurs. The theory is in itself very simple – indeed, that has probably been one of the reasons why it has been considered so often to be inadequate, but often the most powerful scientific theories are characterized by an elegant simplicity.

Natural Selection
Darwinian evolutionary mechanisms are based on four conditions, each of which builds successively on the other. Natural selection – the differential survival of genes – is the outcome of certain conditions that have to be fulfilled. The first of these is that organisms reproduce. If there is no reproduction, then the game of life would have to start afresh with each deceased generation. In the early days of life forms perhaps this happened, when the replicating molecules were less efficient, although natural selection would still be operating, selecting for the most efficient replicating molecule.

The second condition is that there should be some mode of inheritance – that is, offspring should resemble their parents more than they do the population as a whole. This is the field of genetics, but when Darwin wrote the *Origin of Species* it was this aspect that was least well understood and caused him the most critical problems. If information that determines the characteristics of the parent can be transmitted to offspring, then those features which enhance the survival and reproductive potential of the parents will occur more frequently in each subsequent generation, dependent upon the number of offspring. If there is no mode of inheritance, then the advantageous features of a parent would simply be lost in each generation. There could be no evolutionary change. It was the absence of this condition that made Lamarckism (a theory suggested by Jean-Baptiste Lamarck in the nineteenth century of how species were held to be physically altered by their environment during their lifetime, and these alterations passed on to progeny) an unworkable theory of evolution.

There must, thirdly, be variation within the population. Even if the first two conditions are fulfilled, if each individual in the population is phenotypically (i.e., the total observable characteristics of an organism, a result of the interplay between genes and the environment) and genetically identical, then natural selection cannot operate. Differential survival will have no effect because all individuals are the same, and so each generation will be identical. It is for this reason that Darwin was himself so concerned with the problem of variation, and why he devoted the first two chapters of *Origin of Species* to 'Variation under Domestication' and 'Variation under Nature'. This was in fact also one of the principal lines of evidence employed against the theory of a special creation of immutable types – if God had created a number of types of plant and animal, then unless he or she was incompetent there was no reason why they should vary at all. Darwin went to extraordinary lengths to show that even the humblest type of creature displayed variation.

Finally – and this condition is perhaps the one most closely associated with Darwin's own ideas – is competition. Imagine a world in which all the conditions outlined above were fulfilled. However, if the resources needed to support all the populations were infinite, then there will be no differential reproduction. An individual could have all the offspring possible, and so there would be no change from one generation to another, just a constant and everlasting expansion. Clearly, though, such a world does not exist. Indeed it is theoretically impossible as time itself is a resource (time to have offspring, etc.) and so as long as there is time, there will be at least some limitation. In practice of course all resources are limited – energy, water, shelter, potential mates and so on. It was the eighteenth-century demographer Malthus who first pointed out the imbalance between the potential of resources to expand and the potential of populations to reproduce. Darwin harnessed this notion as the central condition necessary for natural selection to operate. If resources are limited, then not all individuals will survive and reproduce or will reproduce at different rates of success. Given the conditions of reproduction, variation and inheritance, then those individuals who are better adapted to acquiring the resources necessary to survive and reproduce will leave more offspring, and those offspring will carry the feature of their parents that gave them this competitive edge.

These then are the conditions under which natural selection must occur. Each of them is independently derived and each of them is easily and empirically tested. Organisms can be observed reproducing, the mechanisms of inheritance have been worked out, the occurrence of variation can be and largely is extremely well established, and the finite nature of the resources of the world is virtually a truism. Looking at the theory of natural selection in this way shows that far from being untestable, it is in fact a logical necessity deriving from a number of simple observations.

Extracted from: R. Lewin and R. Foley, *The Principles of Human Evolution* (Oxford: Blackwell, 2004), pp. 28–30.

2   Explaining the Very Improbable
Richard Dawkins

How does evolution by natural selection explain the complexity of life? Animals are the most complex things in the known universe. Clearly such complicated things require a rather special explanation. In this extract from his book The Blind Watchmaker, *Richard Dawkins contrasts complicated objects designed by humans with organic life, exploring how complicated patterns and processes in nature were once thought to have been the result of design rather than evolution. As he so eloquently concludes, when we examine life in close detail we can see no evidence for any sort of design; and to borrow from his title, if there is a 'designer' it is a non-planned blind one in the form of natural selection.*

The watchmaker of my title (*The Blind Watchmaker*) is borrowed from a famous treatise by the eighteenth-century theologian William Paley. His *Natural Theology – or Evidences of the Existence and Attributes of the Deity Collected from the Appearances of Nature*, published in 1802, is the best-known exposition of the 'Argument from Design', always the most influential of the arguments for the existence of a God. It is a book that I greatly admire, for in his own time its author succeeded in doing what I am struggling to do now. He had a point to make, he passionately believed in it, and he spared no effort to ram it home clearly. He had a proper reverence for the complexity of the living world, and he saw that it demands a very special kind of explanation. The only thing he got wrong – admittedly quite a big thing! – was the explanation itself. He gave the traditional religious answer to the riddle, but he articulated it more clearly and convincingly than anybody had before. The true explanation is utterly different, and it had to wait for one of the most revolutionary thinkers of all time, Charles Darwin.

Paley begins *Natural Theology* with a famous passage:

> In crossing a heath, suppose I pitched my foot against a stone, and were asked how the stone came to be there; I might possibly answer, that, for anything I

knew to the contrary, it had lain there for ever: nor would it perhaps be very easy to show the absurdity of this answer. But suppose I had found a watch upon the ground, and it should be inquired how the watch happened to be in that place; I should hardly think of the answer which I had before given, that for anything I knew, the watch might have always been there.

Paley here appreciates the difference between natural physical objects like stones, and designed and manufactured objects like watches. He goes on to expound the precision with which the cogs and springs of a watch are fashioned, and the intricacy with which they are put together. If we found an object such as a watch upon a heath, even if we didn't know how it had come into existence, its own precision and intricacy of design would force us to conclude that the watch must have had a maker: that there must have existed, at some time, and at some place or other, an artificer or artificers, who formed it for the purpose which we find it actually to answer, who comprehended its construction, and designed its use.

Nobody could reasonably dissent from this conclusion, Paley insists, yet that is just what the atheist, in effect, does when he contemplates the works of nature, for: 'every indication of contrivance, every manifestation of design, which existed in the watch, exists in the works of nature; with the difference, on the side of nature, of being greater or more, and that in a degree which exceeds all computation'. Paley drives his point home with beautiful and reverent descriptions of the dissected machinery of life, beginning with the human eye, a favourite example which Darwin was later to use…. Paley compares the eye with a designed instrument such as a telescope, and concludes that 'there is precisely the same proof that the eye was made for vision, as there is that the telescope was made for assisting it'. The eye must have had a designer, just as the telescope had.

Paley's argument is made with passionate sincerity and is informed by the best biological scholarship of his day, but it is wrong, gloriously and utterly wrong. The analogy between telescope and eye, between watch and living organism, is false. All appearances to the contrary, the only watchmaker in nature is the blind forces of physics, albeit deployed in a very special way. A true watchmaker has foresight: he designs his cogs and springs, and plans their interconnections, with a future purpose in his mind's eye. Natural selection, the blind, unconscious, automatic process which Darwin discovered, and which we now know is the explanation for the existence and apparently purposeful form of all life, has no purpose in mind. It has no mind and no mind's eye. It does not plan for the future. It has no vision, no foresight, no sight at all. If it can be said to play the role of watchmaker in nature, it is the blind watchmaker.

Extracted from: Richard Dawkins, *The Blind Watchmaker* (Harmondsworth: Penguin, 1986), pp. 4–6.

3   What Is Sexual Selection?
R. Lewin and R. Foley

Sexual selection is a theory that was suggested by Darwin to explain how some evolutionary traits can be explained by competition for mates within a species. Darwin described this as the 'struggle between the individuals of one sex, generally the males, for the possession of the other sex'. Many species have sexually divided traits that appear to be the result of this process, such as the peacock's tail or the bower bird's twig-based structures to attract female attention. While we can identify many examples of such things in other species, what about humans? It might be thought that humans have not been greatly subject to the effects of sexual selection. However, when we look closer, a large number of human traits have been suggested to be the result of sexual selection, from males' beards to female breasts right through to the idea that the loss of the penis bone in human males (while it is still present in other primates) results from sexual selection by females looking for healthy mates – since the human erection relies on fully functioning hydraulics, this is a very visible and obvious way of advertising health! In the second extract from their book The Principles of Human Evolution, *the authors outline the concept of sexual selection and how it can affect the evolutionary trajectory of a species.*

In his second major work on evolution, *The Descent of Man and Selection in Relation to Sex*, which was published in 1871, Darwin described a variant of natural selection that has an important impact on the anatomy and behavior of many species. Where natural selection adapts an organism for survival in its environment, sexual selection adapts it to the needs of obtaining a mate. In many species, the females select their mates, and the male's role is to be as attractive as possible. In birds, for instance, this consideration often leads to males having brightly colored plumage, which they show off in elaborate displays. In other species, such as red deer and impala, males fight one another for the possession of a herd of females. (Even in these cases, females often exercise some choice of whether to stay with the herd 'owner'.) Male–male competition often leads to a larger body size in males (sexual dimorphism of body size) and enhanced fighting equipment, such as large antlers. In primate societies, this type of competition (plus social skills) is common and has usually resulted in the evolution of increased body size in males, as well as enlarged canine teeth. This pattern is also [widely] observed among hominins [and humans].

Extracted from: R. Lewin and R. Foley, *The Principles of Human Evolution* (Oxford: Blackwell, 2004), p. 42.

4   Human Evolution: An Overview
Simon Underdown

For many biological anthropologists, human evolution is one of the most intriguing areas of anthropology. By studying how we have evolved we can try to understand more about what makes us human. It is also an area of the subject that can change dramatically with one new fossil discovery or the development of new techniques. Over the last twenty years our understanding of our evolutionary story has gained much from the use of genetic analysis which has filled in some of the gaps left by the fossils of our ancestors, while new dating techniques have revealed more clues about when specific behaviours emerged. Yet it is still a subject that has much to discover – the gaps in the story or the missing pieces of the puzzle are what makes human evolution such a fascinating and frustrating science. In this piece, specially written for the Reader, evolutionary anthropologist Simon Underdown presents an overview of the current state of the discipline and some of the issues that it faces in the twenty-first century (he just hopes it's still up to date when it's finished!).

We, as humans in the form of *Homo sapiens*, have existed for a mere 200,000 years; and the entire course of what we can think of as human evolution took place over the last 7 million years. So human evolution is a process that has a very short history when pitched against – say – the age of the universe or our planet. It is all the more remarkable given our rapid rise to dominate (and deplete) our environment so utterly.

Traditionally we have liked to think of ourselves as 'different' from the rest of the animal world. After Darwin's ideas showed that we are a product of evolution by natural selection, we instead developed a view of our evolution as special or unique from that of all other organisms. We are all familiar with the linear pictures that show the low stooping ape gradually becoming upright until we see a tall man (usually holding a spear and sporting a bushy beard). This created an idea that our evolution was somehow inevitable – that once our ancestors had started down a particular path the end result would always be a walking, talking, thinking human. But this is not how we now understand our evolutionary development.

When the human evolutionary record is examined, the picture that presents itself is one of trial and error. Since the start of the human evolutionary story approximately 7 million years ago with an ape-like species called *Sahelanthropus tchadensis*, there have been somewhere between twenty and thirty species of what we call hominins (us and our ancestors). Today there is one: *Homo sapiens*.

The story of human evolution has changed dramatically over the last hundred years. However, nothing in the history of the discipline can match the developments that have taken place over the last fifteen to twenty years. Within that time we have completely moved away from the idea of a single line of species – *Australopithecus* to *Homo erectus* to Neanderthal to us. Instead we now have a complex picture of multiple species, whose exact relationship to each other is patchy at best. New fossil finds (like the amazing *Homo floresiensis*) continue to make us question our assumptions about what it means to be human – prompting a re-evaluation of many of the assumptions we made in the past about our evolutionary development.

The pattern of human evolution, far from being neat and predictable, is messy, filled with failed 'experiments' and very difficult to understand. In fact we still have a large number of gaps in our thinking about how and why we became human. This is partly a result of the fact that human evolution is a subject that seems to love confounding the expectations of those who study it. One new fossil can radically alter the way in which we interpret the data. As an example, at the start of 2010 we had a clear idea that the Neanderthals died out without passing on any genetic material to us; by the end of 2010 that idea had to be abandoned after data showed the opposite. But 2010 was not an unusual year in human evolution – a casual glance through any textbook from five or ten years ago compared to one from today will show just how much has changed. No other subject has such a rapidly changing set of rules by which the game is played!

To understand how we have evolved from our first ape-like ancestor 7 million years ago to the humans of today, it is simplest to split the story into two halves and to give them different labels. From 7 to 5 million years ago we are not really dealing with anything that would look to us at all human; so we can think of this as hominin evolution, while the period from 2 million years ago to now can be thought of as human evolution.

Almost the whole of our story took place in Africa, and it is not until around 2 million years ago that we first see any of the characters in our story leaving the African continent. Just over 7 million years ago, the forerunners of humans and chimps belonged to the same species (we often refer to this as the 'common ancestor') and would have been approximately one metre tall, very ape-like in appearance, would have eaten a diet very similar to modern chimpanzees and would have lived in the huge tropical forests that dominated Africa at the time. The trigger for the start of hominin evolution seems to have been the large-scale environmental changes that had been taking place during the Miocene period (approximately 24 to 5 million years ago). During this time there had been a gradual decrease in global temperature, which resulted in a decrease in rainfall across the regions of Africa where the human-chimp ancestor lived. This decrease in rainfall created periods of wet and periods of dry (or seasons) shrinking the large rainforests and producing a new type of habitat that filled the void left by the gaps in the large belts of rainforest. It was towards these new areas of habitat that some of the human-chimp ancestors moved, ultimately resulting in a new species (through a process of geographical isolation). So it is that at about 7 million years ago we encounter our first hominin ancestor in the form of a species called *Sahelanthropus tchadensis*.

To our eyes this early hominin would have looked like nothing more than an ape – there was nothing that we would regard as human behaviour at this point. It is in the skeleton that *Sahelanthropus* shows the changes that make it a hominin. The first trait that we see in our hominin ancestors is a shift towards walking on two legs. We can tell this by looking at the base of the skull and examining the position at which the spinal cord enters the brain. However this was not a form of walking on two legs like our own, but merely the beginning of the process that would produce the form of walking that we find around 2 million years ago in the species *Homo ergaster* (which also marks the beginning of human evolution).

The first 2 million years of hominin evolution are not very well understood: we know that the environment was changing with more areas of open forest and savannah appearing but we know of only a handful of hominins, all of which appear to be spending more time on the ground around the edges of the forest. But we have no clear understanding of how these species related to one another – the gaps in the data are problematic. Not until around 4.5 million years ago does the story become clearer with the appearance of the first of the *Australopithecines*. These hominins are amongst the best known of our fossil ancestors. This group of species cover a period of approximately 4 million years and co-existed with many other hominin species such as the *Paranthropines* (a group of hominins that developed huge teeth and jaws to chew hard foods and became extinct around 1 million years ago) as well as the first members of our own genus *Homo*. The *Australopithecines* would have still looked very apelike but they continued the trend started by *Sahelanthropus* by spending more and more time walking on two legs; and by around 2.5 million years ago a member of this group, *Australopithecus gahri*, was even using tools to butcher meat. But we are not entirely clear where these species fit in relation to us – we know we are all hominins, but are we cousins or direct relations? We need more fossils to better answer this question.

It is not until 2 million years ago that we see the start of human-like hominins that, while different from us, shared some of our abilities and behaviours. The title of 'first human' goes to a species from East Africa called *Homo ergaster*. This was a species that was unlike the earlier ape-like hominins and was the first to have a skeleton that closely resembled our own below the neck – their brains were much smaller, about 800 cm^2 versus about 1250 cm^2 for us, and the skull was still very different from our own. In terms of behaviour, *Homo ergaster* exhibited many human-like traits such as using fire, making complex stone tools, probably some form of vocal communication and even perhaps caring for the sick (as we shall see later). The impetus for this dramatic change from ape-like to human-like biological and cultural adaptations appears to have been a shift in habitat use. *Homo ergaster* had a skeleton that was extremely well adapted for life on the open savannah grasslands that dominated East Africa during the Pleistocene period, rather than the tropical forests that the first hominins inhabited. Thick ape fur is of no use in the dry heat and would have rapidly been lost leading in turn to two key adaptations: the pigmentation of skin and the development of sweating as a means of expelling heat from the body (humans can claim the title of best sweating animal). Taller, leaner skeletons completed the suite of adaptations to the hot, dry savannah landscape. Much of our skeleton and physiology can be traced back to this change in habitat use by *Homo ergaster*.

Homo ergaster was the first hominin species to leave Africa. By 1.8 million years ago we find this species on the fringes of Central Asia and as far east as Indonesia (where they are known as *Homo erectus)*. The groups of *Homo ergaster* that left Africa at this time seem to have been very successful, survived in Asia until as late as 50,000 years ago, and evolved into the bizarre species *Homo floresiensis* (nicknamed 'the hobbit' by its discoverers because of its short stature) on the island of Flores in Indonesia, which suggests that at some point *Homo erectus* perhaps made short sea journeys.

Meanwhile, back in Africa groups of *Homo ergaster* evolved into a species known as *Homo heidelbergensis* by approximately 600,00 years ago. This is the species that was the common ancestor of both the Neanderthals and us. Like *Homo ergaster* before it, this species showed many human-like traits, and would have been a formidable predator that used projectile weapons (spears) to hunt very large prey many times their own size. Groups of this species left Africa and found their way to Europe by about 500,000 years ago, and lived across Europe from the British Isles to Greece. By around 250,000 years ago we see in the fossils from Europe traits that we associate with the Neanderthals. In Africa we see our own species *Homo sapiens* appear from 200,000 years ago in the Omo region of Ethiopia.

The Neanderthals have an unfair reputation for stupidity, but in fact they were an advanced human species that wore clothes and jewellery, buried their dead and cooked their food – sound familiar? Many of the behaviours that we think of as distinct to us were found in the Neanderthals and in earlier species. Why the Neanderthals became extinct (and we didn't!) remains one of the most compelling questions in human evolution: climate change, extermination by *Homo sapiens* arriving from Africa and disease have all been suggested, but the answer remains tantalisingly out of reach.

Our own species, *Homo sapiens*, spread south across Africa before leaving the continent some time around 100,000 years ago. Initially heading to the east and Australia, we arrived in Europe around 45,000 years ago, went on to colonise the Americas and then moved across the rest of the globe. Intriguingly it would appear that the species that first walked the earth at Omo was exactly the same as us both in terms of biological adaptation and thought processes – the same types of worries and fears, but with fewer technological developments. In other words, they were us but without the gadgets.

Human evolution was once thought to have been inevitable, and it was assumed that we represented the summit of what evolution could achieve. We now know this to be nonsense, but the question remains: are we still evolving and if so in what way? This is one of the most interesting questions in biological anthropology, and addresses the very core of the subject. We can safely suggest that we have largely stopped evolving biologically – although the effects of natural selection still act on us, they are no longer solved with biological adaptations (as indeed they have increasingly not been since the first tools were used). Instead, we use culture and technology, such as sunscreen, antibiotics and IVF, to solve the problems we encounter in our existence. Human evolution has not stopped but it has ceased to be a biological game and has become one of culture – and what could be more human than that?

5	**Were the Neanderthals So Different from Us?** *Chris Stringer*

The next article, written specially for the Reader, looks at new evidence bearing on the boundary separating the human species from our extinct relatives the Neanderthals. The Neanderthals have seemingly always had a bad press. Ever since the discovery of the first Neanderthal fossils in the nineteenth century, they have often been held up as examples of lumbering, stupid cave dwellers who by comparison make us look even more sophisticated. Yet the Neanderthals could lay equal claim to the term 'human'; many of their behaviours and skills were similar to our own, and we increasingly understand the Neanderthals' extinction and our own survival as the result of luck rather than evolutionary advantage. As we shall explore later in the Reader, our own species Homo sapiens *is closely associated with the creation of groups and the drawing of boundaries. We only need think about the different types of criteria we use to create distinct groups that act as very real boundaries to see this – be it ancient Roman chariot teams or modern football teams through to 'racial' and cultural distinctions. In the following piece, Chris Stringer considers the identity of the Neanderthals and our relationship to another human species that has traditionally been dismissed as good, but not quite as good as us!*

The first point to make in response to the question is that Neanderthals were human too, and like us so-called modern humans, they were one of the last evolutionary experiments in how to be human – we represent the sole survivor of those experiments. Why are we the sole surviving human species, and was *Homo sapiens* directly or indirectly responsible for the extinction of other late-surviving human species such as the Neanderthals?

So who were these Neanderthal cousins of ours? They have certainly had an image problem over the years, and brutish behaviour is often still called 'Neanderthal'. Yet they were actually highly evolved humans who walked as upright as we do, and whose brains were as large as ours. Fossil and DNA evidence suggests that their lineage split from ours about 400,000 years ago, and over the next 370,00 years in Europe and western Asia, the Neanderthals developed their own bodily (and no doubt behavioural and social) characteristics, following their own evolutionary path until they disappeared about 30,000 years ago.

We modern humans (*Homo sapiens*) have features that distinguish us from the other humans that came before: for example, we have high rounded skulls, small brow ridges and a chin, and we also show behavioural traits like making complex tools and art, and using language and symbolism. Over the last twenty years, the Out of Africa model (OOA) has risen to dominance as an explanation of how modern humans evolved, supported by discoveries in fossils, archaeology and genetics. OOA argues that there was only one place (rather than many) where our species originated – Africa – and having developed there recently, *Homo sapiens* spread out during the last 100,000 years or so, replacing archaic species like Neanderthals and *Homo erectus*, who were living outside the continent in regions like Europe and East Asia. As modern humans spread out across the world in small numbers (and remained in Africa), our 'racial' features began to develop in each region.

While recognisably human, the Neanderthals would have appeared rather different to us. Above the neck, the Neanderthal skull was particularly distinctive. Their brain cases were big, but long and low, with a large brow ridge instead of the domed forehead of modern humans. Neanderthal faces were dominated by an enormous and projecting nose, which was accentuated by sweptback cheekbones and a receding chin. As to their intelligence, we have no direct data on the quality of their large brains, but the Neanderthals were clearly capable hunters, gatherers and tool-makers. While it does not seem they were great innovators, nevertheless during the final 30,000 years of their existence they started to make more advanced tools, showed increasing use of pigments, and developed jewellery. These changes have been the source of much debate – were the Neanderthals becoming increasingly inventive, or were they under the influence of modern humans who had emerged from Africa?

Because, like us, they buried their dead, many of their remains in caves have been saved from erosion and damage, and so we have a good idea of their bodily form – they were relatively short, wide-shouldered and hipped, and barrel-chested. Their physique looked more suited to short powerful bursts rather than endurance running, and it is thought they were mainly ambush hunters, armed with thrusting spears. Their stocky body shape may also reflect their evolution through the ice ages, although they probably preferred temperate weather and environments.

So did these two human populations overlap, and how did they interact, if and when they encountered each other? Despite recent claims that we screwed, speared or sometimes even ate the Neanderthals, we need many more data on these questions. It is difficult with our existing dating precision to place them together in the landscape in one time and place, and given their inferred low numbers, perhaps they did not encounter each other that often. Nevertheless, considerable recent progress on dating has confirmed that modern human fossils and sophisticated cave art (attributable to modern humans) date from the period from 35,000 to 40,000 years ago in Europe, while Neanderthals may have persisted in regions such as Gibraltar until about 30,000 years ago (here I am using various dating methods, including radiocarbon dates which are calibrated – adjusted – using other techniques), so there must have been at least occasional encounters. If they were different species, could they have interbred if they met?

The answer to this question lies in the recovery of ancient DNA from Neanderthal fossils. The first tiny piece of DNA from a Neanderthal fossil was published in 1997, and since then, with improvements in recovery techniques and computing power, 20 Neanderthals have yielded up increasing amounts of ancient DNA. Until recently, the results had matched interpretations of the fossil record indicating that Neanderthals formed a separate evolutionary lineage from our species *Homo sapiens*, and that they split from us about 400,000 years ago. Now, at last, a complete Neanderthal genome sequence has been reconstructed, and the results have produced an intriguing twist to our evolutionary tale. On the one hand we modern humans have mutations linked with the brain, skeleton and bodily tissues that are not found in Neanderthals, and may explain some of the differences we show compared with them. But on the other hand, if you are European, Asian or from New Guinea, you may have some Neanderthal blood racing through your veins (but probably not, according to the latest research, if you are African). These surprising results are probably only the first of many, as the results of fossil genomics start to build momentum.

As one of the architects of OOA, I have regarded the Neanderthals as representing a separate lineage, and most likely a separate species from *Homo sapiens*. Although I have never ruled out the possibility of interbreeding, I have considered this to have been small and insignificant in the bigger picture of our evolution – for example, the results of isolated interbreeding events could easily have been lost in the intervening millennia. Now, the Neanderthal genome strongly suggests those genes were not lost, and that many of us outside Africa have some Neanderthal inheritance. Any functional significance of these shared genes remains to be determined, but that will certainly be a focus for the next stages of this fascinating research.

6   An Evolving Tale
Simon Underdown

The course of human evolution has been strongly influenced by changes in the environment. Climate change is a massively important issue in the twenty-first century; and individuals, the media and governments around the world are concerned about how changes in global temperature will affect us. No one can really deny that a change in average global temperature of a few degrees could cause widespread and potentially catastrophic disruption to life on this planet. Yet the degree of change is small when compared to the amount of variation we see in the past during the course of hominin and human evolution. In this article, Simon Underdown examines the role that changes in climatic conditions in the past have played in shaping the evolution of the human body and the effect it had on some of our evolutionary cousins. Ultimately we can see that climate change in the past was an important factor in making us who we are, but human cultural adaptations since the Industrial Revolution are beginning to manipulate our whole planet on a large scale and in ways that we can only just begin to understand.

There really seems to be very little doubt that human activity is responsible for climate change: atmospheric concentration of CO_2 (a major cause of global warming) is now significantly higher than at any time over the last 600,000 years. The start of this massive increase coincides very closely with the genesis of the Industrial Revolution.

We should be worried about the effects of climate change, not just because of the short-term problems it will undoubtedly lead to, but also because of the long-term issues we can only guess at. The media is full of speculation about the effect of relatively short-term climate change, such as rising sea levels and desertification.

Yet it is worth examining just how powerful a hold climate really has on our species from an evolutionary perspective. It would not be going too far to say that climate change has been one of the major factors in human evolution (the other is, of course, technology). A drop in global temperature during the Miocene epoch, approximately 8 to 10 million years ago, resulted in the fragmentation of the large African forests, which in turn led to the development of savannahs (wide open grassland). It was this incidence of climate change that seems to have kick-started human evolution.

Around 7 million years ago our early ancestors ventured out of the forests and onto the savannah, slowly adapting to this new environment (while the ancestors of chimpanzees stayed within the forests). The key adaptation caused by this shift in habitat was that our ancestors began to walk on two legs (bipedalism), probably to reduce the surface area exposed to the sun. This left the hands free to do other things, aiding the development of stone tools, which could be used to scavenge and butcher meat, which in turn provided energy for bigger brains. Without that change in the global climate, it is fair to suggest that we might not have become the species we are today.

Human evolution continued to be highly influenced by the environment over the next 5 million years, but this changed dramatically around 2 million years ago when our evolutionary ancestor, a species called *Homo ergaster*, first started to significantly manipulate its environment. Over the last 2 million years we have been gradually lessening the hold that climate has on us, but never removing it.

The extinction of the Neanderthals around 30,000 years ago seems to have been closely related to climate change. Our own species, *Homo sapiens*, has been able to populate almost every area of the planet, using technology to exploit areas our biological make-up would not be able to cope with.

The process has now come full circle: the environment had a massive impact on our evolution, we evolved strategies to reduce this impact, but these technological innovations have now caused the environment to start moving beyond our control once again. The lessons from our evolutionary past are very clear: humans are part of the environment, not masters of it.

Originally published in the *Guardian*, 3 April 2007.

I.2   The Body

Ways of Thinking about 'Race' and Ethnicity

7	**Race against Time** *Simon Underdown*

*In this article, Simon Underdown explores the concept of human races
from a biological perspective. Biologically speaking, 'race' is a term that
effectively means sub-species (enough difference to separate one group
from another). But when dealing with humans, 'race' is a term that is
often used in a very generic way to describe abstract and outward
differences between human groups. Popular media continually refer to
large groupings such as the 'European race' or the 'Black race' all the
way down to much smaller units such as the 'British' race. Yet genetic
analysis and the study of fossil materials point towards a very recent
common ancestor in Africa and a remarkable lack of genetic variation
– in other words, no room for different races. How then can we best
explain why and how the term 'race' has come to be used and
understood? As this article suggests, we have no biological basis for
using the term but should instead reflect on the rich cultural variation
that we have developed over the course of our shared history.*

Race is one of the most misunderstood terms in modern science, misused
by seasoned scientists and laymen alike. Put simply, there are no human
races, just the one species: *Homo sapiens*. The idea of human races is a
totally artificial concept, a sloppy form of shorthand that refers to an ill-
defined mish-mash of surface differences, such as skin colour (probably
controlled by a small number of genes), as well as different cultural
practices, especially religious ones. Humans have an innate need to define
and categorise, but race is a dangerous and outmoded idea that just can't
keep up with modern science.

The concept of different human races is an old one. From the nineteenth
century onwards, Darwinian ideas of natural selection were misused to
justify erroneous concepts of Victorian racial superiority and nationalism.
To still talk about separate human races in the twenty-first century is at best
misguided and at worst woefully ignorant of biology.

Our own species is remarkable for our lack of genetic variation. The eruption of the super-volcano Toba approximately 74,000 years ago is thought to have wiped out much of our genetic diversity by causing the extinction of many human groups. All of the differences that we now see in humans are a mixture of small genetic variations, built up over time, and of environmental effects. The Maasai and the Inuit have almost identical genes but the differences in their environment have greatly influenced how those genes are expressed, producing different outward appearances.

Yet many researchers continue to prop up this sick old man of biology, suggesting that 'human races' in different parts of the world are becoming genetically more distinct. The fact that we are one species does not mean that we should not expect variation between populations, especially ones separated by large distances. Differences do exist, but the shared similarities are far greater. We all remain *Homo sapiens* but the outward and genetic differences we see between populations are retained because of sexual selection and allegorical mating, the simple concept that like attracts like. Similarly the idea that we will all end up looking the same given long enough is just as flawed as the idea of human races.

The study of human evolution has done much to show up the fallacy of separate human races. Indeed, when we examine the work carried out on DNA from Neanderthal fossils (a separate species), huge areas of shared genetic information emerge, not least the FOXP2 or 'speech' gene which is identical in humans and Neanderthals. If such little variation exists between two species that last shared a common ancestor over 500,000 years ago, then how comfortable can we be with the idea of separate human races today? Surely it is at last time to put away the idea of different races, celebrate our cultural differences and warmly embrace what makes us all *Homo sapiens*.

Originally published in the *Guardian*, 12 December 2007.

8   Dem Bones
Simon Underdown

The study of human skeletons has traditionally been an important part of biological anthropology. Bones can tell us a great deal about the way populations lived in the past and the relationship that people had with the environment they lived in. However, many of the large human skeletal collections held by institutions in Western countries were collected during the colonial period, often with little or no regard for indigenous traditions and beliefs. Compounding this issue is the way that many of the collections were originally used to prop up ridiculous ideas of European racial supremacy. However, the collections today provide a rich record of human diversity, and their study by modern biological anthropologists has contributed massively to our understanding of this. Yet some indigenous populations would like to see all such material returned to them and reburied, effectively destroying the material forever. In this piece, Simon Underdown considers the history of the issues surrounding these collections and discusses why the sensitive preservation of human skeletal collections is crucial for a better understanding of our shared human journey.

One of the saddest but often untold stories of the eighteenth and nineteenth centuries was the huge loss of human life, and diversity, as European empire builders spread 'civilisation'. Tragically, this 'civilisation' took the form of enforced Western modes of behaviour, and all too often the extermination of populations that were considered troublesome or occupied regions rich in valuable natural resources. Within a relatively short space of time whole ways of life were wiped out: millennia of rich human diversity were gone forever.

Most of the indigenous populations that suffered had traditions of oral history, and as they died so too did their histories. Pockets of indigenous people remain but the process of 'Mac-Disneyfication' continues unabated. What we are left with, however, are the skeletal remains of indigenous groups that were collected during the same period, albeit in ways abhorrent to modern standards, now residing in museums.

In many cases these skeletons are the last representatives of populations that were utterly destroyed. Analysis of these skeletal remains by scientists, always with extreme reverence and respect, gives us a last chance to better understand the story of humanity. Human skeletons are an invaluable source of information for the understanding of recent human evolution, or how we came to be who we are. The data that can be collected ranges from sex, age at death and disease right through to dietary make-up and DNA profiles.

However, over the last few years there have been increasingly vocal calls from minority groups for the repatriation and reburial (i.e., destruction) of many of the remains held in British institutions. These bones allow every single human being to better understand our shared history. Genetic analysis of human bones has shown that we are a very closely related species of primate. Surface differences, like skin colour, are insignificant when seen in the light of how recently we evolved in Africa (*circa* 200,000 years ago), demonstrating how little genetic difference exists between us all. Analysis of these human bones has done much to show up the flaws in racist arguments.

Institutions that hold collections of human skeletons are generally happy to work with those seeking repatriation of remains and simply ask that they be allowed to carry out tests first. The research that anthropologists carry out is generally non-invasive, and when samples are collected they are usually very small. DNA analysis or radiocarbon dating can be performed with a single tooth. Groups that seek repatriation try to demonise those of us who work with human skeletal remains, recently stating that these

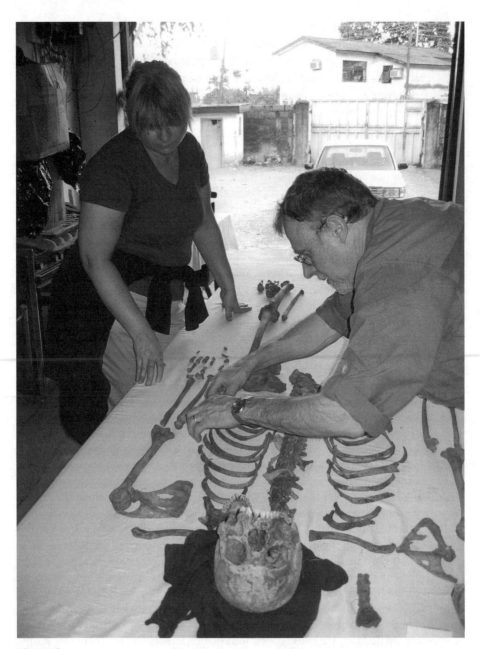

The Seeker
American forensic anthropologist Bill Haglund has travelled worldwide to investigate genocide and war crimes. By unearthing and analyzing the physical remains of victims of these atrocities, Haglund works to identify the victims and establish the circumstances surrounding their deaths.

Filmstill from *The Seeker*. © Philippe Cornet (RAI Film Festival 2007).

experiments were nothing more than 'mutilation' and were causing 'torment to the souls of the dead'.

The most vocal calls for destructive repatriation generally come from groups who disagree with the story scientific analysis presents, which often sharply contrasts with indigenous creation myths (which are so central to land claims). Preventing the analysis of these bones through reburial won't just stop the current generation from better understanding our global history, but will make it impossible forever. Can one generation of people be allowed to rule this out for all that come after them?

Originally published in the *Guardian*, 7 March 2007.

9　Representations of Non-European Society in Popular Fiction
Brian Street

The second half of the nineteenth century in England was a period of exploration and colonial expansion, coinciding with the scientific debates then raging over the theory of evolution. Concepts of race, and beliefs about the supposedly 'lower' evolutionary status of non-European peoples, were not confined to the scientific writings of the time, but were also widespread in popular fiction. In this extract, Brian Street maps out the ways in which fiction writers in the late nineteenth century drew upon stereotypes of non-European society in their accounts of life in distant parts of the world. He argues that these stereotypes derived not simply from popular prejudice but also from the science of the day, especially theories of evolution, race and debates concerning 'primitivism' versus 'progress'. We might at first think that this is all in the past and that both science and popular accounts of the 'other' have moved on. However, if we follow Street's argument and look back at some of the novels he describes – Rider Haggard on parts of Africa; Kipling on India; The Tarzan stories, and so on – we may find familiar issues in the representation of other people that are still to be found today. Anthropologists would argue that they have indeed moved on – for instance the notion of 'race' is now seen as 'unscientific' and not a valid category for describing cultural and social differences (see the earlier articles by Simon Underdown) – and that part of the discipline's job is precisely to challenge these older ideas. However, it may be that popular fiction, the media, film and so on are still putting forward some of these ideas, and a course of study in anthropology today might provide a good starting place for challenging such misconceptions. It might be a fruitful exercise, then, to take some books or films published recently and search in them for the kinds of images and stereotypes Street is describing for nineteenth-century fiction. Despite the work of contemporary scientists, anthropologists and others in demonstrating that all human beings share capacities and abilities, though they express them often in different ways, do contemporary sources, and the popular media more generally, still represent people from non-European societies as 'backward', as 'nearer to nature' or as belonging to 'inferior races'? Are the 'idyllic lands which travellers struggle to find' still 'left in the charge of enlightened Englishmen'? Anthropologists set out to describe social and cultural differences and their complex relationship to biological factors without making such value judgements about the 'superiority' of one culture or group of people over another. How far do current representations of the 'other' take account of such balanced approaches?

The 'Ethnographic Novel'

The origin of popular representations [of non-European society] is to be found, in the nineteenth century, not only in popular literature but also in contemporary science and imperial politics, so that all three continually derive from and contribute to the changing image of 'primitive' man.

In the 1840s, publishing techniques were developed which enabled large quantities of very cheap fiction to reach the newly educated working classes. Novels were brought out in penny parts, the 'penny dreadfuls', and in 1847 the first successful attempt was made to produce cheap reprints of these serials in volume form. The themes of these first mass-produced novels were domestic, and conventions grew up which restricted the author to a stereotyped pattern of events and characters in limited contexts.

By the 1870s writers were trying to break out of this strait-jacket. The growth of Empire at this time and the experiences of so many travellers in distant, exotic lands provided a ready-made alternative, and from the 1870s onwards fiction took up this theme. The 'ethnographic novel', estranged in time and space from the claustrophobic Victorian drawing-room, became popular. For the first time, information on other cultures, expressed in vivid, exciting tales, was available to the mass public of England. Such romances, with their large circulation and appeal to a recently literate general public, are appropriately termed 'popular fiction'.

There is a unity in this period noted by students of literature: 'The end of the nineteenth and the beginning of the twentieth century make up a single literary period'. ...There is a unity, likewise, in the particular kind of literature with which we are dealing; Dalziel (1957: 3), describing the early 'popular' novels, justifies her generalisations about them on the strength of a few examples by claiming: 'The descriptions of these novels and periodicals ...

are acceptable only on the assumption that one quality of mass-produced fiction at any date is its great sameness.' While Dalziel is referring to the domestic novel, the same is true of the 'ethnographic novel'. The mass-produced stories of far-off lands and their inhabitants, so popular during this period in England, are similar in style and content and, most significantly, in the assumptions they share with regard to 'primitive' peoples.

There is a unity in the scientific thought of the period, based on common interest in evolutionary and racial theory and the nature of 'armchair anthropology', and there is a unity in the political interests of the time, in the concern with overseas territory and the eventual emergence of an Empire.... Killam (1968: 2–3) dates 'ethnographic fiction' from 1874 because in that year Henty published his first boys' books on the Ashanti campaign. He too agrees that the writers of this period perpetuated an older image:

> Addressing themselves to a general public caught up in the enthusiasm of the overseas venture in Africa, they knew what their readers wished to read and to that taste they catered. Thus the generality of authors adhere strictly in their treatments of the African setting to an image of Africa which was in large part formed before they came to write their books. (Killam 1968: x)

The image was not confined to Africa. Since the ideas stemmed from nineteenth-century views of the world beyond Europe, it was easy enough to apply descriptions of African inferiority or 'savagery' to natives of South America, Asia or Malaysia, with the same lack of discrimination.

Images of Non-European Society

By the mid-nineteenth century, then, the details of the image were fairly explicit. 'Primitive' peoples are considered to be the slaves of custom and thus to be unable to break the despotism of their own 'collective conscience'. Any custom 'discovered' among a 'primitive' people is assumed to dominate their whole lives; they are unconscious of it and will never change it themselves. This provides the basis for the analysis of many customs being reported back to nineteenth-century England by the growing number of travellers. And their reporting is already conditioned by the scientifically backed metaphors of the chain of being and the ladder by means of which all other cultures were ascribed their place in a universal hierarchy. A people was given its appropriate rung on the ladder according to race. It was assumed that one's place in the hierarchy was determined by heredity; the ladder represented stages of social evolution, with Anglo-Saxon at the top, and reporters looked for criteria by which to determine how far other races had climbed up it.

Since the races were thus divided up by various criteria and characteristics, a particular 'character' could be attributed to a whole people on the strength of casual personal observations; a 'race' might be gullible, faithful, brave, childlike, savage, blood-thirsty, noble, etc., and these qualities were assumed to be hereditary. Likewise, the Anglo-Saxon race had certain qualities which were inborn in all its members and it was these qualities which enabled it to dominate the rest of the world.

'Primitive man', on the other hand, spent his whole life in fear of spirits and mystical beings; his gullibility was exploited by self-seeking priests and kings, who manipulated religion to gain a hold on the minds of their simple subjects; he worshipped animals and trees, tried to control the mystical forces of nature by means of ceremony, ritual, taboos and sacrifices, and explained the wonders of the universe in imaginative but 'unscientific' myths. Politically, the 'primitive' was in the grip of either anarchy or despotism; social control, if any, was exercised by the most savage tyranny, by the despotism of custom or by religious trickery. And his economic life consisted of either primitive communism in which everything was shared, or a system of each man for himself, 'grab and never let go'. Life was a perpetual struggle against harsh nature and harsher men, and only the fittest would survive.

Whilst much of this may, in fact, seem 'true' up to a point, such descriptions lack the sense of proportion that can only be achieved by putting them in their full context alongside the mass of orderly life and alongside the many other, less exotic or dramatic, aspects of the religious, political and economic life of Englishmen and 'primitive' peoples alike. Needless to say, most popular reporting and novels dealing in such matters fail to do this, and their presentation is correspondingly distorted.

While the 'ignoble' side of 'savage' life tends to be thus distorted, so too is the 'noble' side. The tradition of the 'noble savage' was not entirely rejected in nineteenth-century thought, and many writers struggle with the conflicting theories presented by the literary tradition on the one hand and contemporary reporters and scientists on the other. In Rider Haggard, for example, the conflict between primitivism and progress causes inconsistencies within the novels and often affects the story itself: while he criticises many features of his own culture in contrast with the pristine goodness of primitive life, he ultimately ascribes to the doctrine of 'progress' and believes British influence will raise the native higher in the scale of being; thus the idyllic lands which his travellers struggle to find are left in the charge of enlightened Englishmen.

References

Dalziel, M. *Popular Fiction 100 Years Ago* (London: Cohen and West, 1957).

Killam, G.D. *Africa in English Fiction, 1874–1939* (Ibadan: Ibadan University Press, 1968).

Extracted from: Brian V. Street, *The Savage in Literature: Representations of 'Primitive' Society in English Fiction, 1858–1920* (London: Routledge, 1975), pp. 2–8.

10 Unravelling 'Race' for the Twenty-first Century
Faye V. Harrison

In the previous passage, we looked at ways in which the notion of fixed 'races', as well as being part of scientific discourse, coloured much of English popular fiction in the later nineteenth century. The passage which follows argues that the idea of race, far from disappearing, is mutating into new forms in the twenty-first century. In this edited extract from an article by Faye V. Harrison she shows how distinctions based on ideas of race have been employed over time to legitimise social injustices by relating them to supposedly fixed and 'natural' categories of human beings. Concentrating on the U.S. experience, Harrison traces the history of racial theories and of anthropologists' responses to them at different times. She argues that in today's globalising world, racial ideas are fragmenting and interacting with other forms of discrimination to generate new, equally violent forms of structural disadvantage.

As a social/cultural anthropologist, I have studied comparatively forms of social inequality in which 'race' is a significant marker of positioning and power. At a juncture when its status as a biological concept – or, in some circles, even as an anthropological concept – is seriously contested, race can be understood as an ideologically charged distinction in social stratification and as a social and often legal classification applied to people presumed to share common physical or biological traits. Racial categories may be used to mark so-called natural differences even in contexts of ostensible homogeneity. In these cases, the racially designated populations are believed to share, at least in part, some socially salient ancestry (and, hence, presumed heritable characteristics transmitted through the 'blood') construed to be of social significance and consequence to the dominant social order. Racialized societies vary in the extent to which socially salient ancestry, appearance, and sociocultural status (e.g., education, income, wealth) are used as criteria for assigning race.

Anthropological studies of the intellectual and social construction of race have proliferated over the past decade, partly as a response to the intensification of racialized tensions and identities in a number of settings around the world. The topic of race has proven to be particularly significant in my career because my ethnographic area speciality is in the Caribbean and the broader African diaspora. In settings such as these, where peoples of African descent predominate or figure prominently in other ways, social definitions and legal codifications of racial and related color distinctions have historically played a major role in 'naturalizing' or representing as naturally produced and unchangeable the markedly unequal and unjust distribution of wealth, power and prestige over the past four centuries of colonial – and now postcolonial or, more accurately, neocolonial – order. Of course, any sense of 'order' – and the structure of domination supporting it – has favored the interests, world-view, and structural location of the most privileged strata of people descended mainly from north-western Europeans and their allies around the world. From the vantage points of the subordinate segments of racially stratified societies, the orderliness, lawfulness and 'natural' guise of structured racial inequalities are often experienced as profoundly problematic assaults against their dignity, life chances and human rights. For them, 'race' is frequently experienced as a form of symbolic as well as … [material] violence. However, they may also experience 'race' as an identity they embrace and mobilize in everyday life as well as in more broadly based struggles for civil rights, socioeconomic mobility and political empowerment.

In some contexts, 'race' is an … [unemphasised] and, in some cases, adamantly denied dimension of lived experience and social identity whose subtlety and unsystematic quality disguises its injuries and displaces them onto more socially acknowledged and politically charged axes of difference such as class, religion or ethnicity. Especially at a postcolonial – or neocolonial – juncture, when racism has been widely discredited and its heinous human-rights consequences exposed, 'race' is often the ugly, embarrassing undercurrent of ethnic conflicts that rises to the surface only when tensions explode.

The more I reflect on my work, the more I realize that my decision to study anthropology as a university student and then later on to become a professional anthropologist may well have been influenced by the profound impact of race and racism on my formative experiences and my subsequent social identity as an American of African descent. Stigmatized in an especially dehumanizing manner, African origins and 'blood' have symbolized to many Euro-Americans the social bottom and an ever-threatening contagion to white purity. In my case as well as that of many other black people, the greater social salience of my African heritage relative to my other ancestral origins is consistent with a cultural logic that anthropology has helped me understand.

…

As I reflect upon who I am, what I do, and what my lived experience has been, I cannot escape the hard 'social fact' that I, like many of the anthropological subjects whom I have researched in the field and in the library, live a racially marked existence. The invidious racial distinctions around which my natal community's life was organized and constrained impelled me to think critically about social and cultural differences, and being a particularly inquisitive youngster, violated by 'Jim Crow' segregation and inspired by the movement that dismantled it, I yearned to be able to think beyond the limits of folk theory and common sense. Moreover, I yearned to see and travel – both physically and metaphorically – beyond the local, state and national boundaries that restricted most people's, including my own kinfolk's, gaze.

As a child, my curiosity and hunger to understand race and racism prompted me to raise questions about how the United States fit into the larger world of diversity. Why had one of the most rigid systems of race relations developed in the United States? Does the 'racial democracy' that Brazilians and other Latin Americans tout really exist, and, if so, does it represent a model that Americans or South Africans should emulate? I eventually learned that these questions as well as the many others I would eventually ask are amenable to the kinds of inquiry that social and cultural anthropologists undertake, which, for the most part, are modes of investigation that take ordinary people's voices and everyday experiences seriously.

A Brief History of the Concept and Social Phenomenon: The Only 'Race' is the Human Race!

Ironically, while my youthful interrogation of race and racism may have led me to anthropology, the anthropology I encountered in the 1970s and 1980s was largely silent on the question of racial inequality and the ideological and material relations that constitute and sustain racism. However, a few anthropologists continued the tradition of anti-racism that had been so much a part of the Boasian school of thought that defined prominent trends within the discipline during the first half of the twentieth century. Franz Boas and his associates and students played a strategic part in dismantling scientific racism and defining the parameters for an anti-racist mode of inquiry. Boas's work was probably informed by his experience as a German Jew, whose stigmatized 'subracial' status was marked and problematized by anti-Semitic folk ideologies that were eventually elevated by Nazism.

...

Just before I discovered anthropology as a university student, a vigorous debate on the biology and social significance of race occurred during the 1960s, perhaps paralleling and informed by the struggles for and against racial discrimination and its alternative, desegregation, or integration. Due to its operational ambiguity, arbitrariness, artificiality and erroneous and harmful assumptions, the concept declined in usage. The intense debates over race's scientific status led many anthropologists to adopt a devout 'no-race' position which, unwittingly, resulted in a failure to investigate racism along with race as a socially constructed phenomenon deeply grounded in ... realities. To rid the field of its problematic biological baggage, those anthropologists, with Ashley Montagu in the lead, jettisoned any notion of race and embraced the culture-centered concepts of 'ethnicity' and 'ethnic group' as alternatives. Interestingly, although many biological anthropologists attempted to make a conceptual shift away from species- and subspecies-centered thinking to clinal approaches (which examine cross-cutting gradients of populations varying in gene frequencies), they were not completely successful. A sizable minority of physical anthropologists continue to use the race concept, and, for the most part, even those who do not use it have, nonetheless, failed to generate new terminology and a substantial body of research acknowledging the complex nature of human population variation and biohistory. ...

By the early 1990s race as a social and an intellectual construction re-emerged as a major focus in anthropological analysis, especially in the United States. Perhaps it is better understood today that, as a dimension of socially defined difference intersecting with and often indistinguishable from ethnicity, race encodes social and cultural differences presumed to be unbridgeable and unchanging ... Ethnicity and race can be thought of as interrelated but distinct dimensions of identity formation, and, depending on the context, one dimension can modify or take precedence over the other. Anthropological analysis now recognizes that, despite the present state of considerable biological knowledge disproving the existence of natural races, *racism,* as an oppressive structure of inequality and power, remains prevalent and persistent with the resilient capacity to alter and disguise its form in response to changing social, political and economic conditions. Despite an absence or a suppression of race-centered prejudice, racism can be the unintended outcome of everyday discourses, behaviors and institutional arrangements ...

Race Reconfigured in an Era of Global Restructuring

Many scholars are observing that during this age of globalization human societies are becoming more tightly integrated into a nexus of intercultural and transnational fields of power, knowledge and commodification. Advanced telecommunications, the increased mobility of capital and labor, and rapid flows of culture and commodities compress time and space across an uneven political and economic geography, giving the impression that, in some respects, the world is becoming smaller and more accessible. The world as 'global village', however, is not set against an idyllic background. Unlike the principles of reciprocity and redistribution which once governed everyday life in the typical village of the ethnographic record, the global community is marked by, among other things, a decentralization of capital accumulation and an upward reconcentration of wealth in[to] the hands of a few. Within this global community we also find a heightening of differences and a deepening of identity politics, often along life-threatening lines of conflict. In many instances, these volatile lines of differentiation relate to shifting dynamics of race as they interact with and mediate those of class, ethnicity, nationality and gender.

...

Today, racial meanings and practices are changing, becoming less stable and more contradictory, and ranging in visibility from subtle, hidden subtexts to flagrant acts of hate speech and genocidal violence. Racial tensions and politics are not at all confined to societies, such as those of the United States and South Africa, in which the most blatant and rigid forms of racial formation developed in contexts of white supremacy. As anthropological studies of intergroup tensions in Fiji, Sri Lanka and Rwanda illustrate, racialization, or the social processes that give rise to new racial identities or the transformation of old ones, is not limited to social orders structured around the (immediate) dominance of 'whites'. While in the overall global scheme of things, whiteness in its cross-cultural varieties has certainly come to be a principal locus of domination, it is important to note that there are also other racisms – subordinate racisms – which, nonetheless, ultimately feed into the structural power of whiteness.

To underscore the severity and far-reaching scope of the problems caused by deepening disparities and conflicts around the world, some researchers have used the concept of *global apartheid* to characterize the troubling gaps in wealth, power, military control and life expectancy that are widening as neoliberal, free market, global integration proceeds. ... For the most part, those most adversely affected are peoples of color whose subordinate positions within international fields of power and political economy have historically been rationalized in terms of class and nation as well as race. Even at this neocolonial juncture, virtually all over the world dark skin still correlates with the brunt of social inequality and structural violence. However, despite race's global reach, [we should not] assume any overarching uniformity in patterns of racial formation. Anthropologists, with their comparative research orientation, are likely to contribute a great deal to our understanding of the diversity of racial formations.

Edited extract from: Faye V. Harrison, 'Unraveling "Race" for the Twenty-first Century', in J. MacClancy (ed.), *Exotic No More: Anthropology on the Front Line* (Chicago: University of Chicago Press, 2002), pp. 145–66 (extracts from pp. 145–51).

A Source of Meanings and a Site of Social Discipline and Control

11	**The Body: Subjugated and Unsexed** *Judith Okely*

The human body is subject to many forms of socially imposed discipline and control. Examples are readily found. Elaborate rules govern covering and revealing the body, from formal uniforms to less formal (but equally binding) dress codes and fashions. The body itself is frequently moulded and modified according to social norms and requirements. A person's very handling of their body (for example in a stiff, relaxed or 'sexy' way, or through gesture and posture) is often socially enjoined or condemned. This is an extract from an article by the social anthropologist Judith Okely, in which Okely reflects from the perspective of her later anthropological training on her memory of her own education at an English girls' boarding school in the 1950s.

The concern with demeanour and carriage is one aspect of a total view of the body which reflects the extent of the institution's invasion and the ambivalences of its intentions. Marcel Mauss (1936) has discussed the ways different societies, groups and forms of education make use of the body. These may change over time and there are individual variations. Mauss isolates three factors: social, psychological and biological: 'In all the elements of the art of using the human body, the facts of education are dominant ... The child, the adult, imitates actions which have succeeded and which he has seen to succeed among persons in whom he has confidence and who have authority over him' (Mauss 1936: 369). In the girls' boarding school, the pupils must acquire such movements. They may give the longed-for anonymity, as well as conspicuous selection as a team member. Within our school there could be no 'natural' movement which might contradict what the authorities considered correct. 'Bad' ways we had learnt elsewhere had to be changed. We did not merely unconsciously imitate movements and gestures, we were consciously made to sit, stand and move in uniform ways. We were drilled and schooled, not by those in whom we had confidence, but by those who had power over us. Our flesh was unscarred, yet our gestures bore their marks. Even when outside the classroom or off the games field, we were to sit, stand and walk erect, chin up, back straight, shoulders well back. At table when not eating, our hands were to rest in our laps. During the afternoon rest period, matrons ordered us not to lie on our backs with knees bent. The games mistresses watched girls at meals, at roll call and in chapel, and would award good and bad 'deportment marks', recorded on a chart, and with house cups. If you were consistently upright you won a red felt badge, embroidered with the word 'Deportment'. This, sewn on your tunic, was a sign of both achievement and defeat. Our minds and understanding of the world were to reflect our custodians. With no private space, we could not even hide in our bodies, which also had to move in unison with their thoughts.

The authorities observed accurately the language of the body. However much a girl might say the right things, do and act within the rules, and however in order her uniform may be, her general carriage, her minutest gesture could betray a lack of conviction, a failure in conversion. I remember (after yet another term's anxious waiting for promotion) being called to the headmistress who said that I needed to improve my 'attitude' before I could be made a sergeant. I was baffled because I thought I had successfully concealed my unorthodoxy. I had said and done what appeared to me to be in order. But they must have seen through me, just by the way my body spoke. It also had to be tempered. I eventually won my deportment badge, and then soared from sergeant, to sub-prefect, to prefect. But my conformity over-reached itself; the games mistress took me aside and said I was now sitting and walking too stiffly, too rigidly. I was becoming conspicuous again.

Eventually the imitating child becomes the part. To survive in a place which beats down diversity, the victim has to believe in the rightness of his or her controller. Children and adolescents are most vulnerable, their minds and growing bodies may be permanently shaped. Apparently insignificant details such as bearing and posture are emphasised because, to use Bourdieu's words, the body is treated 'as a memory'. The principles of a whole cosmology or ethic are 'placed beyond the grasp of consciousness, and hence cannot be touched by voluntary, deliberate transformation' (Bourdieu 1977: 94). At an Old Girls' meeting, I talked with an old form-mate who had tried to train as an opera singer, but who could never breathe deeply enough. She spontaneously laid the blame on her schooling – her chest had, as it were, been too rigidly encased, and later she couldn't free herself, couldn't project her voice. In our bodies, we carried their minds into the future.

The presence of corporal punishment in boys' schools and its absence in girls' schools indicates differing attitudes to bodily display and contact, and possibly a differing consciousness of sexuality. Connections have been made between the childhood beatings of English males and their adult predilections for flagellation in brothels. Although our deportment was continually viewed, our corporal modesty nevertheless stayed intact. In punishment, the girls were fully clothed and untouchable. In this sense, our bodies were invisible, anaesthetised and protected for one man's intrusion later.

As skeletons, we were corrected and straightened, ordered to sit and stand in upright lines. As female flesh and curves, we were concealed by the uniform. Take the traditional gym slip – a barrel shape with deep pleats designed to hide breasts, waist, hips and buttocks, giving freedom of movement without contour. My mother wore such a tunic. Previously women wore clothes which revealed the 'hourglass' shape, but one made rigid and immobile by 'stays' or corsets. From the gym slip of the 1930s, we had graduated to the tunic of thick serge ('hop-sack' we called it), without pleats, but again skilfully flattening the breasts and widening the waist. While my mother's legs had been hidden and desexualised by thick black stockings, we wore thick brown ones, 'regulation shade', and called them 'bullet-proofs'.

In those days before tights, our movements were further constrained lest we expose our suspenders beneath our short tunics. There was no risk of any greater exposure. We had to wear two pairs of knickers – white 'linings' and thick navy-blue baggy knickers complete with pocket. For gym we removed our tunics and any girl in linings only was shamed and punished. In summer the navy knickers were replaced by pale blue ones.

A friend still recalls being given a 'disobedience' for doing handstands and, unknown to her, exposing her knickers to a nearby gardener. She was told only to say 'for handstands' at roll call. Thus her unmentionable exposure was effectively treated by psychological exposure. For games, our shorts concealed the existence of a split between the thighs. Two deep pleats in front and back made them like a skirt, but one which did not lift and reveal the thighs or buttocks as we ran or jumped. The lower abdomen retained its mystery.

This was the fifties when the dominant female fashion meant long full skirts. Yet our tunics had to be 'three inches above the knee when kneeling' (note the supplicant pose), even for girls aged seventeen years. I have been informed by a girl at another boarding school in the 1960s, when the miniskirt symbolised fashionable femininity, that her tunic had to be 'touching the floor when kneeling'. Thus the girls' schools demand the opposite to the notion of sexuality in the world outside. Our appearance was neutered. Our hair could not touch the backs of our shirt collars; in effect we were given the male 'short back and sides'. The crucial inspection time was the daily march-past at roll call. The dilemma was whether to bend forward and be rebuked for 'poking' the head (and not marching in the male military fashion) or whether to straighten up and risk being summoned for mutilation by the hairdresser. We were caught between conformity to the school, and saving our female sexuality as symbolised by longer hair.

The girls' uniform also had strange male traits: lace-up shoes, striped shirts, blazers, ties and tie pins. Unlike some of the boys' uniforms, ours was discontinuous with the clothes we would wear in adulthood. To us the school tie had no significance for membership of an 'old boy network'. We were caught between a male and female image long after puberty, and denied an identity which asserted the dangerous consciousness of sexuality. Immediately we left school, we had to drop all masculine traits, since a very different appearance was required for marriageability. Sexual ripeness, if only expressed in clothes, burst out. The hated tunics and lace-ups were torn, cut, burnt or flung into the sea. Old girls would return on parade, keen to demonstrate their transformation from androgyny to womanhood. To be wearing the diamond engagement ring was the ultimate achievement. There was no link between our past and future. In such uncertainty our confidence was surely broken.

References

Bourdieu, Pierre. *Outline of a Theory of Practice* (Cambridge: Cambridge University Press, 1977).

Mauss, Marcel. 'Les Techniques du Corps', in M. Mauss, *Anthropologie et Sociologie* (Paris: Presses Universitaires de France, 1938).

Extracted from: Judith Okely, 'Privileged, Schooled and Finished: Boarding Education for Girls', in S. Ardener (ed.), *Defining Females: The Nature of Women in Society* (London: Croom Helm, 1978), pp. 109–39 (extracts from pp. 128–31). Reprinted in Judith Okely, *Own or Other Culture* (London: Routledge), pp. 147–74.

Braveness and the Gaze of Others

This wrestling match has become a rare site in northern Philippines. The men are not competing on physical strength. Instead, it is a joint venturing, a dance, where both men by exposing their bodies defeat their *angbetang* – the shyness of the young.

Photographer: Henrik Hvenegaard (Body Category Finalist of the RAI's International Anthropology of Sport Photo Competition 2010). © Henrik Hvenegaard.

I.3 Ways of Thinking and Communicating

Language Evolution

12	**How Humans are Different** *Robin Dunbar*

Language is perhaps the most strikingly human of all of our behaviours – we might go so far as to say it is what makes humans human. In this extract, biological anthropologist Robin Dunbar explores the role that language plays in making humans so very different from our cousins, the other great apes. On a genetic level we are very similar to the other great apes, yet there is unquestionably some tangible difference that marks us apart. Dunbar argues that it is our ability to not only conceptualise complex imaginary ideas but to communicate them to others using language that provides the basis of this difference. If we take this as a starting point we can begin to understand the massive impact that the development of language has had on the course of human evolution.

Let's begin with an easy question: in exactly what ways are humans different from other species? I want to argue that the real differences lie in our capacity to live in an imagined world. In respect of almost everything else, including the basic features of our cognition – like memory and causal reasoning – we are all but indistinguishable from [the other] great apes. What we can do, and they cannot, is step back from the real world and ask: could it have been otherwise than we experience it? In that simple question lies the basis for everything that we would think of as uniquely human. Literature depends on our capacity to imagine a set of events, a world that is different from the one we personally inhabit on a day to day basis. Science depends on our capacity to imagine that the world could have been different, and then to ask why it has to be the way it is. Curiosity about distant places has led us to explore the furthest reaches of the planet, and even to venture hesitantly out into space.

By contrast, all other creatures alive today seem to have their noses thrust so firmly up against the grindstone of everyday experience that they cannot step back far enough to ask these kinds of questions. The world is as it is, and that seems to be all there is to it. They cannot explore the world of the imagination in the way that is so fundamental and so necessary to everything we would identify as being the core to the human condition – what it means to be human.

But there is one aspect of our cultural life that merits particular comment in this context. And this is our capacity to contemplate alternative universes. As a result of this, we have developed theories about transcendent spirit worlds, about life before birth and after death, about beings who live in a parallel universe who can influence the world in which we live. In short, it is the world of religion. There is something genuinely odd about our apparent capacity to live our lives partly in an inner world that is half-connected with the real world. I would argue that this capacity has a particularly close association with our capacity to produce literature. Both share the curious feature of requiring us to imagine fictional worlds with such intensity that we can believe in their veracity.

Given this, the question we have to ask is why apes, for example, cannot create these imagined worlds. At least, so far as I know, no one has yet produced convincing evidence that they can do so and pretty well most scientists working in the area are rather pessimistic that anyone is ever likely to do so in the future. Apes certainly do not produce any of the externally visible signs of being able to do so. They do not build structures, or organise festivals to worship gods or plan (never mind go on) expeditions to far distant places. And, crucially, they do not speak. Language is critical in this context, because if we do not communicate our ideas and thoughts about this inner world, it might as well not exist. This is not to say that language creates or gives rise to these inner worlds. Far from it: my point is only that language is necessary to communicate our discoveries about these inner worlds to each other. If we cannot share these experiences with others, we cannot build those communal intellectual edifices that we think of as the essence of human culture – dramas, histories, the rituals of religion, metaphysics and theologies. So, what is it about apes' minds that prevents them from doing so?

Extracted from: Robin Dunbar, 'Why are Humans not just Great Apes?', in C. Pasternak (ed.), *What Makes Us Human?* (Oxford: Oneworld Books, 2007), pp. 38–40.

13   Technical Difficulties and Hopeful Monsters
Terrence Deacon

To what extent is it reasonable to think that humans were somehow 'prefigured' for language ability? How does an idea like this sit with our understanding of how evolution works and the history of human evolution? In this extract, Terrence Deacon considers the evolution of language in humans. It has often been erroneously thought that humans are the 'most evolved' of all animals, that our communication abilities reflect this, and that given enough time perhaps other animals would also develop complex language skills like ours. Deacon demonstrates why the idea of human language being somehow 'evolutionarily predetermined' is flawed, and discusses the idea that the rich variety of vocal communication seen in animal species are far from being under-evolved forms of language, but instead reflect something quite different from what humans do. From this starting point he argues that human language and complex symbolic thought form a symbiotic relationship that allows our species to access a bewildering range of cognitive abilities, which truly make us the 'symbolic species'.

One of the most common views about language evolution is that it is the inevitable outcome of evolution. Evolution was headed this way, our way. As the only species capable of conceiving of our place among all the others, we see what looks like a continuous series of stages leading up to one species capable of such reflections. It goes without saying that a more articulate, more precise, more flexible means of communicating should always be an advantage, all other things being equal. In terms of cooperative behaviours, a better ability to pass on information about distant or hidden food resources, or to organise labour for a hunt, or to warn of impending danger, would be advantageous for kin and the social group as a whole. Better communication skills might also contribute to more successful social manipulation and deception. The ability to convince and mislead one's competitors or cooperate and connive with one's social and sexual partners could also have provided significant reproductive advantages, particularly in social systems where competition determines access to defendable resources or multiple mates. In fact, it's difficult to imagine any human endeavour that would not benefit from better communication. Looked at this way, it appears that humans have just developed further than other species along an inevitable progressive trend towards better thinking and better communicating.

Surely we must be part of a trend of better communication in some form? It seems to be an unstated assumption that if biological evolution continues long enough, some form of language will eventually evolve in many other species. Are chimpanzees the runners-up, lagging only a little behind on the road to language? As in *Planet of the Apes*, a science fiction movie in which our more hairy cousins catch up to a human level of mental and linguistic abilities, we imagine that if given sufficient time, something like language is prefigured in evolution.

Of no other form of communication is it legitimate to say that 'language is a more complicated version of that'. It is just as misleading to call other species' communication systems simple languages as it is to call them languages. In addition to asserting that a Procrustean mapping (making the data fit the standard model) of one to the other is possible, the analogy ignores the sophistication and power of animals' non-linguistic communication, whose capabilities may also be without language parallels. Perhaps we see other species' communication through the filter of language metaphors because language is too much a natural part of our everyday cognitive apparatus to let us easily gain an outside perspective on it. Yet our experience of its naturalness, its matter-of-factness, belies its alien nature in the grander scheme of things. It is an evolutionary anomaly, not merely an evolutionary extreme.

My point is not that we humans are better or smarter than other species, or that language is impossible for them. It is simply that these differences are not a matter of incommensurate kinds of language, but rather that non-human forms of communication are something quite different from language.

Edited extract from: Terrence Deacon, *The Symbolic Species: The Co-evolution of Language and the Human Brain* (London: Penguin, 1997), pp. 28 and 33.

Language and Classification

14 The 'Savage' Mind
Claude Lévi-Strauss

Probably the best known account of classification – how human beings name and organise categories of things in nature and in social life – is that by the French philosopher and anthropologist Claude Lévi-Strauss. His book The Savage Mind *might nowadays need the term 'savage' to be clearly put in italics, as would his use of the term 'primitive' when he is describing the many peoples around the world whose complex ways of classifying he describes; but, of course, he was trying to challenge the dominant view in Western society that such people were 'savage' or 'primitive', that is 'backward', behind 'modern' society and so on. His evidence shows the key anthropological theme that all peoples in the world have elaborate, intellectually profound ways of making meaning – and that it has just been a Western misapprehension that their ways of thinking and knowing were somehow inferior to those of Western 'scientific' society. The examples indicated below and the arguments Lévi-Strauss makes help us to see that such prejudice is untenable. In particular, if we pay attention to the complexity of language in different cultures, we will see how they all involve levels of abstractness and complexity that we might miss if we view it only from our own point of view. Indeed, Lévi-Strauss begins with the argument: 'richness of*

*abstract words is not a monopoly of civilized languages'. The modern
anthropologist starts, then, from the premise that language
classification is universal and that we cannot simply place the different
ways of putting things together and of explaining their relationships
into a hierarchy (with our own at the top). Such ethnocentrism is
exactly what the field of anthropology has spent the past fifty years
challenging, and represents a key starting point for any study of the
discipline and its account of cultural variety around the world. The
opening passage of* The Savage Mind *brings these points home both
concretely and theoretically.*

It has long been the fashion to invoke languages which lack the terms for
expressing such a concept as 'tree' or 'animal', even though they contain
all the words necessary for a detailed inventory of species and varieties.
But, to begin with, while these cases are cited as evidence of the supposed
ineptitude of 'primitive people' for abstract thought, other cases are at the
same time ignored which make it plain that richness of abstract words is not
a monopoly of civilized languages. In Chinook, a language widely spoken
in the north-west of North America, to take one example, many properties
and qualities are referred to by means of abstract words: 'This method', Boas
says, 'is applied to a greater extent than in any other language I know'. The
proposition 'The bad man killed the poor child' is rendered in Chinook: 'The
man's badness killed the child's poverty'; and for 'The woman used too small
a basket' they say: 'She put the potentilla roots into the smallness of a clam
basket' (Boas 1911: 657–58).

In every language, moreover, discourse and syntax supply indispensable
means of supplementing deficiencies of vocabulary. And the tendentious
character of the argument referred to in the last paragraph becomes very
apparent when one observes that the opposite state of affairs, that is, where
very general terms outweigh specific names, has also been exploited to
prove the intellectual poverty of Savages: 'Among plants and animals he [the
Indian] designates by name only those which are useful or harmful, all
others are included under the classification of bird, weed, etc.'

In fact, the delimitation of concepts is different in every language, and,
as the author of the article 'nom' in the *Encyclopédie* correctly observed in
the eighteenth century, the use of more or less abstract terms is a function
not of greater or lesser intellectual capacity, but of differences in the interests
– in their intensity and attention to detail – of particular social groups
within the national society: 'In an observatory a star is not simply a star but
of Capricorn or of Centaur or of the Great Bear, etc. In stables every horse
has a proper name – Diamond, Sprite, Fiery, etc.' Further, even if the
observation about so-called primitive languages referred to at the beginning
of the chapter could be accepted as it stands, one would not be able to

conclude from this that such languages are deficient in general ideas. Words like 'oak', 'beech', 'birch', etc., are no less entitled to be considered as abstract words than the word 'tree'; and a language possessing only the word 'tree' would be, from this point of view, less rich in concepts than one which lacked this term but contained dozens or hundreds for the individual species and varieties.

The proliferation of concepts, as in the case of technical languages, goes with more constant attention to properties of the world, with an interest that is more alert to possible distinctions which can be introduced between them. This thirst for objective knowledge is one of the most neglected aspects of the thought of people we call 'primitive'. Even if it is rarely directed towards facts of the same level as those with which modern science is concerned, it implies comparable intellectual application and methods of observation. In both cases the universe is an object of thought at least as much as it is a means of satisfying needs.

Every civilization tends to overestimate the objective orientation of its thought and this tendency is never absent. When we make the mistake of thinking that the Savage is governed solely by organic or economic needs, we forget that he levels the same reproach at us, and that to him his own desires for knowledge seems more balanced than ours.

… Among the Hanunoo of the Philippines a custom as simple as that of betel chewing demands a knowledge of four varieties of areca nut and eight substitutes for them, and of five varieties of betel and five substitutes. Almost all Hanunoo activities require an intimate familiarity with local plants and a precise knowledge of plant classification. Contrary to the assumption that subsistence-level groups never use but a small segment of the local flora, ninety-three per cent of the total number of native plant types are recognized by the Hanunoo as culturally significant (Conklin 1954: 249).

Editorial note:
Lévi-Strauss goes on to show how such classification is linked to explanations: for instance different classes of animal and contact with them may be associated with cures for different kinds of ill health, such as

Contact with a woodpecker's beak, blood of a woodpecker, nasal insufflation of the powder of a mummified woodpecker, gobbled egg of the bird *koukcha* (Iakoute), against toothache, scrofula, high fevers and tuberculosis respectively);

…

The precise definition of and the specific uses ascribed to the natural products which Siberian peoples use for medicinal purposes illustrate the care and ingeniousness, the attention to detail and concern with distinctions employed by theoretical and practical workers in societies of this kind.

Examples like these could be drawn from all parts of the world and one may readily conclude that animals and plants are not known as a result of their usefulness; they are deemed to be useful or interesting because they are first of all known.

It may be objected that science of this kind can scarcely be of much practical effect. The answer to this is that its main purpose is not a practical one. It meets intellectual requirements rather than or instead of satisfying needs.

The real question is not whether the touch of a woodpecker's beak does in fact cure toothache. It is rather whether there is a point of view from which a woodpecker's beak and a man's tooth can be seen as 'going together' (the use of this congruity for therapeutic purposes being only one of its possible uses), and whether some initial order can be introduced into the universe by means of these groupings. Classifying, as opposed to not classifying, has a value of its own, whatever form the classification may take.

References

Boas, Franz. *Handbook of American Indian Languages*, Part 1 (Washington, DC: Bureau of American Ethnology, 1911).

Conklin, H.C. 'The Relation of Hanunoo Culture to the Plant World', Ph.D. dissertation (New Haven, CT: Yale University, 1954).

Extracted from: Claude Lévi-Strauss, *The Savage Mind* (London: Weidenfeld and Nicolson, 1966), p. 9ff.

Explanation of Events

15 Witchcraft Beliefs
Godfrey Lienhardt

The passage by Lévi-Strauss showed not only that different societies classify the natural world in complex and often very different ways, but also that the link between different classes of phenomena may serve the purpose of explaining such issues as misfortune, ill health and so on. The example quoted was that of the woodpecker's beak and its association, for Siberian people, with a cure for toothache. The passage below, by Godfrey Lienhardt, takes this argument further by showing how the Azande people in Africa likewise offer explanations for misfortune that again are associated with different classes of natural life – in this case diagnosis is achieved with reference to feeding poison to chickens. But Lienhardt, drawing upon seminal work by Evans-Pritchard, takes us further into Zande thinking so that we don't just see such links as 'mistaken' but rather understand the internal logic as actually being not unlike the logic we use in our own attempts to explain accident and misfortune. The term 'witchcraft' used to describe the overall process is perhaps misleading, if it leads us to see Azande as 'non-scientific'; rather, we can follow the anthropologist's lead in attempting to describe what actually happens, the language used for labelling classes of natural and social life being addressed here, and how different levels of explanation are brought to bear before an Azande takes action. Moreover, these beliefs are not just linked to actual harm or misfortune but also associated with issues of power and princely rule – the authority to determine the explanation for a problem ultimately lies with leaders, as in other societies. And a further complexity in our understanding of what is going on is that Azande are quite aware that poisons administered to chickens might not always work in the way expected, but this need not bring the whole system into doubt – there are checks and balances just as with any system of belief. It is this comparison with belief systems in general, including our own, that enables us to move beyond seeing 'witchcraft' as simply an exotic or 'non-scientific' belief and instead recognising the underlying principles of belief and explanation that can be compared across societies.

The Azande's beliefs in witchcraft, like those of other peoples, start from the observed facts of misfortune and differential luck; the desire to explain these; and the assumption that the reasons for them are in other people. 'Witchcraft' for Azande is thus a term used to some extent like 'providence' or 'chance' in England; but behind it is a more searching explanatory intention. 'Witchcraft' accounts primarily for the particular manifestations, rather than general characteristics, of human unhappiness.

A Zande who has cultivated his garden to the best of his ability, let us say, following all locally prescribed procedures, has a bad yield because of some pest. He recognizes that it is the pest that has ruined his crop, but he is not content to let the matter rest there. He wants to know why it is his particular crop that has failed when others promise a fine harvest. Brought up to explain misfortune and death by 'witchcraft', and to believe that witches and other secret enemies may be identified by the consultation of oracles, he turns to the oracles to discover who may be responsible for his bad luck.

Of the several kinds of Zande oracle, the most authoritative is *benge*, a poison administered to chickens whose reactions to it vary and are interpreted as positive or negative answers to questions asked of the poison oracle. The following text gives some indication of how this works: *Benge* is the wood from which [Azande] derive oracles. If a man's relative dies he consults *benge* about his death in order to find out the witch who killed him. … A Zande catches some chickens today and takes them to *benge*. He mixes *benge* with a little water and he seizes a chicken and pours *benge* into its beak, and addresses *benge* thus: '*Benge, benge*, you are in the throat of the chicken. I will die this year, *benge* hear it, twist the fowl round and round and lay down its corpse. It is untrue, I will eat my eleusine [*a genus of grasses sometimes called by the common name goosegrass*] this year and the year after, let the fowl survive'. If he will not die the fowl survives. If he will die the fowl dies in accordance with the speech of *benge*.

Such beliefs can be shown to have several important functions and effects in Zande society. For instance, witchcraft beliefs represent a kind of popular psychology and moral philosophy, since the people whom a Zande expects to bewitch him, and whose names are likely to be put before the oracle, are those whom he thinks have reason to dislike him. These also are likely to be those whom he himself dislikes. To suspect witchcraft, then, is to assess motive and intention. Also (since the wing of a fowl that has died from *benge* in an oracular consultation may be sent to the witch identified by it, to blow upon to 'cool' his witchcraft) the result is to deal openly and frankly with the minor irritations of human relationships before they accumulate into determined hatred. Writing of a very different people, the Navaho Indians of North America, the late Clyde Kluckhohn concluded that: 'In a society where the relative strength of anticipation of punishment for overt aggression is high, witchcraft allows imaginary aggression. Witchcraft channels the displacement of aggression, facilitating emotional adjustment with a minimum disturbance of social relationships'. Therefore also: 'Witchcraft belief allows the verbalization of anxiety in a framework that is understandable and that implies the possibility of doing something' (Kluckhohn 1944).

Whilst witches are potentially controllable by the society, since they are living individuals, the caprices of the environment are not, since they are part of nature. …

Zande acceptance of witchcraft and oracles has another function more specific to Zande society. When legal cases lie for injury – for witchcraft, adultery, or other wrongs which it is easy to suspect but difficult to prove – and the evidence from different primary consultations of the oracle are contradictory, then the oracles of princes are regarded as final. Thus the regressions of doubt and conflict of opinions in matters which, by their very nature, cannot become clear by demonstrable proofs, have an end in the attribution of infallibility to the oracles of rulers. The princes' oracles then have legal and political functions, in bolstering the system of rule and providing a means of settling issues which must otherwise, to the detriment of effective law, remain in dispute.

Evans-Pritchard emphasized that the Azande were not able or not prepared to put their whole system of beliefs in witchcraft, oracles and magic to any test which would call the validity of the whole into question.

They would not, for example, test the poison on the fowl as though it were simply a natural poison, without putting any question to it at all, for this would be a foolish waste of poison. When an oracle contradicted itself, answering 'yes' and 'no' to exactly the same question, they would not doubt the value of oracles in general. They would merely argue that in this particular case there had been some fault in the procedure or the poison.

... [Michael] Polanyi has considered the implications of this Zande system of belief for our understanding of the stability of belief and the 'fiduciary basis of knowledge', as he calls it, more generally. The Azande accept on traditional faith the assumption upon which their whole system of thought rests, and which, since it involves circular argument, defeats particular doubts:

> So long as each doubt is defeated in its turn, its effect is to strengthen the fundamental convictions against which it was raised. 'Let the reader consider (writes Evans-Pritchard) any argument that would utterly demolish all Zande claims for the power of the oracles. If it were translated into Zande modes of thought it would serve to support their entire structure of belief'. Thus the circularity of a conceptual system tends to reinforce itself by contact with every fresh topic.

The stability of belief, then, is shown by 'the way it denies to any rival conception the ground in which it might take root':

> a new conception, e.g., that of natural causation, which would take the place of Zande superstition, could be established only by a whole series of relevant instances, and such evidence cannot accumulate in the minds of people if each of them is disregarded in its turn for lack of the concept that would lend significance to it. (Polanyi 1958: 123)

Such is a philosopher's and scientist's account of what anthropologists have called 'collective representations', categories of thought which are absolutely assumed among members of a given society. In Polanyi's terms, 'by holding the same set of presuppositions they mutually confirm each other's interpretation of experience'.

References
Kluckhohn, Clyde. *Navaho Witchcraft* (Boston: Beacon Press, 1944).
Polanyi, Michael. *Personal Knowledge: Towards a Post Critical Philosophy* (London: Routledge, 1958).

Edited extract from: Godfrey Lienhardt, *Social Anthropology* (Oxford: Oxford University Press, 1966), pp. 124–26.

The Ethnographic Study of Language and Communication

The authors in extracts 16 to 19 provide an introduction to how ethnographers might study the varied ways that humans communicate. These include both spoken and written language and also non-linguistic 'modes' of communication, such as visual, gestural, and so forth. The dominant view of these modes of communication tends to focus on spoken language, which we illustrate via an extract by Rampton of how linguistic ethnography shows the complexity and range of language varieties, beyond simple associations of one language with one people. Here both language and identity, such as that associated with ethnicity or with nationality, are shown to be multiple and varied rather than fixed and static, as a more formal account might suggest. Before this we address a major dimension of communication that has acquired high status in some societies, namely literacy. In a book *On Ethnography*, written for researchers in language and literacy, Heath and Street explain how dominant understandings of literacy in many Western societies, especially in educational contexts, do not capture the full and rich range of uses of reading and writing that are evident across cultures. In a book written by adult literacy educators working in Ethiopia, Gebre et al. show how applications of an ethnographic perspective on literacy might lead to more awareness of local cultural uses and meanings and the importance for educators to build on the local – that is to take account of local knowledge and ideas – rather than simply impose outside views. Finally, we include recent texts that recognise the importance of other 'modes' of communication besides language and literacy, including visual and gestural modes. Kress and van Leeuwen remind us that in making meaning we always invoke a variety of such modes, combining for instance the layout of a text with colour and visual design in addition to the classic forms of written script on which education has traditionally focused. Again an ethnographic perspective enables us to track such complex patterns of communication cross-culturally and to put our own particular uses into broader and comparative perspective – the classic approach of anthropology.

16	**The Ethnographic Study of Language and Communication** *Shirley Heath and Brian Street*

In the first extract, Heath and Street each describe their own entry into this field, in both cases a classic example of the ethnographer keeping their ears and eyes open to 'what is going on' and thereby recognising different practices than they might have expected given their respective backgrounds. Understanding aspects of communication such as language and literacy require us, then, to reflect on the ways in which we 'find out' about such topics and not just describe them from some apparently 'neutral' standpoint. Heath, for instance, describes how as an anthropologist she entered the field, curious to know what is going on and with some prior questions she wanted to find answers to. A key question was how local people, blacks and whites, in the Piedmont Carolinas in the southeastern U.S.A., handled language. Dominant stereotypes referred to them – and to their children as they entered school – as in 'deficit' and 'lacking' many language skills. Heath had been brought up in this part of the world and knew this not to be true. But how to represent what was going on, to describe the 'ways with words' of such people and earn them the respect their complex knowledge deserved – a classic anthropological position as researchers attempt to challenge dominant stereotypes and describe the complex skills of the people they study. Such a study appears to start from knowledge of language, dialect, switching between varieties of language, and so on. However, Heath came to realise that to understand language we need also to know about 'integrity and quality of life and the need to understand how long-standing personal human relationships slip away under political and social pressures'. This insight has now become a classic way in which anthropologists, sociolinguists and others have come to see language – that we need to understand the social context in which speaking, listening, reading and writing are embedded rather than trying to isolate a thing called 'language' (or, as Street shows below in an extract from the same book, 'literacy'). Heath's study has proved particularly important in educational contexts, where perhaps the isolation and separation of skills is a frequent part of the way subjects are taught. Researchers in the U.K. as well as the U.S., and in many other countries, are coming to address 'ways with words' from a more anthropological perspective. To follow through the implications of this for our own involvement in education in the U.K., for instance, would lead us to listen to the varieties of language and dialect that we all encounter in daily life, in and out of school, as the Rampton extract indicates and also, as the Kress and van Leeuwen example shows, including paying attention in the present digital era to how we use a variety of signs to communicate on the internet, via mobile phones and so forth. There is considerable scope here for applying such anthropological ideas to our own everyday practices.

Shirley Goes to Trackton and Roadville

What opens ethnographers to the idea of undertaking their particular study? If pushed hard enough, most ethnographers admit that a sense of curiosity and adventure, a desire to know, a sense of 'real' unknowns take them to the field. Moreover, within every such researcher rests a core concern about the quality and integrity of human life.

We thus begin ... not with the usual advice that ethnographers start with a 'good' research question but rather the reminder that is a refrain throughout this volume: As you collect data, know the company you keep as ethnographer and get to know yourself as constant learner – ever curious and open to what's happening. Remember always that we study something because we already know something. The opener that led to *Ways with Words: Language, Life and Work in Communities and Classrooms* (Heath 1983), a book often seen as centred on language, came from knowing that the political dimensions of the late 1960s were wiping away social and historical realities. When the civil rights movement and desegregation came to the southeastern United States in the late 1960s, most White teachers had had lifelong and almost daily interactions with Blacks of their region. Yet the communicative underpinnings of these relationships suddenly seemed to disappear when White teachers claimed they could not understand the talk of Black children in their classrooms. Further 'new' proclamations came in local newspapers and from Black and White teachers alike: Black children could not speak 'proper' or 'standard' English; they did not listen well; and they came to school without skills in counting, identifying, and classifying. Yet in all rural and small-town areas of the Southeast, every radio station carried programs in which local and national Black speakers shifted back and forth across varieties of English. The civil rights movement had generated more widespread attention to the oratorical powers of Black speakers than at any other time in American history.

Moreover, every merchant in small towns knew well the counting, identifying, and classifying skills of children, Black and White, who were sent to stores by their caregiving grandparents with whom the children stayed while parents worked. In the springtime, these children knew how to distinguish one type of plant seedling from another, one kind of hoe from another, and what the count should be on certain pharmaceutical prescriptions they were sent to the drugstore to collect. In many parts of the Southeast, every White knew members of the Black middle class whose linguistic repertoires exceeded their own. Periods in military service, residence in northern cities, or extensive travel in connection with their professions had expanded the number of dialects, languages, and styles of talking of the numerous Blacks who sought opportunities outside the Southeast after World War II.

Shirley's study of language socialization in southeastern communities, both Black and White, initially seemed to be about language. *Ways with Words*, however, ultimately proved to be about integrity and quality of life and the need to understand how long-standing personal human relationships slip away under political and social pressures. This illustration of what can open a desire for fieldwork in a particular place and time underscores the fact that within ethnography, the researcher is the instrument.

Though much is said about *participant observation* as the key means of collecting data as an ethnographer, the truth is that only rarely can we shed features of ourselves to be a 'real' participant. ... Ethnography forces us to think consciously about ways to enter into the life of the individual, group, or institutional life of the 'other.' ...

What ethnographers really want to know is 'What is happening here in the field site(s) I have chosen?' This question asks not just for a description of events and actions that people create, react to, assess, and learn within but also for history and explanations informed by and leading to theories. What does the ethnographer find when tracing the lines of connection for what is heard, said, and done by an individual? What about the study of groups that interact in their own communities in historically established ways while meanwhile denying knowledge drawn from habits they have followed all their lives? How do people adapt when their daily lives shift radically as a result of decisions brought about by social forces and institutions over which they have little or no control?

Following the account of how Shirley Heath entered the field and addressed language and literacy issues in their social and political context, the authors go on to describe how Brian Street came to do fieldwork in Iran. As with Shirley, his previous experience, in this case having studied literature, writing and literacy, may have helped direct his view of local language and literacy practices in villages in Iran. He had not necessarily gone to the village to conduct this kind of study, but the power of that past experience and the conflict it threw up with dominant views of language and literacy led him, as with Shirley in the earlier account, to focus more closely on the everyday uses and meanings of language and literacy. Again it was not enough to simply isolate literacy, as previous scholars according to Shirley had isolated language; rather, the practices of reading and writing needed to be seen in their social context. The uses of reading and writing in Qur'anic schools and in trading arrangements were quite different from those evident in the village school, and constant comparison across these practices, and then with the dominant theories about them, led to a fuller and richer account than a more isolated or culturally biased view might have done. Again we might consider how these ideas could be applied to our own local contexts in the U.K.: How do schools view 'literacy'? What account do they take of the literacy practices of pupils outside school? What different social varieties of literacy might we identify in our own localities?

'What Really Happens Here?'

When Brian undertook the fieldwork in Iran that led to his book *Literacy in Theory and Practice* (Street 1984), he had a sense of contradictions between sweeping theories of literacy. He also knew what some ethnographers reported from their fieldwork about how reading and writing 'actually' happened. Brian describes how this prior knowledge went with him to Iran.

> When I went to Iran in the 1970s to undertake anthropological field research, I did not go to study 'literacy', but I found myself living in a mountain village where a great deal of literacy activity was going on. Maybe part of my interest derived from having done my first degree in English literature. I had moved into anthropology because of dissatisfaction with looking only at 'texts'. I wanted to locate texts with respect to 'practices'. I attempted to bring English literature together with anthropology through a Ph.D. on 'European Representations of Non-European Society in Popular Fiction'. I looked at popular stories of adventure in exotic places: the Tarzan stories, Rider Haggard, and John Buchan as popular authors and Rudyard Kipling, D.H. Lawrence, and Joseph Conrad as more established authors. I arrived in Iran as my field site already excited by the ways that writing and anthropology could be brought together. Perhaps it was this sense that led me to focus closely on the literacy practices of the villages I lived amongst and even more on the 'representations' of these practices by different parties.

> I was drawn then to the conceptual and rhetorical issues involved in representing the variety and complexity of literacy activity at a time when my encounter with people outside of the village suggested the dominant representation was of 'illiterate' backward villagers. Looking more closely at village life in light of these characterizations, I saw not only a lot of literacy going on but several quite different 'practices' associated with literacy – those in a traditional 'Quoranic school', those taking place in the new State schools, and the inscribed means that traders used in their buying and selling of fruit to urban markets. Versions of literacy by outside agencies (e.g., State education, UNESCO, and national literacy campaigns) did not capture these complex variations in literacy happening in one small locale where the people were generally characterized as 'illiterate'.

What happened in Brian's case repeats in certain ways for every ethnographer: a host of questions emerge from initial curiosity about patterns of symbol structures and their uses.

In terms of keeping track of 'decision rules' that will surely follow on from initial planning and entry to a field site, we see that Brian's approach and interest rest in his own earlier intellectual background. Decision rules within the field site led him to focus more tightly than expected on the variety and complexity of literary uses by the villagers. The ideas, judgments, and practices from accounts of outsiders also became data. The constant comparative principle behind decision rules led Brian to compare the insider world of the villagers with the outsider perspectives on that world.

As Brian moved forward, he compared his own findings with those of other scholars of literacy. He studied the work of anthropologist Jack Goody and many international literacy program developers who held to a theory of the 'great divide' between literacy and orality. He checked his own data through these theories and began to develop new ideas.

The theoretical validity of his account rests on ongoing negotiation with earlier accounts of literacy as well as research that he found when he returned to England from Iran. Eventually, a new hybrid theoretical position emerged from the testing of empirical data that he terms an 'ideological' model of literacy (Street 1984). Had Brian held to the 'great divide' theory that dominated literacy studies before and while he was in the field, and had he taken at face value ideas that outsiders had about the villagers' 'illiteracy', he would have interpreted his data merely to confirm these notions. Ethnographic work is dialogic between existing explanations and judgments (whether held by scholars, outsiders, or insiders) and ongoing data collection and analysis.

References

Heath, Shirley B. *Ways with Words: Language, Life and Work in Communities and Classrooms* (Cambridge: Cambridge University Press, 1983).

Street, Brian. *Literacy in Theory and Practice* (Cambridge: Cambridge University Press, 1984).

Edited extract from: Shirley Heath and Brian Street, *Ethnography: Approaches to Language and Literacy* (New York: National Council for Research in Language and Literacy, 2008), pp. 29–32 and 55–57.

Language and Ethnicity

17 **Language in Late Modernity**
B. Rampton

In the following extract, Rampton argues that notions of language and ethnicity are no longer seen as a fixed aspect of 'cultural inheritance' in which a particular language is associated with a particular ethnicity. Rather, it is now recognised that membership of a group and group identity are not always clear or permanent and that the language aspect of this is more fluid than used to be thought. Instead we need to ask about the 'social life of language' so that terms such as 'Asian' or 'youth' need to be located in particular circumstances, localities and conditions rather than taken as given or fixed. Language then is a resource that people use to achieve particular ends using categories and classification, as we have seen earlier in the accounts by Lévi-Strauss, Lienhardt and so on.

These ideas are especially relevant to educational views of language and ethnicity, and Rampton – like Heath in the earlier example from the U.S. – shows how traditional views of student uses of language tended to put them down and treat them as in 'deficit', just as traditional views of non-Western society tended to treat them as less competent thinkers. A more anthropological perspective has helped to shift education away from such ethnocentric views towards a more sophisticated view that people cannot be 'allocated unambiguously to one group or another' and that their language and thinking skills are equally complex, if we take the trouble to listen and watch using an ethnographic perspective. A further aspect of this classic anthropological approach is that the local specificity of language, ethnicity and so forth has to be seen in the larger context of institutions, economic and political systems and ideology. The concept of 'discourse' is used to describe these processes, rather than simply 'language'; people engage in different 'discourses' or uses of communication, according to context, drawing upon whatever communicative resources are appropriate – local dialects, standard language, literacy practices, visual modes and so on. It would be interesting to work through how far these ideas might be applied to contemporary experiences of students both in school and in their out of school lives.

There have been shifts in the view of ethnicity, where it is no longer enough to see ethnicity as either cultural inheritance, or as the strategic/political accentuation of inheritance. It is also necessary to reckon with the ways in which language can be used to extend ethnic co-membership as well as the ways in which ethnic forms, products and symbols are marketised, disseminated and appropriated as desirable commodities, life-style options and aesthetic objects. All in all, whether it is age- or ethnicity-based, belonging to a group now seems a great deal less clear, less permanent and less omni-relevant than it did twenty-five years ago, and this makes it much harder to produce an account of 'the language of such-and-such a social group', or 'language use among the —', than it used to be. The critical reflexivity associated with [an ethnographic perspective] asks where these claims are 'coming from' and where they fit in ongoing processes of political argument and policy formation; and it scrutinises them for what they leave out, why and with what consequences. Along with other approaches, it wants to know more about the social life of the language forms clustered under the label 'Asian', 'youth' or 'such-and-such a locality'; under precisely what conditions are these forms produced, doing what, when and where, in relation to who else is doing what in the vicinity, within what interactional and institutional histories? And so instead of investigating how old people, or Afro-Caribbeans, or Yorkshire folk, use language, analysis turns to the role that language plays when humans interact together in situations where (a) discourses of language group membership, age, ethnicity, region, etc., have currency, ... where (b) these categorisations are relevant to the participants (classifying and rating them differently), where (c) the participants may need, want or happen to orient actively to these categories and their associations, but where (d) they might also have other things on their minds, or have come to an understanding that temporarily neutralises the personal impact that these discourses can have.

These ... shifts also have major implications for our conceptualisation of the politics of language and culture. For much of the twentieth century, three very general perspectives have been highly influential in attempts to account for inequalities in the distribution of knowledge, influence and resources within stratified societies. The first perspective, 'the deficit position', has stressed the inadequacies of subordinate (out)groups and the importance of their being socialised into dominant (in)group norms. The second, with difference as its key word, has emphasised the integrity and autonomy of the subordinate group's language and culture and the need for institutions to be hospitable to diversity. In the third, the focus has shifted to larger structures of domination, and the need for institutions to combat the institutional processes and ideologies that reproduce the oppression of subordinate groups is stressed. There has obviously been a great deal of conflict between these interpretations of the basic character of inequality, and different perspectives have gained ascendancy at different times in different places. But they are all similar in treating the conflict as a relationship between groups and communities conceived as separate social, cultural and/or linguistic blocs.

More recently, however, they have been joined by a fourth very general perspective which challenges the assumption that people can be allocated unambiguously to one group or another. This view accepts the role that larger social, economic and political systems play in structuring dominant–subordinate, majority–minority relations, but argues that their impact on everyday experience cannot easily be predicted. Instead, the emphasis is on looking closely at how people make sense of inequality and difference in their local situations, and at how they interpret them in the context of a range of social relationships (gender, class, region, generation, etc.). This perspective is wary of seeing culture exclusively either as an elite canon or as a set of static ethnic essences or as a simple reflection of economic and political processes; it takes the view that the reality of people's circumstances is actively shaped by the ways in which they interpret and respond to them; and in line with this, it lays a good deal of emphasis on the cultural politics of imagery and representation.

Edited extract from: B. Rampton, *Language in Late Modernity* (Cambridge: Cambridge University Press, 2006), pp. 17–19.

Anthropological Approaches to Literacy and Numeracy

18 Everyday Literacies in Africa
A.H. Gebre, A. Rogers, B. Street and G. Openjuru

One of the ways in which anthropological ideas about ways of communicating have been applied in practical circumstances has been in adult education programmes in different countries. We illustrate this via an extract from a comparative study of literacy and numeracy in Ethiopia. The authors came from Ethiopia, Uganda and the U.K., and they worked through the implications of a more culturally sensitive view of learning and education for the ways in which such programmes can be taught. In particular, international organisations such as UNESCO and the World Bank, as well as national policy makers, tend to focus strongly on literacy as a central mode of communication. They argue that if the 'illiterate' are made 'literate' then the society as a whole will progress, 'take off' economically, 'modernise', and so on. The work of Heath and Street from an ethnographic perspective, as we saw, has already shown that such centralised ideas about literacy are not always well tuned to local meanings and reading and writing practices, and a number of educators are beginning to build upon their insights in order to develop more culturally sensitive education programmes. This requires educators to start from where the learners are – and this of course requires them to be able to recognise local reading and writing practices in the first place. The programme from which this excerpt is taken involved exactly such an attempt to help educators 'see' local literacies by developing an ethnographic perspective. This did not, of course, involve training them to be anthropologists, but rather helping them adopt a perspective of the kind evident in ethnographic study and applying it to their own particular circumstances as adult educators. In the present case, Gebre and his fellow trainers in Ethiopia gathered educators for a workshop in which they exchanged experiences of using an ethnographic perspective in order to observe and describe the variety of ways in which people read and write in different cultural contexts.

In southern Ethiopia, where this particular workshop was set, the participants were invited to go out into the streets and market places, to look more closely at the signs evident in public spaces, and to notice the variety of languages and scripts in use. This raised important questions regarding education and policy; it was not possible after this to claim that local people were 'illiterate' and that the outsiders were bringing them literacy. Instead, the questions became: Which scripts and languages were appropriate for different purposes? How did local people read the signs around them? And how could educators build on this prior knowledge and experience to help them extend their knowledge of literacy?

Taking an ethnographic approach to literacy and numeracy means that we start from the premise that people already have literacy practices. The question for adult educators is: How do we build on these practices? This question is different from assuming that people have no pre-existing literacy. But when we look at literacy in real life, we see that the word 'literacy' is used in many different ways. For example, some staff in some universities say, 'The students these days are illiterate'. This usage is different from the use of the word 'illiterate' in other contexts, particularly in a developing-country context.

An ethnographic approach to literacy then does not start by assuming that people are not literate. Rather, it seeks to discover what literacy activities there are in any society and how different people relate to these activities. Our first question will then be: Are they using literacy in some ways? There are many different modes of communication, but people may not use all of them; which mode a person uses is a choice, whether conscious or unconscious. Our researches have shown us that there are local literacy and numeracy practices, what a recent book has termed 'hidden literacies', that have been overlooked. When adult and non-formal educators try to persuade people to become 'literate', the question arises: Which literacy? We need to recognise the different kinds of literacies people have.

For instance, along the drive from Addis Ababa to the training centre in Yirgalem, a variety of languages were seen being utilised. Brian Street questioned the use of scripts when he noticed that Isuzu cargo trucks had the word Isuzu inscribed in both Arabic and Latin scripts on the back of many trucks. Multilingualism and multi-scriptism are then built into the experience of being literate in Ethiopia in a way that it is not in other places. If we walk around the town of Bahir Dar, what can we learn about literacy practices? Are local people taking for granted that signs will be written in a number of different languages and scripts whilst to outsiders this needs explaining and is not necessarily 'normal'? Which script is used for which kind of sign? Local people are making complex choices all the time but visitors need help with understanding what they mean.

Extracted from: A.H. Gebre, A. Rogers, B. Street and G. Openjuru, *Everyday Literacies in Africa: Ethnographic Studies of Literacy and Numeracy in Ethiopia* (Kampala: Fountain Publishers, 2009), pp. 15–16.

Multimodal Discourse

19	Multimodal Discourse *G. Kress and T. van Leeuwen*

Recent work in the field of communication has suggested that another Western preoccupation with ways of making meaning – namely the dominant emphasis on language – also needs to be revised, along with the approach to classification, categories, explanation and so on that we saw earlier. In the following extract, Kress and van Leeuwen address this ethnocentric view and argue instead for a notion of 'multimodality' in which a variety of modes are called upon to make meaning – visual, aural, gestural, and so on. Mass media and new technologies, such as digital communication and the internet, have shifted the balance away from written language and towards this variety of ways in which we make meaning – ways in fact which have always been present in our own and other societies, although perhaps the balance has shifted recently, as they say, away from 'a preference for monomodality' towards 'multimodality'. The study of signs – which they refer to as 'semiotics' – needs, then, to move beyond the separate 'camps' in which researchers either looked at visual or language or sound and so on and instead it needs to recognise that 'the "same" meanings can often be expressed in different semiotic modes'. One multi-skilled person can invoke a number of modes and may then choose which one is appropriate – such as music, spoken language, visual imagery. The answer to 'Shall I say this visually or verbally?' depends upon the context and the particular meanings the person has in mind.

We reproduce here two examples that the authors provide to illustrate this point. One is that of a famous painting, Noli me Tangere by Titian, in which the frame around the picture is seen as a key part of the way the artist communicated his meanings; we can 'read' the picture by looking not only at the visual images themselves – the figure of Christ, Mary Magdalen, a tree in the background – but also the placing of different lines, the staff and the tree, in such a way as to create boundaries. The visual separation between Christ and Mary Magdalen, for instance, is broken by her arm moving across the line of the tree and of the figure of Christ. Kress and van Leeuwen suggest that this interpretation is not just a matter of artists looking at high culture but can actually be extended to more everyday ways of making meaning; the 'search for common principles can be undertaken in different ways'. To illustrate this, they offer a more everyday example, that of families in England and Australia knocking down walls in their homes. This action, by mostly middle-class families, at a particular time from the 1970s onwards, can be interpreted as being about ways of expressing value systems – such as the separation of private and public space, high and low status. The 'ideology' of living was changing and the design and changing of space in houses provided a way of representing this. As with the other anthropological examples we have seen, this local and specific practice is linked by the authors to larger social patterns – changes in social hierarchy, status, economic positions and so on. It is possible here to apply these ideas to our own experience – whether our home spaces, the layout of classrooms, or the clubs and bars we frequent. Again an ethnographic perspective can help us to link concrete detail to these larger social theories and ideas.

For some time now, there has been, in Western culture, a distinct preference for monomodality. The most highly valued genres of writing (literary novels, academic treatises, official documents and reports, etc.) came entirely without illustration, and had graphically uniform, dense pages of print. Paintings nearly all used the same support (canvas) and the same medium (oils), whatever their style or subject. In concert performances all musicians dressed identically and only conductor and soloists were allowed a modicum of bodily expression. The specialised theoretical and critical disciplines which developed to speak of these arts became equally monomodal: one language to speak about language (linguistics), another to speak about art (art history), yet another to speak about music (musicology), and so on, each with its own methods, its own assumptions, its own technical vocabulary, its own strengths and its own blind spots.

More recently this dominance of monomodality has begun to reverse. Not only the mass media, the pages of magazines and comic strips for example, but also the documents produced by corporations, universities, government departments etc., have acquired colour illustrations and sophisticated layout and typography. And not only the cinema and the semiotically exuberant performances and videos of popular music, but also the avant-gardes of the 'high culture' arts have begun to use an increasing variety of materials and to cross the boundaries between the various art, design and performance disciplines, towards multimodal *Gesamtkunstwerke*, multimedia events, and so on.

... The 'same' meanings can often be expressed in different semiotic modes. ... [Here] we make this move our primary aim; and so we explore the common principles behind multimodal communication. We move away from the idea that the different modes in multimodal texts have strictly bounded and framed specialist tasks, as in a film where images may provide the action, sync sounds a sense of realism, music a layer of emotion, and so on, with the editing process supplying the 'integration code', the means for synchronising the elements through a common rhythm. ... Instead we move towards a view of multimodality in which common semiotic principles operate in and across different modes, and in which it is therefore quite possible for music to encode action, or images to encode emotion. This move comes, on our part, not because we think we had it all wrong before and have now suddenly seen the light. It is because we want to create a theory of semiotics appropriate to contemporary semiotic practice. In the past, and in many contexts still today, multimodal texts (such as films or newspapers) were organised as hierarchies of specialist modes integrated by an editing process. Moreover, they were produced in this way, with different, hierarchically organised specialists in charge of the different modes, and an editing process bringing their work together.

Today, however, in the age of digitisation, the different modes can be operated by one multi-skilled person, using one interface, one mode of physical manipulation, so that he or she can ask, at every point: 'Shall I express this with sound or music?', 'Shall I say this visually or verbally?', and so on. Our approach takes its point of departure from this new development.

Let us give one specific example. ... [Elsewhere we have discussed] 'framing' as specific to visual communication. By 'framing' we meant, in that context, the way elements of a visual composition may be disconnected, marked off from each other, for instance by tramlines, pictorial framing devices (boundaries formed by the edge of a building, a tree, etc.), empty space between elements, discontinuities of colour, and so on. The concept also included the ways in which elements of a composition may be connected to each other through continuities and similarities of colour, visual shape and so on. The significance is that disconnected elements will be read as, in some sense, separate and independent, perhaps even as contrasting units of meaning, whereas connected elements will be read as belonging together in some sense, as continuous or complementary .... [A] discussion of Titian's *Noli Me Tangere* provides an example: '[Christ's] staff acts as a visual boundary between the figures ... and Magdalen breaks the visual separation by the aggressive act of her right arm' [see figure on p. 71].

But clearly framing is a multimodal principle. There can be framing, not only between the elements of a visual composition, but also between the bits of writing in a newspaper or magazine layout, ... between the people in an office, the seats in a train or restaurant (e.g., private compartments versus sharing tables), the dwellings in a suburb, etc., and such instances of framing will also he realised by 'framelines', empty space, discontinuities of all kinds, and so on. In time-based modes, moreover, 'framing' becomes 'phrasing' and is realised by the short pauses and discontinuities of various kinds (rhythmic, dynamic, etc.) which separate the phrases of speech, of music and of actors' movements. We have here a common semiotic principle, though differently realised in different semiotic modes.

Noli me Tangere. Titian. Bequeathed by Samuel Rogers, 1856. © The National Gallery, London.

... Let us look now in more detail at an example of 'practically lived texts'. From the 1970s onward, middle-class families began knocking down walls (or rather, and more usually, paid a builder to do so) in the inner-city houses into which they were beginning to move at that time, whether in the inner-city suburbs of Sydney or of London. It is essential to see this as ideologically and therefore socially, economically and aesthetically driven. The British terraced house is basically a structure of 'two (rooms) up, two (rooms) down', with various kinds of elaboration on this 'two up, two down' structure developed over the course of the nineteenth century (in somewhat distinctive ways in tropical Singapore, hot Sydney, or cooler London), in finely articulated nuance in relation to class (and income) difference.

... [P]recisely articulated notions of social practice and of their value systems – of who did what, where, when – were set in bricks and mortar in the endless rows of such houses in the British Empire. ... One of the elaborations of the 'two up, two down' structure was the addition of a 'service section' at the back of the house, in which kitchen and scullery could be accommodated. This elaboration was not merely practical in its effects, but accentuated a distinction between 'front' and 'back', where 'front' was the public part of the house, and 'back' the more private, with 'front' higher in social status than the back. Hence in such houses, beyond a certain size, the back section was inhabited by the maid, working downstairs in the scullery and kitchen and sleeping upstairs usually in a tiny room also in the back section, built above the back section of the ground floor.

One form of 'middle-class knocking down' reflected the changed relation and valuations of front and back, public and private, high and low status. The ideology of 'living' of the 1970s had begun to stress the possibilities of living outside, even in Britain, and so an opening to the garden, now no longer used for growing vegetables, drying clothes and accommodating an outside toilet, was derived – a glass door or a big window out onto, or better still into, the garden. This shift around, this realignment of the house, a turn through 180 degrees, literally and metaphorically, in the social orientation of values around living, went with or realised a realignment, a shift in the social orientation of the family, and therefore of the house, and amounted to a fundamental transformation. ... It was accompanied by other social changes of the 1960s and 1970s, such as the vast rearrangement of status hierarchies involving the reconfigurations of the distinction of public and private, and their effects on the relation between adults and adults, and between adults and children in the family structures of these societies.

Thus the knocking down of the wall between kitchen and scullery, for instance, opened a space where the family could ... hark back to an unspecified past, or gather to 'eat, chat, and even entertain' in the kitchen, whether surrounded by 'heavenly aromas' or not. The opening out to the garden not only allowed in much more light but also gave a view out into 'nature', and permitted the cook to pick herbs freshly from the obligatory pots of parsley, thyme and chives on the paved back patio, where meals could be had – informally – in the right weather.

The knocking down, ubiquitously, of the wall between the front room and the room behind (in some Victorian houses there was already a partition formed by wooden doors which could be opened) responded in part to different ideological motives but also paralleled the rearrangement of the distinctions of public and private. Motives such as 'larger space', 'lighter', 'airier' rooms, and in general the falling out of the use of certain kinds of formal entertainment ('receiving' visitors in what real estate agents in their written descriptions still call 'reception rooms') which had marked the rigorous framing of public and private, and the shift to informal, less strongly bounded and framed activities, declared the changed discourses of family and the family's relation to the world. In general, all these were signs of the turning away from a focus on the public to a focus on the private (where both domains are of course social/cultural/semiotic constructs). Literally and semiotically, it was a turning away from the public road, the place of public communication, and a turning in to the space of the family, of the house, and of socialised nature, the private garden.

The fact that this movement occurred right across the Anglophone world shows its ideological character and the significance of public organs of ideological dissemination such as magazines. ... In projecting and proposing a 'lifestyle' they establish a certain stability ('this is how one lives') and give stability to discursive arrangements and their attendant practices. In this they perform a broadly pedagogic function – telling readers what values and practices to adopt, how to think of themselves, who and how to be. Nevertheless, it is the 'family', or those in the family who have the task of ideological/discursive management, which is the agent of implementation of the discursive/ideological projections – 'designs' in our theory – of the magazines.

If the transformative act of knocking down walls is a fundamental remaking of the house-as-complex-sign, of the house-as-text, it has to remain a relatively rare semiotic act even for the most ardent home improver. Other acts of semiosis transform parts of the sign complex. Social practices in the house are associated with physical spaces: the spaces where the family watches television, e.g., in the kitchen, in the dining room, in the living room; the spaces where meals are had (whether with or without television), e.g., 'informally' in the kitchen, or in a formal space set aside for all meals eaten by all the family together; spaces which are given over to specific purposes such as sleeping, entertaining, study, whether these are integrated into other spaces or not (a study in a corner of a living room). There is also the question of who is entitled to their own spaces, and at what age (provided the space is available) children will have 'their own' spaces; or, if space is not available, the question of how spaces are marked off for each child, and for each adult.

In other words, a house is a highly flexible set of signifiers, available for the constant making of new signs in the transformative acts of social living. It is far from rigidly static and varies with family types in the pace and extent of its dynamic as well as historically. It is a set of signs which is constantly transformed. The house signals the social relations and value systems of the family itself as well as its relations with its social group. A visitor may be entertained in the kitchen, a sign of informality, solidarity, intimacy; or in the dining room, if the family has made the decision (and has been able to make the decision) to allocate space in that manner. The decision not to have a large eating space (the house which one of us purchased had at that time a tiny table in the kitchen for eating at, sufficient at most to seat three people uncomfortably, and had no other space for eating) will signal certain social practices and relations, for instance the practice of eating and entertaining in the public spaces of restaurants rather than at home, so that eating other than with the closest family members becomes largely an activity of the public domain.

These transformative actions on the house are closely related, as we stress, to other social practices and value systems. They are (trans)coded in magazines and television programmes as well as articulated in the house through actions and materials – knocking down, reshaping, painting, wallpapering, carpeting, taking carpet out to restore original wooden floors, etc. They are projected in magazines and television programmes, but transformatively implemented, acted out, articulated by individuals, and these actings-out are never just direct implementations, 'copies of the original'. Work of whatever kind is always transformative.

We have here mentioned transformations which might be regarded as taking place at the macro- (or meso-) level of signs. But transformations take place at every level, including the micro-level, and incessantly so. The decision to entertain a friend for dinner in the kitchen is one transformation if last time we entertained her or him in the dining room. To set the kitchen table with a white tablecloth is a transformation if usually we use place-mats, making the informal slightly heightened as a sign of our sense of the friend and of the occasion. To use one set of plates rather than another (if choice is possible) is another transformation. To serve three courses for that meal in the kitchen rather than two or just one is yet another one, etc. ... Entertaining in the kitchen may lead to 'We need a larger table in the kitchen', which may lead to 'We can't accommodate a larger table in the kitchen' and 'We need to extend the kitchen'. Changes to the arrangements of rooms fall into this category, as do re-decorations: 'I can't stand that postmodern green and blue in the kitchen anymore'.

... The house, however rigid as a text/complex set of signs it may seem to be due to its material aspects, is a complex sign which is constantly transformed. Even the shopping bag hastily put down in the hall and the bicycles parked there or hung up in the entrance corridor are transformative actions, and experienced as such. 'Don't turn this into a pigsty, workshop' ... are expressions precisely of that. As children grow older they may retain their space, but the space may get re-decorated to signal a transition in a phase of the child's life – from toddler to young person, from young person to early teenager.

The decision to turn around the physical, social semiotic orientation of the house from the street to the garden, from facing the public arena to turning in to the private, would no doubt have been utterly shocking to the Victorian social theorist, architect, builder and family. We think that such transformations are in every way akin to the transformations we perform with sets of signs such as the texts of (written) language. When, in the 1960s, rock 'n' roll bands strove for distinctiveness, they did it largely by means of using existing modes – music of course, but also clothing and language. The shock felt at the 'violence done to language' by using an interrogative pronoun as a count noun, as in The Who, was every bit as strong as our imagined shock of the Victorian builder and house owner. What is at issue in these transformations is the complex of discourse and modal articulation, in which both are always transformed: hence the shock and at times – when the transformation is too sudden, too great, or too revealing – the outrage.

Edited extract from: G. Kress and T. van Leeuwen, *Multimodal Discourse: The Modes and Media of Contemporary Communication* (London: Arnold, 2001), pp. 1–3 and 37–39.

I.4 Organising Social Relations: Kinship and Gender

<table>
<tr><td>20</td><td>The Semantics of Biology
Kirsten Hastrup</td></tr>
</table>

All societies make some differentiation between what men and women are expected to be and do, although the details and the sharpness of the division vary considerably from one culture to another. Anthropologists, and other social scientists, make a fundamental distinction between biological sex – physical, neurological, hormonal and chromosomal maleness and femaleness – and gender, which refers to the social identities and roles associated with being a male or a female person. This distinction, as well as the significance of kinship as an organising principle of social life, is clearly set out in the edited extract we reproduce here, in which Kirsten Hastrup shows particularly clearly how social categories and relations are mapped upon biological facts such as those of sex and reproduction, but are not reducible to those facts. She shows, further, how particular terms and categories, such as those of virginity or paternity, can only be fully understood in relation to other elements within the total framework of meanings within a particular society.

A recurring theme in discussions of the position of women in different societies is the role played by biology. The question is to what extent biology, and notably the difference of sex, can be said to determine sexual behaviour and sexual ideology in any one culture. Often biology has been dismissed altogether, because any universalistic claims for its determining effect have been held to obscure the issue at a point where clarification was badly needed. The aim here is to reinstate biology as an important factor in our comprehension of the position held by women (and men), but as a set of social, rather than 'natural', facts. The 'facts of life' in themselves only operate at the level of biology: as biological facts they tell people how to reproduce the species. But these facts may take on a particular cultural meaning and a specific social significance in different societies. The task of the social anthropologist and anyone else concerned with a total apprehension of the position of women is to analyse how socially significant distinctions are mapped on to basic biological differences, and vice versa. In any social context we must study 'what difference the difference makes', since this will yield information about the social and ideological organisation of the society in question.

In short, I shall enquire into the 'semantics of biology'. My aim is to demonstrate how biological and cultural perspectives on women constantly merge. The method chosen is to present some ideas on the relationship of mutual dependence between nature and culture, and ... virginity.

... 'The facts of life' refer basically to the biological facts of sexuality and reproduction. As indicated by the brief introductory remarks, biology here denotes the facts given by nature, and in this sense it is opposed to what is given by culture. When it comes to an analysis of sexuality and reproduction as social facts, these concepts are not, however, referring to biology, or nature, alone; they are loaded with a specific meaning, which is by no means given by nature itself. We should be careful to note that this is also true for the medical models of this society, even though we tend to regard medical knowledge as consisting of objective, that is natural, truths.

Medical models are specialists' models, but this fact does not in itself guarantee that they are culture-free, in the sense of being objectively true and universally valid. Like lay models, specialists' models are expressions of particular conceptions of interrelationships between certain elements of a whole. In terms of women's reproductive forces, the case of abortion that has been so vividly discussed during recent years clearly demonstrates how even medical models differ, reflecting the different values attached to a biological problem. The attitudes towards abortion as a social fact cannot be understood without reference to the different (ideological) conceptions of when life starts, and who is responsible towards whom for this new life, and what is the social organisation into which the child may be born and in which the woman becomes a mother. Virginity can be seen as an aspect of female sexuality which is likewise subject to different interpretations; maybe not so much within our own society, but certainly under a cross-cultural perspective. The significance of virginity cannot be understood all by itself. As a biological fact, yes, but not as a social fact, a fact that enters into the lives of young women as a demand or as a virtue. We have to know the meaning of virginity in relation to a larger social whole, and in relation to the evaluations attached to different stages of a woman's life.

This is a general point: we cannot understand the meaning and significance of one single aspect of sexuality and reproduction without knowing its relationship to related concepts within the same semantic domain, as we cannot deduce the significance of this particular domain without reference to the social context in which it leads its meaningful life. Stated in very general terms, it is part of anthropological knowledge that the meaning of specific categories depends on their position within a larger system of cultural categories. Virginity as a category is no exception to this theoretical axiom. The semantic load of this concept is defined by its position within a larger semantic field of 'female sexuality', and this field, again, is defined in relation to society at large.

The importance of relationships in the mapping of the meaning attached to biological facts can hardly be over-estimated. This is already well documented in at least one major field of anthropological investigation, namely that of kinship. Kinship is a way of conceiving of and representing biological facts, but we must stress that kinship by itself is by no means just biology. It is a cultural extension of universal (natural) facts of reproduction. The parts played by men and women in different kinship systems vary greatly from one culture to the next. Even in our own society kinship is an important parameter in the daily lives of most people, if not explicitly, then at least implicitly. Notions of kinship play a role, for example, in many discussions of sexual matters; the discussion of abortion is a case in point (e.g., whether the woman alone has the right to decide). Early anthropologists tended to confuse facts of biology with facts of society, but we now know that the use of biological models, such as notions of kinship, is just a way of marking out culturally significant categories. When Malinowski stated in 1929 that the people of the Trobriand Islands in Melanesia were unaware of the role played by the father in procreation, this was not the same as saying that they collectively believed in virgin birth. But as descent was matrilineal (kinship was traced predominantly through women) the actual role played by the father was not important. ... Here it suffices to note the fact that biological models are used to mark out culturally or socially important categories, and this, again, stresses the general point that apparently biological explanations may be objects for semantic analyses.

Kinship is one way of ordering society into distinct categories. There are other ways of organising oneself, but it is a basic knowledge of social anthropology that all societies use distinctions of some kind in order to operate. No society is completely amorphous, making no difference of the differences between people on grounds of sex, age, access to power or anything else. Everywhere the conceptions of society are in terms of distinct categories. In so-called primitive societies the most important distinction seems to be that of sex and, by extension, that of kinship. This is no great surprise, since biological differences are always at hand when organising society becomes acute.

Edited extract from: Kirsten Hastrup, 'The Semantics of Biology: Virginity', in S. Ardener (ed.), *Defining Females* (London: Croom Helm, 1978), pp. 49–65 (extract from pp. 49–51).

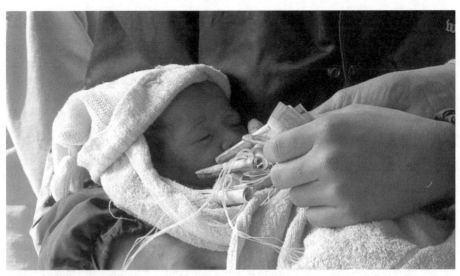

Bunong's Birth Practice

On the basis of a social anthropological case study, this film documents the birth practices of the Bunong in Mondulkiri province, located in the northeast of Cambodia. Social, economic, and political changes are transforming the province and affecting villagers' beliefs, perceptions and habits regarding pregnancy, delivery and early motherhood.

Filmstill from *Bunong's Birth Practice*. © Tommi Mendel (RAI Film Festival 2011).

21 **'Ladies' behind Bars: A Liminal Gender as Cultural Mirror**
John M. Coggeshall

> *In the previous extract from Kirsten Hastrup's work, we saw how social relations and meanings are characteristically mapped onto the biological contrasts of sexual and reproductive roles. Gender identities and performances can, however, be even more elaborated in particular social settings. In this edited version of an article by John Coggeshall, the author shows how, in a rather brutal prison environment organised around power and control, images of maleness and femaleness, and of sexual orientation, prevalent in the surrounding society are transformed and played upon. Individuals may choose, or have forced upon them, patterns of behaviour that accord with these gender stereotypes and expectations – albeit in distorted and exaggerated form.*

'You here to see the show?' the inmate leered. The focus of attention was the tall blond then receiving her food in the prison cafeteria. The workers filled her plate with polite deference, and as she walked between the tables her fine blond hair bounced over her shoulders. 'Make you want to leave home?' the guard next to me teased. His joke clarified the significance of the episode I had just witnessed. The object of attention was genetically a male, reconstructed as female according to the perception of gender within the cultural rule system of prison. Behind bars, certain males become redefined as 'ladies'. … The process by which this transformation occurs reveals not only clues about gender construction in prison culture, but also suggests perceptions of gender identity in American culture in general.

Prison culture involves one predominant theme: control. To establish identity, males profess a culturally defined image to defend themselves from oppression by guards and other inmates. Men define themselves as males by juxtaposing maleness with femaleness, fabricating gender identity from the reflection. For inmates, the concept of female emerges from the concept of male. To borrow a well-known metaphor, the rib for Eve's creation is taken from Adam's side, and draws both its cultural significance and social status from the extraction. Woman is defined in contrast to man, and takes a lesser place at his side. In prison, males create females in their image, and by doing so, dominate and subjugate them.

The fieldwork upon which this study is based was conducted in two medium-security prisons in southern Illinois between 1984 and 1986. Within that time span I taught three university-level courses to about thirty adult inmates, constituting a range of racial-group and criminal-record diversity representative of the overall prison population. Their perceptions provided a portion of the field data, supplemented by my observations of and conversations with guards and staff. …

Prison culture is extremely complex, and deserves much more detailed study by anthropologists. Even my relatively brief 'incarceration' has suggested numerous leads for future research. Gender identity in prison could be explored in much greater detail, describing for example the abusive context whereby young males might become pawns by an administration concerned with pacifying gangs. Another productive line of inquiry might explore the overall cultural context of gender identity in prison culture, for themes of sexuality pervade prison, indicating its cultural significance for staff as well as inmates.

Gender Perceptions of Convicts
… Inmates have provided various estimates for the amount of homosexual activity in prison. All agree that long-timers are more likely to engage in such practices, for they have less of a future to anticipate, more opportunities, and relatively lenient punishments for violations. For example, Paul and Sandy, homosexual lovers, and Frank, Paul's straight friend, believe that about 65 per cent of their prison population engages in homosexual activity, an estimate supported by Dr B, an incarcerated medical doctor. While such numbers reveal the amount of control and coercion in prisoner culture, they

also reveal the 'need for love, affection, [and] intimate relationships' denied by the system, another inmate observes. Some ties are based on affection, but these are relatively rare. Homosexual behaviour fulfils numerous functions in the social and cultural system of prison. Thus most inmates see it as at worst a repugnant necessity and at best a tolerable alternative.

Despite varying views on prevalence, prisoners agree on the general gender constructs in prisoner culture. Males in prison adopt a 'masculine role', inmates assert. Robert describes 'a big ... macho weight-lifting virile Tom Selleck type guy' as typical of the stereotype. Weight lifters, in fact, seem to predominate in the category, for strength suggests masculinity. Real men vigorously protest sexual advances from other males by exhibiting a willingness to fight. Men are also seen as preoccupied with sexual gratification, and will obtain it at all costs.

Real men in prison are perceived as those who can keep, satisfy and protect 'women'. The dominant sex partner is termed a 'daddy', who watches out for and protects his 'kid' or 'girl'. For some men, the acquisition of sex partners strongly resembles courting, where the pursuer flirts with and purchases commissary (snack foods, cosmetics and similar items) for the object of his interest. Others acquire submissive sex partners by force. Ultimately, with either type, sexual partnerships are based on power and control, the complete domination of one person and one gender by another. In fact, domination defines the structure of the relationship which distinguishes the genders in prison.

However, in prison, since the culturally defined females had been males at one time, this presents 'real' men with a gender identity problem: reconciling having sexual intercourse with males while maintaining a masculine self-concept. This adjustment is accomplished by means of a unique folk explanation of the origins of gender development and orientation. Basically, males in prison redefine selected males as females.

In direct contrast to these self-perceptions of males, men portray women in a painting of their own creation. Males see females as passive, subordinate, sexual objects. According to Robert, women are 'sweet and charming', 'fluid of movement', with 'seductive gestures'. ... Women are also viewed as attractive, and they use that allure to their advantage by feigning helplessness; this allows women to maintain a 'certain power' over men. ... Women often tease to coerce men, and sometimes withhold what had apparently been promised.

Of course, nearly all female staff in prison culture do not meet these stereotypes. By inmate definition, then, they must not be women. Such 'non-women' do not challenge gender constructs but reinforce them further. Female guards and staff occupy positions of power and authority over inmates, decidedly atypical for women from a prisoner's perspective. Moreover, most of these women dress in ways to deliberately de-accentuate anatomical differences and to resemble their male counterparts uniformly. Because these women dress as 'non-women' and control men, they cannot be women and must therefore be homosexuals or 'dykes', as the convicts term them. To inmates, this can be the only explanation for women who do not act like women. Cultural reality persists as potentially disruptive anomalies disappear through redefinition.

Trapped between Male and Female Roles

The process by which certain males become redefined as females in prison provides an example of Victor Turner's concept of liminality. Prisoner culture perceives certain males as being trapped in between male and female, thus necessitating the release of their true gender identities. The period of incarceration provides the 'time out of time' necessary for the transfiguration to occur. In fact, inmate terms for the metamorphosis reveal this gender ambiguity: males 'turn out' these non-males, transforming them into the cultural equivalent of females. The liminal gender is actually 'male as female', betwixt and between both. Such individuals figuratively 'turn out' to be females, reconstructed according to the prisoner cultural stereotypes of 'female'. They thus become their 'true' selves at last. This duality creates additional complications in self-identity for such men. ... The homosexual in prison must convince herself that this new self-perception had been her true identity all along. Thus she now has adopted the normal role befitting her identity and gender adjustment.

Vindication for the transformation comes as those forced to become homosexuals remain as such. The acceptance by the homosexual of her new gender identity and associated behaviour justifies the conversion in the eyes of the rest of the prison population. If the 'male becoming female' had no natural proclivity or had not been submissive by nature and thus also female, she would never have agreed to have adopted a feminine identity. As Frank (an inmate) explains, those who surrender are weak, and females are weak. Therefore, those who surrender must be female by nature. ... Not resisting, or not resisting aggressively enough, merely validates this gender liminality. In a sense, it is only appropriate that those trapped betwixt and between be released, to unfetter their true natures. Even coercive gender conversion restores the natural order.

Prisoner culture divides homosexuals into several types, each defined on the basis of degree of sexual promiscuity, amount of self-conceptual pride, and severity of coercion used to turn them out. Generally, status declines as sexual promiscuity increases, self-concept decreases, and the types and intensity of coercion used in the conversion process increase.

The highest status category of homosexuals in prison is that of 'queens' or 'ladies', those who had come out both voluntarily and willingly. Prisoner cultural belief suggests that these individuals had been homosexual on the outside but may have lacked the freedom to have been themselves. Prison has provided them with a treasured opportunity to 'come out', and they have accepted the freedom gratefully. Such individuals maintain a high status by remaining in control of their own lives and of their own self-concept.

Other individuals volunteer to be females, transforming themselves in order to acquire material comforts or social prestige. Terms for this general category vary, depending on the amount of coercion or force needed to 'turn out' the female image. 'Kids', 'gumps', or 'punks' describe individuals who in effect have sold their male identities, surrendering their culturally defined masculinity to be redefined as females.

Many other inmates, however, are forced to become homosexuals against their initial will. ... Those unwilling or unable to control others are thus themselves controlled. According to the cultural rules of gender identity in prison, those who dominate, by natural right, are males, and those who submit, by natural temperament, are females.

A Forced Female Role

Individuals forced to adopt a female role have the lowest status, and are termed 'girls', 'kids', 'gumps', or 'punks'. Kids are kept in servitude by others, as a sign of the owner's power and prestige. Gumps are generally owned or kept by a gang, which collects money by prostituting the sexual favours of the unfortunate inmate. A gump may at one time have volunteered to come out to her feminine identity, but due to lack of personal status or power she has been forced to become sexually promiscuous for money or her physical survival. A punk, most agree, initially hesitates, and is turned out by coercion. However transformed, most homosexuals in prison take on a feminine persona and appearance, even assuming a feminine name and requesting feminine pronouns as referents. The external transformation from male to female often is remarkable. Despite the formal restrictions of a dress code in prison, clothing styles may be manipulated rather patently to proclaim gender identity. Hair is often styled or curled and worn long. Even cosmetics are possible: black felt-tip pens provide eye liner and shadow; kool-aid substitutes for blush; and baby powder disguises prominent cheekbones. The personal appearance of homosexuals enhances their identity by demarcating them as obviously different from men.

Homosexuals perform numerous functions depending upon their status and relative freedom. Generally, the higher the status the more control one has over one's activities and one's life. High status individuals such as Sandy select their own lovers. These couples live as husbands and wives, with the 'little woman' providing domestic services such as laundry, cell cleaning, grooming and sex.

Those with less status perform much the same tasks, but less voluntarily and with less consideration from their daddies. Once an inmate has been forced to adopt a submissive lifestyle, the nightmare of domination becomes more intense. For example, gumps might be forced to pleasure a gang chief, or may be passed down to soldiers in the gang for enjoyment. A particularly attractive kid might be put 'on the stroll', forced to be a prostitute, for the financial benefit of the gang. Business may prove to be so lucrative that some homosexuals must seek protective custody (solitary confinement) to get some rest.

...

Hated and abused, desired and adored, ladies in prison occupy an important niche: they are the women of that society, constructed as such by the male-based perception of gender identity. In prison, females are termed 'holes' and 'bitches', reflecting the contempt of what Dr B believes to be characteristic of society's view of lower-class women in general. In prison, he adds, a homosexual 'is likely to receive much of the contempt [and] pent-up hostility that would otherwise be directed at women'. Herein lies the key to unlocking the deeper significance of gender construction in prisoner culture.

Gender Construction in Prison

... Homosexuals are owned and protected by daddies, who provide for their material and social comfort. In exchange, they provide sexual gratification. They often sell themselves and their bodies for material objects, promiscuously using their allure to manipulate men and to improve their social status. They feign helplessness in order to control their men. Ladies are emotional, helpless and timid, while at the same time petulant, sassy and demanding, nagging their men for attention. Best suited for certain tasks, homosexuals provide domestic and personal services for their daddies, serving their every whim.

Most fundamentally, homosexuals are sexual objects, to be used, abused and discarded whenever necessary. Passive recipients of male power, they even enjoy being dominated and controlled. Males do them favours by releasing their 'true' female identities through rape. In prison, sexuality equals power. Males have power, females do not, and thus males dominate and exploit the 'weaker sex'.

Ultimately, in whose image and likeness are these 'males as females' created? Female staff and administrators do not fit the stereotypical view, and thus provide no role models for ladies in prison. Males themselves draft the image of female in prison, forming her from their own perceptions. Males 'turned out' as females perform the cultural role allotted to them by males, a role of submission and passivity. In actuality, males produce, direct, cast and write the script for the cultural performance of gender identity behind bars.

In prison, woman is made in contrast to the image and likeness of man. Men define women as 'not men', establishing their own self-identity from the juxtapositioning. Gender as a cultural construct is reflexive; each pole draws meaning from a negation of the other. ... [F]olk concepts reinforce the differences, emphasizing maleness at the expense of femaleness and the powerful at the expense of the powerless. By means of sexual domination, women remain in a culturally defined place of servitude and submission.

Prison Culture as a Distorting Mirror

It is precisely this concept of gender identity that has proven most disquieting about the status of homosexuals in prison. Granted, prison culture fosters a terribly distorted view of American culture. Nevertheless, one sees a shadowy reflection in the mirror of prisoner culture which remains hauntingly familiar. As ladies are viewed by males in prison culture, so are females perceived by many males in American culture. Gender roles and attitudes in prison do not contradict American male values, they merely exaggerate the domination and exploitation already present. In prison gender constructs, one sees not contrasts but caricatures of gender concepts 'on the street'. Thus, the liminal gender of ladies behind bars presents, in reality, a cultural mirror grotesquely reflecting the predominant sexism of American society in general, despite initiatives by women to redefine their position and change gender relationships.

References
Turner, Victor. *The Ritual Process* (London: Routledge, 1966).

Edited extract from: John M. Coggeshall, '"Ladies" behind Bars: A Liminal Gender as Cultural Mirror', *Anthropology Today* 4/4 (1988), pp. 6–8; reprinted in J. Benthall (ed.), *The Best of Anthropology Today* (London: Routledge, 2002), pp. 26–33.

I.5 Engaging with Nature

22 Social Views of the Environment
Joy Hendry

Human societies have elaborated many different ways of thinking about the external world, whether conceptualised as abstract 'nature' or more concretely in terms of the physical environment. Anthropologists have devoted a great deal of effort in recent years to analysing and comparing different views of nature and the environment, and in doing so have revealed some of the inconsistencies and ambiguities present within notions that Westerners, including conservationists and policy makers, often take for granted. As the following group of extracts illustrates, views of nature and the environment prevalent within a society are often consonant with that society's particular history and culture. It is important to understand that anthropological analysis of environmental ideas does not necessarily oppose the findings of the physical sciences, but it can help interpret those findings by placing them in the context of a society's values, history, local situation and political organisation. In the following edited extract, Joy Hendry shows particularly clearly how the relationship between human existence and the environment is always dynamic and never purely one-way: environmental factors can set limits to human life, but they do not fully determine it.

At the time of this writing, the whole world's 'natural environment' is thought to be under threat from too much development, and the same people whom our forebears thought primitive are admired for their care and techniques of conservation. In practice, problems arise in thinking about the environment because of apparently incompatible views, and an anthropological approach can help to formulate less fiercely opposed alternatives. This, in turn, can help decision-making bodies to take account of all the people involved when they devise plans to make economically advantageous developments.

In a book entitled *Environmentalism: The View from Anthropology*, Kay Milton has collected together a series of articles which offer various contributions to the debate. She points out, in the introduction, that concerns with the preservation of the environment are by no means new in small-scale societies:

> The Australian Aborigine who avoids hunting animals on sacred sites, and performs ceremonies to ensure the continued existence of edible species, is,

like the Greenpeace campaigner, implementing environmental responsibilities. The rubber-tappers of Amazonia, the Penan of Borneo, the subsistence farmers of northern India and many other communities have attempted to defend their traditional patterns of resource-use against what they see as the destructive consequences of large-scale commercial exploitation.

Milton considers the advantages some local discussion and interpretation could have when governments and international NGOs (non-governmental organisations) formulate their environmental policies. An understanding of each other's motives and expectations would go a long way towards easing in changes perceived as globally important at a local level, but a greater understanding of local views might even offer an opportunity for a better system of conservation to be put into place. As Milton explains, ideas about the environment are constituted through discourse, and this draws on all kinds of ammunition depending on the point of view being advocated. Aboriginal people may be credited quite falsely with environmental concerns if it suits an argument for them to be so cited. On another occasion, the same people may be painted in a negative light for the same set of practices. Before we pursue this line of discussion, it is important that we try and see how complicated the issues may be.

In industrialised countries, for the most part, people are able to transcend environmental limitations, except in extremes of weather, such as snow, floods and excessively high wind, and even then they get upset when the forecasters don't warn about the problems in time, or the authorities don't react swiftly enough. Damage caused by environmental phenomena is something that appears on television, and the *tsunami* that caused havoc in South East Asia in late 2004 was particularly shocking to people in the rest of the world who watched chaos hit a normally idyllic holiday zone. Equally shocking was hurricane Katrina, which devastated New Orleans, a place with an international reputation for music and easy living in the heartland of the richest country in the world. Another shock was the stark contrast between technological achievement and the indiscriminate damage caused by the mighty earthquake which hit Kobe, Japan, in January 1995.

People in less highly industrialised regions live in much closer contact with the physical environment, and their view of the world may well reflect this intimacy. The various Inuit groups have a multitude of ways of dealing with the snow and ice in which they spend so much of the year, reflected in their words for different forms of it, and the Bedouin of the Sahara desert have a similar understanding of the sand. An anthropologist living amongst such people must consider environmental factors as a prime feature of their study, but novelists and film-makers have sometimes better captured the feel of a way of life so alien to a cosseted twentieth century city dweller. The novel by the Danish writer Peter Hoeg, *Miss Smilla's Feeling for Snow,* presents a Greenlander's view of the snow, for example, and some passages of Michael Ondaatje's book *The English Patient* forcibly illustrate the importance in the desert of understanding different types of wind. Both of these works have now been made into films that well illustrate the environmental exigencies of life in these extreme circumstances, and an early anthropological film known as *Nanook of the North* makes clear the stark daily life of a traditional Inuit family.

Anthropologists must look at environmental conditions wherever they work, but they realise that the world-view of the people they live with may involve quite different perceptions to those which they themselves classify as 'the environment'. The anthropologist must aim to unearth this view ... Another aspect of the subject is the way in which people place themselves in the context of their surroundings and, in this environmentally conscious contemporary world, the extent to which their ideology is reflected in practice.

In the opening of the book *Japanese Images of Nature*, the authors write:

> It is often claimed that the Japanese have a particular love for nature, a love often reflected in their art and material culture. But today equal notice is being given to the environmental degradation caused by the Japanese at home as well as abroad. How can these phenomena be reconciled? The aim of this volume is to address this question through an in-depth analysis of the human-nature relationship in Japan.

In the book, much attention is devoted to Japanese ideas which are translated as 'nature', demonstrating again the problems of definition, as well as conceptions of human interaction with the rest of the world.

In another article in Milton's book, developed further in a fascinating collection of his own essays entitled *The Perception of the Environment*, Tim Ingold makes a point very apt in this context about our whole notion of the environment as a global phenomenon. To think of the world we live in as a globe implies a view taken from the outside, as opposed to an earlier (European) view of humankind being part of a series of spheres which surrounded as well as included human activity. We learn of the world at school in global terms, although few of us have actually seen more than a photograph of this version of our environment, and we also study maps which colour the land masses in nation states which represent a history of colonialism and voyages of discovery and exploration.

Ingold refers to an idea that this view represents a triumph of technology over cosmology which, in contrast, 'places the person at the centre of an ordered universe of meaningful relations ... and enjoins an understanding of these relations as a foundation for proper conduct towards the environment' ... Seeing the world as a globe puts human society 'outside what is residually construed as the "physical world" ... and furnishes the means for the former's control over the latter' ... Japanese often argue that they think of themselves as 'one with nature', an idea which they oppose to a Western desire to control it, although, in practice, the Japanese clearly make efforts to control natural forces too.

In an indigenous system of Indian thought, too, a person is seen as integrally connected with the cosmos. According to Tambiah:

The Ayurvedic system we have in mind postulates that the constituents of nature and of man are the same, and that processes such as the ingestion of food and medicine and the excretion of bodily waste products are part and parcel of the flow of energies and potencies between man and nature. Physical illness is the result of imbalances that can be corrected by exchanges at various levels, by ingestion of the right substances and diet, by exposure to or protection from climatic conditions, by maintaining proper relations with other persons – family, kin, and the gods.

It is important not to fall into the temptation of explaining the whole of social and political life in environmental terms, however. Several explanations of Japanese idiosyncratic 'character' seek causes in the rugged mountainous scenery, or the predominance of rice cultivation. There are mountains elsewhere, however, and plenty of people grow rice. It is important to avoid a determinist view. The physical environment undoubtedly limits the social arrangements a people are able to make, but it cannot be said to *determine* them. If it could, there would always be the same social system in the same environment and this is by no means the case. A glance at the variety of Mexican ethnography will illustrate the point, for there have been highly centralised, artistically and technologically advanced peoples living in precisely the area now populated with societies much more diffuse in political organisation, and much less developed in technological terms.

To take one environmental factor, one 'problem' for a people to solve, usually reveals a variety of solutions, and these will depend on cultural differences. Everyone needs water to live, and a shortage of water can be a serious issue. Some hunter-gatherer and pastoralist people ... solve the problem by moving around, by seeking water sources to resolve their needs immediately. Their response to the 'problem' is the nomadic way of life, and the transhumance of people like the Nuer [of the Sudan] is a more stable possibility. Elsewhere, a long-term response to the same 'problem' may be achieved through the building of irrigation systems, which in turn involves a social organisation capable of maintaining and administering them, as well as sharing out the supplies. Rules of land ownership are then likely to characterise economic life, and access to water will very likely be regulated.

The environment cannot be said to *determine* the social system because the environment is no objective reality. It is always categorised by the people who live in it and make use of it, according to their view of the world. One last example of different views, which has become a highly contentious international issue, involves the varying perceptions of the problems of whale conservation found in Japan and among members of different Western nations. According to a Japanese view, based on their own independent research – a view which is shared by Norwegians and Icelanders – there are enough whales to be harvested for consumption; indeed, if they are not harvested they will eat up food supplies for fish which could otherwise also have been caught to feed the Japanese population. Whale meat is a valuable source of protein, and the catching and preparation of whales are specialist occupations, which have been passed down through generations.

The predominant Western view, however, is that the whale population is threatened with extinction, and if the Japanese (and others) keep catching them, they will soon be no more. Many of the people who take this view have been brought up on stories about [humanised] whales such as Moby Dick, and the tale of Jonah, and very few of them regard whale meat as part of their diet. Japanese commentators remark that if the whales were called 'cows' there would be no problem, and criticise the Western world for being sentimental. A very similar, but measured, anthropological view is presented by Niels Einarsson (in Milton's collection), who set out the case of Icelandic fisherman who were losing their entire livelihood for reasons seen locally as quite indefensible. A Norwegian anthropologist, Arne Kalland, even took a place on the International Whaling Commission to try and present a more objective viewpoint.

I have no idea whose scientific figures are more accurate, and this is not the place to take up the issue. A demonstration of differing perceptions is the aim at this point. The whaling issue emphasises the importance of seeing how the environment is classified by those who live in it, and also how views of the environment may be created through discourse about it.

Tenere-Mapping the Desert
The film *Tenere-Mapping the Desert* portrays the differing attitudes towards the 'cultural landscape' of the Libyan Sahara held by a group of European visitors to the region as well as the Tuareg 'locals' who guide them.

Filmstill from *Tenere-Mapping the Desert*. © Ed Owles (RAI Film Festival 2011).

References

Asquith, P. and A. Kalland. *Japanese Images of Nature: Cultural Perspectives* (London: Curzon Press, 1997).

Ingold, Tim. *The Perception of the Environment: Essays in Livelihood, Dwelling and Skill* (London: Routledge, 2000).

Milton, Kay (ed.) *Environmentalism: The View from Anthropology* (London: Routledge, 1993).

Tambiah, Stanley J. *Magic, Science, Religion and the Scope of Rationality* (Cambridge: Cambridge University Press, 1990).

Edited extract from: Joy Hendry, *An Introduction to Social Anthropology: Sharing Our Worlds*, 2nd edn (London: Palgrave Macmillan, 2008), pp. 247–53.

23 Death on the Farm: Badger Culling in North Pembrokeshire
Pat Caplan

The next edited extract from an article by Pat Caplan takes a highly topical controversy – that surrounding the culling of badgers in Wales – and places it in relation to local and national concerns as well as contrasting views of 'nature' and the symbolic and literary associations of badgers. Note in particular the ways in which, as she shows, the proponents of conflicting views appeal to science in support of their positions.

> 'Who can tell?' said the Badger. 'People come – they stay for a while, they flourish, they build – and they go. It is their way. But we remain. There were badgers here, I've been told, long before that same city came ever to be. And now there are badgers here again. We are an enduring lot, and we may move out for a time, but we wait, and are patient, and back we come. And so it will ever be.'
> —Kenneth Grahame, *Wind in the Willows*

It is the finale of the Eisteddfod in Cardigan town in the summer of 2009 and a large audience has gathered to hear some of the finalists. ... The compère announces the arrival of the chief guest. She is the Minister for Environment and Rural Affairs in the Welsh Assembly and she is introduced as 'the person who is going to do something about bovine TB and the badgers.' There is an instant round of loud applause. The Minister ... had recently announced that there is to be a complete cull of badgers in north Pembrokeshire, just across the county border. When she speaks to the Eisteddfod audience, it is to state that she is a farmer's daughter and she knows how farmers are suffering from bovine TB. She also argues that the *eisteddfod* system, and the perpetuation of Welsh culture generally, is dependent upon the continuation of farming in Wales. ...

Farming here, as in much of the rest of the U.K., is in the doldrums. Farmers complain of the low prices paid for their products, especially by the supermarkets, of the restrictions imposed by government ministries and EU regulations, of the endless form-filling, and of the Welsh weather, with 2009 seeing exceptionally high summer rainfall for the second year in a row. ... Moreover, in the recent past, farmers have endured several waves of animal diseases: BSE (bovine somatropin encephalitis), foot and mouth disease, blue tongue and bovine tuberculosis (bTB), the last two of which are still problematic.

In north Pembrokeshire, such problems are often exacerbated because many farms are small and some of the hill land can only be used for grazing. As in other parts of the U.K., many farmers are leaving the industry, or their sons (and daughters) are not entering it. Many of those who stay in the business have to find off-farm work to supplement their farming income. Small wonder, then, that a disease like bTB, the incidence of which is increasing in some areas ('hot spots') like north Pembrokeshire, causes great concern in the farming community. Farm animals are regularly tested for bTB, and if a cow tests positive it has to be slaughtered.

...

One farmer in north Pembrokeshire explained its effect on his farm:

> I have lost cattle to bTB and it is very upsetting. I lost a number of good heifers, and some of them had just calved. They took the heifers away for slaughter because they had tested positive ... and so then I had several newborn calves on the yard. I had to feed them for several days of course until the lab tests came back proving whether or not the mothers had indeed had bTB. It would have been kinder to shoot them immediately, but they wanted them kept. When the confirmation came, they took them away.

...

Culling Badgers

Badgers are one of the largest mammals found in the wild in the British Isles; they are also one of the most secretive, with nocturnal habits. They are social animals who live in large setts underground. They have achieved a curious status in popular perception, perhaps fostered by the classic children's novel *Wind in the Willows*, in which the Badger, represented as a wise and down-to-earth character, plays a major role. ... Such enthusiasm on the part of some does not, however, mean that there is no 'badger-baiting', which, although illegal, as badgers are currently a protected species, continues in some country areas, including north Pembrokeshire. ... Badgers are also carriers of bTB and, as they share fields and pastures with cattle, have been held by some to be largely responsible for its transmission and the recent increase in incidence and prevalence.

... There has been official concern in the U.K. for some years about bTB, and several studies have been carried out seeking to identify both causes and remedies. In England, the government set up an Independent Scientific Group which, after a decade of work, issued its report in 2007 and concluded that culling badgers would be unlikely to solve the problem of bTB. ... Subsequently the Westminster government decided not to go ahead with a cull in England. Shortly thereafter, however, the U.K. government's then Chief Scientist, Sir David King, used both the Independent Scientific Group's final report and a number of other studies to argue for a cull of badgers. ... It is the King Report which has been used by the Welsh Assembly to justify the decision to cull all badgers in the 'intensive action pilot area' (IAPA) of north Pembrokeshire.

North Pembrokeshire and the Welsh Assembly Government

... This is traditionally a Welsh-speaking area, although the overall proportion of native Welsh speakers has diminished with the arrival of large numbers of English-speaking incomers who have moved into the area over the last generation. Some of these are affluent retired people or those simply wishing to live in less pressured surroundings, while a few are 'alternatives' ('hippies' in local parlance) who have set up smallholdings and communities where they can practise some form of self-sufficiency. ... Relations between locally born Welsh and English incomers here, as elsewhere in Wales, have sometimes been fraught, as the former argue that the latter have pushed up the price of housing and rendered it unaffordable for their children while also diluting the local culture and its most important manifestation, the Welsh language. Recently, this situation has improved somewhat as many of the earlier demands of the Welsh nationalists have been met: there are now Welsh TV and radio stations, road signs prioritise Welsh, and all children learn Welsh in school. Language remains, however, a major issue, and even people who define themselves as Welsh born and bred, but are not able to speak Welsh fluently because they are originally from non-Welsh-speaking parts of Wales, may find their credentials questioned in certain contexts. ...

The Pembrokeshire National Park is funded by the Welsh Assembly Government (WAG), a body set up some years ago as the result of the British government's policies on devolution. The Assembly has far fewer powers than the Scottish Parliament, but among the powers that it does possess is a degree of control over matters to do with the environment and agriculture. This enabled it to propose, in the spring of 2009, that there should be a cull of all badgers over a period of several years in north Pembrokeshire.

...

Reactions to the Badger Cull

In the 1990s, together with Janice Williams, I had carried out research in this area on people's ideas about the relation between food and health. ... This was the period when BSE was a major concern and even after the food and health project was finished, I continued to work on BSE and monitor its local impact, becoming interested in perceptions of risk as a result. ...

One of the findings was that, unsurprisingly, perceptions of the risk of BSE depended largely on who people were: for example, farmers – most of them Welsh-speaking – did not stop eating beef … whereas other people in the area did, at least for a time. It occurred to me that the issue of the badger cull was similarly likely to arouse fairly predictable reactions among different social categories of the local population, notably rural as opposed to urban and Welsh as opposed to English speakers. … I was to find, however, that the situation was somewhat more complex.

During the summer of 2009, I talked to a range of residents in north Pembrokeshire about their reactions to a possible badger cull. … Since then I have continued to monitor the situation virtually, and over the Christmas and New Year period I also conducted a number of lengthy telephone interviews with local people. From all of this data, it is clear that views vary considerably and sometimes rather unpredictably.

Unsurprisingly, given the support of the Welsh farming unions … and much of the farming press for the cull, a number of farmers and smallholders were unequivocally in favour of the cull:

> I am in favour. They are nice to look at but they are a nuisance, and something has to be done. People's livelihoods are involved. Farming is a hard business and this is making it worse. I know this will cause problems – some people will not want the badgers killed. There will be protests. And the police don't want to know. … (Welsh-speaking farmer)

But some English-speaking farmers and smallholders were also in favour:

> Q: Would you be in favour of a cull?
> A: Yes, I would, the badgers are a damned nuisance. They block drains, they dig up land. They can have the mountain [to live on]. (English-speaking smallholder)

However, not all of those engaged in farming favoured the cull, nor was it always the case that all Welsh farmers did so:

> As a farmer I am not in favour, our farm has badgers but we raise cattle and we have not had bTB. My father has farmed here for decades and lived alongside the badgers – he says that badgers are not a problem. (Welsh-speaking farmer)

> To tell the truth, I think it's [bTB] more to do with the farming methods these days [than badgers]. They move them [cattle] around so much. (Woman from Welsh-speaking farming family)

> …

In several conversations with people opposed to the cull, it was thought that it posed a major risk both to the tourism industry and to the sale of Pembrokeshire food products. One interviewee who worked in a food shop told me: 'People are already asking about the sourcing of some of our products. For example, they don't want to buy Daioni milk now because of its very public stance in favour of the cull'.

At a meeting of people opposed to the cull, which included (English-speaking) farmers and smallholders, there was considerable emotion expressed. People talked about 'loving my badgers'. Some saw them as part of the locality and of nature, and argued that badgers had 'always been there' and therefore should remain so. Their solution to the problem of bTB was vaccination of badgers: 'if they can trap them in cages to shoot them, why can't they trap them and vaccinate them?' The converse of their opposition to the cull was often criticism of modern farming methods: increasingly large herds, cattle confined to sheds throughout the year, frequent movement of animals (sometimes illegally), in-breeding, and lack of bio-security on farms. But there was also criticism of the policies proposed by the WAG, since it planned to introduce a raft of measures all at the same time, thereby making it impossible to distinguish cause and effect at a later date.

There is also a middle position taken by people who would accept a limited cull in areas where there were deemed to be both too many badgers and infected herds, but refuse to countenance a blanket cull. ...

Potential Responses to the Cull
How do people think they will react if the cull starts? Will they try and stop access to their land to prevent 'their' badgers being killed? Will they join a local campaign group ... or the UK-wide Badger Trust, which has six local groups in Wales, and which in late 2009 launched an application for a judicial review of the WAG decision to cull badgers?

...

Here the issues are complex, and pertain not only to identity as farmer/ smallholder or non-farmer, but also to identification with a particular community. For example, a Welsh townswoman said that, while she did not like the idea of the cull, she understood why many farmers were in favour. Similarly, some Welsh-speaking farmers who expressed scepticism or even opposition to the cull were well aware that joining an anti-cull campaign might be construed as failing to support neighbours who had lost cattle and thus were unwilling to 'break ranks' and criticise the cull in public. The same situation applied equally to some English speakers who were long-time residents of the area, especially those who had made the effort to learn Welsh, sent their children to Welsh-medium schools and saw themselves as part of the local community.

> I have badgers and would not want them culled. And I think it [the cull] could be very confrontational. But if you resist [the cull], you would be deemed a 'daffy English' – is it worth the aggro? I just hope our area won't be included. (English-speaking smallholder)

Clearly, then, the ground is set for the possibility of confrontations between those sent to carry out the cull and those who would defend badgers. But there is also the possibility of splits in communities whose inhabitants have tried hard in the past few decades to get along together: English speakers who have learned Welsh, Welsh speakers who have come to accept incomers who have been there for a long time and proved their commitment to local communities. Thus differences in language and perceived ethnicity become all too readily available channels for the expression of difference of views about the cull. In other words, the popular perception is that the debate divides neatly along ethnic and linguistic lines, whereas this is far from being the case.

...

Badgers and Other Animals

... One of the questions which interested me was why badgers evoke such strong reactions, being sometimes 'loved' and bearing a heavy weight as symbols of wildlife, and in other cases, viewed as pests and fair game for sport. I asked a number of people about their views on other wild animals in the area such as wild ponies, rabbits, grey squirrels and foxes, and also used my own long-term local knowledge. The first two are both used for human consumption, while grey squirrels and foxes are deemed to be pests and are sometimes shot or hunted ..., as indeed are mink and otters. Yet in this area there has been no sustained campaign against any of these practices similar to that against the plan to cull badgers. ...

So why has the proposal to cull badgers provoked such strong reactions, and what did people have to say about these animals? On the positive side, badgers were described as 'iconic', 'beautiful', 'mysterious', 'interesting', 'our largest wild mammal'. Some of those who spoke in this way recognised that badgers (like other animals) have been anthropomorphised in English-language literature and mentioned their portrayal in *Wind in the Willows*. ... Some noted that it was precisely for such reasons that there had been pressure to give badgers the legal protection which was enacted in the 1990s. Several people noted that badgers had survived and even prospered in the face of increasingly intensive agriculture, so they had become a symbol of resilience, 'a bastion of wildlife resistance' to the profound changes which have taken place in the countryside over the last few decades, so that 'If badgers go, what are we left with?'

On the negative side, some (particularly farmers) described them as a 'nuisance' regardless of bTB, and as having increased in numbers as a result of their protected status. Several people noted that farmers used to cull badgers on their land when they thought there were too many of them, but now they are not allowed to do so. However, since the WAG had made the decision to move towards a cull, the local press reported a noticeable increase in the number of dead badgers found in the area and it was widely thought that some farmers were taking matters into their own hands.

Science, Emotion, Economics and Politics

Both sides of this debate adduce scientific arguments to support their stance. Although there is a great deal of literature available, much of it on the web, the likely effects of a cull are as yet unknown, particularly as it is proposed to implement it in conjunction with a much more frequent testing regime and improved bio-security on farms. Studies have been carried out of culls conducted in other countries, but the evidence from these is not conclusive, and they are often cited by both sides. … In other words, the use of scientific evidence is highly selective. …

The second aspect of many arguments is the emotional, although in the case of the pro-cull lobby, it is not the fate of the badgers but the devastation caused to farming families by bTB. … But in the case of those who oppose the cull, it is primarily the badgers who are the subject of emotional responses, even where these are tempered, as they often are, by recognition of the plight of farmers. Paradoxically, each side accuses the other of using emotional arguments, while claiming that its own stance is based on science not emotion.

Economic arguments in favour of the cull are frequently adduced both by the WAG and by farmers. … Cattle, both dairy and beef, are a very important part of the Welsh rural economy, and the policy of the Assembly has been to improve the 'branding' of animals reared in Wales, so that Welsh beef, like Welsh lamb, is synonymous with good quality. … But equally, it is suggested by the anti-cull lobby that the cost of the cull (some £9 million over five years) would be better spent on improving bio-security and testing regimes, and on developing and rolling out vaccines for badgers.

More rarely discussed openly are the underlying politics of this situation. The Assembly is currently governed by a coalition of Plaid Cymru and Labour, and both these and the opposition Conservative party have, with few exceptions, supported the cull. Some argue that the WAG's decision to have a cull is precisely because its devolved powers allow it to do so, and that its members have the 'guts' to do what the Westminster government has refused to do in England. …

Yet paradoxically, for citizens on both sides of the debate, the bTB, badgers and the cull have also come to symbolise the intrusive state. For those against the cull, the Control Order recently passed by the WAG, which allows access to land for the purposes of culling regardless of the owner's wishes, is seen as draconian, and as threatening civil liberties and human rights. But for those farmers wanting a cull, it is precisely the (English) state's legal protection of badgers which has led to the present situation. Several people also explained the WAG's decision to have a cull as being a 'sop' to the farmers to persuade them to comply with the ever tighter regulations on testing and cattle movement – 'buying off the farmers' and at the same time playing to the Welsh rural vote, the heart of support for Plaid Cymru.

Badgers thus sit at a fault line in world views. For those who wish to put nature, the environment and sustainable farming first, and for incomers who came to live in West Wales with 'a dream', as one of them put it, badgers are its most powerful symbol, and killing them is emblematic of lack of care and caring for the environment, for wildlife, and thus 'the end of the dream'. For those who see their farming livelihoods threatened, and thus their communities and culture, and who are convinced that at least part of the blame lies with badgers, killing them is seen to be the only way out. Those who oppose the cull are labelled as finding wildlife more important than people, being 'hobby farmers', incomers who do not understand the situation. This polarisation is a tragedy, and one made worse by the frequent perception that it is primarily the 'Welsh' who support the cull and the 'English' who do not, whereas, as I have tried to demonstrate in this article, things are far from being so simple.

Postscript

On the day I finished writing this article, the announcement came from the Minister in the WAG that the badger cull was to go ahead, starting in April of 2010.

Edited extract from: Pat Caplan, 'Death on the Farm: Culling Badgers in North Pembrokeshire', *Anthropology Today* 26/2 (2010), pp. 14–18.

Going for the Kill
Ditchling, a small village in rural Sussex, struggles with the economic and political issues affecting the livelihoods of the villagers brought about by the banning of fox hunting with hounds in England.

Filmstill from *Going for the Kill. A Very English Village.* © Luke Holland (RAI Film Festival 2007).

24 The Whaling War: Conflicting Cultural Perspectives
Adrian Peace

In this edited extract, Adrian Peace takes up the theme of international conflicts over whaling, which we met earlier in the passage from Joy Hendry's book. Peace traces the contrasting views held by Australians and Japanese of the boundary between human society and nature, and the place of whales in relation to that boundary. Just as, in the preceding passage, Caplan argued that badgers stand at a kind of fault line in Welsh and British perceptions of the human and natural worlds, whales seem here to occupy a similarly ambiguous position in conflicting international views of humanity's responsibility towards the non-human environment.

The political ritual generated annually by Japanese whaling in the Southern Ocean captures the Australian imagination and at least the attention of international audiences. Shortly before Christmas, the fleet comprising six vessels steams southwards and is soon picked up by environmental organisations and the Australian navy. Public interest and anger rise as details are broadcast about the whalers' regular target of about 900 cetaceans. The stage is set for 'drama on the high seas'.

...

Amid all this maritime mayhem, little attention is paid when the whalers reach their target and all protagonists limp back to the northern hemisphere. But they leave behind in Australia widespread resentment that this conflict remains unresolved after several decades. Political parties in opposition repeatedly indulge in sabre-rattling over the whaling issue; once in office, the realpolitik of Japan being Australia's second largest trading partner prevails. The current Labour government was elected in late 2007 with an explicit and determined anti-whaling platform; in power, it fast retreated behind a screen of diplomatic negotiation, where it was roundly condemned as weak and hypocritical. ...

These costs are small beer by comparison with those incurred by the Japanese. Whaling is subsidised to the hilt by the Japanese state. The return from meat sales is meagre when set against grants and loans: only a few hundred workers are directly employed; recurrent costs constantly escalate. The most important cost by far is the diminution of Japan's international stature, for continued Antarctic whaling attracts widespread international condemnation, especially from New Zealand and the United Kingdom, Australia's closest allies.

The whaling war has become one of the longest running conservation issues. How has it come about that the end point is little more than a diplomatic stalemate? How has Australia become the self-appointed guardian of Antarctic whales while Japan resolutely continues to kill them? ...

The Politics of Anti-whaling

The ecological proximity of the two populations is crucial to understanding the close identification of the Australian public with whales in the region. Interest in whale behaviour seems insatiable in Australia. Through books, videos, magazines, museums and tours, whales have entered into public culture. But those from Antarctica are routinely referred to as 'our whales', and protecting them has become a national responsibility. Currently, about 13,000 whales migrate up the coast of Western Australia, and 7,000 along the eastern coast: many are humpbacks, which typically swim close to the shore. As regional media provide regular updates on whale movements to Australia's predominantly coastal population, the scale of casual observation is huge as families head for promontories, beaches and jetties to watch the whale migration. Radio and television are also at the forefront of elaborating a discourse of possession where whales are concerned. Since Australia has no physical boundary with other countries, there is a naturalness to commentators talking about 'our whales', 'our visitors from the south' and 'our gentle giants', labels which have entered everyday vocabulary. Explanations as to why there are increasing numbers of whales in Australian waters are similarly naturalised: since females calve in warmer waters to the north, it is said they know they will be secure there. According to a talkback radio host in Queensland: 'It's incredible they keep coming back to the same place. I suppose it's because they're so intelligent they know somehow our whales are totally protected'.

This is the opening gambit to an anthropomorphic discourse which lasts throughout the annual migration. Whales are considered to have a range of senses and an intelligence to which we can relate, as well as being defenceless and vulnerable to all manner of predation. By comparison with the decidedly muted reception accorded to desperate refugees from the north, the much-heralded arrival of defenceless cetaceans brings them firmly within our moral orbit. An Aboriginal girl included in a delegation to an International Whaling Commission (IWC) meeting in Alaska displayed 'wisdom far beyond her years' ... when she said: 'These are our humpbacks ... The first thing they see when they come from their mother's womb is the Australian coastline. So if anyone should determine what happens to them, it's us'.

Given these circumstances, it is not surprising that when whales are rescued by members of the public, identification with and responsibility for them assumes heightened significance. When 'lost whales' end up in Sydney harbour, crowds several thousand strong assemble and speculate anthropomorphically on the reasons for their presence. ... Newspaper reports strive to capture the emotion and empathy generated by such occasions. One 'mercy mission' that attracted 1,500 volunteers to save eighty killer whales involved 'a tremendous show of community spirit. The mammoth effort saw wet-suit clad volunteers cradle whales in shallow waters, working tirelessly to keep them wet, upright and facing the beach as they became increasingly distressed' ... Massive lifeless bodies silently observed by children and parents have become a stock image, reinforcing emotive terms like 'cradle'. When an entire pod dies, much can be made of the human-like sociability which has proved its undoing. In their altruistic efforts to save the first victim, the rest have become beached too.

It is, however, above all in the multi-million-dollar industry of whale-watching that the notion of a close bond with whales is most elaborated. Below-deck presentations on whale-watching boats intersperse brief mention of Australia's whaling past with stunning video images, rendering the country's currently humane, enlightened position all the more impressive. By joining a whale-watch tour, it is explained, ordinary people are playing their part in the national project to 'save the whales'.

... So the whale has become a contemporary totem to be approached with affection, respect, even adulation. In relation to them, we express our contemporary humanity, our commitment to civilised standards, as seems imperative when relations between society and nature are substantially awry. Since we have 'saved the whale' in our part of the world, this small but significant reversal suggests that a broader equilibrium between the two can be salvaged.

It follows that pro-whaling countries can lay no similar claim to being enlightened and humane, and since only the Japanese kill 'Australian whales', they are the target of sustained demonisation. As the fleet enters the Southern Ocean, the media describes it as 'an invasion' down to the last detail. ... 'Butcher', 'massacre' and 'torture' are terms routinely deployed to describe the killing of 'defenceless' and 'gentle' whales. Video clips are endlessly replayed to demonstrate the destructive force of the harpoon. ... The dominant message is unambiguous: the Japanese are a barbaric and cruel lot, ... they are deceitful in claiming to be engaged in scientific research, they are unreliable in providing data on their catches, they buy the support of bankrupt Third World nations, above all they are cruel and callous in the way they go about their whaling business.

In brief, the totemic relationship between charismatic megafauna and ordinary Australians is reproduced in multiple contexts. This is why government failure to realise a satisfactory outcome grates so badly with the public: having promised so much, those in power have failed to deliver and lag behind public opinion. Meanwhile, identification with the totemised whale has become part of how Australians imagine themselves as decent and enlightened citizens in the contemporary world. The image has an especially sharp definition because it is constituted against a damning, even racist, portrayal of the Japanese.

The Politics of Pro-whaling

On the other side of the conflict, pro-whaling is similarly embedded in the everyday world of the Japanese. But as unswerving political policy, it is thoroughly driven by institutions within the Japanese state. One explanation given for this is that the whaling industry and the consumption of whale meat are recognised as significant traditions which must be honoured. This heritage, it is said, goes back to the Jonan period (1000 to 300 BC). But by the late eighteenth century, advances in technology and expansion of trade routes helped the industry to become fully commercialised in southern and northern Japan, where whale meat eating (*gyoshoku bunka*) became a significant part of ritual life.

A more frequent claim is that in the early twentieth century, a period of exceptional rural hardship, the northward spread of whaling provided inhabitants with protein. Then canned whale meat became part of the military diet, and after 1945 food shortages were avoided by the expansion of whaling on the advice of the American military occupiers. ... Continuity was then maintained as whale meat became a regular item in the carefully prepared *obentos*, or lunch boxes, which children take to school.

The Australian anti-whaling lobby makes much of surveys which find that only a small proportion of the Japanese population consumes whale meat. But this is somewhat irrelevant when *gyoshoku bunka* is considered a distinctive part of a culture generally unparalleled in its uniqueness. It is likewise unimportant that whale consumption occurs in other countries, such as the Faeroe Islands. What matters most is that the exceptional elements of Japanese culture, including eating whale meat, are valorised and preserved across the board. Eating whale meat represents an integral part of how the Japanese locate themselves in a world geared to the destruction of regional differences.

The anti-whaling rhetoric of countries like Australia and the United States is thus interpreted as a challenge to the right of the Japanese to live as they choose. While the language of cultural imperialism is not much used in the West nowadays, the stridency of anti-whaling rhetoric from overseas keeps it current inside Japan. A complementary argument has it that the Japanese do not attach the same significance to the whale as Westerners do because of the way it is culturally categorised. The whale falls into the category of fish rather than mammal: the character for 'whale' (*kujira*) has two parts, the first being the sign for a fish (*uo-hen*). ... When reduced to just another species of fish, whales possess none of the aura which nowadays surrounds mammals in the West. Even when killing whales is considered problematic, traditional Buddhist rituals carried out by the whalers aim to appease the deceased creature's spirit. ... Whaling carries none of the heinous qualities which Australians attribute as a matter of course.

For these reasons, prominent analysts agree, attempts to mobilise a minority opinion against whaling consistently prove unsuccessful and the field is left open for pro-whaling views to thrive. [One analyst] maintains that eating whale has assumed significance in recent times precisely as a response to the 'cultural imperialism' of anti-whaling propaganda. ...

This kind of prioritisation of varying cultural considerations is, of course, one of the strong points of an anthropological perspective. But in order to explain Japan's resolute refusal to budge where whaling is concerned, accounts from other quarters appropriately focus on the variable of institutional power. We should recall here that whaling is heavily subsidised, generates no profit, employs few workers and faces rising costs. Modern nation-states everywhere subsidise unprofitable ventures, but not many are prepared to incur the opprobrium of other powerful countries with which they have their most important relationships as a consequence.

Several social analysts who problematise Japan's unmoving position return to the point that the whale is categorised as mere fish. For this means that the whaling industry in its entirety comes under the conservative Ministry of Agriculture, Forestry and Fishing (MAFF) and its Fisheries Agency. The agency is the powerhouse that has directed all aspects of whaling since the late 1980s, when several commercial enterprises were amalgamated into one, Kyodo Senpaku Kaisha, and the government of the day established the Institute for Cetacean Research (ICR).

These arrangements were made in response to the IWC's moratorium on commercial whaling, promulgated in 1982. At the time Japan saw this as a highly provocative decision. It came as IWC membership was being broadened to facilitate stacking the commission with anti-whaling interest groups, and the United States had threatened Japan with the loss of access to the lucrative Alaskan fishery if it did not go along with the moratorium. Eventually Japan agreed, but only because it was possible under the moratorium to continue whaling for scientific purposes. ... The ICR was established for precisely this purpose: it was to provide the data needed to justify whaling by Kyodo Senpaku Kaisha on lines laid down by MAFF and the Fisheries Agency. ... Needless to say, the value of this scientific data is the subject of intense international disagreement.

...

Conclusion

The concept of culture often surfaces in Australian print and electronic media to account for the depth and duration of the conflict over Japan's continued whaling. But it is used in broad-brush fashion to characterise, and sometimes caricature, behavioural patterns and values purportedly commonplace across each society.

... By contrast, I have tried to draw out some of the more salient cultural influences that have contributed to the political divide between Australia and Japan. In metaphorical terms, the whaling war is best conceived of not so much as the contemporary political drama with which I began, but rather as an archaeological site in which factors of varying cultural significance have become sedimented over time. Some historical factors have been discreetly forgotten, some traditions have been enthusiastically revived. Some market forces have been eliminated, other economic factors have flourished. Some loci of power have gone into decline, others have become undeniably influential. But, as with real archaeological sites, it is possible to specify particular times at which the course of history was effectively changed.

The first date is 1978, the year in which Australia's last whaling station, at Albany in Western Australia, closed down. From that time onwards, there was little impediment to Australia emerging as the most vocal anti-whaling nation-state in its hemisphere. As the country entered a phase in which long-established myths lost their potency, the politics and morality of anti-whaling became part of the forging of a reconstituted national identity. The second date is 1982, when the IWC declared its moratorium on commercial whaling, thus forcing Japan to reorganise the industry as a state enterprise. Whaling was effectively removed from the marketplace and turned into a bureaucratic and scientific exercise. In this intensely capitalist country, the profit motive could neither drive nor legitimise the continuation of whaling, especially a long way from home. At the same time, whenever the fleet set sail, whalers and the country to which they belonged ran the gamut of a vituperative 'cultural imperialism'.

So the killing of whales is nowadays only part of the problem. Over time, it has become entwined with a diversity of economic, political and cultural considerations. As well as pinpointing dates, it is important to emphasise that throughout this lengthy period of conflict both Japan and Australia have consolidated their status as significant players on the international stage, to the point at which national reputations are of inescapable significance. National identity and cultural integrity have become potent forces as globalization has rendered spatial boundaries relatively unimportant. Inside Australia, it is often asserted that the main reason Japan continues whaling is because of 'the loss of face' which an end to the practice will entail. This argument is part and parcel of the … 'Orientalist' discourse which informs the annual demonisation of the Japanese. On both sides of the whaling war, the combined force of national identity and cultural integrity may well prove as great an impediment as any other to the resolution of this long-running transnational conflict.

Edited extract from: Adrian Peace, 'The Whaling War: Conflicting Cultural Perspectives', *Anthropology Today* 26/3 (2010), pp. 5–9.

25 Ducks Out of Water: Nature Conservation as Boundary Maintenance
Kay Milton

In the previous extract from Peace's article on whaling, we looked at international contrasts in views of nature – and in particular, of natural environments as threatened by human activities. In our next passage, which again has an international scale, Kay Milton looks with an anthropologist's eye at the values and beliefs about what is and is not 'natural' that drive a conservation campaign such as the one to prevent the spread of the ruddy duck population in Britain and Europe. We encountered the themes of classification and categories earlier in the Reader, with the extract from Lévi-Strauss's classic work, The Savage Mind. *As Milton points out in this extract, anthropological studies over many years have revealed how a wide variety of cultural practices can be interpreted as directed to the maintenance of categories and boundaries. By placing a conservation campaign within this frame, Milton shows how an anthropological perspective can contribute to our total understanding of the issues in question.*

...

One of the most useful insights to emerge from structural anthropology was Mary Douglas's definition of dirt as 'matter out of place' and of pollution as the confusion of categories (Douglas 1966). As Douglas and others have demonstrated, this idea can lead us to see many cultural norms and activities as instances of boundary maintenance. The incest taboo, for example, maintains the proper boundaries between categories of kin and prevents roles from becoming confused; the act of tidying the house or garden, of putting things in their proper place, re-establishes boundaries which, in the state of untidiness, have become blurred. For post-structuralist and postmodernist anthropologists, one of the main difficulties with this approach is its reliance on the subconscious. Unless people explicitly describe their own activities as boundary maintenance, it is difficult to argue that this is what they are 'really' doing without implying that it is, for them, a subconscious preoccupation. The analysis, as a consequence, looks more like an imposition than an interpretation.

There are some activities, however, in which the maintenance of boundaries appears to be conscious and explicit. Gardening is a good example: weeds are often described by gardeners as 'plants in the wrong place'. ... I suggest that nature conservation might also be understood in these terms. ... I shall consider whether a campaign in which conservationists are currently engaged makes sense as an effort to maintain particular boundaries and, if so, what role those boundaries play in the way conservationists think and act. My chosen case study is the campaign to reduce (and, if possible, eradicate) the population of ruddy ducks in the U.K., which is part of an international effort to halt their spread across Europe.

...

Ruddy Ducks: The Problem

The ruddy duck (*Oxyura jamaicensis*) is native to North America, where it is relatively common. A few pairs were introduced into wildfowl collections in the U.K. during the 1940s. Captive wildfowl normally have their wings clipped to prevent them from flying away, but young ruddy ducks proved difficult to catch for this purpose. Some escaped from the Wildfowl Trust's collection in Gloucestershire in the 1950s, since when unknown numbers have escaped from this and other collections. A feral population became established and, over the next forty years, spread through the U.K. and on to the European continent. ...

At first, the presence of ruddy ducks in the U.K. appeared to pose no problem. ... But by the early 1980s conservationists were concerned that it might spread to Spain and compete or interbreed with the rare, native white-headed duck (*Oxyura leucocephala*). ... By the early 1990s these fears had been realized. Ruddy ducks were first recorded breeding in Spain in 1991, and in the same year, the first ruddy-duck/white-headed-duck hybrid was seen. ...

Hybridization among ducks is not uncommon, and is considered a problem by conservationists because it can cause one or other of the parent species to lose its genetic distinctiveness and become, effectively, extinct in its original form. ... Conservationists fear that [this] fate awaits the white-headed duck, if the spread of ruddy ducks across Europe is not reversed. ... Conservationists are afraid that the expanding ruddy-duck population will not only overwhelm the white-headed duck in Spain, but will also spread east and eventually threaten the white-headed duck throughout its current range.

The Campaign

Ruddy ducks and hybrids have been shot in Spain since their first appearance there in 1991, but the Spanish authorities requested that action be taken throughout Europe to halt and reverse the spread of the ruddy duck. This request is consistent with the understanding that the conservation of biodiversity is an international obligation, sanctioned by European law. ... The U.K. is seen as bearing particular responsibility in this instance, because of the understanding that ruddy ducks first entered Europe through British wildfowl collections. ...

Killing animals is always a sensitive issue in the U.K. ... My purpose here is not to discuss the rights and wrongs of the campaign, nor to present a fully balanced account of it, but to explore what it can tell us about the way conservationists understand the world. ... [T]he opposition to the campaign ... provide[s] a context for contesting, and thereby testing, the boundaries identified below as part of the culture of conservation.

The Boundaries

I suggest that three culturally defined boundaries are recognized and invoked by conservationists engaged in the ruddy-duck campaign. The least inclusive is the boundary between the two species. Without the explicit recognition that white-headed ducks and ruddy ducks are distinct from one another, the campaign would simply make no sense, because it would have no purpose. The second boundary, more inclusive but no less explicit than the first, is the boundary between natives and aliens. The white-headed duck is a native of Europe while the ruddy duck is an alien from North America. In the literature that surrounds the campaign, the ruddy duck is presented as an alien twice over. From a Spanish and European continental viewpoint it is not only American but also an invader from the U.K.: if ruddy ducks had remained there, they would not currently pose a threat to Europe's biodiversity.

The third boundary, the most inclusive of the three but also the least explicit, is that between human and non-human processes (often referred to in the social science literature as 'culture' and 'nature' respectively). The presence of the white-headed duck in Europe is a 'natural' phenomenon; it is there because it either evolved there or arrived under its own steam or was assisted by some other non-human power. The ruddy duck was brought to the U.K. by human agency and permitted to colonize Europe through human carelessness. Thus its presence in Europe is not natural; as one conservationist stated during a discussion, it has 'nothing to do with nature'.

I have referred to these boundaries as 'culturally defined'. It is worth spelling out what I mean by this, given that culture is understood in several different ways both within and outside anthropology. I treat culture as having both a general and a specific meaning. In its general sense, it refers to people's understanding of the world, the sum total of human perceptions and interpretations. ... In this sense, the boundaries identified above are culturally defined simply because they are part of human understanding. In its more specific sense, a culture is a way of understanding the world that is associated with a particular society or category of people. In this sense we can speak of 'English culture' or 'youth culture'. The boundaries identified above belong, in this sense, to a 'conservationist culture', a way of understanding that is held by conservationists and which is continually reinforced and modified through their ongoing discourse about conservation. None of this is intended to imply that the boundaries are not 'real' – I do not consider it part of an anthropologist's role to judge the truth of the ideas they analyse. But like all ideas they can be contested, as they have been in the context of the ruddy-duck debate.

Keeping the Species Apart

... The boundary between the two species provides the campaign with its central focus. The objective of the campaign is to maintain this boundary, by reducing the opportunities for ruddy ducks and white-headed ducks to mix, and ultimately by keeping them apart altogether. This objective is rationalized as part of the commitment to conserve biodiversity, which is said to mean 'the variety of life'. ... The loss of a species amounts to a reduction in biodiversity, so a great deal of conservation effort is aimed at preventing this. Many of the species that attract the attention of conservationists are endangered because their habitat is being destroyed, or because they are the victims of human activities such as hunting. In such cases, conservationists concentrate their efforts on protecting and restoring habitat and campaigning to change the human activities that present a threat. They also try to return endangered species to areas from which they have disappeared. These are precisely the measures that have been taken over the past twenty years to conserve the white-headed duck, both in Spain and in Eastern Europe ... . Thus, conservation does not always require species to be kept physically apart, but when the threat comes from another species, through predation or, as in the case of the white-headed duck, competition and hybridization, keeping them apart becomes an important objective.

...

A slightly different but closely related argument employed by some critics of the campaign is that the boundary is not significant outside science, and certainly not in the world outside human understanding. The implication is that the conservationists are seeking to preserve their own categories, rather than something of significance in the 'real' world. ... Such arguments come close to what some anthropologists say about culture in general. An important part of Douglas's (1966) model is that cultural categories are by definition symbolic; their function is to make the world meaningful by representing reality to us. When we seek, through our actions, to protect those categories, by maintaining the boundaries that separate them, we are preserving our own understanding of the world. ... [T]he question of whether that understanding is accurate, of whether the categories are 'real', is not an anthropological issue, though it is clearly very important in the context of everyday life and in the work of scientists who set out specifically to understand the real world.

...

Natives and Aliens: Ruddy Ducks as 'Dirt'

In virtually all the literature generated by the ruddy-duck campaign, its status as an alien species is conspicuously reported. The conservation organizations, from the start, presented the duck as an import from America; its alien status within the U.K. was, for them, a central consideration. In the general media, and particularly in the popular press, ruddy ducks were presented initially as British and only later as American. Although much of this coverage is contradictory and inaccurate when judged against the conservation literature and official reports ..., it nevertheless reflects the shifting emphases in the conservationists' own presentation of the issue.

In 1993, when the first major decisions in the campaign were being taken, conservationists were concerned to stress the U.K.'s responsibility for the threat to white-headed ducks in Spain. At that stage, it was not clear what action might be appropriate, but the important message was that, since the ducks causing the problem appeared to have spread from Britain, the U.K. must be prepared to act. In many of the press reports from 1993, ruddy ducks were presented as a British nuisance abroad, and inevitably compared with another famous British nuisance, the 'lager lout', a stereotyped rogue male holiday-maker who invades Spain each summer. Surprisingly, this comparison appears to have originated, not with the popular press, but with a government official, who was reported to have said: 'Ruddy ducks are the lager louts of the bird world. They have been mating their way across Europe' (*Sunday Express*, 24 January 1993).

In 1995, when the decision was taken to attempt a regional cull of ruddy ducks, conservationists had a different priority: to persuade the British public to accept the deliberate shooting of birds, during the breeding season, in the name of conservation. Part of the justification for this was the argument that the ducks did not really belong in the U.K. In the resulting wave of publicity, they were described (misleadingly) as a 'U.S. invasion'. At least one writer, who opposed the campaign, noted a comparison with American GIs stationed in the U.K. during the Second World War, and modified a famous descriptive phrase to suit the situation: 'Over-plumed, over-sexed and over here'. ...

The impression created by the ruddy-duck campaign is of conservationists concerned to restore an order which has been disrupted by things getting out of place. Ruddy ducks belong in America. As a result of being brought to Europe and allowed to get out of control, they are threatening the proper order of things by confusing the boundary between themselves and another species. This image accords well with Douglas's model of dirt as 'matter out of place' (Douglas 1966). According to this model, our definition of something as 'dirt', as a polluting influence to be eliminated, depends on its location. Soil in the garden is appropriate, but soil on the carpet is dirt; food on our plates is desirable, but food on the floor should be cleaned away; dandelions in a hedgerow are wild flowers, but in a garden lawn they are weeds. A dirty world is a disordered world, one in which our understanding of what should be is challenged by what we see around us. When we tidy up our environment we re-order our world, re-establishing the proper boundaries and protecting our understanding of what should be. It would be easy to see the ruddy-duck campaign as precisely this kind of activity: an attempt to restore order by eliminating a transgressor of boundaries.

But would this be a realistic characterization of the campaign or of conservation in general? Is this what conservationists are 'really' doing? There are two main points to be made in response to this question. First, there are instances of alien species whose presence, while not necessarily considered desirable by conservationists, is tolerated. These include the pheasant, introduced into Britain by the Normans (or the Romans) and now one of the most common birds in the U.K., and the Egyptian goose, of which a population of around 1,000 has become established in eastern England. ... And, of course, the ruddy duck itself was tolerated before its threat to the white-headed duck was recognized. ...

Second, there are instances in which the presence of an alien species is not only tolerated, but welcomed as a contribution to its own survival. These include the golden pheasant, which is rare in its native China and has a U.K. population of 1,000 to 2,000 birds, and the Mandarin duck, also a native of the Far East, whose U.K. population exceeds that in any other country except Japan. ... The implication is that, if the ruddy duck were endangered in its native land, then some other way of removing its threat to the white-headed duck would have to be found, one that did not involve eradicating the U.K. population.

A more detailed understanding of the values conservationists place on alien and native species can be gained by comparing their responses to problems caused by aliens with their responses to problems caused by natives. When an alien species poses a threat to biodiversity, then provided that species is not, itself, endangered, its eradication is treated as an option. This is clear in the case of the ruddy duck and also in cases where islands are cleared of introduced predators, such as cats and rats, which threaten ground-nesting birds. Attempts have been made over several years to remove ferrets from Rathlin Island, off the north coast of Ireland, and conservationists are currently discussing ways of removing hedgehogs from the Western Isles, in Scotland, where they threaten the breeding populations of wading birds. In both these instances, the total eradication of the offending predators is considered desirable, if not necessarily feasible.

When native species are seen as posing a threat, eradication is not treated as an option. If the problem species is a common one, as in the case of foxes or crows in the U.K. preying on rare birds, then killing the predators is considered an acceptable solution, but the objective is not to eradicate, since this would, in itself, reduce biodiversity. If the problem species is itself rare or vulnerable, conservationists seek a solution which does not involve reducing its population. For instance, when peregrines began to prey on roseate terns on the island of Anglesey a few years ago, the terns were provided with shelters under which they could keep out of sight of the peregrines.

It appears, then, that the removal of alien species is not the overriding consideration for conservationists. Their primary objective remains the conservation of biodiversity, which requires them to value species, above all, in terms of their rarity and vulnerability to extinction. Nevertheless, the distinction between aliens and natives is important in conservationists' perspective on the world, in giving them a clear understanding of which species belong where. It also provides a secondary criterion (rarity being the primary one) for valuing some species more highly than others, and therefore guides their responses to specific conservation problems.

...

The Human and the Natural

The distinction between natives and aliens, which is so central to the ruddy-duck campaign, depends on the more fundamental distinction between human and non-human processes. ... Under natural circumstances, the ruddy duck would have remained in its native land; its presence in Europe is not 'completely natural' because it is a product of human activity. By enabling species to be identified as native or alien, the distinction between human and non-human processes guides the actions of conservationists in the manner described above. Whenever the overriding consideration, the protection of biodiversity, allows, it helps them to decide which species take priority over others.

But this is not the only use conservationists make of the distinction between human and non-human processes. For nature conservationists, as distinct from conservationists in general ..., it defines the limits of their concern. Nature conservationists, by definition, conserve what is natural and without an understanding of what is natural and what is not, they would have no basis for taking decisions about which issues to become involved in. This is not to say that the products of human activity are not considered worthy of conservation. There are organizations dedicated to the protection of historic buildings and of rare varieties of domestic animals and plants. But these are not the concerns of those who regard themselves and are regarded by others as nature conservationists.

... What gives the distinction between human and non-human processes a greater importance for conservationists is the fact that 'naturalness', in the sense of freedom from human interference, is seen as a quality worth conserving in itself. ... For more than a century biologists have observed that, in general, human management of the land significantly reduces the number of species able to survive on it .... So naturalness came to be used as a shorthand indicator of species richness. In other words, even when naturalness appears to be a primary criterion for conservation, in reality it is subordinate to biodiversity. But ... naturalness is [also] valued because it is rare. In the U.K., conservationists have long recognized that almost the entire landscape bears the mark of human use, so it is not surprising that naturalness should, itself, have acquired rarity value. ...

Once naturalness is, itself, an object of conservation concern ... , then it becomes important to conservationists to maintain the boundary between the natural and the non-natural, between human and non-human processes, just as it is important to maintain the boundaries that separate different species. This was emphasized, for me, during a discussion about the ruddy-duck campaign, when I suggested that the genetic purity of the white-headed duck might be preserved through cloning (assuming, of course, that the technique could be made sufficiently safe and reliable). One participant in the discussion said that this would be like building a replica of a cathedral while allowing the original to be destroyed. What makes the difference, the only difference, between a 'natural' white-headed duck and its clone is the human intervention involved in the production of the latter. What is implied here is that this also makes the difference between 'real' nature and 'artificial' nature, between what is authentic and a degraded and devalued copy.

There are two ways in which the boundary between the human and the non-human is contested in conservation discourse. First, the significance of the boundary is questioned by the observation that conservation is, itself, a human activity, a form of intervention in nature, and that the management of habitats for biodiversity, the captive breeding and reintroduction of species to areas from which they have disappeared, are no less artificial than techniques such as cloning. Second, the foundations of the boundary are questioned by the argument that humanity is a part of nature rather than separate from it. ... Those who oppose the ruddy-duck campaign present it, metaphorically, in human terms, as ethnic cleansing, xenophobia and genocide ..., challenging the morality of treating non-human nature in ways that are condemned when directed at human beings. This challenge is issued, not surprisingly, by those who seek to extend our sphere of moral concern to non-human animals. But it is also supported by the more ecocentric thinkers within the environmental lobby, who argue that, from an ecological viewpoint, humanity is just one species among many, with no special right to dictate the fate of the others.

... [In the Western concept of nature, n]ature is seen as separate from humanity; the boundary between human and non-human processes defines the natural. The conservation of nature, as conservationists understand it, thus requires the preservation both of the separate things that constitute nature (the species, sub-species and ecosystems) and of the quality that makes them natural (their independence from human influence).

This makes conservation, inevitably, a boundary-maintaining exercise. In order to conserve the things that constitute nature, the boundaries that separate them must be maintained ... , and in order to conserve nature's 'naturalness', the boundary between the human and the non-human must be preserved. So it is not surprising if conservationists sometimes appear, when viewed through the filter of Douglas's model of symbolic classification, to be acting like nature's housekeepers, obsessively restoring order by putting things where they belong – eliminating species that are in the wrong place, returning them to where they used to be – tidying up the mess that others (sometimes, ironically, other conservationists) have created. This appearance is particularly strong in cases such as the ruddy-duck campaign, in which several boundaries come into play at once. The objective is to maintain the boundary between two species. The measures required to do this are justified in terms of the boundary between the human and the natural, through the mediation of yet another boundary, between natives and aliens.

But the boundaries with which conservationists concern themselves do not always coalesce in this way. Sometimes it is necessary to tolerate an unnatural situation, such as the presence of an alien species, in order to serve the higher purpose of conserving biodiversity. Thus the Mandarin duck is accepted in the U.K., where it does not naturally belong, because to eradicate it would make its global extinction more likely, and so would threaten biodiversity. And ultimately, the very project of nature conservation is contradictory, since it seeks to conserve what is natural through unnatural means (human agency). If a species can be conserved only through human intervention, in what sense can conservationists regard its continued existence as a natural phenomenon? In other words, in what sense can they claim, in such instances, to be conserving nature?

These observations suggest that, while conservationists in the U.K. are reasonably secure in their understanding of nature as a collection of things that should be preserved, they are much more ambivalent about its separation from humanity. In the practice of conservation, the boundary between the human and the natural is often obscured in the interests of conserving biodiversity. And yet, if they were to abandon this distinction ..., conservationists would lose an important source of value and justification for their work, and their main criterion for defining their area of concern. Indeed, without a distinction between human and non-human processes, nature conservation as we know it would become a meaningless exercise. For this reason we can expect conservationists to cling to their understanding that nature is distinct from the products of human activity, even though that understanding is continually challenged by their own activities.

References
Douglas, Mary. *Purity and Danger* (London: Routledge and Kegan Paul, 1966).

Edited extract from: Kay Milton, 'Ducks out of Water: Nature Conservation as Boundary Maintenance', in J. Knight (ed.), *Natural Enemies: People–Wildlife Conflict in Anthropological Perspective* (London: Routledge, 2000), pp. 229–43.

I.6   The Humanity of Things

26	**Feminine Power at Sea** *Silvia Rodgers*

Our next group of extracts focuses on the ways in which anthropologists approach the making and use of things, or material culture. As we saw with regard to nature and the environment, it is a characteristic of human societies to incorporate things and products within the human world. It is not an exaggeration to say that the things created and used by humans participate in deep ways in the social world. The passage which follows by Silvia Rodgers describes some of the ways in which, within a British naval tradition, ships have been given a human and feminine identity. Some of the practices and beliefs she describes are no longer current, but her account still offers a vivid example of a widespread general phenomenon.

The ceremony that accompanies the launch of a Royal Navy ship is classified as a state occasion, performed more frequently than other state occasions and to an audience of thousands. But until now it has never been the subject of research, either historical or anthropological.

If the ceremony of launching looks at first sight like the transition rite that accompanies the ship as she passes from land to water, it soon becomes clear that the critical transition is from the status of an inanimate thing to that of an animate and social being. From being a numbered thing at her launch, the ship receives her name and all that comes with the name. This includes everything that gives her an individual and social identity, her luck, her life essence and her femininity. … My research into the ceremony sheds light not only on the nature and development of the ceremony itself but also on the religious beliefs of sailors, on the symbolic classification of a ship by sailors, on the extensive and reincarnating power of the ship's name, and on the relationship between women and ships and mariners. It is the last aspect on which I want to concentrate here.

Most of us know that sailors refer to a ship by the feminine pronoun. But the extent of the metaphor of the ship as a living, feminine and anthropomorphic being, is not, I think, appreciated. Furthermore, it is this metaphor that shows up the quintessential and extraordinary nature of the launching ceremony. I say 'extraordinary' because this ceremony is unique in our society and any of its auxiliary societies in that it symbolically brings to life an artefact. It looks more like a case of animism than of personification. Its status in the Royal Navy as a state occasion makes all this even more remarkable, particularly as it is accompanied by a service of the established Church.

There are of course other new things that are inaugurated by secular or sacred means. But in none of these instances does the artefact acquire the properties of a living thing, let alone a feminine person. There is the proclivity to personify virtues and institutions in the feminine, but these are not conceptualized as living and human beings. Personal articles are given human attributes, with a name and even a gender. But this is not a social rule, nor a rule of grammar, as in the case of the personified ship. Nor is life, name and gender instilled through the public enactment of a prescribed ceremony.

Members of the Royal Navy, and indeed the merchant navies, talk about a ship as having a life, a soul, a spirit, a personality and a character of her own. These notions are not necessarily differentiated, and the terms are used interchangeably. Whether the word 'soul', 'life' or 'spirit' is used depends on the informant. What is constant is the gender of the ship. In the English language, which allows gender only to human beings and animals of determinate sex, it is the rule to refer to a ship as 'she' or 'her'. While reflecting the strength of the metaphor, the rules of grammar also indicate its limit. The linguistic boundary lies in the region of the relative pronoun. According to Fowler it is correct to say: 'The ship that lost her rudder' and 'the *Arethusa* that lost her rudder' or '*Arethusa* who lost her rudder'. Sailors frequently drop the 'the' in front of the name of a ship. They explain that if I went to see a friend I would not say 'I am going to see the Sally' but 'I am going to see Sally' and that this applies to a ship.

The image of the ship as a fictive woman is established in diaries and chronicles, is legally encoded in naval and legal documents, and celebrated in poetry and prose. It survives masculine names, figureheads and the labels East Indiamen and men-of-war. In the current Royal Navy, as I have indicated, the metaphor is as strong as ever. But what kind of woman is she? A ship is represented as possessing the attributes of more than one category of woman. All are stereotypes that are idealized by sailors. Two images predominate: the all-powerful mother who nurtures and offers womb-like protection; and the enchantress of whom a man can never be certain. Other images intrude, but all inspire romantic and consuming love, awe and constant devotion. When [the novelist] Joseph Conrad ... writes of 'the mysteries of her [the ship's] feminine nature' and how the love of a man for his ship 'is nearly as great as that of man for a woman, and often as blind', he expresses the sentiments of modern sailors.

Conrad not only depicts vividly the ship as a woman, but brings out the whole environment of being at sea. My informants frequently explain to me, with some emotion and with interesting detail, the reality at sea. It is disorienting, frightening as well as awe-inspiring. This environmental context is crucial when we look for reasons for the feminine nature of the ship. In an environment which is not the natural habitat of human beings, a man may feel himself to be especially vulnerable if as a species he is incompletely represented. That vulnerability could well account for the partnership of an all-male crew with a feminine ship. It is significant that the male and secular principle is complemented not by a secular and natural woman, but by her metaphysical and metaphorical manifestation. ... It is easy to understand that the oceanic environment exacerbates the need for mystical protection that emanates from women. In addition, in circumstances where uncertainty and the likelihood of sudden death is increased, the symbol of rebirth in the form of the mother would be particularly welcome.

...

In western societies, from the coasts of pre-classical Mediterranean to Catholic Europe, patron saints of mariners are usually feminine. Figureheads, now no longer extant on British ships, were particularly efficacious if the image was a woman, especially if she was bare-breasted. There is some ground for concluding that this icon symbolized the mother who suckled the infant god, and that this made her a powerful intercessor especially against the Devil. However, one hardly needs this evidence to recognize the existence of a special relationship between women, ships and mariners in British fleets.

First and foremost is the irrefutable feminine nature of the ship. Then there is the launch at which the two most important personages are both feminine: the ship and her sponsor. It is the role of the sponsor, a woman of high rank by ascription, to exercise her mystical powers to imbue the ship with luck and life by naming her in strict adherence to the ritual detail: the bottle must move, the ship begin to move, the name (the generator of the luck and life) be pronounced – all at the same moment. Anything else augurs bad luck for the ship. Unfortunately, a ship at her launch is hypersensitive towards her sponsor and may react with self-destructive wilfulness to any lapse by the sponsor in her manner of dress or rendition of the formula. There are many accounts of instances when a ship has refused to move or moved too soon, making it impossible for the bottle to break at the right moment. When a ship behaves in this way she puts her own luck at risk, but it is always the sponsor who is blamed. The sponsor's power to bless has inadvertently turned into the power to curse.

There are several ethnographic examples where positive power co-exists with negative power in one and the same person. ... But negative power, where ships of the Royal Navy are concerned, usually emanates from ordinary women. Strict taboos attempt to restrict this harmful influence. A woman on board a ship at night is regarded with particular misgiving. She is bound to bring bad luck, and sophisticated technology is no proof against this. On the contrary, it may itself be a target. This is nicely demonstrated by the true story of the Rolls-Royce engine of a destroyer that blew up when a woman computer programmer had spent the night on board. It was perfectly true that the manufacturers had omitted to drill a critical hole, and the engine could have blown up at any time. But why, the officers wondered, had it blown up on the one night that a woman was on board? ... The taboos excluding women from critical areas extend to the part of the dockyard where ships are under construction. We know that equivalent taboos are described in a host of ethnographies. They also operate on oil rigs and down coalmines in Britain, and are very stringent in fishing communities here and across the world.

With modern technology no match for the vicissitudes of luck, it is not surprising to find that the ceremony of the launch is as indispensable as ever, and part of the regulations of the Royal Navy. Nor is it surprising that it is still believed that if the bottle fails to break at exactly the right time, the fate of the ship is in doubt.

At the launch of a destroyer in 1975, a distinguished naval officer was alarmed when he thought that the sponsor had failed to break the bottle across the bow. 'After all', he told me, 'I might be in command of her one day'. The role of the sponsor has if anything increased. Advanced technology has made it possible for her to be seen to control not only the mystical but also the technical part of the launching. From 1876, engravings in the *Illustrated London News* portray Royal sponsors setting the ship in motion and releasing the bottle with just a touch of the finger. It may have been coincidental that this overall control mechanism was installed at the same time as the Christian service was added to the ceremony.

But the very existence of a Christian service presents a puzzle. The critical part of the launching ceremony is concerned with imbuing the ship, an artefact, with luck and the soul and personality of a feminine entity – hardly in accord with Christian doctrine. Although this naming ritual has always been called a 'christening', the term is misleading: the subject of the ritual is not a human being but an artefact; the liquid is not water but wine; the celebrant is neither ordained nor male. The duties of the sponsor (or godmother as she is sometimes referred to) are in any case not consistent with that of a Christian godmother, apart from the secular obligations that start after the launch. The puzzle comes no nearer to solution when one looks at the varying attitudes of ministers of the Church to this ceremony. Some clergymen in the nineteenth century voiced strong disapproval of the naming ritual and of it being called a baptism. Today, incumbents of parishes local to the shipyards are happy to conduct the service at a launch.

...

To understand the religious beliefs of sailors one has to look beyond the tenets of Christianity. The power of a ship's name, the naming ceremony, the metaphor of the ship as a fictive woman, the taboos relating to women: all are part of the beliefs of sailors which they themselves call 'superstitious'. It is well known in our own society that sailors are superstitious. What is not appreciated is that when sailors describe themselves as being superstitious, and they do so frequently, it has none of the usual pejorative connotations. They explain it as a natural consequence of life at sea, which makes them see things in a different way. An acceptable part of their syncretic religion, it comes near to the sense that adhered to *superstitio* in early Classical Rome: a valued and useful quality.

Historical investigation shows that this so-called superstition has always existed in British navies, though specific manifestations may have changed. A ceremony to mark the launch of a new ship seems to have been imperative for centuries. But it has undergone such transformations that it is unrecognizable from, for example, the one performed in Pepys's time. The ship has always been feminine, but the relationship between women and ships has shifted over time. That the power of women has remained confined to the supernatural plane will come as no surprise.

With so much emotion invested in a ship, one may well ask why the demise, unlike the launch, of a Royal Navy ship, is marked only by routine, and not by ritual. The answer must surely lie in the name through which the life, luck and personality survive the body of any one ship. The choice of names is vast, but the same names recur time and again: the present *Ark Royal* is the fifth ship of that name; the first belonged to Elizabeth I. If a name is outstandingly lucky and illustrious, it is reincarnated more frequently than others. ...

Edited extract from: Silvia Rodgers, 'Feminine Power at Sea', *RAIN* (*Royal Anthropological Institute News*) 64 (1984), pp. 2–4; reprinted in J. Benthall (ed.), *The Best of Anthropology Today* (London: Routledge, 2002), pp. 20–25.

27 Why Clothing Is Not Superficial
Daniel Miller

In this passage, Daniel Miller discusses the relationship between clothes, style and the essential or inner 'self' which is sometimes assumed to be more 'real' than the external trappings in which we choose to present ourselves. Through an extended treatment of three examples (drawn from fieldwork in Trinidad, India and London), he shows that this notion of a detached inner 'self' is often misleading. In different ways and different places, he argues, our 'self' is embodied in the styles and disciplines (or absence thereof) that dictate what we wear and how we wear it. So, for example, the discipline of wearing a sari, and how the body feels in it, become an inseparable part of a woman's experience of herself as she wears it – or it 'wears' her.

Dancing Kathmandu
Sangita, a dancer of Czech-Nepali origin, journeys to Kathmandu to explore how
practitioners in the Himalayan Kingdom negotiate Nepal's dance traditions in a period
of rapid cultural change. In Nepal, dancers are sometimes viewed with suspicion as they
straddle the uncomfortable border between the sacred and the profane.

Filmstill from *Dancing Kathmandu*. © Sangita Shresthova (RAI Film Festival 2007).

When I began my career as an academic, committed to the study of material
culture, the dominant theory and approach to the study of things was that of
semiotics. We were taught that the best way to appreciate the role of objects
was to consider them as signs and as symbols that represent us. The example
that was most commonly employed to illustrate this perspective was that
of clothing, since it seemed intuitively obvious that we choose clothing for
precisely this reason. My clothing shows that I am sexy, or Slovenian, or
smart, or all three. Through the study of the differentiation of clothing we
could embark upon the study of the differentiation of us. ... Clothes might
represent gender differences, but also class, levels of education, cultures
of origin, confidence or diffidence, our occupational roles as against our
evening leisure. Clothing was a kind of pseudo-language that could tell us
about who we are. As such, material things were a neglected adjunct to the
study of language: an apparently unspoken form of communication that
could actually speak volumes once we had attuned ourselves to this capacity.

...

There is no doubt that material culture studies was significantly enhanced
by the arrival of this semiotic perspective; but ultimately it became as much
a limitation as an asset. ... Consider one of the best-known clothing stories.

'The Emperor's New Clothes' is a morality tale about pretentiousness and vanity. The Emperor is persuaded by his tailors that the clothes they have stitched him are fine to the point of invisibility, leaving him to strut naked around his court. The problem with semiotics is that it makes the clothes into mere servants whose task it is to represent an Emperor – the human subject. Clothes do our bidding and represent us to the outside world. In themselves, clothes are pretty worthless creatures, superficial, of little consequence, mere inanimate stuff. It is the Emperor, the self, that gives them such dignity, glamour and refinement.

But what and where is this self that the clothes represent? In both philosophy and everyday life we imagine that there is a real or true self which lies deep within us. On the surface is found the clothing which may represent us and may reveal a truth about ourselves, but it may also lie. It is as though if we peeled off the outer layers we would finally get to the real self within. But what was revealed by the absence of clothes was not the Emperor's inner self but his outward conceit. Actually, as Ibsen's Peer Gynt observed, we are all onions. If you keep peeling off our layers you find absolutely nothing left. There is no true inner self. We are not Emperors represented by clothes, because if we remove the clothes there isn't an inner core. ... At first this sounds odd, unlikely, implausible or just plain wrong. To discover the truth of Peer Gynt, as applied to clothing, we need to travel to Trinidad, from there to India, and then to use these experiences to re-think our relationship to clothing back in London.

Trinidad

The problem with viewing clothing as the surface that represents, or fails to represent, the inner core of true being is that we are then inclined to consider people who take clothes seriously as themselves superficial. Prior to feminism, newspaper cartoons had few qualms in showing women as superficial merely by portraying their desire to shop for shoes or dresses. Young black males were superficial because they wanted expensive trainers that they were not supposed to be able to afford. .... Such assumptions ... [create] a problem for an anthropologist going out to Trinidad. Because the point of anthropology is to enquire empathetically into how other people see the world, dismissing them as superficial would represent a rather disastrous start to such an exercise, for Trinidadians in general were devoted to clothes, and knew they were good at looking good....

I worked much of my time in Trinidad with squatters who had neither a water supply nor electricity in the house. Yet women living in these squatters' camps might have a dozen or twenty pairs of shoes. A common leisure activity was to hold a fashion display, on a temporary catwalk, along one of the open spaces within the squatters' encampment. They would beg, borrow, make or steal clothes. It wasn't just the clothes, it was also the hair, the accessories and the way they strutted their stuff; knowing how to walk sexy and to look glamorous or beguiling. Movements were based on an exaggerated self-confidence and a strong eroticism, with striding, bouncy, or dance-like displays. In local parlance there should be something 'hot' about the clothing and something 'hot' about the performance. ...

As evident in the description of the local catwalk, what mostly concerned Trinidadians was not fashion – that is, the collective following of a trend – but style – that is, the individual construction of an aesthetic based not just on what you wear, but on how you wear it. ... Trinidad style, in turn, has two components, individualism and transience. The individual has to re-combine elements in their own way. The source of these elements is unimportant. They may be copied from the soap operas or the fashion shows which appear on television, sent from relatives abroad or purchased while abroad. They may simply re-combine local products. But the various elements should work together, be appropriate to the person who carries them off well, for ideally just one particular occasion. It didn't matter what clothes cost or even whether the clothes worn on the catwalk belonged to them or were borrowed for the occasion. This wasn't about accumulation, but about transience. The stylist may learn from fashion but only as the vanguard. Then they must move on. Trinidad's best known cultural export, Carnival, enshrines this transience. Individuals may spend weeks, if not months, creating elaborate and time-consuming costumes. But these must be discarded and re-made annually. What is celebrated is the event, the moment.

... [I]nstead of trying to ask where such a relationship to style comes from, instead of seeing it as a problem that requires explanation, we can turn the lens back onto ourselves. Why do we think that a devotion to clothing is a problem anyway? Why do we see it as a sign of superficiality and what does the very term superficiality imply? The problem with a theory of semiotics and of treating clothing as superficial is that we presume a certain relationship between the interior and the exterior. .... The assumption is that being – what we truly are – is located deep inside ourselves and is in direct opposition to the surface. A clothes shopper is shallow because a philosopher or a saint is deep. The true core to the self is relatively constant and unchanging and also unresponsive to mere circumstance. We have to look deep inside ourselves to find ourselves. But these are all metaphors. Deep inside ourselves is blood and bile, not philosophical certainty. We won't find a soul by cutting deep into someone, though I suppose we might accidentally release it. My point is that there is simply no reason on earth why another population should see things this same way. No reason at all why they should consider our real being to be deep inside and falsity on the outside. The argument here is that Trinidadians by and large don't.

...

So demolishing our presumptions about superficiality can only be a start. Next we need to look in more detail at how things, such as clothing, come not to represent people, but to actually constitute who they are. In pursuit of that goal we are now going to shift from Trinidad to India. Once that was hard to imagine. But thanks to Google Earth, just zoom out a little, move the globe a little, and now zoom right back in.

The Sari

A sari is a single piece of entirely unsewn cloth, usually around 6 metres, worn by being draped around the body. Usually these days it is worn in association with a petticoat, a blouse piece, and beneath these, pants and a bra. The aim of this section is not to tell you how Indian women wear a sari, or how the sari represents their identity. Quite the opposite. The intention is to explain how the sari wears the Indian woman, how it makes her what she is – both woman and Indian. … [B]eing a woman is quite different if it is accomplished through wearing a sari rather than through wearing a skirt or dress. Clothes are among our most personal possessions. They are the main medium between our sense of our bodies and our sense of the external world. First then, let's consider how it feels to wear a sari.

In the now widespread Nivi style, the sari is draped from right to left, passing over the lower body twice – the second time in a cluster of fan-shaped pleats – and the upper body once. The *pallu*, the free and usually more decorated end of the sari, falls over the left shoulder down to the waist. Given the asymmetry of the sari, no sensation in one part of the body is repeated in any other. The right leg does not feel like the mirror of the left. The two shoulders and the two breasts are touched by the garment in quite different ways. The right shoulder can remain untouched by the sari, while the left bears the weight of the *pallu*. The right breast feels the pressure of the pleats of the *pallu* pulled across the bosom, whereas the left one feels exposed, covered from the front but visible from the side. The right side of the waist is hot from the pleats passing over it, but the left side is uncovered and cool.

The centre point of the sari – the navel – carries the sensation of being a focal pivot around which the security of the whole garment revolves. Here the pleats are tucked into the drawstring of the petticoat. About a metre of cloth is gathered, with a good 12 cm tucked inside the string, against the belly. This causes perspiration, and a *zari* or starched cotton border may scratch …, but these sensations also give reassurance that the pleats are not spilling out. The thighs help define the graceful folds of the pleats that fan out from between the legs. Here again the sensations are asymmetrical. The pleats often lie from right to left in such a way that the first pleat rests on the right leg while the last pleat rests against the left leg. It is how one holds the right leg and knee that defines the shape of the pleats, but it is from the left leg that the sari curves from mid-thigh around towards the back of the body, resting in folds on the back of one's waist to then be brought around from the right side as the *pallu*. So the curve of a woman's hip and waist is accentuated on the left side. A slight bend at the knee can create a horizontal break in the vertical folds of the sari, giving a woman a more feminine and statuesque look. The ankles always feel slightly crowded as the gathers of the folds of the sari rest against them, their touch made heavier by the 'fall'. When walking, the right leg determines the length of the stride, which is kept in check by the warning tension at the ankle when the stride is too long for the sari. The left leg needs to move a little bit out and forward so as not to trap the pleats between the knees. The *pallu* may slide off with the movement, in which case the right arm comes up to restore it to the left shoulder, but carefully so as not to crush the cloth. After a few strides the sari may slip down from the left waist, and the left arm needs to pull it back up in order to retain the fan shape of the pleats.

...

Clearly then, wearing a sari has a specific feel. But this is only a hint of much more profound differences. To appreciate these we need to zoom in upon just one part of the sari – the *pallu*, the often highly decorated end of the sari that falls over the shoulder. The *pallu* represents a prosthetic quality to the garment that is not shared by any Western clothing. This is most obvious in its functional usage. As a woman does her household chores, the *pallu* is in constant use as a kind of third hand, lifting hot vessels in the kitchen, wiping the seat she is about to sit on in a public place, cleaning her spectacles, gathering up rupee notes in a purse-like knot, or protecting her face from smoke and smog. The *pallu*'s presence is so constant and available, so taken for granted, that it almost seems part of the body itself. Yet the same quality that extends the capacity of a person also gives the *pallu* the power to betray them. When something happens that represents the unwelcome intrusion of the external world upon the self, it may well have the *pallu* at the end of it. The *pallu* gets jammed in a car door, flies in your face so that you cannot see, or falls off your head when you are trying to be modest. The same *pallu* that is used to hold a hot *karhai* (cooking pot) of food may actually catch fire when cooking. Such accidents are all too common, and can result in horrible injury and death. They are not always accidents either. In many instances of dowry deaths, the groom's family claim that her *pallu* caught fire 'accidentally' while she was cooking. On the other hand, desperately unhappy brides typically end their misery by hanging themselves from the ceiling by their *pallu*.

The close identification between people and the *pallu* starts with the initial relationship between mother and infant. Most Indians have their first encounter with the sari before the time of memory. Mothers use it as a multi-purpose nursing tool. When breast-feeding they cradle the baby within it, veiling the operation from the outside world, and use the cloth to wipe the surplus milk from the baby's lips.

...

For the child, the *pallu* becomes a physical embodiment of their mother's love, a love they can literally take hold of. ...

For adults, the ambiguity of the *pallu* being simultaneously part of someone, yet separate from them, continues when it comes to their own attempts to form relationships. Given the natural propensity of the *pallu* to slip down from the bosom, the action of constantly covering up one's chest can have the effect, if done well (and some do it *very* well), of constantly drawing attention to the area that is ostensibly being protected. So a man has no idea whether a woman is re-covering herself because of what she does not want him to see, or is pointing out what she *does* want him to see. Another provocative form of manipulation deftly exploits the property of a sari as a draped garment, and consists of swiftly tightening it to accentuate the tautness of the bottom or the smallness of the waist. There is the additional potential for beauty and eroticism in a fabric which may appear transparent when in a single layer but is opaque when worn in several layers. The same subtlety that applies to flirtation is even more commonly applied to the institution of modesty, in which the *pallu* plays a central role. Most Hindu women have to cover their heads in the presence of certain family members, while most Muslim women have to cover theirs before strangers. Women have considerable scope to manipulate the precise way the *pallu* is held between the teeth or placed over their head, leaving the observing male quite uncertain as to the attitude that lies behind the action: it might be demure or respectful, tantalizing or truculent. These nuances of modesty and eroticism are used to great effect by those making Bollywood films and television soap operas.

...

This intimate relationship between person and cloth is not simply given, by virtue of being born in South Asia. All of this has to be learnt and mastered by each individual. A typical girl in Delhi is not brought up wearing a sari. She will first attempt this intimidating feat at the special 'school farewell' ceremony, which marks the end of the final school year, for girls aged around seventeen. The girls fumble around, scared stiff of the unfamiliar folds, dangerous-looking pins and sudden extrusions of loose cloth. They are continually worried about the risk of slippage, exposure and shame before highly competitive peers, their parents and their teachers. The girls' ability to tame and inhabit this fearsome flood of fabric will be taken as an indicator of their future ability to perform the social roles that will be expected of them. Not surprisingly at this point saris often stay in place thanks largely to discreetly placed safety pins. A girl may then wear the sari a few more times at the weddings of relatives, only to be faced with the occasion in her life when she is most subject to constant scrutiny, her own wedding, where her sari wearing becomes the centrepiece of the performance.

Once married, the neophyte sari wearer strives for social respectability. She must learn to move, drape, sit, fold, pleat and swirl the sari in an appropriate way. She may live in constant fear of embarrassment on moving to her husband's home. She can hardly sleep because she is so afraid that loss of consciousness will lead to her head or knees being uncovered, and as a result she feels stifled in the summer nights. ... At the level of safety and practicality, she must try to avoid the frequent injuries that arise from getting the sari caught in doors, machines or, worst of all, the stove.

...

Just as the sari starts off as far more oppressive than most Western garments, it now has the capacity to be far more powerful. Men working in offices complained that they could not compete with some women, simply because men don't wear a sari. A woman at one with her sari knows exactly how to place her *pallu*. While everyone else looking at her thinks it is just about to fall from her shoulder, she knows it isn't. She has command of a tool that allows her to express a variety of subtle emotions and claims, manipulating the sari's particular capacity for ambiguity especially with respect to eroticism. The sari by this stage becomes an instrument of power. No one ever achieved such a political mastery of this garment as Indira Gandhi. Somehow her wardrobe represented every region, group and aspiration of hundreds of millions of ordinary Indian women.

London

The presumption of anthropology lies in such comparative analysis between Trinidad and India. [It is by r]ecognizing that we take for granted our own ways of doing things, and that it is only through coming to appreciate how other people have entirely different experiences and expectations, that we can start to challenge our own. ... It is only by paying attention to the relationship between people and clothing in Trinidad and in India that a Londoner, such as myself, can in turn find people's relationship to clothes in London extraordinary, exotic and in need of explanation. Why should we think clothing is superficial, why do we wear such static clothing when there are alternatives that are more dynamic? Finally, we become ready to acknowledge why, from other people's perspective, it is we who may be seriously weird.

In its initial conception, anthropology tended to treat the places from which anthropologists then came, such as London, as given, ... [in] contrast with all other places that required explanation. Today we have an anthropology based on a global equality of amazement and exoticism. Just because I was born, brought up in and now live in London doesn't mean that I understand it. Quite the contrary, in some ways as a Londoner I am the least qualified person to engage with London, because it has, for me, this taken-for-granted quality. In other disciplines, the fashion is to suggest that if we seek to understand the experience of, for example, a transsexual Argentinian shop assistant, we need mainly to give voice to transsexual Argentinian shop assistants. But anthropology has always resisted this kind of politics, [i]nsisting instead that we need an exchange of understanding, where it is the others who can see much more easily the conventions and suppositions upon which we found our daily lives. This implies that we need to treat cosmopolitan sites such as London with the same respect of intense observation and analysis as anywhere else. It is all too easy to sink back into glib generalization when we return to familiar surroundings. Even in Western Europe there are profound distinctions in regional relationships to clothing if we examine them systematically.

...

... London is striving today to be a capital of cool partly in refutation of a previous time when it was a capital of Empire – now seen as extremely uncool. To merely conform to a generic public fashion, or to resort to designer labels, is likely to see the wearer branded as sartorially incompetent. Styles that deliberately repudiate respectability are often the vanguard of fashion. In London individuals are exhorted to express themselves, even find themselves, through their clothes. As most women in London will attest, this is a hell of a lot harder than it sounds. It does, however, lead to a very different understanding of what fashion itself is. Most theories of fashion, most studies of fashion, look to the fashion industry, its organization, pressures and patterns to account for fashion. But actually there is good evidence that most people choose their clothing as much despite as because of that fashion industry. If one glances across the range of clothing actually worn on London underground trains or in the street, things look very different from the fashion magazines that those same people are reading.

...

So perhaps we need to look elsewhere for a theory of women's fashion in London. Just as in India and Trinidad, we need to take seriously the experience of the women who wear it. The critical moment in that experience may well be when a woman gets up in the morning, examines a full wardrobe and yet feels an overwhelming fear that she has 'absolutely nothing to wear'.
...[I]t is possible to document and characterize this anxiety at the core of fashion, but we also need to account for it. Why has it grown over the last few decades so that people feel unable to wear much of what is easily available in the shops? Here anthropology can step in with its comparative perspective. What makes the situation in London so different from the previous examples?
In India, women who wear a sari are subject to a very well-established set of rules and social conventions. A woman who wears something inappropriate will soon be made well aware of her faux pas. By comparison, clothing in London is much less guided by order and social convention. It has become quite extraordinarily diverse and subject to rapid changes. So both the constraint, but also the support, of social convention have diminished. Advice from the fashion industry is much harder to use. Once there was some consistency and one was confident in how long skirts should be worn that year. Hemlines around the country went up and down in

unison. Now advice is as voluminous as it is contradictory, and despite reading multiple magazines, most people are not too sure what fashion actually is at any point of time.

...

If in London people bear individual responsibility for developing their own sense of style, this makes London seem much more like Trinidad. But there are separate issues which make London very different from Trinidad. People in London are relatively circumspect in expressing their opinions about how others look. Strangers would never shout out comments on the street to a passing woman, in the way they seem to do in Trinidad every few minutes. Comments in London are rarely direct; they are more often based on banter, or irony or said to a third person, rather than directly to the individual in question. As a result, individuals in London find it much more difficult to gain a purchase on this external presentation of themselves. They simply feel unsure about what other people think about them, and then in turn they become increasingly insecure that they even know what they think about themselves. At least with overt criticism you know where you stand. In London this is replaced with paranoia about what people might be saying behind your back – from where they can get a clear view that one's bottom really is too big. It is perhaps no surprise that the key television programme was called not *What to Wear* but *What Not to Wear*.

Without the social norms of India and the explicit critical comments of Trinidad, women feel a lack of support in developing their own personal preference. ... All of this culminates in a situation where the heart of fashion becomes anxiety. So for London, paradoxically, freedom ends up as a conformity that can be quite drab.

...

In three very different instances it becomes clear that we cannot regard clothing as a form of representation, a semiotic sign or symbol of the person. It is this form of analysis, not the clothing, that may now appear to us as superficial. Instead we have discovered something really quite profound. That the concept of the person, the sense of the self, the experience of being an individual, are radically different at different times and in different places, partly in relation to differences in clothing. In each case we have found that clothing plays a considerable and active part in constituting the particular experience of the self, in determining what the self is.

In Trinidad people use clothes to find out who they are at that particular moment of time. In India the experience of being a woman is different, when one is expected to constantly shift appearance in relation to each shift in circumstance. .... [I]n London clothing was found to be a source of anxiety, precisely because of the increasing pressure on individuals to express themselves, combined with the growing difficulty in determining one's own individual taste. So notwithstanding our increasingly common expectations of education and lifestyle, the supposed homogenizing effects of global capitalism, we have found striking regional differences in our relationship to clothing. This in turn has shown us that there remains also considerable diversity in who and what we think we are. That is not something that strikes me as superficial at all. So even if the same retail clothing chains are now to be found from São Paulo to Seoul this doesn't mean that the experience of wearing that clothing has been reduced to a single expressive form. One further conclusion is that the role of anthropology, committed to learning from comparative studies of humanity, is by no means diminished by global capitalism and modernity. In some ways the fun is only just beginning.

Edited extract from: Daniel Miller, *Stuff* (Cambridge: Polity Press, 2010), pp. 12–41.

SECTION II

BECOMING A PERSON
IDENTITY AND BELONGING

The Joy of Belonging
A sports team celebrating a victorious game on Krishna's birthday helps to reinforce the men's identities as athletes, Hindus and Indians.

Photographer: Kabir Orlowski (Identity Category Winner of the RAI's International Anthropology of Sport Photo Competition 2010). © Kabir Orlowski.

Introduction to Section II

Hilary Callan, Brian Street and Simon Underdown

In Section I we looked at a range of anthropological writings illustrating the complex nature of unity and diversity in human life. This second section moves us on through the themes of personhood, identity and belonging, which are treated in the second unit of the A Level course described in the General Introduction, and are focal to the discipline of anthropology generally. Sections III and IV will deal with the wider issues associated with 'Global and Local Societies: Environments and Globalisation', and with the practice of anthropology.

Once again, we illustrate these themes with extracts drawn from a wide range of anthropological literature, both from the past and also more recent examples. We suggest that you draw upon the extracts and discussions across the Reader in order to begin to build a cross-cutting understanding of the range and complexity of an anthropological approach to these fundamental features of human experience. You should quickly recognise that the separate sections are not water-tight units, but overlap and interweave in elaborate and complex ways. As we stated at the outset, this recognition can allow you to enter and engage in 'a series of conversations – sometimes of debates – between different anthropological interpretations of the themes we touch on'.

II.1 Personhood

A biological human becomes a social actor, or person, by acquiring a position in a society – by taking on an identity, statuses and roles that are socially recognised. But ideas of personhood are themselves variable from one society to another. The first passage of this section, taken from T.H. Eriksen's book *Small Places, Large Issues: An Introduction to Social and Cultural Anthropology*, outlines the essentially social character of human action, and indicates how concepts of personhood differ across cultures. This observation is taken further in the extracts from Brian Morris's book *Anthropology of the Self: The Individual in Cultural Perspective*, which present a contrast between Confucian and Tallensi concepts of the person. Reflect on your own assumptions of what it is to be a 'person', as distinct from a 'human being'. Do we in the West see personhood primarily in individual, rather than relational, terms?

One's standing as a person normally undergoes a series of socially recognised changes over the course of life – and in some cases, as we shall see, full personhood is not attained until after physical death. Typically, changes of status are marked by ritual means. These rituals are often called 'rites of passage', a term first coined by

Arnold van Gennep in 1909. They are quite familiar to us in contemporary life: think of our ceremonies marking birth, naming, graduation, coming-of-age, marriage, change of job or retirement. The work of anthropologists has consistently shown how widespread these rites of passage are across the world, and how they fall into several recognisable patterns. These are described in our second extract from Joy Hendry's book *An Introduction to Social Anthropology: Sharing Our Worlds*. The passage also shows how the rituals differentiating the different stages of a person's life reflect the ways in which time, space and the physical world are socially classified and ordered. Can you think of more examples of rites of passage, in addition to the ones Hendry gives? You may also have noticed that, in the developed world especially, people sometimes feel a *lack* of suitable rites of passage to mark significant life changes. For example, from time to time efforts are made to invent 'divorce ceremonies'. And in cases of still-birth or late miscarriage, medical services are nowadays urged to give bereaved parents an opportunity to mark ritually the passing of a baby who never became, in society's eyes, a 'person'.

We have referred to the taking on of a socially recognised identity. The concept of 'identity' is used in more than one way in anthropology, but it broadly refers to who you essentially think you are, how you define and place yourself in relation to your social world, and how you are regarded and placed by others. Identity in this sense is not exclusive: a person can have more than one identity (for example, as British, black, female, student) and these identities can become more or less significant or emphasised in different situations. To illustrate the many factors that enter into the construction of identities, we include an extract from an article by Gaynor Cohen, 'A Sense of People and Place: The Chapel and Language in Sustaining Welsh Identity'. Taking a historical perspective, Cohen shows in this article how the traditions and economic importance of the Nonconformist chapel, the Welsh language, music and performance, and the fortunes of mining and industry, interacted to shape ideas of 'Welshness' through the nineteenth and twentieth centuries and into the present day. The article also illustrates how the suppression of an indigenous language by a dominant authority (in this case, the English government) is experienced as an assault on a people's cultural identity. There are historical parallels to this from other parts of the world, as you may know from reading about the suppression of native languages in North America and Australasia in the past. Overt policies of language suppression are rare in the West today. But are there more subtle means by which ways of using language in a person's home environment – such as accent and dialect – may be discouraged or downgraded in education or employment; and what might be the effect of this on the person's sense of cultural identity? In reflecting on this question you may find it particularly helpful to look back at the passages on language and literacy practices and education, which we included in Section I.

II.2 Drawing Boundaries and Defining Groups

The tendency to create and maintain social boundaries and borders, and to define 'in-groups' and 'out-groups', appears to be a human universal, against which more high-minded ideals of human equality and moral universalism compete with difficulty. The boundaries themselves, however, and the means by which they are sustained, are highly variable. Perhaps the most universal boundary is that between what is considered 'human' and what is not; but even this is far from self-evident or constant. In some languages, the term the people use to refer to themselves as distinct from outsiders is also the term for 'human'; and at various times in history, foreigners, slaves and women have been thought of as excluded from the 'human' community. Conversely, attitudes to domestic animals – especially pets – in the Western world show that in some contexts the 'human community' can be stretched to include the biologically non-human. Earlier, in Chris Stringer's article on the Neanderthals, we met an example of scientific advance making it necessary to reconsider our ideas of where the human boundary should be placed. Bringing Neanderthals into the human fold may well make a difference in the long term to the ways in which we can think about ourselves and our humanity. Moving forward in time, we include an article 'What's in a Name? Creating Identities in Britain' by the historian and archaeologist Jemma Underdown, also specially written for the Reader. Continuing the discussion of identity we looked at earlier, Underdown gives us a glimpse into how these issues are addressed in archaeological and historical research covering long periods of time. Her article describes a remarkable instance of local continuity of descent traced through mitochondrial DNA; but it also demonstrates how far cultural identities can shift over time, and how distorting it is to think in terms of 'Britishness' (and by extension, other national or ethnic categories) as permanently fixed and bounded.

Social boundaries and borders are constructed and kept in being in an almost unlimited number of ways, from military fortification to social inclusion and exclusion based on ethnicity, religion, class or gender. Of particular interest to anthropologists are symbolic boundaries associated with ideas of pollution, and maintained through ritual observances. We include an excellent example, extracted from a study of English Gypsies conducted by Judith Okely (whose work on her boarding school we met earlier). In this article, Okely looks at the cultural boundary between Gypsies and the surrounding Gorgio (settled) society. She analyses the economic relationship between the two groups, and shows how the boundary is maintained through ideas of cleanliness and ritual pollution. Because of their need to engage economically with Gorgio society, Gypsy women are a potential conduit for pollution and a threat to the integrity of the boundary. They are therefore subject – and subject themselves – to tight disciplines in dress, behaviour and sexual expression that serve to maintain the symbolic separation and contain the danger.

II.3 Ritual and Social Relations

Our closing extract, in this section of the Reader, takes us to the heart of the anthropological approach to ritual as well as offering a prime example of a classical ethnographic study. In this passage taken from Victor Turner's *The Ritual Process*, published in 1966, the author gives us a deep insight into how the ethnographer goes about his or her task: gaining trust, cross-checking information with different informants, making use of opportunities and observations as they present themselves, and refining questions and interpretations until a deep structure of thought and practice among the people studied emerges. This painstaking process, as Turner's study of the Ndembu of what is now Zambia shows, reveals the intimate relationship of ritual to other areas of social life such as economic and political organisation. One of the things anthropological research does best is to illuminate this ultimate 'connectedness' between domains of human life which, at first sight, might appear entirely disparate.

Duka's Dilemma
Anthropologist and filmmaker Jean Lydall has been working with the Hamar of southern Ethiopia since 1970. In 2000, she and her daughter, Kaira Strecker, visited Duka, featured in the Hamar Trilogy, to bring Duka's life story up to date. Their film, *Duka's Dilemma*, reveals complex family dynamics, Duka's husband, Sago, having taken a second wife.

Filmstill from *Duka's Dilemma*. © Jean Lydall (Winner of RAI Film Festival 2003).

II.1 Personhood

Contrasting Concepts

28   **The Social Character of Humanity**
Thomas Hylland Eriksen

In this section of the Reader, we consider anthropological approaches to personhood: that is, how a biological human being comes to be transformed into a socially constituted person, with a publicly recognised status, roles, obligations and entitlements. We begin with an edited extract by Thomas Hylland Eriksen, who reiterates the theme we have seen in earlier passages: that while our existence is importantly rooted in, and to some extent limited by, our biological constitution, human action of even the simplest kind (such as dressing, walking or eating) is fundamentally social in character. Echoing (from a very different direction) the argument of Robin Dunbar which we met earlier, attributing human uniqueness to the evolution of language and the capacity to imagine alternative realities, Eriksen here discusses 'agency' as the essentially social ability of human persons to reflect on what they do and to imagine other choices. Towards the end of the extract, he discusses the differences between concepts of the person as a bounded individual, and as an amalgam of that individual's relationships with others.

The press occasionally reports stories about 'jungle children' who are discovered after allegedly having spent many years in a forest or similar wilderness, isolated from culture and human society. According to such stories – Kipling's novel about Mowgli, *The Jungle Book*, is the most famous one (and one of the few which does not claim authenticity) – these children have been raised by animals, usually monkeys, and are therefore unable to communicate with humans. Normally, 'jungle children' are said to reveal a pattern of acting similar to animal behaviour; they growl, they are terrified of humans and they lack human language, table manners and other capabilities which render the rest of us culturally competent. In all probability, stories of this kind are myths, but they can nevertheless be useful as illustrations of a crucial anthropological insight, namely the fact that human beings are social products....

What we think of as our human character is not inborn; it must be acquired through learning. The truly human in us, as anthropology sees it, is primarily created through our engagement with the social and cultural world; it is neither exclusively individual nor natural. All behaviour has a social origin: how we dress (for that matter, the mere fact that we dress), how we communicate through language, gestures and facial expressions, what we eat and how we eat – all of these capabilities, so self-evident that we tend to think of them as natural, are acquired. Of course, humans are also biological creatures with certain unquestionably innate needs (such as those for nourishment and sleep), but there are always socially created ways of satisfying these needs. It is a biological fact that humans need food to grow and to survive; on the other hand, the food is always prepared and eaten in a culturally determined way, and food habits vary. Ways of cooking, seasoning and mixtures of ingredients which may seem natural to me may seem disgusting to you; and – a topic of great interest to anthropologists – food taboos are nearly ubiquitous but differ from society to society. High-caste Hindus are not supposed to eat meat at all; rule-abiding Jews and Muslims do not eat pork; many Europeans refuse to eat horse meat, and so on. It is also a biological fact that hair grows on our heads, but our ways of relating to this fact are socially and culturally shaped. Whether we let it grow, cut it, shave it, dye it, curl it, straighten it, wash it or comb it depends on the social conventions considered valid in our society.

In order for humans to exist at all, they depend on a number of shared social conventions or implicit rules for behaviour. For example, there is general agreement in Britain that one speaks English and not Japanese, that one buys a ticket upon entering a bus, that one does not wander naked around shopping centres, that one rings the bell before entering one's neighbour's house and so on. Most social conventions of this kind are taken for granted and are therefore frequently perceived as natural. In this way, we may learn something about ourselves by studying other societies, where entirely different conventions are taken for granted. These studies remind us that a wealth of facts about ourselves, considered more or less innate or natural, are actually socially created.

...

Above all, social life consists of action, or interaction: if people ceased to interact, society would no longer exist. It may be useful for our purpose to distinguish the concept of action from the related concept of behaviour: behaviour refers to observable events involving humans or animals, whereas action (or agency), the way the concept is used here, implies that actors can reflect on what they do. It calls attention to the intentional (willed, reflexive) aspect of human existence. As far as we know, no other species apart from humanity is able to reflect upon its behaviour intentionally. Marx referred to this fact when, in *Capital*, he compares a human master-builder with a bee ... The beehive may be more perfectly fashioned and more functional than the house constructed by the builder (at least if he happens to be mediocre), but there is a qualitative difference: the human builder has an image of the house in his consciousness before starting on his work, and we have no reason to suppose that the bee starts from a similar image. It acts directly on pre-programmed 'instincts', and human actors do not.

The notion of agency thus implies that people know that they act, even if they do not necessarily know the consequences of their acts. In other words, it is always possible to do something different from what one is doing at the moment. This indeterminacy in agency makes it difficult to predict human agency; indeed, many social scientists hold that it is in principle impossible.

In anthropology and sociology, an acting person is frequently spoken of as an actor (or agent). This term can also include collective actors and is therefore more encompassing than words like 'person', 'individual' and so on. The state, for example, may be an actor. Further, *corporations* frequently appear as actors in anthropological studies. A corporation is a collective of humans which appears as an acting unit in one or several regards. In many societies, political parties and trade unions are typical actors; in others, kin groups make up corporations. ... The concept of the corporation must be distinguished from that of the *category:* a category of persons who have something in common at the level of classification without ever functioning as an acting unit.

The concept of agency, or action, can usually be replaced by the concept of interaction. Conceptualising whatever people are up to as interaction calls attention to the reciprocal character of agency, and most acts are not only directed towards other agents, but shaped by the relationship. The smallest entity studied by social anthropologists is not an individual, but a relationship .... In other words, the mutual relationship between two persons may be seen as the smallest building-block of society.

...

Comparative research has indicated that all human groups have a concept of the self or the person, ... but this concept varies in important ways. In European societies, the self is usually conceived of as undivided (as in the word 'individual'), integrated and sovereign – as an independent agent. In many non-Western societies, however, the self may be seen rather as the sum total of the social relationships of the individual. Indeed, as [Marilyn] Strathern (1992) has argued in a comparison between the English and Melanesian kinship systems, the typical Melanesian view of the self is, sociologically speaking, the more correct one. In highland societies in New Guinea, a human being is not perceived as a fully fledged person until he or she has acquired the basic categories of local culture. Personhood, in other words, is acquired gradually from birth onwards as the child becomes increasingly familiar with the shared customs and knowledge of society. In many central African societies we may discern a similar notion, since children who die do not turn into proper ancestral spirits: as their cultural competence is limited, and as they have yet to forge a wide array of social relationships, their personhood is still only partial. Further – to return to Melanesia – a person is not considered dead until all debts are paid and the inheritance has been distributed. Only when all of the social relationships engaged in by the deceased have been formally ended can he or she be considered properly dead. Strathern concludes that Melanesians conceive of persons pretty much as social scientists do, as the sum of their social relationships – unlike the English, who tend to see persons as isolated entities.

...

Personal names may give a clue as to the concept of personhood prevailing in a society. Among the Curia of Central America, ... children do not acquire a proper first name until they are about ten years of age. Geertz (1973) has described naming in Java as an extremely bewildering and complex affair to the outsider, where each person has seven different names pertinent in different situations. Compare this to the informality of North American society, where even complete strangers may address each other with a diminutive of their first, or Christian, name (Bill, Bob, Jim, Tommy, etc.).

References

Geertz, Clifford. *The Interpretation of Cultures* (New York: Basic Books, 1973).
Strathern, Marilyn. *After Nature: English Kinship in the late Twentieth Century* (Cambridge: Cambridge University Press, 1992).

Edited extract from: Thomas Hylland Eriksen, *Small Places, Large Issues: An Introduction to Social and Cultural Anthropology*, 2nd edn (London: Pluto Press, 2001), pp. 40–57.

29 Anthropology of the Self
Brian Morris

The previous passage from T.H. Eriksen's work indicated the extent to which cultures differ in their conceptualisations of the person. These two edited extracts by Brian Morris add detail by comparing views of personhood in the Confucian tradition and among the Tallensi people of Ghana. The two passages illustrate contrasting notions of personhood in different parts of the world and historical traditions.

The Confucian Tradition
Confucianism has, for most of Chinese history, been the dominant ideology, and intimately connected with the support of the imperial state. Its influence on Chinese culture has, with the present century, been profound. The

Confucian tradition suggests ... a very different ethos, and a very different self-conception to that of Taoism. Essentially Confucian selfhood entails not only a conception of the self as a centre of relationships – particularly with significant others – but also as a dynamic process of spiritual development. While Taoism situates the self in the organic processes of the natural world, Confucianism proclaims an ethical humanism, and situates the self in society. But ... the social order envisaged by Confucians implied a hierarchical order. The Confucian conception of the self thus takes as its model the aristocrat or superior man (*Chun Tzu*), who is implicitly a ruler of others. It is a conception, however, that puts a fundamental stress on sociality and on social ethics.

According to Confucian doctrine all things derive their being from a common source (Heaven); all therefore possess a 'heavenly nature' (*T'ien-Nsing*). Confucians thus accept the concept of a human 'Nature' (*Jen-Hsing*) that is common to all humans, and suggests that there is an ethical imperative in all humans to love one another. In a Confucian book of rites the human being (*Jen*) is defined as 'the expression of the virtue of heaven and earth, the intersection of yin and yang, the meeting place of ghosts and spirits, and the vital energy (*Ch'i*) of the five elemental movements or agents of all phenomena (*Wu Hsing*)'. Thus the human subject is considered both a material and spiritual being, ...[with] sociality and ethical propensities different from the animal world. ... The word *Jen* originally referred only to the aristocratic class, as opposed to the common people (*Min*), but over time this distinction was dropped and *Jen* became a general term for human being. The term also means 'good', 'humane' and is used as an adjective to refer to human conduct as opposed to that of animals. ...

The Chinese character *Hsing* (nature) is composed of two elements, the 'heart' radical (*Hsin*) which by itself denotes 'mind' or mental activity, and *Sheng* which has a variety of meanings, including 'to give birth' and 'life'. Human nature therefore involves life and vitality and 'mind' which is seen as a unique attribute of humans. In Confucian thought the 'mind' (*Hsin*) was not seen as a metaphysical entity separate from the body, but was rather understood functionally with reference to certain types of activity. It referred to the spirit or vital force, to the heart and the emotions, and to the mind as a cognitive organ. The term *Hsin* was therefore used to denote many things, including 'intentions', 'feelings', the location of desires, cognitive activity, and importantly for Confucians, the discrimination of what is ethically proper and required as a duty in a given situation. ... 'Mind' was seen as the origin of goodness, and a specifically human attribute. ...

Confucian conceptions of the human person focused ... around several key virtues: ...: *Jen* (humaneness), *I* (righteousness), *Li* (ritual propriety), *Chung* (loyalty), *Shu* (reciprocity) and *Hsiao* (filial piety).

Jen has been translated ... as 'goodness' and the 'perfect virtue'. It has a wide range of meanings: benevolence, compassion, sympathy, kindness, generosity. Confucius defined it as the love of other people. *Jen* was seen as an expression of the human heart, and to be human-hearted was to be a person. ... In essence *Jen* (humanity or humaneness) is the characteristic of an ideal person, or the norm of what a person should be – although it is evident that Confucius saw this ideal as embodied in the male person.

I (or *Yi*) means 'righteousness' and is used by Confucius as a standard of judgement. In the *Analects* he says: 'The superior person is concerned with what is right, just as the small man is concerned with profit.'

...

Li (ritual propriety): The term *Li* originally meant 'to sacrifice' to the ancestors or spirits, but later came to mean or have connotations of social order. 'The sage teaches people *Li*, by which all circumstances can be governed in the proper way'. Although Confucius was an expert on religious ritual, and the *Li Chi* ('Book of rites') is considered one of the classic Confucian texts, Confucius himself seems to have been agnostic in matters of religion. What he stresses is the value of ritual in promoting good conduct and orderly social life. Confucius, then, advocates ritual in terms of social order and government by a benevolent, saintly ruler.

Chung (loyalty): This is another social virtue stressed by Confucius. Originally the term meant the loyalty that officials and the people owed to the ruler of the state, but it was later extended to include loyalty between friends. It then came to have association with sincerity and a concern for others. 'To do one's very best for the sake of others is Chung'.

Shu: This virtue has been translated variously as compassion, altruism, forgiveness and reciprocity. In the *Analects*, Confucius's disciple Tzu-Kung asks, 'Is there any single saying that one can act upon all day and every day? The Master said, perhaps the saying about consideration: "Never do to others what you would not like them to do to you"'. ... Like *Chung*, the virtue of reciprocity is intrinsically connected with *Jen* (humaneness).

Hsiao: Filial piety is a major virtue in Chinese culture and a central pillar of Confucianism. It originally meant piety or reverence towards spirits of the dead, including one's dead parents, but it came to be applied to the duties towards one's living parents. It eventually came to be regarded as the root of all other virtues. Obligations towards parents involve not only obedience to them, but caring for and supporting them in old age, providing a worthy funeral for them, and offering proper sacrifices to them thereafter. ... But filial piety goes beyond relationships between parents and children, and in Confucian philosophy it is not only an ethical imperative but a function of a universal hierarchical order. To respect the father is to be in accord with Heaven. The *Hsiao Ching* ('Classic of filial piety'), a Confucian work of the Han dynasty, describes filial piety (*Hsiao*) as a principle penetrating the universe. ... But in general such piety implied respect and obedience not only of children towards parents, but of people towards the emperor or official, a wife towards her husband, and a younger person towards an older person. Towards people of superior status a person should show obedience, respect, reverence and a pleasant demeanour. *Hsiao* was not seen as an exclusive virtue but it did play a central role in Confucian ethics, and was seen as 'the primary and most fundamental unit of mutual connection between two or more persons'.

    ... All these virtues – ritual propriety, righteousness, loyalty, humaneness, filial piety, consideration of others – are encompassed in the abstract conception of the perfect man, *Jen* in the broadest sense. And importantly they are all social virtues. The Chinese conception, or rather the Confucian conception, of the person therefore is essentially based ... on an individual's transactions with his or her fellow human beings. The central focus of the concept *Jen*, therefore, is 'the place of the individual in a web of interpersonal relationships'. The Confucian self can thus be seen as a configuration of role relations with significant others, and there is a suggestion that the self has little meaning outside these rigidly defined social contexts. The self was thus constructed within a collectivity of kinship networks and strongly bolstered by such cultural ideas as loyalty, filial piety and consideration for others.

...

Confucianism ... [thus] suggests a feudal state, and a self-conception that is essentially sociocentric. The ideal person for Confucius was the scholar-bureaucrat (*Shih*), governing wisely through moral example. ... [F]or Confucius, self-realisation was an ethical task, conforming with the dictates of social status, and developing the *Jen*, the humanity, the 'heavenly nature' within each person.

The Tallensi

Editors' Note
The Tallensi are a Ghanaian people. The anthropologist Meyer Fortes
worked with them and recorded their life in a series of important
studies during the 1940s and 1950s.

The religion of the Tallensi is focused around ancestral spirits, referred to as 'fathers' or 'forefathers'. These are the dominant supernatural agencies believed to control human existence, and as their shrines are situated within the homes and settlements of living people, they are in all important senses incorporated into Tallensi social order. ... Although for the Tallensi the ultimate source of everything on earth is Heaven (*Naawun*), there are no shrines or myths associated with this 'being'. Moreover, unlike many African communities, witchcraft and sorcery are only marginal to the Tallensi scheme of mystical thought, as is their belief in bush spirits and ghosts. It is their ancestral spirits that have social significance, and as Fortes writes: 'Every important activity and every significant social relationship among them is expressed and sanctioned by the ancestor cult' ... . The ancestors are continuously involved in the affairs of the living and make their powers felt by inflicting misfortunes on or even slaying their descendants. Retribution is seen as just, and is due to the neglect of the ancestral spirit or to the flouting of kinship norms. The spirits are concerned with upholding not morality in a general sense – with theft or adultery say – but rather with transgressions of the rule of kinship amity. What the ancestors demand, writes Fortes, and enforce with pain of death 'is conformity with the basic moral axioms in fulfilling the requirements of all social relationships'. ... Thus Fortes suggests that the Tallensi and the ancestral spirits belong to the same moral universe and are linked together in complementary opposition that is mediated by sacrificial rites. ... Fortes regarded the facts of kinship, particularly as these relate to relationships between parents and children, as axiomatic, and as crucial in the understanding of Tallensi social life. The Tallensi ancestors, he wrote, 'are essentially projections of the jural authority vested in parents'.

... Fortes's analysis of Tallensi religious conceptions therefore attempts to go beyond a ... functional description. Stressing the importance of psychoanalytic theory, he suggests that a focus needs to be put on primary kin relations. He thus writes: 'The binding force of custom among the Tallensi depends, in the final analysis, on their ancestor cults, and ... the key to this lies in their family and kinship system'.

... But more than this, Fortes is also concerned that functionalist ethnography does not enable us 'to see how ritual or belief is actually used by men and women to regulate their lives'. It is important therefore to situate religious ideas not only in the context of social relationships, but also in the context of personal history. ... In his important study of Tallensi religion Fortes therefore interprets the religious beliefs of this community in terms of two analytic paradigms drawn from Western culture, those of Oedipus and Job.

The myth of Oedipus is centrally concerned with the notion of fate or destiny. This finds its counterpart in Tallensi culture, Fortes suggests, in their notion of prenatal destiny (*vin*). Soon after a child's birth its father ascertains from a diviner which configuration of ancestral spirits desires to take the child as its ward. Each Tallensi thus has a guardian spirit to watch over and preserve his or her life, and this may be for good or ill. A person's destiny then 'consists of a unique configuration of ancestors who have of their own accord elected to exercise specific surveillance over his (or her) life-cycle'. .... Given a good destiny a person's life will prosper and if a man, he may achieve full personhood. An evil pre-natal destiny may negatively affect one's life and may have to be propitiated or exorcised. Such beliefs not only recognise the individuality of human life – and the Tallensi have a shrewd understanding of individual differences in character and disposition – but they serve as a legitimate alibi for personal misfortunes. They relieve the person and his or her kin of responsibility and guilt for the misfortunes and tribulations that are inflicted upon them. The result is, Fortes writes, 'that the Tallensi can accept responsibility on the personal level for the good and ill in their lives without feeling morbidly guilty'. ... It is important to note of course that unlike the Greek concept of destiny or fate (which is impersonal), the Tallensi concept of pre-natal destiny involves personal agencies with whom social relations can be established.

The paradigm of Job – the old testament figure whom god punished – is represented, Fortes suggests, in Tallensi culture by the ancestral spirits who are 'the jealous guardians of the highest moral values', those axiomatic values associated with filial piety and kinship amity. Thus Fortes concludes that the cult of ancestors among the Tallensi 'is an institutionalised scheme of beliefs and practices, by means of which men can accept some kind of responsibility for what happens to them and yet feel free of blame for failure to control the vicissitudes of life'.

...

But Fortes explores the relationship of the ancestral cults not only with Tallensi kinship structure, but also with their conceptions of the human personality. ... Fortes is centrally concerned with the relationship between the individual and society but he is free of the rigid dualism that pervades the work of earlier scholars, ... and sees the relationship as essentially a dialectical one. Although he stresses the fact that the human subject is intrinsically a social being and that the achievement of personhood is a social process, the human individual is crucially involved as an agent in this process. As he writes: 'One cannot emphasise too much the principle that familial and lineage status is an inescapable determinant of personhood at every stage. The person emerges through the dialectic interplay of individual and social structure'.

...

... Fortes showed with great insight how among the Tallensi ... [the concept of the person] involved a complex process that incorporated many different aspects of social life. He summed up the Tallensi concept of the person in the following extract:

> A person (as distinct from his or her personality) in Tallensi thought is a complex socio-psychological entity. Rudimentary components are the body, the life and the soul, which emerge at birth. To these must be added identity, which is rooted in ancestry, and achievements which are ruled by destiny. And as these accrue through the life-cycle, so personhood grows and develops. But personhood is not regarded as complete and fulfilled until ancestorhood is assured, and for this one must have surviving children, at least a son, to install one as an ancestor.

...

It is characteristic therefore of Tallensi thought and institutions that full personhood is only attained by degrees over the whole course of life, and is focused on the male elders who are transposed after death into an ancestor.

Genuine personhood is thus validated retrospectively in the attainment of ancestral status.

Edited extracts from: Brian Morris, *Anthropology of the Self: The Individual in Cultural Perspective* (London: Pluto Press, 1994), pp. 112–17 and 124–28.

Transitions

30	**Rites of Passage** *Joy Hendry*

In the previous extracts from anthropological writings on notions of the person, we saw that, in some cultures, personhood is a 'process' rather than an all-in-one attribute. In other words, personhood is acquired over the course of life – and sometimes not until after physical death – through a gradual accumulation of relationships, responsibilities and reputation. In fact, the human life-course seen as a passage through birth to death and the afterlife, with key stages marked by ritual, has been a key theme of anthropological study since the notion of 'rites of passage' was introduced into the discipline by Arnold van Gennep in 1909. The following edited extract by Joy Hendry shows clearly the power of the 'rites of passage' concept in revealing the common structure linking otherwise very different ritual practices across the world.

Much has been written on the subject of ritual, and there have been many theories about its interpretation, but there is one classic work that has stood the tests both of time and of further research. This is the study by Arnold van Gennep, first published in 1909, in French, and translated into English in a book called *Rites of Passage* (1960). ... [T]his writer refers to the people under discussion as 'primitive'; and he talks mostly of people in small-scale society, but his theories have been shown to have applicability in any society in any part of the world. ...

These rites of passage are those which accompany the movement from ... one social category to another, the passage of a person or persons in a society from one class to another. There are four main types of move:

1. The passage of people from one *status* to another (for example, marriage or initiation to a new social or religious group).
2. The passage from one *place* to another (for example, a change of address or territory).
3. The passage from one *situation* to another (for example, taking up a new job or starting a new school).
4. The passage of *time* (when the whole social group might move from one period to another, for example at New Year, or into the reign of a new king/queen or emperor).

If we think of occasions in our lives, and in those of people around us, when we might engage in some form of ritual, they are very often precisely the sort of passages which fit these descriptions. For example:

- birth, marriage, death
- christening, initiation, bar mitzvah
- changes of school, job or house
- going away, coming back
- birthdays, anniversaries, graduation
- changes of the seasons, New Year.

We ritualise these occasions in various ways, but some elements on which we draw are:

- dressing up
- sending cards
- giving presents
- holding parties
- making and consuming special food
- making resolutions
- ordeals.

By examining reports of rites of passage from various parts of the world, van Gennep noticed that certain characteristic patterns recurred in the order of the ceremonies even from places much too far apart to have influenced one another. First of all, there would be rites of separation from the old class or category, and these, he argued, are very often characterised by a symbolic death. There would also be rites of incorporation into the new class or category, and these would be characterised by a symbolic rebirth. Most striking, however, was the fact that these sets of rites would almost always be separated by a transition period when the participants would belong to neither one nor the other.

These rites he named as follows:

- Rites of Separation or Preliminal Rites
- Rites of Transition or Liminal Rites
- Rites of Incorporation or Postliminal Rites

… Let us examine some examples of the types of rite of passage he proposes.

Territorial Rites of Passage

…

Van Gennep discussed passages from one tribal area to another, or between different inhabited regions, but his ideas also work in a consideration of the bureaucratic rituals associated with making a passage from one nation to another. First of all, it is necessary to acquire a passport, sometimes quite a complicated and time-consuming process. In the case of many countries, it is also necessary to acquire a visa for entry. If the journey is to be of a considerable duration, friends and relatives may hold a farewell party and offer gifts and cards of good wishes. The moment of parting, at the airport, dock or station, will be marked with kisses, embraces and/or handshakes, and the passenger will be exhorted to telephone, text or e-mail on arrival.

In an airport, one is then forced to pass through a series of physical barriers involving the showing of passports and visas, the checking of luggage (and the body) through security screens, and, until arrival at the point of destination, one is quite literally in a zone of transition. Airlines use a technical explanation to account for their requests for mobile phones and other electronic equipment to be turned off during a flight, but the fact of doing it adds to the sense of liminality. The rituals of departure are repeated in reverse on arrival, and if friends or relatives are waiting, despite a high probability of fatigue and overindulgence in food and drink, it would be regarded as most unfriendly to refuse the welcoming rituals of hospitality. The phone call of arrival is a reassurance for those left behind that the zone of transition is thus safely crossed, that the traveller has entered another world. It may be a world relatively dangerous and unknown, but at least it is a world!

... Van Gennep also discusses rites for crossing thresholds. ... The zone of transition is most clear at the entrance to a Japanese house, and it is often filled with shoes, but there are parallel rites for entering a Jewish house, where the mezuzah must be touched, and churches, mosques and temples have some form of ritual act as one moves from a profane space to a sacred one. This may involve the removal of pollution, with a touch of holy water; it may involve a bow, a sign of the cross, the removal or donning of shoes or headgear, or simply a lowering of the voice. Again, the crossing of the threshold involves a passage from one cosmic world to another, and visitors might be expected to observe the conventions regardless of their own religious allegiances.

...

These rites also represent a form of security for the world which is being entered. In the case of countries, the checking of the passport is a way of controlling immigration; in the case of a sacred building, there is an opportunity to remove the pollution of the mundane outside world. In any house or community a stranger may represent a threat, and ritual is a way of neutralising the potential danger. Van Gennep describes society as 'similar to a house divided into rooms and corridors' ... and territorial rites of passage associated with entering and moving about in a house may thus be seen as a model in spatial form of the rites which accompany moves from one section of society to another.

Pregnancy and Childbirth
The arrival of a completely new member of society is an occasion for ritual observance anywhere, and it also provides a threat to the mother who will give birth. In some societies women are regarded as polluting throughout

their pregnancy and they must live in a special hut removed from the public arena. They are thus removed physically from their normal lives to live in a 'liminal' part of their social world. They participate in rites of separation before they go, rites of transition while they are there, and only become incorporated back into society after the baby has been born. The baby, too, must be welcomed into society through rites of separation from the mother and rites of incorporation into the new social world it has joined.

Although there are few formal periods of separation for pregnant mothers in the cosmopolitan world, the English language does still contain the telltale word 'confinement' which refers back to a period when it was considered inappropriate for heavily pregnant women to be out in the world at large. Moreover, pregnant women in almost all societies do observe various restrictions on their usual behaviour, perhaps in variations to their culinary practices, … or the avoidance of alcohol and smoking, as well as the careful control of drugs and other remedies. Others who are aware of their condition will carry heavy objects for them, seek out titbits for them to consume, and generally offer special care during this transitory period. Women who suffer high blood pressure and other serious complications may be literally removed from society to hospital for the waiting period.

…

In most societies there is some form of celebration following a birth. Amongst Christians, the christening is a formal naming ceremony in the church as well as a presentation of the child to God, and the Church of England used to have a ceremony for mothers known as 'churching', which incorporated them back into normal life. During the christening service the baby is taken from its mother by the minister, who holds it throughout the most crucial part of the ceremony, and it may be handed to a godparent as well. Elsewhere, there is a rite of separation of the baby from its mother associated with the cutting of the cord, and the cord itself may be buried in a special place with some significance for the future. The Jewish practice of circumcising a baby boy is also an important early rite of passage.

In some societies in South America, the father of a baby goes through a series of rites parallel to those undergone by the mother, partly as a way of expressing and confirming his paternity. This practice, known as couvade, implies the idea that the father shares substance with the mother and the unborn child, and they restrict their behaviour to avoid illnesses, particularly to avoid the child taking on the characteristics of animals eaten by humans. Although for very different reasons, this practice could be compared to the way fathers in the U.K., U.S.A. and elsewhere attend and participate in antenatal classes with their pregnant partners so that they may assist at the birth of their children. These classes sometimes demand quite serious commitment on the part of the fathers, who must carry out breathing and relaxation exercises along with the mothers.

…

Initiation Rites

During childhood, rites are held in different societies to mark various stages of development that are regarded as important. These may include regular events such as birthdays, or accomplishments such as a first outing, first food, first haircut, first teeth (or loss of same), first day at school, and so forth. In some societies physical changes are made, such as circumcision or ear piercing. The periods which are marked reflect the local system of classification of life into stages, and some societies are divided into age sets where children born within a particular period move through the stages together. Others move through on an individual basis. In either case, there will be rituals to mark the passages from one stage to another.

Social recognition of the physical changes of puberty provides widespread examples of clearly defined rites of passage which ritually turn children into adults, and these may again involve a substantial period of separation and/or special treatment. Amongst African tribes such as the Maasai of the Kenya/Tanzania border, and the Ndembu of Zambia, for example, young men are turned out to fend for themselves in 'the bush', and they may be regarded as dead for the duration. Special rites precede and follow their absence, and their physical appearance will reflect their stage in the process. ... The Maasai allow their hair to grow long and unkempt in the bush, but shave completely on their return, painting their bare heads with shining ochre to mark their rebirth into society. The Ndembu have female puberty rituals which take place when a girl's breasts begin to form. They are confined to the village, but the girl is wrapped up in a blanket and lain under a tree where she must remain motionless for the whole of a very often hot and clammy day while others perform ritual activities around her. ...

This kind of ordeal is characteristic of many initiation rituals, which may again involve mutilations of the body of one sort or another. The proximity of these events to the flowering of sexual maturity may focus attention on the genitals in the practice of circumcision again, or even clitoridectomy. This last practice has incurred something of a backlash from women around the world, although there have been fewer protests about the former, male practice. In some societies, incisions in the face will leave permanent scarring, indicating membership of a particular tribe or lineage. Undergoing the ordeal associated with these practices is supposed to demonstrate the readiness of the child for adulthood, and the permanent markings left behind will illustrate their new status once and for all.

Education of some sort is also often involved, and youths may be taken for the first time into the men's hut to be shown ritual objects, or taught tribal lore to be kept secret from the women and children. Likewise, girls may be taught certain esoteric elements of female life. In many societies, these young initiates are regarded as immune to social sanctions for the period of transition, and they may engage in all sorts of outrageous antisocial behaviour. Even if they are not in the bush, they may live for a period in a special house where they can experiment with adult activities and practise various social aberrations while they are in the intermediate stage between two categories. ... Something of the same tolerance is accorded to youths for certain periods in many societies. For example, in universities in Britain, Holland and Ireland, an annual institution known as 'rag week' is the occasion for the tolerance of all kinds of scrapes and usually illegal activities in the interest of raising money for charity.

...

Other forms of initiation to secret societies or esoteric bodies such as priesthood, as well as the enthronement ceremonies for a king or emperor, follow the same principles as initiation to adulthood. There are rites of separation of the principals from their previous lives, periods of transition involving education and training, and rites of incorporation representing a rebirth into their new roles. In some societies the period of interregnum between one ruler and his successor allows antisocial behaviour for the whole people, and steps are sometimes taken to keep the death of a king secret until the arrangements are in place for a quick succession, in order to cut down on the disorder.

Marriage Rites

Marriage is a most important transition in most societies and it may coincide with the attainment of adulthood so that the rites associated with the wedding come at the end of the period of separation associated with the initiation into adulthood. In other societies there will be a long period of betrothal, which may be regarded as a period of transition with rites at the beginning and end. In any case, this is a passage well marked with rites of separation, transition and incorporation in most societies, although the details may differ.

In Mexico, for example, a party held for girls who have become engaged is called the *despedida de soltera*, or seeing off of the state of being single. Friends of approximately the same age gather to drink and eat together, and they dress up and act out some of the events which will follow for the bride, an occasion usually of considerable laughter and frivolity. The 'shower' for girls in the U.S.A. serves a similar role, and in the U.K. there is a 'hen party'. These rites separate the bride from her previous life in preparation for the new state to come. The version for the bridegroom is also commonly an all-male occasion known as a 'stag party' where serious drinking seems to be the order of the day.

...

[A] bride in Japan wears a white garment under her colourful wedding kimono and this is said to represent a clean slate for her new life. In this way she resembles a corpse, as she dies to her old house, and a baby, to be born again into the new one. After the ceremony itself, the bride goes through a series of rites of incorporation into the new house and community, greeting her new ancestors, visiting the new local shrine, and being introduced to the new neighbours.

...

In many parts of the world it is customary for the bride and groom to go away for a honeymoon after their wedding and this practice can be seen as a rite of transition for the couple as a new unit. This time they will be formally separated from the crowd of family and friends who have come to wish them well, and various rites may be practised as they leave. Throwing of confetti is one example, tying boots to their car another. Some people go much further, and in Scotland my brother was kidnapped by his old friends, who tied his hands and feet together and hailed a passing van to drive him away around the streets of Glasgow. Again, this is a period of liminality when few rules apply. Later the couple will be regarded as properly married and treated as such. In the meantime, there would seem to be no end of fun to be had.

...

Funerals

Rites of separation are highly developed at a funeral, but there is again a period of transition, both for the deceased on his or her way to the afterlife, and for those who remain behind to come to terms with their loss. At Christian funerals, the custom of throwing a little earth into the grave is a way of saying farewell, as is the practice in Japan of adding a pinch of incense to the burning pile. In Roman Catholic and Afro-Caribbean communities, the custom of holding a wake allows a more elaborate venue for the final farewells, and elsewhere there is open house for the bereaved to receive the condolences of their friends and relatives.

During the period of mourning, people may alter their lifestyles, refraining from celebrations and jollification perhaps, and making regular visits to the grave of the loved one. In Japan, a notice is pasted to the door which not only identifies the house as one in mourning but also makes explicit the idea of pollution associated with the period in question. During this time, no meat is to be eaten, and there is a special diet for the bereaved. Various rites are held to mark stages in the progress of the soul, and these coincide with gatherings to thank those who helped at the funeral, and generally to redefine the social relations of the members of the family left behind. In some countries in southern Europe, a widow continues to wear black for the rest of her life, but in most cases there is a means of incorporating the living back into normal life.

Festivals and the Passage of Time

Finally, most societies have regular rituals to mark the passage of time. These reflect the classification of time in the way that the rituals associated with territorial passage reflect the classification of space into homes, villages, countries and so forth. As with the rites of passage through life, these events regularise in a social form natural cycles, though this time of the earth and moon, rather than the human body. Thus, the year is divided in various ways depending on the local climate, though provision is usually made for a festival to mark the harvest, at least in agricultural communities, and in countries with a severe winter there is usually a rite to herald the arrival of spring.

In the summer, in Europe, the year is clearly broken with holidays, and this ritual break in the normal routines of life is especially marked in countries such as France and Italy where there is a long and serious period of play which is virtually compulsory in its effective interruption of the ordinary. In France, the motorways are cleared of large trucks and roadworks, and it seems as though the entire population heads south to the sea and the sunshine. Certainly it is difficult to get anything done in government buildings, or, indeed, any number of other city offices. ...

The pattern of breaking work with play is of course repeated weekly in many parts of the world, but this is a system of classification originally based on the biblical story of the creation of the world. Elsewhere the breaks will come at different times. The lunar month is a more universal segment, and, especially before the advent of electricity, many people would organise events to coincide with the light of the full moon. Approaching the equator there is little difference in the climate between winter and summer, and seasons and their markings may be organised instead around wet and dry periods, or some other local climatic variable.

In many parts of the world, the year is broken clearly during the season of Christmas and New Year, when schools close and many government activities are suspended for a period of about two weeks, all preceded by preparations which may last for a couple of months. This 'festival' is, strictly speaking, a celebration of the birth of Jesus Christ, but it takes place at a time chosen by early Christians to coincide with winter solstice celebrations in northern Europe, and for many of its participants it is characterised as much by feasting and resting from usual routines as for any religious rites. Moreover, followers of other faiths observe their own rituals, such as the Jewish Hanukah and Hindu Diwali, close to the winter break, and a popular greeting card message, especially in the United States, has become 'Happy Holidays'.

...

[Thus] [r]ituals, wherever they are found, mark out the social categories for the people in question. They may be more or less related to the natural cycles of the seasons, the moon and the human body, but they will always order them in a cultural way related to ideas about the social world in which they are found.

References
Van Gennep, Arnold. *Rites of Passage* (London: Routledge and Kegan Paul, 1960; originally published in 1909).

Edited extract from: Joy Hendry, *An Introduction to Social Anthropology: Sharing Our Worlds*, 2nd edn (London: Palgrave Macmillan, 2008), pp. 77–90.

Juarke Boys Made Men in Mboum Society
The Mboum people of Northern Cameroon have practiced male circumcision for decades.
Until the middle of the last century, male circumcision was highly regarded as a period of
initiation leading to a man's status.

Filmstill from *Juarke Boys Made Men in Mboum Society*. © Mohamadou Saliou (Student
Film Prize RAI Film Festival 2011).

Identities

<table>
<tr><td>**31**</td><td>**A Sense of People and Place**
Gaynor Cohen</td></tr>
</table>

*Our next passage returns us to Wales, the location of Pat Caplan's
analysis of the controversies over badger culling that we encountered
earlier in the Reader. This is an edited extract from an article by Gaynor
Cohen, which focuses on the concept of identity, and the strands that
go into a person's sense of where they 'belong'. A social anthropologist,
she knits together her own family history with the broader record of the
chapel, the Welsh language, nationality, performance traditions and
economic fortunes to build a complex and subtle picture of 'Welshness'.*

Within Britain, the Welsh language is often presented by the English media
as controversial. In some cases it is seen as the instrument through which
the minority, namely Welsh-language speakers, impose their will on the
majority. Promoters have been accused of encouraging linguistic racialism
in Wales in the context of bilingual education policy. Yet few would deny
the importance of language in a person's identity: 'For a man to speak one
language rather than another is a ritual act, it is a statement about one's
personal status; to speak the same language as one's neighbours expresses
solidarity with those neighbours, to speak a different language from one's
neighbours expresses social distance or even hostility' (Leach 1954 cited in
Fishman 1966: 7). ... This chapter discusses the role of the Welsh language
and the chapel in sustaining Welsh cultural identity during the growth of
mining and industrialisation in the Welsh countryside over the nineteenth
and twentieth centuries.

Outsiders often dichotomise Wales's identity and culture relative to that
of England. This can lead to a false picture of a homogeneous and cohesive
community, which does not exist in reality. ... This dichotomy is also
operative within Wales. For many Welsh people, being Welsh means being
different from the English. The majority of the population are conscious of
the need to affirm their Welsh identity in relation to the English, their
powerful neighbours, whom they perceive as potential perpetrators of
cultural genocide. ... The Welsh language is an obvious means of presenting
this difference, although it is not the only or even necessarily the main
mediator for 'Welshness'.

...

In the South Wales area, to which my case study refers, there is ambiguity
today over the definition of 'Welshness'. During the nineteenth and first half

of the twentieth century, the definition of Welshness was closely linked to the Welsh language and the chapel. This chapter traces the Welsh sense of identity back to this period and then throughout the twentieth century through the eyes of my father, Llywelyn Jones, who lived from 1900 to 1986 in Llansamlet, a village situated between Swansea and Neath in South Wales. He lived and worked in two cultures: as an accountant in a British oil firm and as a local Welshman serving as the secretary of the local Welsh chapel.

...

The Building of Bethel Chapel in the Industrial Heartland of South Wales

The building of Bethel chapel in Llansamlet illustrates the link between the chapel, the family and the community. During the eighteenth century, Nonconformism grew in strength in Wales. In 1740 a small group were meeting informally in the front room of a house in Llansamlet. Peripatetic preachers travelled substantial distances to link this house and village with others in the area. The Reverend John Davies was one of these preachers, travelling miles to homes in Neath and Skewen, Ystalafera, Swansea, Llansamlet and Pontardawe. Once a month he held communion for a number of believers at his home in Mynyddbach. Eventually he persuaded the people of Llansamlet and members of Mynyddbach to get together and build Bethel on the site where it stands today. A wealthy coal-mine owner contributed money and land towards the building. The combined membership of farmers and miners who constituted the religious community came to about eighty. The chapel's opening ceremony was held in 1818.

...

This long-term chapel-building effort was undertaken by a small dissenting community with little surplus wealth. Bethel chapel offered a place of worship suited to the needs of families struggling in difficult circumstances as a self-sufficient, independent, religious community. The minister was chosen and paid for by the congregation. In the nineteenth and even the early twentieth century, many ministers were the sons of miners and had received only an elementary education. They empathised with the congregation and relied more on appeals to their hearts than to their minds. The best of them knew how to stir their congregation to great emotional heights with their distinctive oratorical style known as the *hwyl*. It has no exact English translation but would approximately mean 'soul'. It was a style closer to singing than speaking, rising to a crescendo at regular intervals, and guaranteed to move the most insensitive of listeners to fever pitch.

The whole family was likely to attend the evening service, after which the sermon would be the subject of discussion around the supper table in members' homes. The language of the home and the chapel was Welsh and continued to be so during Llywelyn's lifetime.

Llywelyn's Family

Llywelyn Jones was one of seven children brought up on a farm in Llansamlet. They were the Joneses Tai Esther, as the Welsh custom was to identify families by the names of the farms on which they lived. Llywelyn's father, David, had been expected to run the farm together with his brother but the soil was too poor to support two families, so David moved into wage employment as a miner in a local pit. The same pattern was true of other families in the area, who supplemented their farming income with wage employment from the mines or from other industries that had grown up in Llansamlet in the late nineteenth century, such as tinplate or copper smelting.

…

The years between 1914 and 1936 were bleak in South Wales. Once again, the chapel was needed as a haven. It was a time when the chapel gave as well as received donations. When the unemployed could not maintain their donations, they received five shillings each from the chapel funds. Llywelyn recalls: 'If we hadn't done that it would have been like taking bread from the babies' mouths'.

…

Editorial Note:
[In the next section (omitted), Cohen describes the organisation of the chapel, consisting of elders, deacons, secretary and treasurer.]

The Chapel and Employment

The peak of the Nonconformist movement in Llansamlet coincided with Welsh industrialisation during the late eighteenth century. The rural Welsh-speaking Nonconformist movement had spread from the west, while industrial growth, bringing in non-Welsh, English speakers, spread from the east. Welsh cultural symbols were reinforced or even created at this time.

Eisteddfodau (verse competitions) were revived in 1858 when an annual National Eisteddfod was established, alternating venues between North and South Wales every other year. Locally, the chapels took over from the pubs in hosting the events. Some of the finest hymns were written during this time and the Welsh national anthem, 'Yr hen wlad fy nhadau' ('The land of my fathers'), was composed by two weavers from Pontypridd in 1858. Music flourished and *Gymanfa Ganu* (singing festivals) were held annually in chapels, including Bethel. These were frequently supplemented by concerts given by invited artists and choirs. Many Bethel members belonged to choirs attached to other chapels or to clubs such as the rugby club. There was evidence of growing national pride as industry expanded. In Llansamlet iron, tinplate and copper were manufactured. The River Tawe, flowing west into Swansea, ran red with copper. Many Bethel members were employed in such industries as well as in the mines.

This period of prosperity in South Wales was short-lived. The conditions of the workers, especially the miners, became appalling. Trade unions to protect the workers' interests had not developed and, despite severe pit accidents, no compensation was given to the injured. Children and adults worked long days for low wages. Lloyd George, the first Welsh prime minister, agreed to import coal from Germany as part of the reparations for the war, creating a crisis in the coal industry as manufacturers in the Midlands and the North were reluctant to pay higher prices for British coal. This led to semi- and in some cases even total starvation for working-class families in South Wales.

Llywelyn was one of the lucky ones. In his evening classes he had studied and gained qualifications in accountancy. When, in 1921, a large oil refinery opened at Llandarcy, Llywelyn was employed as head of the wages department. As they did not then have a trained personnel manager, this responsibility was added to Llywelyn's employment profile. As many of his acquaintances and some from his own family were unemployed at that time, Llywelyn's post as personnel officer gave him a golden opportunity to find jobs for them. He frequently found himself under considerable pressure to use his position to the advantage of other Bethel members. In the early days of his marriage, fellow members of the chapel would come to his house in the evenings to plead their case. Many had reason to be grateful to him for their livelihood.

Employment at Llandarcy again provided cross-cutting ties between members of the congregation, although their workplace had a significant effect upon the use of the Welsh language. Bethel members spoke Welsh as their mother tongue, while most senior members of the Llandarcy refinery had been recruited from London and spoke mainly or exclusively English. Gradually Welsh became a medium reserved for use with close friends or in the home and the chapel.

As a senior staff member Llywelyn was automatically part of the management team and was expected to side against the workers in their union disputes:

> I never felt really comfortable in those negotiations you know. Especially if they involved men I knew, like Bethel people; even if I knew they were in the wrong. You are forced to take the management's side. I couldn't help feeling I was letting the family down. Because that's what it felt like. Men I've known all my life, who speak my language and pray with me every Sunday; they're like my family.

The associational ties of Bethel chapel helped generate local employment for its members. Ivor Sims owned the sawmills that produced wood which chapel members purchased. Idwal Clements ran a funeral service that Bethel's ageing congregation used. There was one shopkeeper and one greengrocer whom Llywelyn urged his wife to patronise: 'I keep telling Doris it's important. They must be able to rely on Bethel members for support. It's like supporting your own family'. For Llywelyn, the chapel members were in effect an extension of his own family. Their daily welfare mattered to him. Another important feature of this family was the common language they spoke.

Learning Welsh

Llywelyn, like other members of Bethel, began his education in the chapel. There they learnt the alphabet in English and Welsh, the foundations for developing their reading and writing. The Bible had been translated into Welsh in the sixteenth century. Throughout Wales chapel Sunday schools were training grounds for reading, writing and discussion of the Bible in the Welsh language. In the late nineteenth century Welsh writing flourished, both in Welsh newspapers and in literary efforts. The Welsh language lent itself to poetry, as is evident in the focus on poetry writing at the national and local *eisteddfodau* and in the hymns still sung today.

Sunday schools provided a strong base for most people's education, especially in Welsh. In the early part of the nineteenth century, education in Wales was fragmented and elementary. Many children had no schooling outside the chapel. The national schools, supported by the Anglican church, found it difficult to recruit Welsh children, as Nonconformist families feared the influence of the Anglican Church upon their chapels, their language, and their culture.

The Westminster government, concerned about education in Wales, sent three commissioners in 1844 to inquire into the issue. The three were young, male Anglicans who sought advice from the Anglican clergy. Their reports, published as 'blue books' and which became popularly known as *Brad Y Llyfrau Gleision* ('The treachery of the blue books'), became notorious throughout Wales. The reports attacked the medium of education, the Welsh language, which was presented as a stumbling block to learning. To people who believed that true religion was only capable of being taught in Welsh, any attack on the language was an attack on their beliefs.

...

The chapel Sunday schools, as institutions, were not the subject of criticism. It was their teaching of the Welsh language that was blamed for the flaws of education in Wales. The Welsh language was not simply presented as an obstacle to learning and progress but also as a vehicle of immorality and backwardness. In the wake of the reports the English press called for the extinction of the Welsh language and teachers were encouraged to punish the use of Welsh on school premises. Even as late as 1910 Llywelyn remembered having the 'Welsh Not' hung around his neck for unthinkingly reverting to his mother tongue while in the playground. This attack on the language led the Welsh to stigmatise the reports as treachery and engendered a passionate divide, which to this day lingers on.

The passage in the reports that gave the greatest offence to the Welsh was the declaration that Welsh women were almost universally unchaste. In

Wales 'mam', the mother of the family, had significant influence and in many homes, including Llywelyn's, had been instrumental in ensuring that the children attended chapel and Sunday school regularly. The consequences of the reports might have been irredeemable were it not for a young Welsh civil servant called Hugh Owen.

In 1843 Owen addressed his 'Letter to the People of Wales'. An ardent believer in education as the way forward for the Welsh, he urged them to take advantage of any official government money available for education and argued his case with the mastery of the skilled senior civil servant that he was. His knowledge of Westminster and the 'corridors of power' was of the greatest assistance to his Welsh compatriots in their dealings with a Parliament representing Tory, Anglican interests. It was because of Owen that primary and then secondary schools were set up, creating in turn a demand for teachers. The establishment of training colleges for teachers and the University of Wales at Aberystwyth followed. These institutions had grown on the back of Nonconformist Wales.

Editorial Note:
[In the next section (omitted), Cohen examines the role of women in the chapel.]

...

Continuity of the Chapel Networks and the Survival of the Welsh Language

The chapel is now kept alive by about twenty active members. The dwindling membership could possibly be explained within the context of the general decline in attendance at Christian religious institutions. The Welsh language, though, has suffered since Bethel chapel was originally built, by a strengthening of Nonconformism. Nevertheless, the chapels have provided the basis for sustaining and even strengthening the Welsh language through their networks and their support for bilingual education.

The foundations for bilingual education were laid at the beginning of the twentieth century. The impetus for growth came from wider political and socio-economic trends taking place throughout Europe. The first designated Welsh-medium school appeared in 1948. ... By 1982 their number had vastly increased, with the education service itself generating demand and offering support to Welsh-language teaching in the face of subsequent changes in socio-economic and political trends. Major reports ... recommended the effective teaching of Welsh as a first or second language in both primary and secondary schools. In 1977, a consultative document, *Education in Schools*, ... stressed the importance of the Welsh language in the life of the nation and the fact that the use of Welsh as the medium of teaching had no harmful effect on attainment. It therefore encouraged more

Welsh learning by both Welsh- and English-speaking children and better language planning by Local Education Authorities.

The result is that there has been a rise in the number of young people speaking Welsh. … The Welsh language has also gained from the increased popularity of the National Eisteddfod, where it is the main medium of communication. During the National Eisteddfod's lifetime the Bardic chair was consistently won by a man, frequently a Nonconformist minister. Three years ago the chain was broken when a young woman became the first to win the Bardic chair.

Other Welsh-language organisations have grown from chapel roots. Organisations such as *Merched Y Wawr* (Daughters of the Dawn) were women's movements established to foster the language. In 1999/2000, they had 277 branches and 7,500 members from all over Wales. The 277 branches, which hold at least ten meetings a year, have received a grant from the Welsh Language Board and have opened clubs for younger people to socialise through the medium of the Welsh language.

Conclusion

Drawing on the biography of Llywelyn Jones, I have stressed the importance of the chapel in the life of the Welsh community. Llywelyn was born when Nonconformists were a strong force in Wales. Struggling to advance in a difficult and rapidly changing environment, they built chapels like Bethel to support Welsh-speaking communities. At that time, the chapel was an extension of the Welsh-speaking family, training the children in their own language and with cross-cutting ties created by employment, friendship and kinship.

By the time of Llywelyn's death, the chapel's influence had waned. The community did not have the same needs for nurture and comfort. The British welfare state and a developed education system had replaced those requirements. Chapel membership dwindled in the face of strong competition from developments such as the mass ownership of television, motor cars and telephones and the exodus of younger generations in the search for employment in England and elsewhere. … The Welsh language suffered concurrently. Nevertheless, the foundation provided by the chapel has been the source from which language networks have recently grown. The language is now being taken forward through Channel 4C (the Welsh radio channel), the National Eisteddfod and the Welsh Assembly, which has taken over from the former Welsh Office. Bilingual education is now officially supported and increasing numbers of people are communicating in Welsh on a daily basis. Chapels remain important landmarks in the landscape, but the spread of the Welsh language currently is more likely to come through the influence of television and radio rather than public worship. Welsh identity and language have a strong post-industrial foundation. The mines are largely gone, but Welsh culture moves on.

References

Fishman, J.A. *Language Loyalty in the United States* (The Hague: Mouton, 1966).

Leach, E. *Political Systems of Highland Burma* (London: Thames and Hudson, 1954).

Edited extract from: Gaynor Cohen, 'A Sense of People and Place: the Chapel and Language in Sustaining Welsh Identity', in D. Bryceson et al. (eds), *Identity and Networks: Fashioning Gender and Ethnicity across Cultures* (Oxford: Berghahn, 2007), pp. 91–102.

II.2 Drawing Boundaries and Defining Groups

32 **What's in a Name? Creating Identities in Britain**
Jemma Underdown

The concept of 'identity', from an anthropological and historical perspective, was illustrated in the previous extract from Gaynor Cohen's article on 'Welshness'. The next passage brings together the notion of identity with the construction of groups and boundaries in the time scale of early British archaeology and history. In this specially written article, Jemma Underdown, a historian and archaeologist of the early Medieval period, explores the role of identity and change in the British past. The concept of being British and being part of a shared heritage, linked by language, culture and genes, is an idea that at first glance appears quite straightforward. In this article Jemma Underdown explores what 'being British' means. She shows that far from being a homogeneous entity the modern 'British' population is the result of thousands of years of migration and mixing between a huge range of contrasting groups. Underdown's incisive historical perspective makes clear that any attempt to draw strict divisions between groups based on ideas of nationalism is fundamentally flawed. If we extend this line of reasoning it clearly highlights the fact that modern extreme opinions about ethnicity and nationality are more of a social construct than the result of solid historical division.

There is a man living in the Somerset village of Cheddar who is able to visit the grave of an ancestor who died 9,000 years ago. The Mesolithic relation is known as Cheddar Man, and his skeleton was discovered in a cave in Cheddar Gorge in 1903. In 1997, scientists extracted mitochondrial DNA from his teeth and compared it to the DNA of twenty inhabitants of the modern village, including a teacher named Adrian Targett. There was a match: the two men are related on the maternal side. Adrian Targett is a direct descendent of one of Cheddar Man's female ancestors – perhaps his mother or grandmother. It is entirely possible that his family has not strayed far from this picturesque area of rural England in millennia. Mr Targett is a British subject, and may also describe himself as English or, if he wanted to be more specific, a resident of Somerset. Cheddar Man, who shares the same DNA and lived in the same place, would not have recognised any of these identities. Only since 1707 when the Act of Union brought the United

Kingdom of Great Britain into existence would Mr Targett's forebears have been able to use all three of these labels to define themselves. In the preceding 8,700 years the 'Cheddar family' would have taken up and cast aside numerous ethnic, regional and political identities.

We have no way of knowing how Cheddar Man would have described himself. Thousands of years before the idea of the nation-state, his identity is likely to have focussed on a 'clan' or extended family, and perhaps a sense of belonging to a wider tribal group. Without written sources, we are left to reconstruct prehistoric concepts of identity through archaeology. Religion and ritual may have been used to mark who belonged and who did not. 'Cheddar family', along with others from a wide area, may have visited the Neolithic stone circles in the Mendip Hills above Cheddar. In the Bronze Age, members of 'Cheddar family' may have been buried in the round barrows on the hilltops. Visible from a distance, they showed outsiders that their deities and dead watched over their territory.

It is during the Bronze Age that the people who are now commonly, but inaccurately, called the Celts may have invaded the British Isles from continental Europe. Brythonic, the ancient tongue of the British Isles that survives today in Welsh, Gaelic, Cornish and Manx is part of the Celtic family of languages. Archaeologists have identified changes in material culture (such as pottery, jewellery and weapons). However, whether or not the 'Celts' overwhelmed the indigenous people of the British Isles is a matter of debate among experts. Material culture cannot directly denote ethnicity. Perhaps the locals suddenly found themselves dominated by 'Celtic' immigrants with new ideas and ways of doing things, one of whom married a daughter of 'Cheddar family'. Or perhaps through trade and more gradual movement of people the same ideas and cultural changes began to imprint themselves on the native population.

Only in the Iron Age do we hear the names that the people of Britain may have used to describe themselves. However, most of our evidence comes from Roman rather than insular sources so they may reflect how outsiders saw the British Isles rather than how its inhabitants saw themselves. Cheddar was in a border region between the Durotriges (whose name survives in modern Dorset) and the Belgae. Ancient boundaries are difficult to determine – one method is to study coin distribution. In issuing coinage, a central authority guarantees its value, and those using it acknowledge its worth. This is not to say that the use of coins indicates an ethnic identity (think of the Euro). The Durotriges were more a confederation than a single tribe, so people may well have identified much more closely with their sub-group. The neighbouring tribe, the Belgae, appear to have been a British offshoot of the continental Belgae whose territory lay on the other side of the English Channel. Rather than acting as a barrier, the sea was the means of communication and trade between those living on its shores and may have facilitated a shared identity. In fact, all the various inhabitants of Britain seem to have close ethnic associations with their continental neighbours. Tacitus, a Roman writing in the late first century, noted that red-haired people of northern Britain resembled those of Germania; the dark, curly-haired Silures in the south-west bear a strong similarity to the Iberians (modern Spain); and the Britons of the south resembled the Gauls over the Channel. He also comments that Britain had not known long-term peace, and the tribes were incapable of working together against a common enemy. 'Cheddar family' might have sought refuge from raids in the nearby Iron Age hill fort at Dolebury Camp. The people of Britain may have shared an island, but not an identity.

The Roman conquest of Britain formally began in AD 43. Incorporation into the Roman Empire brought soldiers, traders and administrators to Britain from all corners of the *imperium*, some of whom settled permanently. However, a sense of *Romanitas* – 'Romanness', was shared by indigenes and immigrants alike. Roman citizenship bore no relationship to ethnicity: within the Empire the great divide was between slaves and free men. Members of 'Cheddar family' (perhaps benefiting from the wealth generated by the huge temple complex at nearby Bath) may have become citizens and felt a greater shared identity (through a shared Latinate language and culture) with fellow citizens from Gaul or North Africa than slaves from southern Britain or the northern 'barbarian' tribes such as the Picts. Pre-Roman tribal identities and allegiances were not entirely erased though: the *civitates* (centres of Roman administration) were frequently based on ancient tribal units.

The end of the Roman Empire in Britain and the origin of the separate entities of England, Scotland and Wales are subject to much debate among historians and archaeologists as to when, why and how they happened. What is clear is that once again there was a change in material culture in southern and eastern Britain – jewellery, pottery and buildings started to resemble those found across the North Sea. Traditionally, it was understood that the sub-Roman population of Britain were killed, enslaved or forced to flee to the far north and west by hordes of Germanic and Scandinavian invaders (such as Angles, Saxons and Jutes) who brought with them their own language, culture and social organisation. More recently, scholars have started to question whether the British were so comprehensively annihilated in the south-east, or whether they, over time, adopted the language, culture and social organisation of the migrants. A myriad of kingdoms sprung up in the fifth and sixth centuries – some appear to have been based on Roman *civitates* or even pre-Roman tribal units, while others were centred around Germanic warlords and their conquered territory. Some were soon annexed by more powerful neighbours, while others remained independent for hundreds of years.

It is very difficult to disentangle concepts of political and ethnic identity during this period, not least because of the very different experiences of different parts of the British Isles, so let's return to 'Cheddar family' in the south-west. This region is thought to have passed from 'British' to 'Anglo-

Saxon' control after the Battle of Dyrham in 577. However, to consider this as the point that 'Cheddar family' became English is to oversimplify a very complex process. Certainly, after the demise of direct rule from Rome there were British kingdoms in western Britain, who fought with each other and the 'Anglo-Saxon' invaders. According to the *Anglo-Saxon Chronicle*, at Dyrham, three British kings (Commail, Condida and Farinmail) were defeated by King Ceawlin of the 'Anglo-Saxon' kingdom of Wessex. Wessex is an interesting example of a kingdom whose ethnic and political identity was complex and shifting. The West Saxons' own foundation myth involves the arrival of Cerdic in three ships on the Hampshire coast, where he defeated the British king of the area. So far, so Anglo-Saxon. But Cerdic, a figure of great importance from whom all later West Saxon kings claimed descent, has a British name (as does King Ceawlin). Also, archaeological evidence suggests that the origins of Wessex can be found inland at Dorchester-on-Thames in Oxfordshire. Dorchester-on-Thames was a Roman walled town, and a late Roman and an early 'Anglo-Saxon' cemetery have been discovered here that may well have been in use at the same time. The origins of Wessex may in fact be very mixed: perhaps the authorities in the Roman town hired Germanic mercenaries for defence when soldiers were no longer forthcoming from Rome, and gradually the people adopted Germanic customs and material culture. Dyrham may not have been such a clash of cultures.

Despite this mixed heritage, it appears that it was important for the West Saxons to consider themselves 'Anglo-Saxon' rather than British. Over a hundred years after Dyrham, the laws of King Ine distinguish between the *Englisc* and *Welisc* ('Welsh', from an Old English word for 'foreigner'), with a more favourable status in law for the former. This would have encouraged the Britons to cast aside the outward signs of their identity, and effectively take on a new one, through adopting *Englisc* culture and language. This would have taken some time: the last person to speak only Cornish probably died in the seventeenth century. But why were they so keen to emphasise their Germanic heritage and erase their British ancestry? The use of the term *Englisc* for all those who consider themselves as the heirs of the Germanic migrants, whether they were originally Angle, Saxon or Jute, demonstrates a shared identity in opposition to the British. This may have its roots in the conversion of the 'Anglo-Saxon' kingdoms to Christianity after a mission from Rome in 597 and the establishment of an English Church, which from the outset was in conflict with the British Church that survived the end of Roman rule. When Bede came to write his *Ecclesiastical History of the English People* in the early eighth century, he depicted the invasion of the pagan English as God's punishment of the sinful Britons, and their eventual conversion as the fulfilment of their destiny as the people chosen by God to inhabit the conquered land. This concept of 'Englishness' was a religious and political construction.

We cannot tell when 'Cheddar family' ceased to consider themselves British but English, but this identity has now endured for many centuries. Neither can we tell how their view of their own identity will change in the future. What is interesting to consider is how conceptions of past identity may change in the future. In the nineteenth century, Bede-like ideas of the English as a Germanic chosen people, destined to conquer and rule other nations, fitted well with a flourishing and expanding empire. History books depicted the annihilation of the British as an unfortunate but necessary step in creating a great nation. However, after two world wars there seemed to be a decline in considering the English and Germans closest cousins, and instead greater emphasis was placed on our British ancestry. Fixing identity in the past is like standing between two mirrors – our reflection disappears into the distance.

33 Gypsy Women: Models in Conflict
Judith Okely

Earlier in the Reader in Kay Milton's article we looked at an anthropologist's interpretation of a nature conservation campaign as an exercise in the maintenance of boundaries – between species, between 'natural' and 'man-made' phenomena, and between the 'native' and the 'foreign'. Within human society, it is extremely common to find groups maintaining their boundaries by ritual and symbolic means. Ideas of pollution, especially, are frequently brought into play to enforce the separateness of social or ethnic groups. Intermarriage or sexual relations across group boundaries are often thought to be particularly threatening or polluting. Many forms of racism and racial exclusion, for example, can be interpreted in this way. The passage that follows is an edited extract from an article by Judith Okely. In this passage, Okely shows how Gypsy ideas of cleanliness and dirt are linked to the maintenance of the boundary between Gypsy society and the surrounding settled community; and how this in turn places tight restrictions on the movements and behaviour of Gypsy women. In reading the passage, it is also worth recalling that, earlier in the Reader, we saw how pervasively social values and categories are mapped onto the human body. For the Gypsies, according to Okely's analysis, the boundaries of the body itself are a symbolic representation of social and ethnic separateness.

Contradictions

... There is a paradox embedded in the Gypsy woman's role. Within her own society she is hedged in by restrictions, expected to be subservient to her husband and cautious with other men. Yet nearly every day she is expected to go out to 'enemy' territory, knock on doors of unknown people and establish contact with new customers, some of whom will be men. Success in obtaining money or goods will depend on her ability to be outgoing and persistent, and her readiness to take the initiative. She must be aggressive – quite the opposite to some of the behaviour required of her in the camp.

There do exist formal restrictions on the woman's activities outside the camp. Fred Wood, a Gypsy writer, has claimed that in the past, at least, when a woman knocked at a door and a man answered, she was to ask for the mistress of the house, and if she did not appear the Gypsy was expected to leave forthwith. Such restrictions explain the apparent inconsistency in the husband's boasting of his wife's mechanical knowledge, 'She knows all about motors', while at the same time discouraging her from learning to drive a vehicle. The latter would give her considerable independence: 'I'm not having you running about; I want to know where you are'. Mechanical knowledge is acceptable so long as it is not used by the women for independent transportation. When out Calling, the woman is expected to travel on foot, or on the more constricting public transport. Nonetheless, such controls over the woman's activities outside the camp are either trivial or unenforceable. When Calling with the women, I discovered that they frequently conducted business with men alone and actually stressed the advantage of such a procedure: 'If you get the men by themselves and keep them talking, you can sell quite a few flowers. Tell them to get a present for their wives. They don't know what their wives want'.

Pollution

Clearly, external control over the women's sexual activities can only be effected by supernatural beliefs, and ones fully internalised by the women. It is here that fears of ritual pollution have power. In addition to the pollution beliefs which the Gypsies use to erect and maintain boundaries between themselves and Gorgios [non-Gypsies], there are certain polluting powers attached to women which can be fully understood only in the context of Gypsy–Gorgio pollution. The general pollution beliefs are illuminated by an awareness of the special ecological niche which the Gypsies hold in the larger society.

Unlike most nomads, Gypsies are directly dependent on the economy of another society which is usually sedentary, around which they circulate supplying goods and services. By exploiting their mobility and by not restricting themselves to one occupation, they fill occasional and intermittent gaps in the system of supply and demand. To ensure their economic survival and independence, they must initiate regular friendly contact with Gorgios and develop a multiplicity of roles and disguises: those who sell carpets will conceal their Gypsy origins, while fortune-tellers will exploit them. The scrap and rag collector, picking through material which the Gorgio classifies as 'dirt', is prepared to adopt the posture expected of a despised scavenger. The same society that offers a wealth of economic opportunity for nomads simultaneously makes it hard for them to survive in other ways, because they have different patterns of land usage and they resist bureaucratic control. This is temporarily resolved by a policy of persecution by Gorgios and of evasion by Gypsies. However, when confronted by Gorgio authorities, a subservient and humble posture may be necessary. All roles, whether trickster or victim, carry the risk of self-degradation and a dangerous sense of unreality unless the inner self is protected intact, or group integrity is maintained and expressed in an independent society.

The problems arising from this relationship with the Gorgios are resolved and symbolised in the Gypsies' attitude to the body. My suggestion ... is that they make a fundamental distinction between the inside of the body and the outside. The outer skin with its discarded scales, accumulated dirt, by-products such as hair, and waste such as faeces, are all potentially polluting. The outer body symbolises the public self or role as presented to the Gorgio. It is a protective covering for the inside, which must be kept pure and inviolate. The inner body symbolises the secret, ethnic self. Anything taken into the body for its sustenance must be ritually clean. Attention is directed not only towards food but also towards the vessels and cutlery that are placed between the lips. The outer body must be kept separate from the inner: even a person's shadow can pollute food. Washing habits are a crucial arena: food, eating utensils and the tea-towel for drying them, must never be washed in a bowl used for washing the hands, body or clothing.

> He's a real Gypsy. You wouldn't find him washing his hands in the same bowl as he washes his cup.

A washing-up bowl used for other activities is permanently contaminated and can never be made clean. The personal washing and laundry bowls are potentially polluting and are usually placed outside the trailer. A woman explained to me that both her washing-up and personal washing bowls were stainless steel. She sensed that others might accuse her of confusing them. So she threw away the personal washing bowl and replaced it with an old plastic bucket.

Gypsies clearly distinguish between something being dirty and something ritually unclean. The word *chikli* (from *chik* for dust or soil) means 'dirty' in a harmless way. But the word *mochadi* means 'ritually polluted'. ... The Gorgio is condemned as *mochadi* for his eating and cleaning habits and because he does not distinguish between the inner and outer body; for example, Gorgios possess and use kitchen sinks for multiple purposes. Gypsies either board up their sinks or commission caravans without them and instead use a variety of bowls.

> If you look at a Gypsy's trailer, you won't find a sink, that's what Gorgios use.

> People say we're dirty ... they don't see that we think they're dirty .... Sometimes you go to houses and maybe the outside and the garden look all right but you should see what's inside.

In trying to relate pollution beliefs to other factors, Mary Douglas (1973: 132–33) explains the Pygmies' absence of rules of purity and sacramental religion in terms of their social organisation, which is decentralised and fluid. The Gypsies' social organisation is very similar, with one major difference: their need for regular interaction with an encompassing, hostile society. The Gypsies' rules of purity fit with an obsession with an external ethnic boundary. The internal fluidity of their society vanishes when juxtaposed with the external Gorgio society. ... Here the woman's dual external and domestic role is important.

In addition to the paradox in the behaviour required of Gypsy women in the encampment, compared to that outside, there is another with which they are connected. Unlike pastoral nomads or hunters and gatherers, Gypsies must obtain the bulk of their food from a wider society. Gypsies may have been able to obtain more wild game in the past, but even then a large amount of food had to be purchased or obtained from the Gorgio cultivator. With greater urbanisation, this dependence has increased. Thus food, which must be clean for the inner body, is acquired from the potentially dirty Gorgio. The Gypsy woman is the crucial intermediary in this transaction since she has the main responsibility for acquiring or purchasing food, as well as its preparation or cooking. She goes between the unclean, alien, and, by implication, unsocialised or 'wild' Gorgio and the clean Gypsy group: she is the link between uncontrolled 'nature' outside the Gypsy system and controlled 'culture' inside it.

Women must be careful as to their method of obtaining food, the type of food acquired, as well as its preparation, which may involve cooking. One danger is that they might obtain unclean food: a fear often voiced is that Gorgios could either deliberately or inadvertently poison food.

But another danger is that the women might trade their sex for food and thereby threaten the ethnic inheritance of the group. The pollution taboos associated with Gypsy women largely reflect these problems: the woman's need to control her sexuality in certain contexts; the separation between her external, unclean Calling role and her internal, clean culinary role; and the necessity for discrimination between Gorgio and Gypsy males as sexual partners.

[Sexuality and Pollution]

...

The power of the Gypsy female to pollute a Gypsy male I would summarise in these three alternative ways: ...:

1. Female sexuality is inherently polluting if mismanaged.
2. Menstruation is associated with pollution.
3. Childbirth is polluting.

...

Sexuality as Inherently Polluting if Mismanaged

The woman must be careful not to expose certain parts of her body or to bring it into contact with a man (private sexual intercourse within marriage being the only permissible context in which this may occur). Both in the past and today this is exemplified in restrictions in the woman's dress. Today, shorter skirts are permitted than formerly, but not miniskirts. I found that blouses must cover the body up to the base of the neck. Tight sweaters and hot-pants are banned. If trousers are worn by women, the hips and upper thighs have to be covered by a dress or smock. The woman has to be careful in her movements.

...

> When that Gorgio woman first came on this site she didn't understand. She kept bending – in a skirt right up here … … the men had to cover their eyes … … and she had a low neck, that was terrible.

> Travellers don't like girls to sit with their legs apart … … even a girl of that age [6] would be told. It wouldn't be allowed.

… [A] woman had to take special precautions in her toilet habits. A woman's underwear had to be washed separately from the men's clothing otherwise this could be polluted. It had to be dried out of sight. I never saw women's underwear on the crowded lines, except sometimes when hidden inside other clothing. … A woman had to wash her body in complete privacy and ideally from a special bowl reserved also for washing her underwear. Any man inadvertently seeing a woman relieving herself, i.e., exposing herself, was also liable to pollution. In my fieldwork one of the major reasons given by Gypsies against unsegregated toilet blocks was that a man might catch a woman by surprise. Breast-feeding … was also to be done in private. I found that the vast majority of women avoided breast-feeding altogether and opted for bottle-feeding, despite the contrary advice of midwives and health visitors.

> I breast-fed only one of mine. But I locked myself in the trailer first and drew the curtain. We wouldn't let a man see. That's filthy.

...

Traditionally, for cooking or food preparation, the woman had to wear a large white apron encompassing her lower body, front and back. Today these are smaller and patterned, but still considered the mark of a 'true Gypsy'. The apron for a Gorgio housewife has a diametrically opposed function which is to protect the dress from the 'dirt' of food and cooking. For the Gypsy, the apron is to protect the food and cooking from the 'dirt' of the dress, which is ritually contaminated by the outer body and specifically the sexual parts.

...

Uncleanliness comes from illicit sex both before and after marriage. It is said that a husband once had the right to throw his wife on the fire for a transgression. Of one woman believed to be associating with Gorgio men, it was said: 'She's been picking up men. She should be burned, that's what she wants'. To which the speaker's husband replied: 'Time was a *moosh* [man] would put his wife in the canal or push her in the fire if she did that'.

More recently it was reported that a Gypsy branded his wife 'with a red hot cleaver when she refused to answer questions about her sex life' (*The Times*, 27 February 1974). Fire is considered to be the suitable purifier for *mochadi* articles (e.g., the possessions of the dead), and so presumably also for impure women. The possibility that illicit sex is more polluting for the female may be where the symbolic and biological potential of the body is used: for a man, sexual intercourse involves temporary absorption into the other, while for the female it may entail permanent absorption, by conception, of the 'other' into the inner body. Since the Gorgio is generally considered *mochadi*, there is the implication that sexual relations between a Gypsy female and a male Gorgio are especially polluting. Moreover, the offspring from a casual sexual encounter between Gypsy and Gorgio is more likely to be born into the Gypsy group, if the mother rather than the father is Gypsy. Thus sexual infidelity with Gorgios by Gypsy women is more threatening to the group than that by Gypsy men.

...

Menstruation as Polluting

... Only among some groups was the woman not supposed to cook during menses. Then, either her husband or other women took over this task. I was able to confirm this from only two such cases, but the occasional trips I noticed to fish-and-chip shops by husbands may have been to protect themselves from pollution. Sexual intercourse seems to be prohibited at this time. Specific mention of menstruation is not supposed to be made in front of men, because they might risk pollution. ... [E]ven the technical problem is not solved by a modern invention: one married woman who, together with her family, showed no inhibition about dispersing all manner of rubbish and uncovered faeces a short distance from their camping spot, told me: 'I never throw them [sanitary towels] out. I don't believe in that. I always burn them'. The implication was, perhaps, that these articles were especially ritually polluting.

Childbirth as Polluting

... Traditionally the woman retreated to a special tent during labour and for a time after the birth. She had her own crockery and was not allowed to prepare food for men for some weeks. Later the tent, bedding and utensils were burnt. The new-born baby was also considered *mochadi* for a time and had to be washed in a special bowl, and so also its clothes. Today the woman and baby are still regarded as temporarily *mochadi*, and cooking must be done by other women or older children. Moreover the woman is forbidden to discuss her experience with any man or even to tell any man other than her husband (which she will do only reluctantly) the fact that she has entered labour and requires aid. A young woman was warned by the hospital to report immediately she had pains as serious complications were expected. One evening, when she was in the company of an uncle as well as her husband and aunt, labour pains began:

> I was doubled up. My uncle asked what was the matter. I couldn't tell him, he was a man. You don't tell men those things ... . They went out for a drink and I had to wait till my husband came back. I walked up and down thinking, 'If only there was a woman I could talk to'.

As in the past, men must not assist women in labour. The almost universal preference for childbirth in hospital has been misinterpreted as a conversion to Gorgio medicine and the Welfare State. Yet women I encountered in fieldwork were reluctant to attend prenatal clinics and often jettisoned any prescriptions such as iron supplements. Any attendance at clinics indicated more a desire to ensure a hospital bed. ... Hospital food is avoided because it has been cooked by Gorgios and in a polluted place. The women usually discharged themselves early, to the consternation of the medical authorities.

> The nurses at the hospital said, 'We're sick of the Gypsies. They never come to the appointments at the clinics'. Mary wouldn't eat the food. She wouldn't let them wash her. She cried a lot.

Many Gypsies even complained of rough treatment and poor attention during the birth. Rather than being a safety measure for the women, hospitalisation is a convenient way of dealing with a polluting act. The Gorgios are given the task of supervising the process and disposing of polluted articles.

[Conclusion]

From the last two sections we can see that at menstruation and childbirth the woman's ability to pollute is temporarily intensified because they are occasions for the outlet of bodily waste. The female sexual orifice is a 'natural' point of exit for polluting bodily waste, in the light of the Gypsies' distinction between the inner and outer body, where rejected matter from the inner body is especially polluting. While, for some families, menstruation may not be considered especially polluting, childbirth seems always so. A certain shame is attached to pregnancy. Women must conceal their shape with coats or other very loose garments (coats are otherwise rarely worn). Pregnancy is proof that the woman has had sexual intercourse. Conception is a dangerous affair and must not be misplaced, i.e., the father must be a Gypsy. The term used by Gypsies is to have 'fallen', or 'when I fell for ...', the added name being that of the child not the father. The baby is ambiguous matter because it has been covered by the blood and waste of birth: the inside come outside. The baby remains polluting for a while, possibly because it has not been 'made' a Gypsy until some socialisation has taken place.

...

It is notable that the women's ability to pollute men, while heightened at certain times, is also ever present, and is not merely associated with certain events or rites of passage. The elaboration and public aspects of precautionary ritual lie in continuing daily observances. Gypsy men are innately pure, almost by predestination, whereas the women have to aspire to an elusive purity by good works, whether as virgins or wives. Since, in their external role, Gypsy women are always vulnerable to sexual contamination by the non-Gypsy, they must be taught that their ever-present sexuality and fertility are dangerous. The woman's dress, deportment and behaviour are matters for constant public scrutiny. They must shield their sexual parts and control their movements and misplaced desires. If women were distinctly polluting merely because of their unique bodily waste, then aprons would presumably be required only at childbirth and menstruation. However, women's sexuality is always potentially polluting to Gypsy men. The Gypsy women must protect all Gypsies from pollution by controlling their sexuality: if indiscriminate and casual with Gypsies, they could be so with Gorgios.

References

Douglas, M. *Natural Symbols* (Harmondsworth: Penguin, 1973).

Edited extract from: Judith Okely, 'Gypsy Women: Models in Conflict', in S. Ardener (ed.), *Perceiving Women* (London: Malaby, 1975), pp. 55–86; reprinted in Judith Okely, *Own or Other Culture* (London: Routledge, 1996) pp. 63–93 (extracts from pp. 67–76).

II.3   Ritual and Social Relations

34	**Extract from** *The Ritual Process* *Victor Turner*

The previous extract from Judith Okely's study of English Gypsies illustrated the role of pollution beliefs and ritual practices in maintaining social boundaries. Our final passage, by Victor Turner, shows vividly how an anthropologist in the field is able to work through the study of ritual practices towards an overall understanding of a community's total social fabric. This early account shows how Victor Turner, doing anthropological fieldwork amongst the Ndembu people in Zambia, gradually came to realise that he needed to study and understand the rituals he was surrounded by in order to better understand other activities, such as kinship, village structure, marriage and divorce, family and individual budgets, tribal and village politics, and the agricultural cycle, which at first sight to a Western observer might seem to belong to a different space than ritual. The ways in which groups are formed and identities located in different groups, with the accompanying inclusion and exclusion that is familiar in all societies, is here linked more closely to ritual practices than perhaps we are used to doing. These insights have since been applied to societies across the world and it is interesting to consider how they might be applied to our own society too. To what extent might the everyday politics and economics of lives in contemporary Britain be likewise linked, in profound ways that are not always apparent, to ritual activities and meanings? And how might we identify such rituals and come to understand them? And what role do they play in defining in-groups and out-groups?

Turner's account of the way he did field work also offers helpful insights into how ethnography can be conducted, where the fieldworker keeps their eyes open for unexpected and unfamiliar things going on and gradually comes to see how observing such practices can be crucial to understanding the more obvious ones. At first Turner 'felt uneasily that I was always on the outside looking in,' but then he spoke with the village chiefs and to local 'experts,' coming to understand their own view of what was going on. He gradually came to realise that 'it was one thing to sit outside describing such things but quite another to reach an adequate understanding of what the movements and words mean to them'. This, for many anthropologists, is the heart of the discipline and what distinguishes it from other 'ways of knowing'. But Turner also describes the difficulties that the anthropologist encounters as they try to get such information from different local people. He firstly asked Ndembu local government employees, such as messengers and clerks, and he came to realise that these were not sufficient to explain the complex rituals he was encountering; so he then engaged with a local English-speaking Chief, whose insights were very helpful; but there were limits, both practical and political, to how much this man could work with Turner. So he turned to Ndembu ritual specialists who already had their own accounts of what was going on and what it meant; and finally he came to live with local people, to become part of their community, he and his wife offering medical support in ways that led to comparative discussions of how illness and misfortune might be explained. Engaging in such relations, Turner and his wife 'began to perceive many aspects of Ndembu culture that had previously been invisible to us because of our theoretical blinkers'. Again we might apply this method to our own understanding of the society and the social groups we live with – listening to what they have to say, and coming to see their meanings and interpretations rather than just our own as 'outsiders'. What groups do we belong to and which are we excluded from, and how are these differences represented – in symbols, rituals, language – and how do we become familiar with them and confident in our knowledge of what counts?

[At first I felt a] reluctance to collect ritual data. For the first nine months of fieldwork, I amassed considerable quantities of data on kinship, village structure, marriage and divorce, family and individual budgets, tribal and village politics, and the agricultural cycle. I filled my notebooks with genealogies; I made village hut-plans and collected census material; I prowled around to catch the rare and unwary kinship term. Yet I felt uneasily that I was always on the outside looking in, even when I became comfortable in my use of the vernacular. For I was constantly aware of the thudding of ritual drums in the vicinity of my camp, and the people I knew would often take their leave of me to spend days at a time attending such exotically named rites as *Nkula*, *Wubwang'u* and *Wubinda*. Eventually, I was forced to recognise that if I wanted to know what even a segment of Ndembu culture was really about, I would have to overcome my prejudice against ritual and start to investigate it.

It is true that almost from the beginning of my stay among the Ndembu I had, on invitation, attended the frequent performances of the girls' puberty rites (*Nkang'a*) and had tried to describe what I had seen as accurately as possible. But it is one thing to observe people performing the stylised gestures and singing the cryptic songs of ritual performances and quite another to reach an adequate understanding of what the movements and words mean to them. To obtain enlightenment, I had recourse at first to the District Notebook, a compilation of random jottings by officers of the Colonial Administration on events and customs that struck them as interesting. Here I found short accounts of Ndembu beliefs in a High God, in ancestral spirits, and of different kinds of rites. Some were accounts of observed ceremonies, but most of them were based on the reports of Ndembu local government employees, such as messengers and clerks. At all events, they hardly provided satisfactory explanations of the long, complicated puberty rites I had seen, though they gave me some preliminary information about the kinds of rites I had not seen.

My next move was to set up a series of interviews with an exceptionally capable chief, entitled Ikelenge, who had a sound knowledge of English: Chief Ikelenge at once grasped what I wanted and gave me an inventory of the names of the principal Ndembu rituals, with brief accounts of the main features of each. I soon discovered that the Ndembu were not at all resentful of a stranger's interest in their ritual system and were perfectly prepared to admit to its performances anyone who treated their beliefs with respect. It was not long before Chief Ikelenge invited me to attend a performance of a ritual belonging to the gun-hunters' cult, *Wuyang'a*. It was at this performance that I became aware that at least one set of economic activities, namely hunting, could hardly be understood without a grasp of the ritual idiom pertaining to the chase. The accumulation of symbols indicative at once of hunting power and virility gave me an insight as well into several features of Ndembu social organisation, notably the stress on the importance of contemporaneous links between male kin, in a matrilineal society, whose structural continuity was through women. [C]ertain regularities that emerged from the analysis of numerical data, such as village genealogies and censuses and records of succession to office and inheritance of property, became fully intelligible only in the light of values embodied and expressed in symbols at ritual performances.

There were limits, however, to the assistance Chief Ikelenge was able to offer me. In the first place, his position and its manifold roles prevented him from leaving his capital village for long, and his relations with the local mission, which were of political importance to him, were too delicate, in a situation where gossip carries news fast, to permit him the luxury of attending many pagan ceremonies. Moreover, my own research was rapidly becoming a micro-sociological investigation of the ongoing process of village life. I moved my camp from the chief's capital to a cluster of commoner villagers. There, in time, my family came to be accepted as more or less a part of the local community, and, with eyes just opened to the importance of ritual in the lives of the Ndembu, my wife and I began to perceive many aspects of Ndembu culture that had previously been invisible to us because of our theoretical blinkers.

I then began to seek out Ndembu ritual specialists to record interpretative texts from them about rites I had observed. Our entree to performances, and access to exegesis, was no doubt helped by the fact that, like most anthropological fieldworkers, we distributed medicines, bandaged wounds, and, in the case of my wife (who is a doctor's daughter and bolder in these matters than I), injected with serum persons bitten by snakes. Since many of the Ndembu cult rituals are performed for the sick, and since European medicines are regarded as having mystical efficacy of the same kind as their own though greater in potency, the curative specialists came to regard us as colleagues and to welcome our attendance at their performances.

I remembered having read in Dr Livingstone's *Missionary Travels* how he had made a strict point of consulting the local medicine men about the condition of patients, and how this had made for good rapport with an influential section of the Central African population. We copied his example, and this may have been one reason why we were allowed to attend the esoteric phases of several rites and obtain what cross-checking suggested were reasonably reliable interpretations of many of the symbols employed in them. By 'reliable' I mean, of course, that the interpretations were, on the whole, mutually consistent. They might, in fact, be said to constitute the standardised hermeneutics of Ndembu culture, rather than the free associations or eccentric views of individuals. We also collected interpretations from Ndembu who were not ritual specialists, or at least not specialists in the ritual immediately under consideration.

Most Ndembu, both men and women, were members of at least one cult association, and it was hard to find an elderly person who was not an 'expert' in the secret knowledge of more than one cult. In this way we gradually built up a body of observational data and interpretative comments, which, when submitted to analysis, began to exhibit certain regularities from which it was possible to elicit a structure, expressed in a set of patterns.

In all this time, we never asked for a ritual to be performed solely for our anthropological benefit; we held no brief for such artificial play-acting. There was, in fact, no dearth of spontaneous performances. One of our major difficulties was frequently in deciding on a given day which of two or more performances to attend. As we became increasingly a part of the village scene, we discovered that very often decisions to perform ritual were connected with crises in the social life of villages. [A]mong the Ndembu there is a close connection between social conflict and ritual at the levels of village and 'vicinage' (a term I use for discrete clusters of villages), and that a multiplicity of conflict situations is correlated with a high frequency of ritual performance.

Edited extract from: Victor Turner, *The Ritual Process* (London: Routledge, 1966), pp. 6–11.

SECTION III

GLOBAL AND LOCAL
SOCIETIES, ENVIRONMENTS AND GLOBALIZATION

Introduction to Section III

Hilary Callan, Brian Street and Simon Underdown

Section III of the Reader brings together examples of the approaches anthropologists have taken to global processes; their impacts on human societies on a large scale; and how they may be experienced, exploited, resisted or transformed in local contexts.

III.1 Anthropological Approaches to the Movement of Peoples, Patterns and Processes

Our first group of extracts looks at approaches from biological anthropology and archaeology, and highlights the fact that the movement and migration of populations is not a new, nor even a recent, phenomenon. On the contrary, it has been integral to the course of human evolution. In 'Human Evolution, Adaptation and Diversity', Simon Underdown returns to the theme of human evolution he discussed in Section I. He shows how the variability of the modern human phenotype (body form) is linked to the spread of early populations through different environments in deep time; but he also stresses the importance of cultural adaptation: the invention of techniques and technologies which can modify the effects of genetic selection. Early environments might well have selected for or against particular physical features such as body shape or the concentration of melanin in the skin. But cultural developments such as clothing and cooking have been equally influential. Similarly, as Underdown argues, some of the differences in average size and appearance between men and women may have come about through sexual selection, as they have in other species. But – as we also saw in Section I – cultural conventions, values and ways of handling the body have a huge influence on what people find attractive in a potential sexual partner.

Our second extract adds detail to the picture by tracing ancient migration patterns as they can be reconstructed through archaeological methods. Fiona Coward summarises the current state of knowledge and opinion about the movement and dispersal of early human populations. As she shows, the picture is complex and not always clear-cut, but this very complexity speaks to the deep interconnections linking all contemporary populations.

Charlotte Roberts next focuses on disease patterns in ancient populations, and the methods by which they can be studied using human remains. As she shows, the relationship between disease patterns and living conditions in human history and prehistory is a two-way one. Disease-driven mortality has had massive economic and social impacts in historical times and into the present day; and it can to some extent be tracked in the distant human past using bones, teeth and (latterly) residual

DNA. Conversely, major shifts in modes of living – such as animal domestication, settled agriculture, the rise of cities and centralised states, and later mass urbanisation – have affected the overall health of populations and fostered the rise of particular infectious diseases.

Anthropologists are often asked by members of the public 'Has human evolution stopped?' The answer seems to be a rather complex one. There are cases – such as the well-known one of the sickle-cell gene discussed by Underdown in our fourth extract – where the effects of selection at genetic level can be traced in modern populations. Again, as Underdown shows, genetic susceptibility to fatal diseases, such as some cancers, tends to remain in a population where the disease mostly strikes individuals after the reproductive years, so that natural selection is muted or absent. But at the same time, the enlargement of the brain and human intelligence (an evolutionary process in itself) that made possible the explosive development of human culture has given the human species tools that arguably drive all our futures for good or ill. Think, for example, of the destructive power of weapons technologies; or (on the more positive side) of advances in medicine that preserve the lives of babies whose genetic blueprints would otherwise be eliminated by natural selection.

This topic of human control over our own evolution has been highly contentious. In the first part of the twentieth century, for example, many intellectuals as well as politicians held that there should be some form of public control over who should have children, in the interest of promoting 'good' features in the population and eliminating 'bad' ones. At its most extreme, the 'eugenics movement' (as it came to be called) was notoriously associated with Nazism. What do you think? Is there ever a moral or social case for intervening in our own evolutionary future? And who decides whether a feature is 'good' or 'bad', or what is to count as 'fitness'?

In our next group of extracts, we switch attention to approaches from social and cultural anthropology to the many-stranded topic of 'globalization'. As T.H. Eriksen argues in the first of these, globalization is a key area of study not only for anthropology but also for other and related disciplines such as economics, sociology, political science, history, media studies and law. The extract we include here, from Eriksen's book on the subject, provides a valuable overview. Globalization is far too complex a cluster of forces and flows for any one discipline to have a monopoly over its study. Anthropology, however, has an important contribution to make to our overall understanding, and this is illustrated in the extracts that follow.

The giving and receiving of gifts, and the moral relationship between giver and receiver created by the act of gift-giving, has been a key theme in social anthropology since it was first explored by the French scholar Marcel Mauss in his study of the gift, first published in 1923 (Mauss 2002). Mauss drew attention to the triple obligations, deep-seated in human societies, to give, to receive and to reciprocate. Gift-giving can set up various kinds of relationships between giver and receiver – for example, relative equality, where a gift of roughly equal value is returned in due course (think of exchanging birthday or festive presents, or repaying hospitality received) or extreme inequality or dependence (think of charity handed out to the destitute). Patty Gray, in the extract included here, makes effective use of the insights of Mauss and his successors in analysing Russia's attempts to move from a 'receiver' to a 'donor' position in what we might think of as the 'moral economy' of international aid and development.

We stay with the subject of international development in the next extract, taken from work by Elisabeth Croll and David Parkin on anthropology, the environment and development. This extract also takes up a theme we explored in Section I of the Reader: that of cultural understandings of the environment, and specifically of the relation between persons and environments. Croll and Parkin argue that the methods of social anthropology, based on long-term deep study, provide a unique way into people's knowledge and management of their local environmental resources – even where the study addresses seemingly unrelated matters such as ritual, spiritual belief or morality. These insights are of central relevance to attempts on an international scale to curb environmental degradation and promote policies for sustainability.

The spotlight moves to another 'globalizing' phenomenon – that of international corporate business – in the next extract, from the research of Jamie Cross and Alice Street on the marketing of Lifebuoy soap in India. This work is an excellent example of the capacity of social anthropology to 'hold in play' events on the large scale of institutional policies, practices and the beliefs on which they rest, and on the small scale of local responses and interpretations. Later in the Reader we will come across more examples of this 'double vision'. Here, Cross and Street document the development within the multinational corporate sector of marketing models emphasising 'social good' as a by-product of commercial success. Such models stand in interesting contrast to the policies based on altruistic doctrines, such as those described by Gray (above). Cross and Street describe in detail a series of marketing initiatives for Lifebuoy soap resting on these models, and the recruitment of local people and interests (such as schoolchildren and women on low incomes) in their service. Research such as that of Cross and Street is particularly illuminating in showing how business-driven understandings of health, hygiene and 'right ways to live' are presented to, and received by, people 'at the bottom of the pyramid'. You may wish to think of comparable cases nearer home. For example, at several points in Section I of the Reader we touched on systems of classification and how these relate to ideas of pollution and contamination. What messages are we constantly receiving through the media of dirt, germs and what to do about them? And how do these messages shape our own ideas of hygiene and good housekeeping?

We next look with an anthropologist's eye at Japanese hip-hop as an instance of the globalization of popular culture. Ian Condry takes us vividly into the environment of Tokyo hip-hop clubs and the teenagers who frequent them, while making us aware of the global reach of this mode of music and performance. Like the work of Cross and Street (above) and Gusterson (in Section V, below), Condry shows that much contemporary research in social anthropology combines highly localised field sites with non-local processes such as flows of knowledge and fashion, and networks of communication and influence. In this example, we glimpse the consumers' active management of the hip-hop 'product', moulding and transforming it in accordance with distinctively Japanese concepts and values.

III.2 Local and Global Processes: Ethnographic Perspectives

In this group of extracts, we look in some detail at ethnographic cases illustrating how global-scale processes feed into, and are moulded within, the relationships and transactions that concern people in their immediate lives. Our first case is that of the international trade in second-hand clothing, analysed by Karen Hansen. As Hansen indicates, this trade receives something of a 'bad press', with the sale of donated cast-offs from rich countries often represented as distorting Third World economies and killing local industries. Hansen's field research shows, however, that the picture is considerably more nuanced than this. Drawing on material from the Philippines and Zambia, she shows that while there may indeed be some negative effects, the trade in second-hand clothing creates local markets that allow new forms of fashion and creativity to thrive, as well as generating direct and secondary employment opportunities. Hansen's article can usefully be read in conjunction with the extract from Daniel Miller's *Stuff* included in Section I of the Reader, where we looked at clothing and style as tools in the cultural construction of identity and the self. We can also, again, consider comparable cases close to home. For example, how might an anthropologist seek to understand local bartering networks in the West, or the recycling movement?

There is widespread public concern – shared by the majority of anthropologists – over the plight of indigenous peoples whose way of life, or even survival, is threatened by global forces and state or commercial interests. This was signalled in the extract from Eriksen included above, and is taken up in our next extract, from Terence Turner's account of the resistance of the Kayapo people of the Amazon basin against encroachments on their land and world. Echoing the piece by Croll and Parkin above, and by Hendry in Section I, Turner emphasises that for the Kayapo the 'environment' is not external to human life but is integral to the creation of persons and human relationships. Environmental destruction therefore entails not just the loss of subsistence resources, although it does entail this – it indeed constitutes the obliteration of their human world. Anthropologists, as well as other activists, have been at the forefront of campaigns to support indigenous peoples facing catastrophic threat; and as we saw above, their most distinctive contribution lies in the ability to provide in-depth knowledge of such peoples' resource use and knowledge systems. Turner offers a narrative with a positive outcome, in that the Kayapo were able at that time to use the opportunities provided by globalization in defence of their threatened interests. But we should note that such struggles are seldom finally over and the threats continue, if not to the Kayapo then to other similarly vulnerable peoples. In the next two extracts we look at the anthropology of tourism; but it is worth considering here whether insensitively managed tourism – for example, the exhibition of indigenous peoples and cultures as 'spectacle' – may be one of the more insidious threats to their powers to determine their own futures.

As just indicated, we now look at contrasting instances of people moving around the world: that of tourists as voluntary travellers, and that of refugees as involuntarily displaced persons. Both have been extensively studied by anthropologists in recent years. Eriksen sets the scene once again, in a short extract comparing these situations. This is followed by an extract from Margaret Kenna's Foreword to a collection of research papers on the anthropology of tourism, published in 2010. Framed partly as an account of the author's own journey between the identities of 'tourist' and 'anthropologist', the piece traces developments over time in the host community's engagements with the tourist presence. Kenna's account also raises deep questions concerning identity, authenticity and performance, which are of central interest to anthropologists. In reading it, you may recall Daniel Miller's account of clothing and identity (in Section I) and Brian Morris's of the anthropology of the self (Section II). Since most of us have some experience of being tourists (whether or not we accept that designation), you may also like to reflect on that experience in the light of your knowledge of anthropology. What deep differences are there between being a (possibly well-informed) tourist in an unfamiliar place and being an anthropologist?

Dianna Shandy's edited piece, which follows, offers an excellent example of the contribution anthropology can make to understanding the situation of refugees and other displaced populations. The Nuer people of the Southern Sudan are well-known to all students of social anthropology through E.E. Evans-Pritchard's groundbreaking studies, conducted in the first half of the last century, of their subsistence, political and kinship organisation, and their religious beliefs and practices. But all human societies are subject to change, which can be profound or even catastrophic. Readers will be well aware of the political violence, social upheaval and displacement of populations that have affected this region of Africa – and continue to do so. The refugee as victim is a familiar figure, and of course this image often corresponds to reality. But detailed ethnographic study, of which Shandy's is a good example, also shows that under some circumstances people preserve a capacity to exercise autonomy, exploit opportunities and find ways through 'cracks' in bureaucratic structures that otherwise oppress and restrict them.

Religious beliefs and practices have been a focus of anthropological study from the beginnings of the discipline in the nineteenth century. At an earlier period, it was most usual for anthropologists to concentrate their attention on the beliefs and spiritual worlds of small-scale societies, and on related phenomena such as 'witchcraft' practices. Many celebrated ethnographies are in this tradition, as we saw in the description of Evans-Pritchard's work on Azande witchcraft included in Section I. More recently, anthropologists have also directed attention to the world-scale, or mainstream, religions, and to the ways in which they impact upon – and are transformed within – local environments and circumstances. The extract from Joy Hendry's book *An Introduction to Social Anthropology: Sharing Our Worlds*, outlines the approaches anthropologists have taken to understanding the rise of new religious movements and 'cults'. Terms such as 'cult' are in themselves judgmental, and it is important to understand that an anthropological approach implies no judgment as to the truth or falsity of religious belief. Rather, the anthropologist seeks to show the coherence or consistency of the belief or practice in its local context, such as various forms of social breakdown and stress.

This principle is well exemplified in the extract that follows, from Anna-Karina Hermkens's account of the figure of the Virgin Mary in Papua New Guinea. Hermkens describes in fine detail how a feature of a global religious institution (the reverence for Mary within Roman Catholicism), which has itself been a subject of concern and legislation by the Vatican, has 'played out' in the specific circumstances and recent history of Papua New Guinea. Reading her ethnography, we see how a global set of doctrines surrounding the figure of Mary has become interwoven with highly local beliefs and experiences – some of which would be considered antithetical to formal Catholic doctrine. Similar transformations are found elsewhere of course where global religion is locally configured; Mexican practices surrounding the 'Day of the Dead' are a well-known example.

The final ethnographic case included here is that of sport; specifically, football's global following. Sport is a relatively recent focus of study for anthropologists, but the 'anthropology of sport' is attracting increasing interest in the discipline. Sport, and some sports in particular (notably football), is of course a major global phenomenon, of far-reaching economic, political and cultural significance. As with the other areas we have looked at in this section of the Reader, international football is followed and supported locally in ways that strongly reflect, and feed into, the circumstances of particular places and communities. Richard Vokes's account of the rise in popularity of English Premier League clubs in rural Uganda illustrates vividly how global sport can create great opportunities for entrepreneurship at a local level. But, because these opportunities themselves rest on the stability of global economies and communication technologies, they can as quickly go into reverse, with sometimes tragic consequences for communities and individuals.

Reference

Mauss, M. [orig 1923] *The Gift: The Form and Reason for Exchange in Archaic Societies*, trans. W.D. Halls (London: Routledge, 2002).

III.1 Anthropological Approaches to the Movement of Peoples, Patterns and Processes

Approaches from Biological Anthropology and Archaeology: Adaptation, Dispersal and Diversity, Migration, Disease

35 Human Evolution, Adaptation and Diversity
Simon Underdown

As humans we appear to be a very diverse group of animals. Different languages, cultures and skin colours, as well as size and shapes, make it hard to imagine that we are anything other than a hugely diverse bunch. In this piece written for the Reader, evolutionary anthropologist Simon Underdown examines how we have expanded from one location in Africa to display so much outward variation while sharing essentially the same genes. A complex relationship between the environment and sex has created the huge range of differences that we see in ourselves from the same genetic blueprint. But genetics is not the only part of human evolution. We are the only animals that are utterly dependent upon cultural adaptations for survival. This can range from simple fire use right through to the latest eco-friendly house-building insulation materials. With this in mind, how far can we consider human biological evolution to have stopped, replaced by cultural solutions to hitherto biological problems?

All living humans share a common ancestor who lived in Africa around 200,000 years ago. This presents us with an interesting question: If we all have such a recent common ancestor and all originate from the same place, how can we explain the differences that we see between humans today? A huge range of skins colours, body types, languages and cultures have grown out of the original ancestral population of *Homo sapiens* from Omo (in present-day Ethiopia) 200,000 years ago. If we examine the range of phenotypic diversity that exists within the human species today we can perhaps identify two main factors in the creation of diversity: environmental factors and sexual selection.

Environmental conditions can exert a huge influence on the human body (or phenotype) that is more than capable of suppressing or reducing the influence of our genes. If we consider a simple example such as skin colour, then we can easily recognise that dark skin is more frequent in hot environments while light skin is more common at northern latitudes. Here there is a clear relationship between melanin concentration (the pigment cells) and sunlight. Ultra violet (UV) radiation is crucial for the synthesis of vitamin D but prolonged exposure can cause severe skin burning. With suncream and the modern diet this would not be a hugely influential selective pressure; but in the past in cold areas, and consuming a hunter-gatherer diet that varied in content and amount (as well as the time spent in the sun), the absorption of UV radiation to produce vitamin D would have been vital for health, while in hot climates the reverse would be true. As our ancestors moved north, less melanin was required to protect the skin from burning and more UV radiation was required to synthesise vitamin D. The skin colour of Arctic groups is not very pale because they use cultural traits (such as special clothing and a high-protein diet) to solve the biological problems posed by living in such an environment. With this very simple example we can see just how much influence our environment has played in developing the variation that exists within our species today. A similar pattern can be seen with body size and shape. Populations of humans living in hot environments developed tall and lean bodies that allowed large amounts of heat to be diverted away from the body while populations living in arctic environments favoured shorter and squatter bodies that better conserved heat.

The second factor that has influenced how human populations differ is that of sexual selection. Specific attributes that are attractive to the opposite sex can become rapidly established within a population. While the classic example is the peacock's tail, we can also see a number of traits in humans. Universal traits such as prominent female breasts (human female breasts are much larger than those of other primates) through to male facial hair are all thought to be artefacts of sexual selection in the past. In relatively isolated populations the effect can become much more exaggerated, leading to traits that look very unusual to an outsider's eyes but are the result of a pattern of sexual attraction altering a small number of genes. However, as is often the case in human evolution, the pattern is not that simple.

One of the most frequently asked questions about humans, and one that allows us to best understand our relationship to the environment, is: Are we still evolving? This is a question that provokes widespread debate. If we are still evolving, how will we look in the future – and if we are not, then what does that mean? On the genetic level it would probably be fair to say that human evolution has stopped. This is based on a genetic view of the evolutionary process; and while it is almost certainly true from a gene-centric perspective, it is really only addressing a small part of what it is to be human. Although it is true enough that we can think of human evolution having stopped when it comes to the slowing down of the effects of natural selection on the human gene pool, human evolution is not a purely genetic affair, and the path of our development as a species cannot possibly be understood without an examination of the role played by cultural adaptations.

The course of human evolution has displayed a complex relationship between biological adaptations (such as bipedalism and brain size) and cultural adaptations (such as tool use) since the development of the first stone tools, around 2.6 million years ago, in East Africa. The appearance of stone tools in the archaeological record was a major cultural adaptation that provided our ancestors with the ability to manipulate their environment – a process that led to ever more complex behavioural innovations, and one that has continued ever since. Our earliest hominin ancestors were very different in appearance to us – if still extant they would look to us very 'ape-like'. This was the case for approximately 5 million years until the appearance, 2 million years ago, of *Homo ergaster* – the first human and the first to rely heavily on cultural adaptations rather than biological ones. The process of human evolution from 2 million years ago onwards was one of relatively small-scale biological changes occurring in tandem with massive and far-reaching cultural developments. It was the development of cultural adaptations that provided the basis for our evolutionary success and produced the current genetic pattern that the geneticist Steve Jones describes as 'largely no longer evolving'.

The use of cultural adaptations, such as a fire and clothing, removed the need for biological adaptation and meant that the basic body plan of the genus Homo has remained relatively unchanged. Although there are of course differences between species such as *Homo ergaster*, the Neanderthals and *Homo sapiens*, the factor that unites us all is the role that cultural innovation played in allowing a wide range of habitats to be exploited without the need for biological adaptation. Massive increases in intelligence, a biological process, provided the raw material for a huge range of cultural adaptation and environmental manipulation. In fact because of this, some would argue that the idea that our genetic evolution has stopped is incorrect, and would highlight the role of genetic engineering which means that we will soon be entering a period of evolutionary dynamism – a result of being able to tweak our genome to remove cancer and other genetic diseases, for instance. This is an interesting idea, but it overlooks the fact that many of these diseases take hold later in life, after reproduction, and as such could be argued to be relatively selectively neutral. Genes are not the only factor; the environment plays a huge role in our make-up. Simply put, genetic pre-disposition to heart disease is not the same as heart disease!

Ultimately, genetics is only part of the story of human evolution. While the process of genetic evolution is clearly slowing down and we are no longer subject to the widespread effects of natural selection, cultural evolution continues to play a crucial role in the development of the human species as it has done for nearly 2.6 million years. The pace of cultural adaptation is still moving rapidly and producing a greater range of variation than at any other time in our evolutionary history. We may be heading for a homogeneous genetic future, but the human evolutionary story tells us that our culture will continue to evolve and flourish as long as humans are around.

Humans are the only animal that is utterly dependent upon culture for its survival; but we also use culture to express ourselves and to ornament our bodies. This means that any biological effects we examine we must also consider what role cultural adaptations have played. For instance, in the Middle East skin colour is often lighter than at parallel latitudes in Africa – this is presumably because of the effect of traditional forms of dress in the Middle East (simplistically speaking, clothes that cover the body to keep it cool and protect it from heat). So when we think about the pattern of variation in living humans today we need to remember that what we see is not the result of deep-rooted genetic variation but rather a combination of environment, sex and culture.

36   Ancestral Migration Patterns
Fiona Coward

Human life began in Africa and we can all trace our ancestry back to the same group of humans living in Ethiopia around 200,000 years ago. Yet today we are a global species of 7 billion and inhabit every corner of the earth. How exactly did this remarkable process of expansion take place? In this piece written for the Reader, archaeologist Fiona Coward describes how humans and their ancestors first left Africa and how we can use a range of scientific techniques to recreate their journey from an African to a global species. As we will see, it is through understanding this journey that we can begin to explore the complex interlinks and ties that we see in the modern world.

Today, humans live almost everywhere. However, our colonisation of the Earth was by no means inevitable. The process involved many stops, starts and sometimes retreats and multiple sequential 'waves' of different groups and even species in some areas. Studying how and why humans and our ancestors spread across the globe can tell us a great deal about how our ancestors evolved the adaptability, intelligence and creativity necessary to develop the skills and knowledge that allow us to survive and thrive in such very different habitats.

The most obvious way in which anthropologists reconstruct ancestral migration patterns is by studying the geographical distribution of fossils of our ancestors. However, only a tiny percentage of our ancestors are preserved in the fossil record, and not all regions preserve fossils equally well. Furthermore, some parts of the world have historically been less easy to reach or to excavate in than others, and a common saying among anthropologists, therefore, is that absence of evidence is not the same thing as evidence of absence. Even when found, fossils are not easily interpreted. They are often poorly preserved, fragmentary or distorted, and because individuals vary and evolution involves constant, gradual change, anthropologists often disagree over which species are represented.

Out of Africa 1

The very earliest hominin fossils are currently only found in Africa. The earliest fossils found outside this continent, at a site called Dmanisi in Georgia, are dated to 1.7 million years ago (Ma). These are currently assigned to the species *Homo georgicus*, but closely resemble specimens of a species called *Homo ergaster*, which lived in Africa from 1.8 Ma. Both these species seem to have been closely related to a third, *Homo erectus*, whose fossils have been found in Indonesia after 1.49 Ma and China after 1.36 Ma.

Further west, the earliest fossils known in Europe date to somewhat later, at 1.2 Ma, and belong to a species known as *Homo antecessor*. Fossils of this species have – so far – only been found at the site of Atapuerca in northern Spain, but stone tools found at Happisburgh in the UK, dated to 0.8mya, suggest that they may have been quite widespread across the continent. After around 600,000 years ago (600ka) a new species appears in Europe, and *Homo heidelbergensis* also spread widely across the continent, reaching even the UK, where a leg bone was found at Boxgrove, together with evidence of quite sophisticated foraging and tool-manufacturing skills.

In Africa, fossil finds are very variable and were initially assigned to a number of different species. However, as a group these are so similar to the European *Homo heidelbergensis* that many anthropologists now consider them to be members of the same widespread species. However, it remains unclear whether or how groups of these species, or others coexisting with them, may have migrated within or between continents. While in eastern Asia *Homo erectus* appears to persist largely unchanged for hundreds of thousands of years, surviving until perhaps as late as 55 to 27ka, at Denisova Cave in Siberia, DNA analysis of bones dated to 40ka revealed genetic material distinct to that of both humans and Neanderthals, suggesting that several groups of species may have migrated and coexisted across Eurasia at different times over the intervening period.

The significance of these early dispersals beyond Africa is that life in these regions requires different ways of life and kinds of skills than those needed on the African savanna. Eurasian climates were cooler – but more importantly they were more seasonal, meaning that food resources varied significantly over the course of the year. Fewer edible plants in particular meant that hominins living in these regions would have had to rely increasingly on animal protein from scavenged or hunted animal prey for food. However, such foodstuffs were scarce and hotly contested by other carnivores. To compete successfully, our ancestors needed to plan ahead and move over much greater geographical distances, requiring sophisticated 'mental mapping' skills. In addition, the complex social skills that allowed them to work together to share resources and information would have been crucial. The use of fire, both to keep warm and also to cook animal protein to gain the most energy from it, was probably also important.

Out of Africa 2

With the appearance of modern humans, anthropologists have another significant line of evidence – DNA analysis – with which to enhance the picture of human migration and dispersal available from study of the bones and stones left by our ancestors. While sequencing of the complete genomes of both modern humans and Neanderthals has allowed us to compare our species directly, the number of geographically disparate samples required to study the dispersal and migration of a species are currently available only for modern *Homo sapiens*. Research has focused in particular on mitochondrial DNA (mtDNA), which is inherited only from an individual's mother, and the Y chromosome, which only men inherit from their fathers. Successive mutations accumulate over time and are transmitted between generations, and as populations 'bud off' during dispersal to different parts of the world, specific mutations become more geographically restricted, allowing geneticists to reconstruct geographically rooted 'family trees' of modern human DNA that can be used to illuminate our understanding of modern human dispersals. For example, the mtDNA L3 mutation is shared by populations both in Africa and beyond, and is therefore believed to pre-date the migration of modern humans out of Africa. Assuming that mutations accumulate at a relatively constant rate (although this is controversial), geneticists have calculated that this mutation occurred, and therefore that widespread dispersals of our species occurred after, around 85ka.

In addition, detailed comparison of the *Homo sapiens* and Neanderthal genomes has revealed that between 1 and 4 per cent of the DNA of modern Eurasians (but not Africans) appears to derive from Neanderthals, suggesting that some contact and interbreeding (though at very low levels) may have occurred between these early human migrants and some of the populations who already lived in the areas in which they arrived as they spread across the globe.

Although some details remain to be fleshed out, and new evidence may also come to light, combining the data obtained from these multiple sources of evidence has given us a good general picture of the spread of modern humans across the globe.

All the evidence supports the theory that *Homo sapiens* evolved first in Africa. Between around 400 and 160ka, the mix of skeletal features characteristic of *Homo sapiens* was gradually accumulating in the fossil record, and by far the greatest diversity of DNA types among modern humans occurs in sub-Saharan Africa, suggesting that these populations have had the longest time for mutations to accumulate. Calculations of the date at which the modern human genome appeared put its emergence at between 200 and 150ka.

By 130 to 100ka, *Homo sapiens* fossils appear in the Near East at sites like Skhul and Qafzeh in Israel. However, Neanderthal fossils from nearby sites date to between only 60 to 54ka, and it seems that these early human dispersals represent a complex pattern of movement in and out of this region by different species as climates and habitats changed over time. Other groups of early *Homo sapiens* may also have followed an alternative route out of Africa across Arabia and the Bab el Mandeb Strait off the Horn of Africa into southern Eurasia, and along the coast from there to India and further east and south. Stone tools possibly made by humans have been found at Jebel Faya near the Horn of Africa and date to 125ka. However, many of the individual 'types' of tool and material culture traditionally seen as characteristic of *Homo sapiens* are now known to have been produced by other species of hominin elsewhere, making any straightforward equation of material culture and hominin species problematic, and it is impossible to identify the manufacturers with complete certainty.

In Asia, some possible *Homo sapiens* fossils are known from Zhirendong in China perhaps as early as 100,000 years ago, but these finds are not well accepted by anthropologists. Some stone tools possibly made by *Homo sapiens* date to 77ka at Jwalapuram in India, 70ka at Kota Tampan in Malaysia and 68ka at Liujiang in China. However, the bulk of the fossil and archaeological evidence, from sites such as Tianyuan in China and Niah Cave on Borneo in Indonesia, dates to after 40ka years ago.

Further south in Australia, until very recently some skeletal remains, from sites such as Kow Swamp and Willandra Lakes, were thought to belong to *Homo erectus* migrants who had arrived in the continent very early. These claims were often used to argue for *in situ* evolution of these hominins into *Homo sapiens*. However, more recent re-dating of these sites using up-to-date techniques has established that all the Australian skeletal finds made to date are those of *Homo sapiens*, and that the majority of sites date to after 40ka. Nevertheless, some archaeological sites do appear to date to earlier than this – Malakunanja rock shelter is currently dated to more than 65ka – and may well represent earlier visits or limited occupations.

In western Eurasia, the earliest *Homo sapiens* fossils in the region, from Peştera cu Oase in Romania, date to only 40ka, and there are very few skeletal remains attesting to the spread of humans across the continent. However, the early Upper Palaeolithic is often defined by a new set of stone tool types (and other kinds of material culture) known collectively as the Aurignacian. At almost all find-spots where Aurignacian tools occur alongside hominin bones, those bones have been those of *Homo sapiens*, and thus the spread of the Aurignacian from around 45ka in Turkey at sites like Üçağizli Cave to ~35ka in western Europe, is often taken to represent the spread of this species across the continent.

Conclusion

There are thus a number of different lines of evidence that anthropologists can draw from in order to reconstruct the dispersals around the globe of our hominin and human ancestors, as well as subsequent migrations, including the study of the distribution of their fossils and the stone tools and other kinds of material culture they made, the modelling of ecological factors involved in their movements, and the modern distribution of variability in DNA and languages. While each line of evidence is individually problematic, and ongoing work is continually producing exciting new finds and refining old research, when all the evidence is studied in conjunction it is possible to reconstruct the spread of our ancestors across the globe and to consider its implications for their intelligence and resourcefulness. Nor is this work purely theoretical: study of prehistoric migration and dispersal reveals the geo-political make-up even of the contemporary world to be the product of complex patterns of migration and dispersal which link all modern human populations, making our differences much less significant than the similarities we all share.

37   The Archaeology of Disease
Charlotte Roberts

Disease is a process that has shaped, and continues to shape, the lives of humans. During our lives we all suffer from diseases – some serious, some trivial. It is an unpleasant fact of the modern world that some diseases that the developed world regard as nuisances, such as diarrhoea, are virulent killers in the developing world. Many of the diseases that we are familiar with today have always been with us and have contributed to shaping the world we live in. In this piece, specially written for the Reader, Charlotte Roberts, a palaeopathologist, explores how we can examine diseases in the past using skeletons; and how this allows us to understand the role of disease in the lives of people in the past.

Introduction

Anthropology is the study of what it means to be human. Part of being human today includes becoming ill, whether that is a minor complaint such as a cough or a cold or a more serious illness such as cancer. Over time, changes to the environment and climate have inevitably led to health challenges to which humans have been exposed, and adapting to being ill has been part of human existence for as long as humans have been on the planet. It is without doubt that no human, past or present, will have escaped, or will escape, being ill, and that very fact raises questions about how this impacts on societies as a whole and how they function all over the world.

Take, for example, the Black Death in the fourteenth century, which killed a significant part of the English population. Its actual impact was much wider than increased mortality; with a reduction in population numbers, the workforce was considerably compromised and reduced, and therefore production, including food for sustenance, was seriously affected. It took years to return to a stable economy. Today in Africa, the impact of the Human Immunodeficiency Virus (HIV) and the development from that into AIDS (Acquired Immune Deficiency Syndrome) has and is similarly taking its toll on the population, especially women, and the population is declining. Thus, productivity is reduced, which in turn affects the very functioning and wealth of society. Exploring and understanding the health

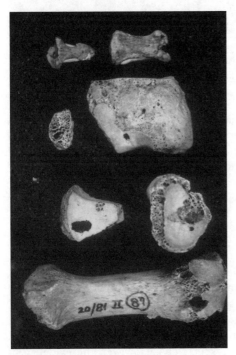

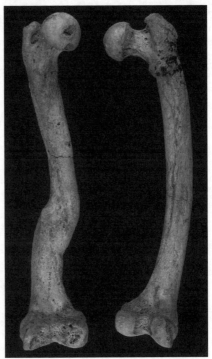

Inflammation of foot bones shown by 'grey' layer of new bone formation; probably the result of infection (1st century BC–1st century AD, Beckford Hereford and Worcester, England).
Photograph by Charlotte Roberts.
Reproduced with permission.

A healed fractured femur from a skeleton showing Paget's disease, possibly a viral infection (8th–10th centuries AD, Jarrow, England).
Photograph by Charlotte Roberts.
Reproduced with permission.

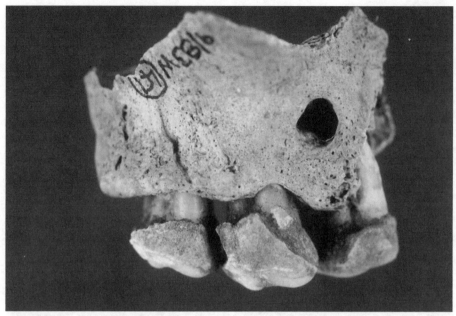

Dental abscess (shown by a sinus or hole) and plaque deposits on the teeth that have calcified into calculus (4th century AD, Gloucester, Gloucestershire, England). Photograph by Charlotte Roberts. Reproduced with permission.

and disease of our ancestors (palaeopathology, or 'old disease') provides a time depth to understand the present and plan for the future. Were the same diseases today around several thousand years ago and what factors led to their appearance, and were they the same as today?

The Study of Our Ancestors' Health through their Buried Remains

Archaeology

Archaeology is the study of people in the past and is carried out by excavating archaeological sites to reveal evidence of past populations. This might include structures that people built (for example, Stonehenge in Wiltshire, England, the Pyramids in Egypt, or Hadrian's Wall and its forts in the north of England), artefacts that people made (such as pottery, jewellery, tools), or environmental evidence that tells us something of the environment in which people lived and the diet they ate (for instance, pollen grains and animal bones, respectively). However, the evidence of the people themselves is revealed in excavated human remains, which may be skeletons or more complete bodies, such as Egyptian mummies. The remains are recovered from different types of archaeological site according to the time period. For example, in Neolithic Britain (between about 4000 and 2500 BC), the common way to bury the dead was in chambered tombs,

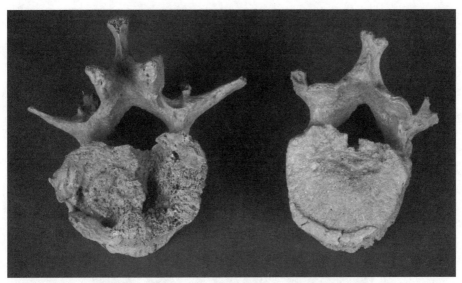

Possible tuberculosis of the spine seen as destructive lesions (6th century AD, Bedhampton, Hampshire, England)
Photograph by Charlotte Roberts. Reproduced with permission.

and bones were placed in the tomb at various times, eventually all becoming mixed up. In later periods of time, for example in the Roman era (AD 43 to 410), large urban cemeteries with individual burials were the norm; this continued into the medieval and post-medieval periods, although for the early medieval era cremation was a common practice at times. The human remains excavated (most commonly skeletons) thus provide physical anthropologists with potential evidence for disease, but also evidence for dietary excess or deficiency. These data can indicate what were the more common health problems our ancestors faced.

How Is It Done?
By looking for abnormalities in the bones and teeth of the skeleton ('lesions'), looking at which bones are affected (distribution pattern), and comparing what is seen with data on how diseases affect the bones and teeth in clinical medicine, it becomes possible to diagnose disease. More recently, researchers use ancient DNA (aDNA) of pathogens that cause disease in diagnosis because aDNA may be preserved in bones and teeth. The more common complaints in the past were those affecting the teeth and joints, and also traumatic lesions such as fractures of bones and head injuries from interpersonal violence. However, this is not just an 'identification' exercise. Like medical anthropologists who study the health of the living, often in developing countries, anthropologists working with human remains have specific questions they wish to answer.

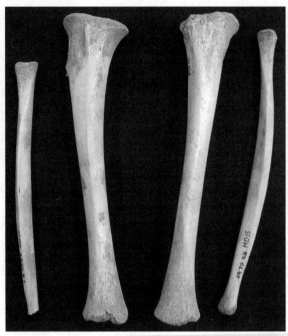

Bending of the lower leg bones (tibiae and fibulae), probably due to rickets (vitamin D deficiency) – 8th–10th centuries AD, Jarrow, England
Photograph by Charlotte Roberts. Reproduced with permission.

Questions to Answer about Past Health

One of the key questions for years has been what happened to health when people started to grow their own food, domesticate animals and live in permanent settled communities. Skeletons from pre-agricultural and agricultural contexts all over the world have generally shown that health declined with this transition; infections, joint problems and dental disease all increased. Diet became less varied with higher amounts of carbohydrates consumed, and there was always the risk of harvest failures and malnutrition, which affected normal human growth. Hunting wild animals and gathering wild foods kept people lean and fit with a more balanced healthy diet, but this economy could not support large populations.

Another transition was that from rural to urban living, as seen in Europe starting around the eleventh century and increasing right through to the post-medieval period and industrialisation (1550 to 1850); this was a time when living conditions changed dramatically, along with technology. Population density increased, infections could be transmitted more readily, hygiene and sanitation levels were very poor, and people lived in closer contact with a wider variety of animals, thus enabling animal diseases to be transmitted to humans. Infections such as tuberculosis increased because conditions were conducive for spreading the causative bacteria (coughing

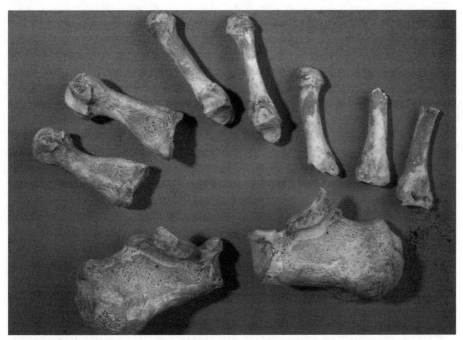

Destructive lesions in foot bones, probably due to gout (4th century AD, Gloucester, Gloucestershire, England).
Photograph by Charlotte Roberts. Reproduced with permission.

and sneezing over an uninfected person), and disorders of the metabolism occurred. One such disorder was rickets, which affected children who did not receive enough sunlight on their skins to manufacture the vitamin; this was because of polluted air but also because children often worked indoors for long periods of time. This in turn affected the uptake of calcium and phosphorus into the bones, with consequent soft bones and bent, deformed legs. Excesses of specific constituents in the diet also led to disease. For example, rich protein diets of higher status people in the Roman period caused gout and produced painful lesions in the joints of the toes. There was also a large increase in dental caries ('rotten teeth') in post-medieval England due to imports of sugar being made available to the wider population, along with finer flours.

Conclusions

Clearly, evidence of disease in human remains begins to tell a story about health through time, but the data only become meaningful when placed in the context of where the remains were excavated, and their time period and geographic location. Some diseases are only seen in certain parts of the world – for example, fungal infections in the Americas and inherited anaemias in Africa and the Mediterranean (sickle-cell anaemia and

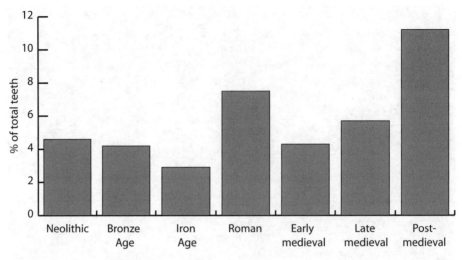

Dental caries rates for Britain through time.
Graph by Charlotte Roberts. Reproduced with permission.

thalassaemia, respectively). Furthermore, males, females and different age groups and ethnicities may be differentially affected, so that knowing this information for the skeletons studied is essential for interpretation. It is also important to understand, as today, that many factors can potentially lead to health problems, including the migration of people, increased trade and contact, quality of the living environment (indoors and outdoors), economy practised and type of work carried out, and concepts of disease and its treatment. Finally, it should be noted that, because most of the data on ancient disease come from skeletons, it is not possible to detect soft tissue diseases (except if aDNA survives to be analysed). That said, human remains provide the primary evidence for disease in the past that, if carefully analysed, can provide a window on past suffering.

38   Patterns of Disease
Simon Underdown

We are all familiar with the wide range of outward human diversity discussed in Chapter 35 above. Yet differences such as hair colour, body shape, language and religious practice are not the only types of difference that we can use to understand human diversity. By examining the global distribution of the different diseases that affect humans we can build up an intriguing picture of how our shared evolutionary history and subsequent movement around the world has

created differences in geographical incidence and occurrence of
disease. In this piece, evolutionary anthropologist Simon Underdown
explores the way in which some diseases can be both harmful and
useful to humans, before reflecting that diseases evolve too – a
salutatory thought, as many diseases that we thought had gone, such
as TB, start to out-evolve our cultural solutions.

Disease patterns give us an intriguing source of data for understanding human variation. The classic example that adorns many a biology textbook is of course sickle-cell anaemia. Sickle-cell is often wrongly thought of as an 'African' or 'black' disease, but in fact it has a distribution that is not restricted to any one skin colour (for as we have discussed above, skin colour is not a particularly good way to differentiate between people!). Sickle-cell disease is an autosomal recessive blood disorder (a genetically inherited condition that occurs when someone has two copies of the recessive gene; having only one would make the person a carrier) that alters the shape of the blood cells from a normal flexible doughnut-like shape to a rigid sickle one. Sickle-cell disease causes a number of symptoms but principally results in obstructed blood flow leading to organ damage. If someone has two copies of the sickle-cell recessive gene, then without medical treatment they have a severely reduced life expectancy. However, if a person has one copy only of the recessive sickle-cell gene, then they have a high degree of naturally occurring protection against malaria (because *Plasmodium falciparum*, the parasite that causes malaria in humans, cannot infect the sickle-shaped blood cells). The global distribution of sickle-cell disease is almost identical to that of the historical distribution of the species of mosquito that carry malaria. Yet once again we can see a crossover with human cultural traits. As humans began to understand the relationship between mosquitoes and malaria, wetlands and marshes were often drained (also providing land for farming) removing the malaria-carrying mosquito's habitat. However, because of this cultural solution, natural selection has not been able to select against the carriers of sickle-cell in the malaria-free areas; and hence the disease is still present. In addition, human cultural adaptations have armed us with a wide range of weapons in the fight against malaria. These range from drugs that have cost millions of pounds to develop through to the humble mosquito net, which costs only a few pounds.

There are other reasons why many diseases that would appear to be disadvantageous from an evolutionary point of view still affect humans. If we take cancer as a generic example, we might ask: Why do humans still get cancer? Or why have the 'cancer genes' not been selected against? The fact is that most cancers do not occur until after humans have reached reproductive age, and in the past would not have occurred before death, since life expectancy was much shorter in the past. For this reason we can actually think of genes that predispose one to cancers as 'selectively neutral' because they do not impact on the ability to reproduce. This is also the reason that we continue to have wisdom teeth and seemingly needless organs like the appendix – to our eyes they may appear pointless because we have modern cultural adaptations such as dental products to prolong the life of our teeth – but there is also no pressure for them to be selected against. It is also here that we can clearly see the impact of our cultural development upon our biological evolution. Simply put, we now generally use culture to circumvent the problems that any other organism must use biological adaptation to solve. A good example is the use of antibiotics to treat infection – although a salutary warning must be taken from the increase in antibiotic-resistant bacteria – just as we have come up with a cultural trick to defeat them, they are biologically evolving resistance. After all, evolution is not just something that happens to us!

Approaches from Social Anthropology: Globalization

39	Globalization Today *Thomas Hylland Eriksen*

In the following two extracts from Thomas Hylland Eriksen's book
Globalization: The Key Concepts, *the author outlines the debates
surrounding the concept of globalization in its contemporary forms, as
a multidimensional phenomenon which transcends the older
boundaries of nation-states, communities and cultures – but can also
enable local identities to be reasserted and reinvigorated. He goes on to
analyse in some depth the connections between globalizing processes
and the rise and spread of various kinds of identity politics worldwide.
The term 'glocalization' has been aptly coined to refer to the
reconstitution of the 'local' within the 'global', examples of which we
shall see in some of the extracts to follow. As shown here and in the
examples that follow, the detailed work of anthropologists is making a
distinctive contribution to our understanding of this many-sided
phenomenon.*

Various parts of the world were interconnected, and there was considerable
awareness of this before the recent coinage of the term globalization. Yet,
it can be argued that there is something new to the present world, that is
to say the world which began with the end of the Cold War in 1989-1991,
which goes a long way to explain the meteoric rise of public interest in
globalization and transnational phenomena more generally. Three factors,
roughly coinciding in time, may be mentioned here.

- The end of the Cold War itself entailed a tighter global integration. The
  global two-block system, which had lasted since the 1940s, had made
  it difficult to think of geopolitics, transnational communication and
  international trade in terms not illustrated by the opposition between
  the USA and the Soviet Union and their respective allies. With the
  dissolution of this conflict, the world seemed to have been left with a
  one-bloc system (notwithstanding the continued existence of a few
  states, such as North Korea, which continue to stay largely aloof). The
  world appeared to have become a single marketplace.

- The Internet, which had existed in embryonic form since the late 1960s,
  began to grow exponentially around 1990. Throughout the 1990s,
  media buzzwords were about bandwidths, Web sites, portals, 'the
  new economy' and its business opportunities. The World Wide Web

was introduced in 1992/93, around the same time as many academics and businesspeople grew accustomed to using e-mail for their daily correspondence. Cellphones became ubiquitous in the rich countries and the middle classes of the poorer ones. The impact of this double delocalization – the physical letter replaced by e-mail, the fixed phone line replaced by the wireless mobile – on the everyday life of millions of people has been considerable, but it remains undertheorized.

- Identity politics – nationalist, ethnic, religious, territorial – was at the forefront of the international agenda, both from above (states demanding homogeneity or engaging in ethnic cleansing) and from below (minorities demanding rights or secession). The Salman Rushdie affair, itself an excellent example of the globalization of ideas, began with the issuing of a fatwa by Iran's ayatollah Khomeini following the publication of Rushdie's allegedly blasphemous novel *The Satanic Verses* … It soon became apparent that Rushdie could move freely nowhere in the world since the fatwa had global implications. Only two years later, Yugoslavia dissolved, with ensuing civil wars based on ethnic differences. In the same period, debates about immigration and multiculturalism came to dominate political discourse in several Western countries, while the Hindu nationalists of the BJP [political party] came to power in India.

These three dimensions of globalization – increased trade and transnational economic activity, faster and denser communication networks, increased tensions between (and within) cultural groups due to intensified mutual exposure – do not suggest that the world has been fundamentally transformed after the late 1980s but that the driving forces of both economics, political and cultural dynamics are transnational – and that this is now widely acknowledged … The compression of the world, in all of its forms, brings us closer to each other for better and for worse. The consciousness about these interconnections gives a sense of both opportunities and of vulnerability. This dual character of globalization – increased interconnectedness and increased awareness of it – can be studied from a myriad of empirical vantage points … The impact of globalization on tribal peoples in Melanesia has … long been a subject in anthropology. Human geographers write about the displacement of people in India as a result of globally driven economic deregulation. Many write about migration, again from a variety of perspectives. Others are concerned with the distribution of economic power in the global economy, or the distribution of symbolic or definitional power in the global media world; some write about standardization of goods and services as an outcome of the globalization of the economy, others about the spread of certain consumer preferences, yet others about the global tourist industry; while others again study international law, human rights as a consequence of globalization or the 'anti-globalization movement' – just to mention a few subject areas. As far as academic disciplines are concerned, globalization is a central topic in sociology, political science, geography, anthropology, media studies, education, law, cultural studies and so on ...

What Globalization Is Not

Before outlining some central analytical dimensions of globalization, it may be a good idea to mention a few things often associated with globalization, either simplistically or wrongly.

- *Globalization is really recent, and began only in the 1980s* ... [T]his view betrays the beholder's poor knowledge of history. World systems have existed earlier, in the sense that people all over the world have participated, often involuntarily, in political and economic systems of a huge, often intercontinental scale. The European colonial era is the most obvious instance but one might argue that the Roman Empire, encompassing as it did most of the known world (for Europeans), or the Aztec Empire, shared many of the characteristics of today's globalization ... However, the inhabitants of such 'world systems' were rarely aware of each other beyond their own experience, and as a form of consciousness, globalization is new as a mass phenomenon. The labour market situation in Oslo has been known to thousands of Pakistani villagers for decades, and the reggae fashion in Melanesia, advertising in Central Africa and the rhetoric of the political opposition in Taiwan all indicate the existence of a global *discourse*, a shared (but not uniform) communicational system. In this cultural sense, globalization is recent, and the number of people who are unaware of the existence of television, chewing-gum and basic human rights is decreasing every year.

- *Globalisation is just a new word for economic imperialism or cultural Westernization.* This view reduces the vast range of transnational processes to certain economic ones. Although it is tautologically true that rich countries are dominant, the situation is not static. China, India, South Korea and other formerly poor countries are emerging as equal players and regional powers such as South Africa and Brazil are both exploited and exploiters in the global economy. However, the main problem with this view is its neglect of the non-economic dimensions of globalization. The direction of transnational flows is not unilateral: some things flow from north to south, others from south to north, and there is also considerable movement between east and west and within the south. Westernization is not a good synonym for globalization.

- *Globalization means homogenization.* This view is simplistic and usually misleading. First, the participation in global, or transnational, processes often entails a vitalization of local cultural expressions, be it African art, Caribbean popular music or Indian novels, which depend on an overseas market for their survival. Second, large segments of our everyday lives are hardly touched by globalization. Although Taiwanese, like people from the North Atlantic, wear jeans and use iPods while eating burgers and drinking cokes, they do not thereby become Europeans or Americans. However ... it is true that similarities between discrete societies develop as an integral dimension of globalization.

- *Globalization is opposed to human rights.* On the contrary, the global spread of human rights is one of the most spectacularly successful forms of globalization experienced in the world. It is true, of course, that transnational companies operating in poor countries do not necessarily respect workers' rights, but it is only thanks to the globalization of political ideas that local communities and organizations can argue effectively against them and canvas for support from transnational NGOs and governments overseas.

- *Globalization is a threat to local identities.* At the very best this is a truth with serious modifications. As tendencies towards globalization (understood as the dissolution of boundaries) usually lead to strong, localizing counter-reactions favouring local food, local customs and so on, some theorists have followed ... [a recent author's] lead in talking about *glocalization* as a more accurate term for what is going on. Local identities are usually strengthened by globalization because people begin to emphasize their uniqueness overtly only when it appears to be threatened. On the other hand, it is evidently true that local *power* is often weakened as a result of globalization. It nonetheless remains indisputable that globalization does not create 'global persons'.

Globalizers and Sceptics

Not everybody who writes about the contemporary world agrees that it has entered a distinctively 'global' era. Some, in fact, argue that the extent of global integration was just as comprehensive, and in some ways more encompassing, in the *belle epoque* of 1890 to 1914 than it is today. Others claim that the nation-state remains, even today, 'the pre-eminent power container of our era' ... Yet others point out that a large number of people, and huge swathes of social and cultural life, are relatively untouched by transnational processes. It may be useful ... to distinguish between globalizers and sceptics, to highlight some of the debates and the positions taken by different scholars.

According to the sceptics ... we are witnessing a process of internationalization and regionalization rather than the emergence of one integrated world of rapid communication, transnational networks and global financial capital, which is the view of globalizers. Sceptics argue, further, that the nation-state remains the most important political entity, while globalizers claim that state sovereignty is on the wane, and that multilateralism and transnational politics are replacing it. Whereas sceptics have identified the development of regional economic blocs like NAFTA and the EU, globalizers see the world economy as 'a single playing-field' ... with diminishing obstacles to truly global competition. Sceptics see a continuation of the classic North–South divide in terms of prosperity and power, whereas globalizers may argue that inequalities are chiefly growing *within* and not between societies. Sceptics believe in the continued or indeed increasing power of national identities and cultures, but globalizers describe hybridities and cosmopolitan orientations as an outcome of intensified interaction.

The sceptics do not deny that changes are taking place but they emphasize continuities with the modern world of the nation-state, whereas globalizers are concerned to show that the world is going through a series of qualitative changes.

There is no reason to take an unequivocal position here. Few of us are simply globalizers or sceptics; and both positions can often shed light on the issues.

For example, the extent of global solidarity in environmental and human rights questions is no doubt enhanced by extensive travel and global communication and media, and this lends credibility to the view that cosmopolitanism and cultural hybridity (mixing) results from increased interconnectedness. Yet at the same time, identity politics based on religion, ethnicity or nationality is also on the rise. Both phenomena co-exist side by side and are possible responses to the opportunity space created by intensified transnational contacts. There can be no 'effects' of say, global capitalism, the Internet or politicized Islam, which are not mediated by human understandings and experiences, and they vary. Most empirical generalizations about globalization are therefore false. At the same time it is possible to delineate a framework for global or transnational processes, objective changes or features of the world to which people everywhere have to relate.

Dimensions of Globalization

Whether we look at global capitalism, trends in consumer tastes, transnational migration and identity politics or online communication, the globalizing processes of the late twentieth and early twenty-first centuries have a few salient characteristics in common ...

- *Disembedding*, including de-localization. Globalization means that distance is becoming irrelevant, relative or at the very least less important. Ideas, songs, books, investment capital, labour and fashions travel faster than ever, and even if they stay put, their location can be less important than it would have been formerly. This aspect of globalization is driven by technological and economic changes but it has cultural and political implications. Disembedding, however, also includes all manners through which social life becomes abstracted from its local spatially fixed context.

- *Acceleration.* The speed of transport and communication has increased throughout the twentieth century, and this acceleration continues. It has been said that there are 'no delays any more' in an era of instantaneous communication over cellphones, Internet servers and television satellites. Although this is surely an exaggeration – delays exist, even if only as unintended consequences – speed is an important feature of globalization. Anything from inexpensive plane tickets to cheap calls contributes to integrating the world, and the exponential growth in the numbers of Internet users since 1990 indicates that distance no longer means separation.

- *Standardization.* Continuing the processes of standardization begun by nationalism and national economies, globalization entails comparability and shared standards where there were formerly none. The rapid increase in the use of English as a foreign language is suggestive of this development, as is the worldwide spread of, for instance, similar hotels and shopping centres, as well as the growing web of international agreements.

- *Interconnectedness.* The networks connecting people across continents are becoming denser, faster and wider every year. Mutual dependence and transnational connections lead to a need for more international agreements and a refashioning of foreign policies, and create both fields of opportunities, constraints and forms of oppression.

- *Movement.* The entire world is on the move, or so it might sometimes seem. Migration, business travel, international conferences and not least tourism have been growing steadily for decades, with various important implications for local communities, politics and economies.

- *Mixing.* Although 'cultural crossroads' where people of different origins met are as ancient as urban life, their number, size and diversity is growing every day. Both frictions and mutual influence result. Additionally, at the level of culture, the instantaneous exchange of messages characteristic of the information era leads to probably more cultural mixing than ever before in human history.

- *Vulnerability.* Globalization entails the weakening, and sometimes obliteration, of boundaries. Flows of anything from money to refugees are intensified in this era. This means that territorial polities have difficulties protecting themselves against unwanted flows. Typical globalized risks include AIDS ... transnational terrorism and climate change. None can effectively be combated by single nation-states, and it has often been pointed out that the planet as a whole lacks efficient political instruments able to deal with and govern the technology and economy-driven processes of globalization.

- *Re-embedding.* A very widespread family of responses to the disembedding tendencies of globalization can be described as re-embedding. In fact, all of the seven key features of globalization mentioned above have their countervailing forces opposing them and positing alternatives. The fragmented, fleeting social world made possible through disembedding processes is counteracted through strong networks of moral commitment, concerns with local power and community integration, national and sub-national identity politics.

Moreover, acceleration is counteracted through social movements promoting slowness in many guises, standardization is counteracted by 'one-of-a-kind' goods and services, transnational interconnectedness through localism and nationalism, movement through quests for stability and continuity, mixing through concerns with cultural purity, vulnerability through attempts at self-determination and relative isolation.

Globalization is not a unidirectional process. It has no end and no intrinsic purpose, and it is neither uncontested, unambiguous nor ubiquitous. If we want the whole picture, it must include both benefactors and victims, both the globalizers and those who are merely globalized, both those who are caught up in the whirlwind of global processes and those who are excluded. Huge, atrocious slums mushrooming all over the poor parts of the world are products of transnational economic processes, but they are generally seen as the debris of the global economy, the people living there cursorily defined as problems, not resources.

...

Globalization can take place, and can be studied, from above or from below. A problematic but necessary distinction, this dichotomy refers to the state, major international organizations and wealthy enterprises on the one hand, and interpersonal relationships on the other hand. I shall argue ... that the interpersonal 'globalization from below' is much more encompassing and more important in shaping the world than often assumed.

A distinction between *objective* and *subjective* globalization, also problematic, must be made initially. Objective globalization means being incorporated into a global, or wide-ranging transnational, system without necessarily being aware of it, whereas subjective globalization amounts to the acknowledgement of such processes taking place (which may or may not be occurring: citizens often blame globalization for changes wrought locally).

Finally ... globalization does not entail the production of *global uniformity* or homogeneity. Rather, it can be seen as a way of organizing *heterogeneity*. ... The local continues to thrive, although it must increasingly be seen as *glocal*, that is, enmeshed in transnational processes.

Research on globalization is sprawling and multidisciplinary ... Yet it may be kept in mind that much of the research about globalization, and indeed much of the public debate in most countries, is concerned with a few central questions.

First, a chiefly academic question: is globalization new or old? I have already commented briefly on this. The answer has to be sphinx-like: it depends on your definition. Sprawling, but well integrated political systems with thriving trade, internal migration, standardized measures and a common 'high culture' have existed in several continents well before the modern era. However, there are so many characteristic features of our present age, even if we limit it to the post-Cold War era, that it merits treatment on its own terms ...

A second question raised in the debates over globalization, academic and nonacademic, concerns the relationship of globalization to neoliberal economics, that is the view that free trade will eventually lead to prosperity everywhere, and that states should encumber the economy as little as possible. Severely criticized ... for not delivering the goods – many countries that have complied with measures imposed by international agencies like the World Bank and the International Monetary Fund have experienced a steep decline in de facto standards of living – neoliberalism is often associated with, indeed sometimes treated as a synonym for, globalization ... Here it must be said that such a usage narrows the concept too much. The global spread of human rights ideas is no less a feature of globalization than the global financial market; the vaccination programmes of the WHO (World Health Organization) are no less global than the lending of the World Bank, and the small-scale lending programmes initiated by 2006 Nobel Peace Laureate Mohammad Yunus and his Bangladeshi Grameen Bank have spread to other countries. And so one could go on. Global governance ... is sometimes posited as an alternative to an anarchic market economy which is in any case imperfect in so far as poor countries rarely obtain full market access in the rich ones. Globalization is form not content; it can be filled with neoliberal market economics, but this is not necessarily happening.

A third, related debate concerns the relationship between globalization and democracy. Many scholars, politicians and commentators are concerned about the loss of political power experienced by nation-states when so much economic power is diverted to the transnational arenas ... Clearly, there are some issues to be tackled here: the institutions of the nation-state arguably lose some of their clout when capital and wealth are disembedded and become transnational. Yet, the spread of democratic ideas, institutions and practices are also part of the global process. In other words, one cannot say that globalization is either favourable or detrimental to democracy; it is necessary to be more specific.

A fourth, important debate deals with the relationship between poor and rich countries – do the poor become poorer and the rich richer as a result of economic globalization? Again, there can be no simple, unequivocal answer. Who benefits in the long (or for that matter short) run from the globalization of economies? The answer is far from clear. Some countries mired in poverty, notably in Africa, are among the least globalized in terms of integration into the world economy. Their exports are modest, and foreign investment is considered risky and therefore is rare. Some rich countries, not least in Western Europe, begin to notice the competition from poorer countries (notably China and Central Eastern Europe) as an unpleasant experience. In other cases, it can be argued that current trade regimes, such as the ones negotiated by the World Trade Organization (WTO), help rich countries to continue exploiting poor ones by buying cheap unprocessed goods from them and selling them expensive industrial products back. This would fit with the dependency theory developed by ... [a number of] Marxist scholars, as well as ... [others]. However this description fits the older neo-colonial trade regime better than the current one, where China is fast making inroads into markets in Asia and Africa with its inexpensive industrial goods and willingness to invest in industrial enterprises ... [T]he poorest countries are not so much exploited as neglected by transnational investors.

A fifth, no less important theme is that of cultural dynamics: Does globalization lead to homogenization or to heterogenization – do we become more similar or more different due to the increased transnational movement and communication? In one sense, we become more similar. Individualism, which we here take to mean the belief that individuals have rights and responsibilities regardless of their place in wider social configurations, is a central feature of global modernity. It is also easy to argue that similarities in consumer preferences among the world's middle classes indicate 'flattening' or homogenization. Yet at the same time local adaptations of universal or nearly universal phenomena show that global modernities always have local expressions, and that the assumed similarities may either conceal real differences in meaning or that they may be superficial with no deep bearing on people's existential condition. Again, the question is phrased too simplistically to have a meaningful yes/no answer.

Related to this problematic is a sixth area of debate, namely that to do with identity politics. Does globalization, by increasingly exposing us to each other's lives, lead to enhanced solidarity, tolerance and sympathy with people elsewhere; or does it rather lead to ferocious counter-reactions in the form of stubborn identity politics – nationalism, religious fundamentalism, racism and so on? This question has, perhaps, a short answer. Globalization does makes it easier for us to understand each other across cultural divides, but it also creates tensions between groups that were formerly isolated from each other, and it creates a need to demarcate uniqueness and sometimes historical rootedness. The more similar we become, the more different from each other we try to be. Strong group identities may serve several purposes economic, political, existential – in a world otherwise full of movement and turmoil. Divisive and exclusionary identity politics are a trueborn child of globalization, but so is transnational solidarity.

Finally, an important question concerns how European (or Western, or North Atlantic) globalization is. The conventional view is that globalization is largely fuelled by the economic, technological and political developments of Western Europe. Those who take the long view may begin with the Renaissance, the Italian city-states, the European conquests of the fifteenth and sixteenth centuries; those who write about the present may emphasize transnational corporations, computer technology and the dynamics of capitalism. However, other perspectives may be useful and indeed necessary. If we look at history, the powerhouses of transnational economies have been located in many places ... Only with the last period of European colonialization in the nineteenth century did that continent become truly dominant in the world economy ... Non-Eurocentric histories of the world ... tend to emphasize important interconnections in the past outside Europe. If a Martian were to visit the Earth in the year 1300 ... he would not be able to predict the rise of Europe as the centre of global power. There were thriving civilizations in Mesoamerica, in the Andes, in West Africa, in the Arab world, in India and in China, easily surpassing stagnant European societies in transnational trade, cultural achievements and political might.

If we restrict ourselves to the present, the picture is also less straightforward than a superficial look might suggest. In popular culture as well as literature, major achievements of global significance come from outside the West; Indian films ('Bollywood movies') are popular in many countries, as are Mexican and Brazilian soap operas, Argentine tango and Japanese 'manga' comics. Major alternatives to Western ideologies, such as political Islam, are expanding, and China and India, which combined have 40 per cent of the world's population, have economic growth rates far surpassing those of Western countries. The division of the world into core, periphery and semi-periphery is thus a model that needs to be tested and which does not always yield the expected results.

...

[T]he main characteristics of globalization [are]: It *standardizes*, *modernizes*, *deterritorializes* and, by dialectical negation, *localizes* people, because it is only after having been 'globalized' that people may become obsessed with the uniqueness of their locality. I emphasize that although globalization is driven by powerful economic and technological forces, it takes place between people, the transnational webs of the world depend on interpersonal trust, and people often use the opportunities offered by globalizing processes in unexpected ways.

Globalization creates a shared grammar for talking about differences and inequalities. Humans everywhere are increasingly entering the same playing field, yet they do not participate in equal ways, and thus frictions and conflicts are an integral part of globalizing processes.

...

The indigenization of modernity

[I]n an important sense, the human world is presently more tightly integrated than at any earlier point in history. In the age of the jet plane and satellite dish, the age of global capitalism, the age of ubiquitous markets and transnational mediascapes, it is time and again claimed that the world is rapidly becoming a single place. Yet, a perhaps even more striking development of the post-Cold War world is the emergence – seemingly everywhere – of identity politics whose explicit aim is the restoration of rooted tradition, religious fervour or commitment to ethnic or national identities, majoritarian and minoritarian.

... [G]lobalization is always *glocal* in the sense that human lives take place in particular locations – even if they are transnational, on the move, dislocated. Anthropologists have written about the *indigenization of modernity* ... showing how modern artefacts and practices are incorporated into pre-existing worlds of meaning, modifying them somewhat, but not homogenizing them. Many of the dimensions of modernity seen as uniform worldwide, such as bureaucracies, markets, computer networks and human-rights discourses, always take on a distinctly local character, not to mention consumption: a trip to McDonald's triggers an entirely different set of cultural connotations in Amsterdam from what it does in Chicago, not to mention Beijing.

...

Globalization is dual and operates, one might say, through dialectical negation: It *shrinks* the world by facilitating fast contact across former boundaries, and it *expands* the world by creating an awareness of difference. It *homogenizes* human lives by imposing a set of common denominators (state organization, labour markets, consumption and so forth), but it also leads to *heterogenization* through the new forms of diversity emerging from the intensified contact. Globalization is *centripetal* in that it connects people worldwide; and it is *centrifugal* in that it inspires a heightened awareness of, and indeed (re)constructions of local uniqueness. It centralizes power and prompts movements, among indigenous peoples, small nations and others, fighting for local autonomy and self-determination. Finally, globalization makes a universalist *cosmopolitanism* possible in political thought and action because it reminds us that we are all in the same boat and have to live together in spite of our mutual differences; but it also encourages *fundamentalism* and various forms of missionary universalism as well as parochial localism, because global integration leads to a sense of alienation threatening identities and notions of political sovereignty.

Third ways or third alternatives are often created through the working out of these tensions. This is, among other things, where the term *glocalization* comes into its own.

An important insight from recent studies of modernities is the fact that modernization and increasing scale in social organization are marked by a complex process of simultaneous homogenization and differentiation. Some differences vanish, whereas others emerge ...

Phrased more generally, *disembedding* is always countered by *re-embedding*. The more abstract the power, the sources of personal identity, the media flows and the commodities available in the market become, the greater will the perceived need be to strengthen and sometimes recreate (or even invent) local foundations for political action and personal identity, locally produced books and songs, products with the smell, the sound, the taste of home. We cannot generalize bluntly about this; many people are perfectly happy to live in a disembedded world, and hundreds of millions are so poor, disenfranchised and marginalized that the problem never occurs to them – or if it does, it appears as a dream of slick affluence. Yet, re-embedding processes are sufficiently comprehensive, varied and influential to justify their place at the end of this, admittedly convoluted and selective, journey through some of the main dimensions of globalization.

While, as a student in the mid 1980s, I was planning my first fieldwork in Mauritius, recognizing the ethnic plurality of its population and the mixed composition of settlements, I imagined Mauritians to have a profoundly reflexive, negotiable and ambivalent attitude to cultural practices and ethnic identity. Being confronted with a bewildering array of options, epitomized in the everyday lives of their neighbours, I expected them to treat group identification with ironic distance. This did not turn out to be the case. In fact, the majority of Mauritians took their own notions and conventions for granted, more or less ignoring what their neighbours were up to. Moreover, the social universe inhabited by most Mauritians was much simpler than an assessment of the actual ethnic diversity of the island would lead one to expect. Categories were lumped and taxonomies were simplified, and group identification was usually taken for granted. This reminds us of the trivial, but often forgotten fact that cosmopolitan societies do not necessarily create cosmopolitans; that globalization does not create global people ...

In other words, millions of people are transnational in the sense that they maintain important ties of obligations across vast distances. Upon close examination of these transnational ties, it often turns out that they resemble the old ties in the sense that they build on similar commonalities and obligations.

Identity Politics as a Response to Globalization

Recent years have witnessed the growth, in societies in all continents, of political movements seeking to strengthen the collective sense of uniqueness, often targeting globalization processes, which are seen as a threat to local distinctiveness and self determination. A European example with tragic consequences is the rise of ethnic nationalism in Croatia and Serbia from the 1980s, but even in the more prosperous and stable European Union, strong ethnic and nationalist movements grew during the 1990s and into the new millennium, ranging from Scottish separatism to the anti-immigration

Front National in France and nationalist populism in countries like Austria, Denmark and the Netherlands. In Asia, two of the most powerful examples from recent history were the rise of the Taliban to power in Afghanistan and the meteoric success of the Hindu nationalist BJP in India; and many African countries have also seen a strong ethnification of their politics during the last decade-and-a half, as well as the rise of political Islam in the Sahel and the north. In the Americas, various minority movements, from indigenous groups to African Americans, have with increasing success demanded cultural recognition and equal rights. In sum, politics around the turn of the millennium has to a great extent meant identity politics.

This new political scene, difficult to fit into the old Left–Right divide, is interpreted in very different ways by the many academics and journalists who have studied them. This is partly because identity politics comes in many flavours: some are separatist nationalist movements; some represent historically oppressed minorities which demand equal rights; some are dominant groups trying to prevent minorities from gaining access to national resources; some are religious, some are ethnic, and some are regional. At the very least, identity politics from above must be distinguished from identity politics from below.

Many writers see identity politics in general as an anti-modern counter-reaction to the individualism and freedom enhanced by globalization, while others see it as the defence of the weak against foreign dominance, or even as a strategy of modernization using the language of tradition to garner popular support. Some emphasize the psychological dimension of identity politics, seeing it as nostalgic attempts to retain dignity and a sense of rootedness in an era of rapid change; others focus on competition for scarce resources between groups; some see identity politics as a strategy of exclusion and an ideology of hatred, whereas yet others see it as the trueborn child of socialism, as an expression of the collective strivings of the underdog.

None of these interpretations and judgements tells the whole story, both because the concrete movements in question differ and because the phenomenon of identity politics is too complex for a simple explanation to suffice. What is clear, however, is that the centripetal or unifying forces of globalization and centrifugal or fragmenting forces of identity politics are two sides of the same coin, two complementary tendencies that must be understood well by anyone wishing to make sense of the global scene at the turn of the millennium.

For a variety of reasons, globalization creates the conditions for *localization*, it is various kinds of attempts at creating bounded entities – countries (nationalism or separatism), faith systems (religious revitalization), cultures (linguistic or cultural movements) or interest groups (ethnicity). For this reason, a more apt term is *glocalization*. Let us now move to a general description of some features that the 'global' identity movements of the turn of the millennium seem to have in common – rudiments of a grammar of identity politics.

First, identity politics always entails *competition over scarce resources.* Successful mobilization on the basis of collective identities presupposes a widespread belief that resources are unequally distributed along group lines. 'Resources' should be interpreted in the widest sense possible and could in principle be taken to mean economic wealth or political power, recognition or symbolic power. What is at stake can be economic or political resources but the *recognition of others* has been an underestimated, scarce resource, as well as meaningful social attachments where one is in command of one's own life to an acceptable degree.

Secondly, *modernization and globalization actualize differences and trigger comparisons.* When formerly discrete groups are integrated into shared economic and political systems, inequalities are made visible because direct comparison between the groups becomes possible. Friction occurs frequently. In a certain sense, ethnicity can be described as the process of making cultural differences comparable, and to an extent, it is a modern phenomenon boosted by the intensified contact entailed by globalization. You do not envy your neighbour if you are unaware of his existence.

Thirdly, *similarity overrules equality ideologically.* Ethnic nationalism, political beliefs, religion and indigenous movements all depict the in-group as homogenous people 'of the same kind'. Internal differences are glossed over and, for this reason it can often be argued that identity politics serves the interests of the privileged segments of the group, even if the group as a whole is underprivileged, because it conceals internal class differences.

Fourthly, *images of past suffering and injustice are invoked.* To mention a few examples: In the 1990s, Serbs bemoaned the defeat at the hands of the Turkish in Kosovo in 1389; leaders of the Hindu BJP have taken great pains to depict Mungal (Muslim) rule in India from the 1500s as bloody and authoritarian; and the African American movement draws extensively on the history of slavery. Even spokesmen for clearly privileged groups, such as anti-immigrant politicians in western Europe, may argue along these lines.

Fifthly, *the political symbolism and rhetoric evokes personal experiences.* This is perhaps the most important ideological feature of identity politics in general. Using myths, cultural symbols and kinship terminology in addressing their supporters, promoters of identity politics try to downplay the difference between personal experiences and group history. In this way, it became perfectly sensible for a Serb, in the 1990s, to talk about the legendary battle of Kosovo in the first person ('we lost in 1389'). The logic of revenge is extended to include metaphorical kin, in many cases millions of people. The intimate experiences associated with locality and family are thereby projected onto a national screen.

Sixthly, *first-comers are contrasted with invaders.* Although this ideological feature is by no means universal in identity politics, it tends to be invoked whenever possible and, in the process, historical facts are frequently stretched.

Finally, *the actual social complexity in society is reduced to a set of simple contrasts*. As Adolf Hitler already wrote in *Mein Kampf*, the truly national leader concentrates the attention of his people on one enemy at the time. Since cross-cutting ties reduce the chances of violent conflict, the collective identity must be based on relatively unambiguous criteria (such as place, religion, mother tongue, kinship). Again, internal differences are undercommunicated in the act of delineating boundaries towards the frequently demonized Other.

Identity politics is a trueborn child of globalization. The more similar we become, the more different we try to be. Paradoxically, however, the more different we try to be, the more similar we become – since most of us try to be different in roughly the same ways worldwide.

Against the view that identity politics is somehow anachronistic, it has been argued many times, always correctly, that although it tends to be dressed in traditional garb, beneath the surface it is a product of modernity and its associated dilemmas of identity. The strong emotions associated with a tradition, a culture or a religion can never be mobilized unless people feel that it is under siege.

Viewed in this way, the collective emotions that identity politics depend on reveal themselves to be deeply modern emotions associated with the sense of loss experienced in situations of rapid change, disembedding and deterritorialization. The need for security, belonging and enduring social ties based on trust is universal and cannot be wished away. Ethnic nationalism, minority movements and politicized religion offer a larger share of the cake as well as a positive sense of self, and these movements are bound to remain influential in large parts of the world.

The Case of Indigenous Peoples
Indigenous peoples are usually defined as ethnic groups associated with a nonindustrial mode of production and a stateless political organization ... The identity politics engaged in by such groups differ from that of nations and migrant minorities in that territorial autonomy and cultural self-determination are their main political goals. Engulfed by dominant states and increasingly incorporated into the global economy, indigenous groups fight legal battles on many fronts, claiming rights to land and water, language, their own artistic production and political autonomy.

The forms of resistance engaged in by indigenous movements are diverse, ranging from institutional politics among the Sami of northern Scandinavia, who have separate parliaments with limited power, to the armed uprising among Maya peasants of Chiapas in southern Mexico, and less spectacular forms of everyday resistance. However ... indigenous struggles against globalized external dominance tend to differ from class-based struggles through their emphasis on local community, identity politics, land claims, and rights to a variety of traditional practices, which include alternative family organizations such as matrilineality and/or polygyny, communal ownership of resources such as land, the use of land for sacred ceremonies, and indigenous knowledge, that occasionally includes use of psychoactive substances ...

Although indigenous groups may occasionally profit economically from global integration, their identity depends on a certain degree of political autonomy ... [W]e may say that states have traditionally subdued indigenous groups through genocide (extermination), ethnocide (their enforced assimilation into the majority) or culturicide (the destruction of group culture, if not necessarily group identity). In defending their group identity as well as the cultural content of this identity, indigenous groups run into a broad range of problems; some of them to do with human rights, national law and the universal rights and obligations of citizenship; some simply to do with the brute force of the state and capitalism – indigenous peoples usually reject private property in favour of the communal ownership or stewardship of resources. A final set of problems pertain to the character and nature of 'indigenous culture', which is, like all other culture, influenced and transformed by reflexive modernity. What exactly does it mean to be a Lakota, a San and an Inuit? Such issues are discussed vividly among scholars and indigenous peoples alike, but it must still be stressed that their main struggle is over land rights with accompanying political autonomy. Paradoxically, perhaps many indigenous peoples have been assisted in their quest for self-determination by transnational agencies and even global organizations such as the World Council of Indigenous Peoples (WCIP), levelling pressure on nation-states from a transnational or supranational point of leverage.

Re-embedding in Diasporas

National and other modern identities founded in traditionalist ideologies (they claim, persuasively, to be pre-modern) have proved to be extremely resilient. The enthusiasm for the proposed European Constitution in the EU member states is very modest, and the Constitution has failed to get a majority in any of the countries that have held referendums. Identification with national football teams in Europe and South America remains very strong, ethnic networks giving career opportunities for members of the in-group in polyethnic societies are thriving in many parts of the world, religions demanding the undiluted loyalty of their followers are on the rise, and everywhere, most people seem to prefer to watch locally produced programmes on TV.

The human need for secure belonging in a community, however abstract (such as a nation or a religion of conversion), seems to be an anthropological constant, but it can be satisfied in many different ways and dealt with politically in different ways, too. Commitment to a group, which forms part of a larger, plural social universe, does not necessarily lead to xenophobia and conflict; it may equally well result in cosmopolitan tolerance ...

Creating a sense of security in an environment that changes rapidly can be hard work and it seems particularly difficult for transnational migrants and their descendants, who are confronted with opposing pressures from their immediate surroundings. The states in which they live may demand their full and undivided loyalty, or they may do quite the opposite and deny them citizenship and political rights. Both alternatives create stress and ambiguity among migrants. The classic modern notion of citizenship as the sole key to political identity is difficult to maintain at a time when dual loyalties, exile and movement are widespread.

Solutions to dilemmas of identity and belonging among uprooted people vary. Some seek to be assimilated in the new country and effectively to change their group identity. This has to a great extent happened over the last 150 years with Poles in Germany and Swedes in Norway, but not with Irish in Britain. With transnational migrants who may have a different skin colour and religion from the majority, full assimilation does not seem to take place anywhere, although New World countries like the US and Canada have a more open-ended national identity than most Old World countries, from Ireland to Japan. As a rule, migrants and their children remain attached to their country of origin. The tie tends to be weakened in the second generation, whose members have more invested in the new country than their parents, but what happens in the third generation depends to a great extent on the ability of the host country to expand its national identity to encompass the descendants of relatively recent migrants.

Whether or not full assimilation is possible, most migrants and their children retain important transnational ties … and draw extensively on ethnic or religious networks in the new country. Far from being the fragmented and alienated people one might expect migrants to be, given their ambiguous political and cultural position, they tend, broadly, to reproduce important aspects of their original culture in the new setting. This is often met with animosity in sections of the majority population, who may insist that the newcomers do their best to 'adapt' to the host society; but at the same time, this option is often closed to immigrants who face discrimination and differential treatment from the majority. A connection to a homeland, be it the tiny Caribbean island of Nevis … or a future independent Kurdistan, gives a sense of attachment that can otherwise be difficult to develop in alien surroundings.

The cultural conservatism often witnessed in migrant populations, not least among Muslims in Europe, is understandable as a reaction to hostility and indifference in the majority population. Moreover … the authority of the state has become increasingly problematic not only with respect to immigrants but in general, because of increased 'turbulence' and uncertainty – what we might call effects of globalization …

…

Disembedding, acceleration, standardization, interconnectedness, movement, mixing: it is easy to conjure up a vision of the world as being in constant flux. I have argued against simplistic version of this view, and even if one is fascinated by the idea of a world in continuous movement, one has to keep in mind that different social and cultural fields are moving at different speeds and at varying length.

Truly global processes affect the conditions of people living in particular localities, creating new opportunities and new forms of vulnerability. Risks are globally shared in the era of the nuclear bomb, transnational terrorism and potential ecological disasters. On the same note, the economic conditions in particular localities frequently (some would say always) depend on events taking place elsewhere in the global system. If there is an industrial boom in Taiwan, towns in the English Midlands will be affected. If oil prices rise, that means salvation for the oil-exporting Trinidadian economy and disaster for the oil-importing, neighbouring Barbadian one.

Patterns of consumption also seem to merge in certain respects; people nearly everywhere desire similar goods, from cellphones to readymade garments. Now, a precondition for this to happen is the more or less successful implementation of certain institutional dimensions of modernity, notably that of a monetary economy – if not necessarily evenly distributed wage-work and literacy. The ever-increasing transnational flow of commodities, be they material or immaterial, creates a set of common cultural denominators that appear to eradicate local distinctions. The hot dog (*halal* or not, as the case may be), the pizza and the hamburger (or, in India, the lamburger) are truly parts of world cuisine; identical pop songs are played in identical discotheques in Costa Rica and Thailand; the same Coca-Cola commercials are shown with minimal local variations at cinemas all over the world, Harry Potter volumes are ubiquitous wherever books are sold, and so on. Investment capital, military power and world literature are being disembedded from the constraints of space; they no longer belong to a particular locality. With the development of the jet plane, the satellite dish and more recently, the Internet, distance no longer seems a limiting factor for the flow of influence, investments and cultural meaning.

Yet, disembedding is never total, and it is always counteracted by re-embedding attempts. Sometimes, re-embedding does not even seem to be required – if one cares to look, the social world in which most of humanity lives remains embedded in important respects, notwithstanding decades of intensive, technology-driven globalization. The impact of globalization – or, rather, its significance for the lives we lead – is considerable but every one-sided account is ultimately false.

...

One consequence of globalization has been the rise or rekindling of various forms of identity politics ... [It has been argued that] al-Qaeda is just as typical a product of globalization as the World Trade Organization ...

Transnational capitalism can bring both wealth and poverty. Millions of people – indeed hundreds of millions – never have access to the wealth because they are simply ignored and squeezed in increasingly marginal areas, like hunter-gatherers encountering armed, well organized, agriculturalists in an earlier period. The suffering of slum dwellers, dispossessed peasants, unemployed men and women in cities, victims of war and of economic exploitation, and their occasionally well orchestrated rebellions or alternative projects seeking autonomy from globalized capitalism, are the trueborn children of globalization, just as the cellphone and the Internet, the proliferation of international NGOs, the cheap tropical holiday and the growth of transnational football fans are results of globalization. The ambiguities and paradoxes of globalization are not going away.

Edited extract from: T.H. Eriksen, *Globalization: The Key Concepts* (Oxford: Berg, 2007), pp.3–14 and 141–53.

40 Looking 'The Gift' in the Mouth
Patty Gray

A number of anthropologists have sought to apply the classic insights of Marcel Mauss's study of the gift (originally published in 1923) and his successors to gift giving on a global (and globalised) scale, notably international aid and development. Anthropologists have looked at the workings of international institutions (such as donor agencies), and also at the local impacts of aid and development programmes 'on the ground'. In this extract, anthropologist Patty Gray draws on her own fieldwork experience to analyse the efforts of the Russian state, since the upheavals following democratisation, to transform itself from a 'receiver' to a 'donor' of development aid. The Russian experience, she suggests, provides an instructive commentary on some of the cultural assumptions taken for granted within more long-established aid agencies.

The Soviet Union in its time was a major player in international development aid, and indeed, the Cold War may be cast as a competition between differing models of development, one capitalist, one socialist. When the Soviet Union was dissolved in 1991, the tables were turned and Russia, once the core of a Soviet empire, was made subject to development initiatives just as was the developing world, aka the 'global South'. However, in this case, the 'global North' shifted to assume the identity of 'the West', and a new terminology of 'transitioning economy' was contrived in order to avoid the awkwardness of referring to Russia and other Eastern European countries as 'developing economies' ... The net effect of being so targeted was the same nevertheless, and Russians themselves knew it – it was not uncommon in the 1990s to hear Russians remark ironically, 'We are not starving Africans!'

A New Concept

Throughout the 1990s and into the 2000s, Russia was obliged to play the role of quintessential eastern recipient of Western aid. But in 2007, Russia officially signalled its intention to reverse the directionality of aid once again by issuing, via the Ministry of Finance, a 'Concept on Russia's Participation in International Development Assistance' ... and thereafter began to participate actively in the global arena of international aid donorship. According to the OECD's Development Assistance Committee ... Russia spent approximately $200 million on official development assistance in 2008 ... According to the Financial Tracking Service, Russia's expenditures on humanitarian aid in 2010 totalled more than $34 million, about a third of which went to Haiti in response to the January 2010 earthquake ...

...

I'm working with a fairly simple argument here, namely that persistent assumptions about the directionality of aid flows are reflected in development discourse and practice, with the 'global North' privileged as a consummate donor and the 'global South' inversely cast as a consummate recipient. The failure to break away from unsatisfactory shorthand labels such as 'global North' and 'global South' and 'the West' and 'the Third World' is symptomatic of these persistent assumptions, as is the fact that South–South and East–East partnerships are treated as titillating novelties (ominous or valorous, depending on one's orientation). I am further arguing that these assumptions about North–South directionality are more fully exposed by Russia's emergence as a donor of aid (which could also be said about India's or China's emergence). Finally, and perhaps most importantly, those assumptions are both challenged and affirmed by Russia's participation in international development assistance. I will come back to this point presently.

Along with the master narrative of North–South aid flows, there are also the assumptions about West–East aid flows that came into play with the changes after 1989, but this is a secondary dyad in development circles (and indeed it seems unlikely that the phrases 'hemispheric West' and 'hemispheric East' will ever catch on). A subsidiary argument here is that development discourse is compartmentalized: one the one hand, there is the discourse about the North developing the South, but on the other hand and separate from this, there is the discourse about the West developing the East. This is a contrived separation that is not helpful – the historical configuration of each is different, but the issues are essentially the same. I am seeking ways to bring these extremely artificial constructions together into one discursive universe, to force them into dialogue with one another, because I think this will reveal some significant patterns that are otherwise not as readily apparent.

The Relevance of 'The Gift'

One conceptual lens through which some insight might be gained is that of Mauss's understanding of the gift (Mauss 2002). Mauss played with the idea that a gift implies obligations and opens up a social relation, noting that if the obligations are not properly observed, then the social relation becomes distorted – and one of the examples he cited was 'almsgiving', or charity. As … [a recent author] has suggested … development aid 'is in fact charity by another name', and mere avoidance of the word 'charity' does not mean the demeaning relationship inherent in one-way flows of development aid is avoided … In the words of Mauss, 'Charity is still wounding for him who has accepted it, and the whole tendency of our morality is to strive to do away with the unconscious and injurious patronage of the rich almsgiver' (Mauss 2002: 83).

Anthropologists have tended to limit their deployment of gift theory to analysis of small-scale societies and face-to-face social contexts, less often applying it to the analysis of charity on a larger scale, such as in the work of international NGOs, or in international development aid … However, gift theory is being picked up by development theorists outside anthropology in disciplines such as international relations … and geography … as a useful tool for unpacking the relations inherent in international development aid. One reason it is so useful in this context is because the 'charitable impulse', that something which makes people want to 'do good' by giving, also compels corporate entities such as NGOs and government aid agencies to couch their actions within the language of such altruistic giving (regardless of how underlying motives might be more cynically understood).

It could be argued that charity – or development aid – becomes wounding precisely in those circumstances when it is framed as a free gift with no return expected (possibly implying the recipient is incapable of return), rather than as a Maussian gift that would imply ongoing mutual obligations. Moreover, there is often a mismatch of expectations between givers and receivers, differing assumptions about the nature of the gift that are mixed up in a single social arena involving many givers, receivers and onlookers (for example, a governmental aid donor, a governmental aid recipient, and the citizens of both countries who observe the flow of aid and are positioned differently in relation to it). Harkening to Mauss's admonition that 'charity is … wounding', could we then see the Russian government's efforts to join the global community of donors at least partly as a defence mechanism against the demeaning experience of being treated as a perpetual recipient on the world stage, and an effort to be seen as a global player with prestige and influence? In order not to be categorized alongside Africans or Haitians, must one be seen to give to Africans and Haitians?

Russian 'Citizens of the World'

My own anthropological field research in Russia was carried out at a time (the 1990s) when Russia was in the position of being an aid recipient, and in a location where the need for humanitarian assistance was genuinely quite acute (Chukotka, a region in the Russian Far North …). My most intense and long-term periods of fieldwork happened to place me alongside residents of Russia (of various ethnicities) just as they were experiencing being targeted by both official development assistance and more informal charity from abroad, and in some ways I found myself implicated in the delivery of some of that aid and charity. The ambivalence of that positionality – both mine and that of my interlocutors – was deeply impressed upon me.

These experiences also impressed upon me the importance of recognizing development aid as a cultural phenomenon, even though it is persistently couched in economic and political terms. The potential for aid to be used as a strategic foreign-policy tool is clear, but to reduce Russia's moves toward donorship to the simple formulae of realist international-relations theory is to miss the point. The challenge is to examine the cultural assumptions that underlie Russia's actions – as well as the cultural assumptions that underlie the international response to Russia's posturing as an aid donor and distinctly not a recipient. Thus, while it is useful to think through the macro-level relations, it is equally if not more important to consider the micro level of Russians' own experiential accounts. How might Russians approach development aid differently from the entrenched 'development apparatus', by which I mean, for example, the G8, the World Bank and its IDA (International Development Association), the OECD and its DAC (Development Assistance Committee), and the countries that acknowledge the authority of such global agencies? This apparatus has been constructed from within the Euro-American context as the only acceptable way to go about development (both the doing of it and the accounting for it), as if development were a common-sense and culture-free category. However, I would argue that it is a category heavily laden with shared cultural assumptions – assumptions not of the culture of any country or region or people, but of a bureaucratic culture of an imagined 'West', perhaps something of a transnational imagined community …

What is shared here in this 'development community' are the bureaucratic practices of development, which I am arguing are cultural practices – techniques for accountability, the way projects are planned and funded, the faith in 'capacity building' to reproduce accountable subjects, the emphasis on 'deliverables' and 'reportables' … These have been naturalized to the extent that participants in this culture proceed as if utterly convinced there is no other possible way of doing development (even as they are constantly discussing what has been wrong with development in the past and exhibit a fervent belief that they are in the continual process of reforming and improving development practices).

Certain countries are placed in a separate category – 'new' donors as opposed to 'traditional' donors – not primarily because they are new on the scene (usually they are not), but because they do not (yet) share the culture of this imagined transnational community. There are all kinds of ways that this difference is discursively marked, such as in the phrases 'emerging donors', 'non-DAC donors', or 'new partners'. To the extent that donor countries in this other category do things differently, that they introduce new cultural practices of development into the global arena, they are held suspect and cause worry, which is also discursively marked in particular ways, for example, in the phrases 'reverse aid' or 'authoritarian aid'. As one article in the *Economist* put it, the spread of aid from these sorts of suspect donors is a challenge to 'Western ideas of the right sort of giving' ... The main worry articulated is that these donors will not be accountable and will therefore cause damage or harm in some way – or, as one think tank has put it, that they will 'undermine democracy' ...

Thus many observers fail to see Russia's emergence as a donor as a cultural, or even economic, phenomenon, but see it rather as a political phenomenon, and a negative one at that. This is in spite of the fact that, if one observes closely, it becomes apparent that the Russian government – or more properly a subset of actors within the government – is bending over backwards to play by the rules of the 'development club', and working with global agencies to develop the technology and accounting infrastructure to make Russia's aid donations transparent and accountable. For example, in May 2008 the Russian Ministry of Finance held a workshop, along with the World Bank, entitled 'Development Aid Statistics: International Experience and the Creation of a Russian Accounting and Reporting System'. The workshop's sponsors included USAID, the OECD, the United Nations Development Programme (UNDP) and the UK's Department for International Development (DFID) ... A recent Russian textbook on international development institutions – the first of its kind ... – argues forcefully that 'Russia's participation in the OECD and the DAC not only will facilitate raising the prestige and increasing the influence of the country in the international arena, but also will allow to a greater degree its integration into processes of global economics' ...

I have only recently begun to explore Russia's emergence as a donor ethnographically, by spending time with participants in the extremely well-developed and sophisticated (Western hand-wringing notwithstanding) Russian NGO sector, encountering volunteering organizations that are beginning to add an overseas dimension to their helping work. These are people in their 20s and 30s who are just coming of age in terms of their international social and political awareness, the first Russians I have encountered who have described themselves not as Russian patriots, but as 'citizens of the world'. They are socially active, either as contributing members of charity organizations or in having spent time as volunteers abroad, and they provide evidence of a blossoming informal volunteering movement in Russia ...

At the same time, some of the people I have spoken to express a certain incredulity about the idea of Russia as a donor of aid abroad. At first, the phenomenon was almost too new to be studied, and many of the people I encountered were surprised to hear that their government was setting itself up as an international aid donor ... A common response was that there are still problems enough inside Russia that need to be addressed, so why would Russia be thinking about sending aid abroad? There is some discussion of these issues on Russian blogs and social-networking sites, much of it sharply ironic about the ambiguities inherent in Russia taking the role of donor or helper in relation to 'the Third World'.

The Relentless Significance of Africa

As I mentioned above, there are two rather separate conversations going on in development discourse: a primary one dealing with North-to-South vectors of aid, and a more recent and subsidiary one dealing with West-to-East vectors of aid. I am entering these conversations from a different perspective altogether: via Russia's entry into the 'development community' as it steps out of the role of recipient and into the role of donor. And here is where I take a perhaps unexpected detour to Africa, because I would argue that it is by using Africa as a fulcrum that Russia attempts to lever itself out of the West–East axis as a transitioning recipient country and into the North–South axis as an emerging donor country.

In what at first was only a very thin official development discourse coming out of Russia, I was surprised to see the extent to which Africa featured in the Russian government's official press releases, which have appeared in both Russian and international media sources. In spite of the fact that Russia's official overseas development activities are primarily targeted at the Newly Independent States, those in Central Asia in particular, statements of government spokesmen are more likely to make reference to Africa as a key recipient of Russia's international largesse – for example, highlighting Russia's contributions to the Millennium Development Goals, of which Africa is an iconic focus, or boasting of Russia's intention to cancel African debt ... They also mention the presence of African students in Russian higher-education institutions as an example of Russia's aid to the developing world, usually pointing out that this dates from the Soviet period.

Here I will state what I think is obvious, but which bears emphasizing at this point: the signifiers 'North' and 'South' and 'West' and 'East' are category markers, and while the content of these categories remains persistently ambiguous, in usage there is an implication that what is signified is a matter of common sense between all interlocutors. One clear assumption in this usage is that the 'North' is already developed and does not need help, while the 'South' is undeveloped/underdeveloped/developing and needs 'our' help. Of significance here is the question of who controls the deployment of the discourse of development, such that who belongs to each category becomes seemingly obvious, and the jargon and practices (aka 'best practices') of the ruling global agencies come to seem natural and beyond reproach. The logical converse of this naturalization is that those who fail to employ the jargon and practices are reproachable.

It is in this sense that Russia's emergence as a donor both challenges and affirms assumptions about the directionality of development aid: Russia challenges them by entering this arena as neither properly of the North nor properly of the South, and as such it is in a unique position to introduce innovative development discourse and practice. On the other hand, Russia affirms entrenched assumptions by the way it positions itself as a donor to 'the Third World', especially to 'Africa' writ large, and also by its near-wholesale adoption of the accepted jargon and practices – at least in most quarters of what remains a not-fully-formed Russian government aid apparatus. It appears that for all states aspiring to be leaders in the world and wishing to join an elite peer group of donors (and this category of aspirants includes China, which decidedly does not kowtow to accepted jargon and practices), Africa is the arena where they can demonstrate their power and privilege by rendering aid to those presumed to be perpetually powerless and underprivileged. Donors need recipients in order to be donors – in order to get to give – and Africa remains the world's most iconic perpetual recipient.

Conclusion

Through both its domestic and foreign policies and practices, Russia seems to be resisting its recent subject placement in the global political economy, refusing to play the role of non-reciprocating aid recipient, and insisting on being taken as a legitimate player in the aid game. For Russia, it seems, incorporation into the global economy, and the continuation of its own development, necessitate its becoming a donor in the global system of givers and receivers. This takes me back to my emphasis on theories of the gift, and the idea of giving on a global scale: for states that are vying for position in a global arena, it is crucial to openly demonstrate one's global 'goodness' and generosity. If there are ideas about the right sort and the wrong sort of giving, then Russia seems to be setting about earnestly to demonstrate that it rightfully deserves to be one of those who gets to give.

Reference

Mauss, Marcel. *The Gift: The Form and Reason for Exchange in Archaic Societies*, trans. W.D. Halls (London: Routledge, 2002[1923]).

Edited extract from: Patty A. Gray, 'Looking "The Gift" in the Mouth: Russia as Donor', *Anthropology Today* 27/2 (2011) pp.5–8.

<table>
<tr><td>**41**</td><td>**Anthropology, the Environment and Development**
Elisabeth Croll and David Parkin</td></tr>
</table>

In this passage from an article originally published in 1992, the authors consider the relationship between human persons and their environments in the context of global debates about resource depletion, conservation and sustainable economic development. As they argue, a key contribution of anthropology to these debates is the insight that 'the environment' does not constitute a self-contained sphere separate from human activities and beliefs. Rather, the relationship between human communities and their material worlds is typically manifested through a wide range of culturally specific beliefs, practices, moralities and cosmologies. This insight, as we saw earlier in Section I of the Reader, is central to anthropological approaches to societies and environments. Here, the authors argue that 'anthropological perspectives on cultural understanding of the environment' also offer a key contribution to global policies and strategies for resource conservation and sustainable development.

As concepts, the environment and development together presuppose an interest in the management of natural resources. Anthropology adds to this a concern with the ways in which peoples bring their cultural imaginations to bear on the utility of such resources. Here, the relationship between humans and their natural surroundings often appears paradoxical. Humans create and exercise understanding and agency on their world around them, yet operate within a web of perceptions, beliefs and myths which portray persons and their environments as constituted in each other, with neither permanently privileged over the other ...

Whether with regard to questions of immediate subsistence or in the name of development, anthropological approaches suggest that environmental transformations can no longer be seen as problems of human activity in relation to non-human physical surroundings. Instead anthropologists question the conventional oppositions between human and non-human agency, or between person and environment, with the result that persons and their changing environments are regarded as part of each other, and as reciprocally inscribed in cosmological ideas and cultural understanding ...

The anthropological emphasis on people's local knowledge and use of their environments, based often on years of painstaking observation carried out in the people's language, provides a perspective that few other disciplines can match. Ethnographies abound in latticed descriptions and analyses of the management of local resources. The anthropological perspective, however, may not seem at first to be addressing environmental issues at all. These are approached, as it were, from the shadows: through ritual, beliefs in spirits and holy sites, ideas of human birth and regeneration, the common origins of mankind and animals, the consubstantiality of human and plant life, the characterization of 'natural' hazards as the wages of sin or the work of malicious non-human forces, or of rain and fertility as the reward of just behaviour or divine beneficence. Anthropologists, then, are not just concerned with technical or ecological questions, but with the construction of knowledge and the power and pressures behind choices and decisions regarding peoples' cultural and physical environments, and with the ways in which these environments 'speak back' either through people or independently. Currently, the increasing interest in the environment generally and also in the specificity of local environments has created and highlighted the potential contributions of anthropologists to our understanding of environment and development issues.

During the past decade, growing awareness and concern with the natural environment has led to the view that environmental issues, choices and problems are popular, political and academic issues of worldwide import. The United Nations has published several seminal reports and convened a series of international meetings on the environment. The World Bank now has an environmental unit; the media have environmental pages or weeks, and universities new and proposed centres for the study of the environment. Much of this concern has focused on the unprecedented demands on land, water, forest and other natural resources. Particular attention has been directed towards the repercussions for the natural resources and the environment of such activities as: the clearing of bush and forest lands, farming marginal lands, intensifying cultivation or herding in the interests of productivity, the effects of irrigation systems and the construction of reservoirs and the redistribution of populations and creation of new settlements, and pollution and the depletion of firewood and other fuels. Most countries face serious economic pressures, both international and domestic, to over-exploit their environmental resource base, and already this is a source of political unrest and international tension. The dimensions of the problem are now considered so acute that it is fashionable to refer to environmental stress, an environmental crisis or even environmental survival.

...

Agriculture, forestry, energy production and mining generate at least half of the gross national product of many developing countries and the capacities of their natural resources very much underlie the maintenance and growth of these economies. They now face enormous pressure to over-exploit their resource base both for continuing growth and development and for sustenance and survival. However, previous concern centred mainly on the negative repercussions of the process of development for the environment. Now it is increasingly recognised that, in turn, environmental deterioration can undermine economic development. Today there is equal concern about the ways in which environmental degradation can slow, halt or reverse economic development. In many regions investigation and documentation reveals how environmental degradation is eroding the resource base of the potential for further development. Presently, much of development aid aims at replenishing the resource base rather than or as a prerequisite to generating new economic activities. That is, the very process of development itself cannot subsist upon a deteriorating environmental resource base; the environment cannot be protected when development ignores the costs of environment destruction and the necessity of replenishment and enhancement.

These increasingly explicit links between economic development and environmental stress prompted the United Nations General Assembly in 1983 to appoint a World Commission on Environment and Development. Its aim was to re-examine the critical environment and development issues and to propose long-term strategies for achieving sustainable development that takes account of the interrelationships between people, resources, environment and development. The resulting Brundtland Report was important in that it officially acknowledged and expanded on the linkages between development and the environment and provided international legitimacy and popular currency for the term 'sustainability' ...

...

Many of the post-Brundtland Report studies have ... focused on two major, relevant areas frequently omitted in the debates about environment and development. The first is the relevance of the framework of global economic relations for the study and protection of the environment ... Second is the relation between person and environment which rejects the previous ways in which the 'environment' was usually regarded as located outside ourselves, as a space inhabited. It was the bounded quality of the environment which was seen as its defining characteristic. Radical ecologists are among those who have taken a renewed interest in people's relation with nature, and for them the solution lies in rejecting previous codes for reading nature, instead pursuing a more spiritual version of ecology, a kind of pantheism in which moral and practical cues are taken from the environment. Such views do not appear to have gained wide currency, but ... they are potentially elements in a new discourse which is more holistic and incorporates a cross-cultural approach. Examining another culture's concept of the environment and sustainability is a logical consequence of considering development and the environment as an integrated process ... In a social and cultural construction of the environment, it is not only a part of nature but also a part of culture which by implication argues for a recognition of cultural diversity.

If anthropologists ... have long argued that the environment and cosmos are inseparable, they have been much slower to incorporate the phenomenon of development into their analytical frameworks ... It is one thing to describe statically or cyclically the role of myth, rite and belief in the shaping of land use and understanding but quite another to include also the influence of a new epistemology premised on changing society through the role and methods of outside specialists. In the modern world, however, it can be argued that development has joined religion as an ideological force of global significance. It does not just refer to methods and plans about how to get things done, but entails moral prescriptions, various collective enthusiasms, different and competing hierarchies of adherents and an overriding assumption that human betterment is society's primary essence, that for which it exists and by which it justifies itself ... It is not peripheral ... but is intertwined with the many other discourses which pattern the anthropological object.

The concept of sustainable development not only provides a framework for the integration of environmental policies and development strategies, but is also a new opportunity for anthropologists to contribute their skills and insights. The concept also embraces and is premissed on many core assumptions o f anthropological interest and analysis such as order, agency, time, space, classification and the deployment of power and knowledge ... The very notion of sustainability is predicated on perceptions of time, aiming to meet the needs of the present without compromising those of future generations. Moreover, conceptions of such needs are perceived to be socially and culturally determined. In deploying the broadest possible definitions of development, the concept of sustainable development incorporates both the material and non-material into a new and holistic conceptual ordering, simultaneously recognising that there can be no fixed or single order ... [T]here can be no single order or blueprint for sustainable development, given the wide cultural variations in ecological, economic and social perceptions and practices.

Finally, international, national and popular bodies increasingly recognize that the achievement of sustainable development rests on the exercise of political agency or will. The Brundtland Report argued that it is the distribution of power and influence which lies 'at the heart of most environmental and developmental challenges'. Indeed, it reiterated that many problems of resource depletion and environmental stress arise from disparities in economic and political power so that sustainable development is conceived not so much to be about natural resources of the physical environment as about issues of control, power, participation and self-determination. Today, it is not so much that environmental difficulties are new, but that previous conceptions of development tended to simplify ecological systems, reduce the diversity of species and strategies and ignore cultural variations in ecological conditions, perception and concepts. These are only beginning to be understood in their complexity and diversity. At the centre lies the difficult, negotiable and contested relationship between person and environment, and crucially, anthropological perspectives on cultural understandings of the environment.

Edited extract from: Elisabeth Croll and David Parkin, 'Anthropology, the Environment and Development', in E. Croll and D. Parkin (eds), *Bush Base, Forest Farm* (London: Routledge, 1992) pp.3–9.

42   Anthropology at the Bottom of the Pyramid
Jamie Cross and Alice Street

In the extract included above from Eriksen's Globalization: The Key Concepts, *the author drew attention to anthropology's power to illuminate global processes through 'studying up' (the practices of powerful elites and large-scale organisations) and 'studying down' (the impacts of, and responses to, these practices at the local level of face-to-face social relations). The following text, extracted from the work of anthropologists Jamie Cross and Alice Street, is an excellent example of this dual vision. Addressing the multinational corporate business sector in the form of Unilever (manufacturers of Lifebuoy soap and many other products), Cross and Street document the growing interest of multinationals in developing profitable models for marketing goods and services to poor people, alongside a doctrine that such marketing is also a bringer of social benefits. In documenting Unilever's campaigns to promote hand-washing – and use of Lifebuoy soap – among poor communities in India, note that Cross and Street do not take a scientific position on the health benefits of using this particular soap. Instead, they position themselves as would most anthropologists, focusing on the strategy, actors and process; and on the ramifications of these within the target communities. Interestingly, their narrative shows that the effectiveness of such 'top-level' strategies has its limits; for example, where (as in one initiative here) community activist groups become suspicious of the motivations at the 'top of the pyramid' and mount a determined resistance.*

Poverty as Opportunity

Search the online business and development media and you will find countless examples of products in the fields of health, energy, telecommunications and banking that are designed for and marketed explicitly to people who live on less than two dollars a day. The well-being of poor people is proving to be a particularly rich seam for global business and is driving innovation in the design and delivery of products and services. High profile 'for-profit' social initiatives include Phillips' smokeless stoves, Ericsson's rural wireless networks, Vesterguard's water-purification tools, Fujitsu's low-power, low-cost laptops and Danone's vitamin-enriched yoghurt.

The US-based management and marketing guru C.K. Prahalad has done much to champion this phenomenon. The essential premise of his 2006 book *The Fortune at the Bottom of the Pyramid* is that the creation of new markets around the needs and aspirations of the poor can be both an efficient technical solution to problems of poverty and an engine for corporate profit. Bottom-of-the-pyramid initiatives are premised on the role of the market as a delivery mechanism and on the logistical capacities of large enterprises. It is a vision that has received accolades from Bill Gates and Madeleine Albright, and is today championed by the United Nations and the British government as a model for private-sector involvement in international development.

One of the inspirations for Prahalad's book came from the Indian subsidiary of Anglo-Dutch multinational Unilever. Since 2000 Hindustan Unilever Limited, India's largest fast-moving consumer goods company, has tied strategies for expanding sales of one its oldest brands, Lifebuoy soap, to educational campaigns focused on reducing diarrhoeal disease and micro-credit schemes aimed at improving rural livelihoods. For Prahalad, the significance of this move was that it made social and economic issues integral to business. Selling soap to poor people, he argued, could be a public health and poverty alleviation project as well as a profitable business venture. Today, Unilever's initiatives in India have become the most commonly referenced case study of business strategy for emerging markets in the developing world. The company's success in increasing revenues while delivering on key international development objectives has provided a new framework for market expansion that is reinvigorating capitalist enterprise. As a result of C.K. Prahalad's book, Unilever's initiatives now circulate through schools of business and management, development agencies and public policy institutes as an exemplary case study in how the search for corporate value and the needs of the poor can be combined. The global influence of Prahalad's work and Unilever's initiatives in India make them particularly relevant for anthropologists interested in the human face of contemporary capitalism. Against the backdrop of social justice movements seeking to reform trade relations and regulatory initiatives concerned with holding business socially accountable ... C.K. Prahalad has emerged as a belligerent champion for the market as a vehicle for moral engagement in the world. His work represents a shift in the language of corporate social responsibility that dispenses with any reference to philanthropy or acts of giving, and makes no distinction between ethical practice and the self-interested pursuit of profit. It is a vision that anchors what anthropologists see as a quintessentially modern desire for a more social economy ... in entrepreneurship and the market.

Soap and the Social Good

In this article we examine three initiatives in South India that have brought Hindustan Unilever to prominence as a pioneer of business at the bottom of the pyramid. Using corporate reports, promotional materials, business case studies, academic papers and newspaper interviews we look at a public–private partnership campaign, a school-based educational campaign and a direct distribution strategy. Our intention is not to advance opinions about the empirical effectiveness of soap against the transmission of disease or human morbidity. Instead we use this article to reflect on the particular constellation of relationships between multiple actors that have enabled Lifebuoy soap to emerge as a 'social good', an object that circulates through international business schools, NGOs, universities and government departments as a convincing composite of both 'social' and 'commercial' value.

Public health has been a particularly fruitful site for bottom-of-the-pyramid innovations. Global companies that sell sanitary towels, contraceptive devices, nutritional supplements, cataract removal services, spectacles and hygiene products have allied themselves to international public health goals through educational marketing campaigns and direct distribution franchises. By appending economic and social development goals to health system privatization, such interventions are reconfiguring relationships between business, science, state and consumer/citizen.

If Lifebuoy soap can be presented convincingly as a 'social good' – to the extent that it has come to circulate globally as a model of successful business practice – it is because the interests of marketing executives, the brokers of scientific knowledge and research, state actors, schoolchildren and women on low incomes have been successfully modified, enlisted and momentarily aligned. The emergence of Lifebuoy soap as a brand-name consumer good associated with the realization of shareholder value and the achievement of specific medical and economic objectives in the fields of public health and micro-enterprise represents a moment of stability in the life of soap as a product ... An anthropology at the bottom of the pyramid, we argue, can provide valuable insights into the hidden work and power relations involved in establishing an everyday commodity – like soap – as a 'social good' that is capable of simultaneously combating disease, tackling poverty and realizing value for shareholders.

Hygiene as a Large, Unmet Consumer Need

Strategies to sell soap have always been at the cutting edge of innovations in marketing. The first mass advertising campaigns of the early 20th century were designed by Lever Brothers to sell their brands of Lux and Sunlight soap. Their campaigns created new consumer 'needs' that tapped into subconscious fears and desires to construct connections between cleanliness, hygiene, social mobility and brands of manufactured soap. Indeed ... their intimate connection to the body has given toiletries a unique role in the construction of modern consumer subjectivities. An early advert for Lifebuoy soap ... emphasized the dangers of invisible germs on doorknobs, public telephones, banister rails and other people in public places, and argued that the only protection against the risk of contagion was the 'perfect scientific cleanliness' offered by Lifebuoy – 'a true health soap'.

As European and colonial histories show, wherever people have embarked on civilizing missions or programmes of social reform to improve indigenous, native or lower-class populations, questions of hygiene have played a major role .... [I]n colonial Rhodesia ideas about cleanliness and the transformation of bodily practices were central to both projects of government and Lever Brothers' commercial expansion ... Little surprise, then, that in the 21st century Unilever has emerged at the forefront of new sales strategies aimed at the fastest-growing markets for consumer goods in the developing world. Today, Unilever's 'bottom-of-the-pyramid' innovations in India have created a new alignment between the commercial value of washing and cleanliness and the goals of international public health policy.

Health in Your Hands

In 2000 Hindustan Unilever was part of 'Health in Your Hands', a global public– private partnership campaign to promote hand-washing with soap, as it launched a pilot project in the South Indian state of Kerala. Based on research which showed that hand-washing could reduce the risk of diarrhoeal disease by 47 per cent ... the partnership harnessed corporate expertise in order to change hygiene habits, increase the use of soap and bring about a significant decline in the transmission of water-borne diseases. With support from the World Bank, the government of Kerala put up 70 per cent of the project costs while a consortium of transnational companies covered the costs of marketing.

Popular conceptions of science as an autonomous realm of knowledge, separate from the social and political domains, make it a particularly crucial ally in the production of soap as a social good ... This is especially the case in public health contexts where the 'social' credentials of a product depend upon evidence of its medical effects. Scientists from the London School of Hygiene and Tropical Medicine have been central to the Health in Your Hands partnership, and their research has provided important evidence of the project's commercial and political neutrality ...

Active-B

For Prahalad, alliances like those between Hindustan Unilever and scientific research institutions are mutually beneficial partnerships. Yet there is nothing predictable or preordained about such alignment of interests. The benign language of partnership obscures the power dynamics involved as global multinationals like Unilever work to recruit other actors and establish themselves as nodal points in emergent market-driven health systems.

At the same time that Hindustan Unilever was participating in the 'Health in Your Hands' initiative, for example, the company was modifying the material qualities of Lifebuoy soap by introducing the anti-bacterial agent 'Active-B', or triclosan. In India this new ingredient was used to market the brand's enhanced health-protecting qualities and heightened effectiveness over other soaps. Yet the same business-school case studies that applauded Hindustan Unilever's involvement in the global hand-washing initiative also noted that the decision to incorporate triclosan was taken despite ongoing debate in scientific and public forums in the US about the health risks associated with adding anti-bacterial agents to household hygiene products ...

Controversy over the risks of triclosan intensified in the late 1990s when findings published in Nature showed that under laboratory conditions triclosan induced genetic changes to bacteria ... The authors suggested that the widespread use of everyday household products containing triclosan could lead to the appearance of multi-product-resistant super-germs. Subsequent laboratory testing and clinical trials ... have both reinforced and contested this research, provoking sensationalist media headlines.

As the business-school case studies report, these US-based controversies have not impinged on Unilever's use of triclosan in household products for markets in India.

Regardless of whether germs in US laboratories are effectively eliminated or dangerously transformed by triclosan, Hindustan Unilever's marketing managers determined that the addition of it to Lifebuoy soap would attract Indian consumers. In the US, public debate over the safety of triclosan reflects increased concern about risk, uncertainty and relationships between science and society in the context of a rapidly developing biotechnology industry. In the context of India's rapidly expanding markets for health-care products and services, meanwhile, the marketing potential of agents such as triclosan reflects the significance of biomedical symbols, treatments, instruments and technologies as ways of legitimizing authority and cultural distinction ...

The processes by which such scientific controversies are settled (or bypassed altogether), and scientific knowledge travels to and is circulated in specific places as universal fact, are central to the way in which commodities aimed at the 'bottom of the pyramid', like Lifebuoy soap, can be marketed as 'social goods'. The high-profile nature of the triclosan controversy in the US media and its comparative absence in India illustrates the intrinsically contingent nature of relationships between business and science and the importance of tracing such alliances as they travel between the laboratory and the marketing department.

Behaviour Change
... [T]he reduction of hand-washing to an instrumental relationship between soap and bacteria belies the multiple ancillary transformations

that occur when public health interventions include commercial partners. Persuading poor Indians that their hands are dirty may be vital if they are to take up a life-saving hand-washing habit. But it is not only bacteria that are being acted on in such campaigns. When health and hygiene are sold as commodities, relationships to the body and understandings of well-being become increasingly mediated by consumption practices. A key motivation for Unilever to encourage hand-washing is that the relationship between hands, soap and cleanliness can be extended to create a 'total hygienic ideal'. As market research for the Health in Your Hands partnership put it, 'the more evolved the market, the more species of soap products will be found in a consumer's household' ... New hygienic consumers will not only wash their hands but other 'dirty' body parts, domestic surfaces and appliances that will each require a unique cleaning product. Just as Unilever's 19th-century campaigns in metropole and colony created new hygienic and consumer subjects, so too their contemporary engagement in international public health initiatives goes well beyond the creation of new hand-washing habits to shape new hygienic sensibilities, aspirations and desires.

Saving Lives or Selling Soap?

The portrayal of the Health in Your Hands global partnership as a purely technical public health intervention, and the involvement of global consumer goods companies as benign and disinterested, ultimately contributed to the failure of the pilot project in Kerala. In Kerala, the Health in Your Hands partnership was construed as an attempt to conceal profit motives with superficial claims about the greater common good. Suspicious that the commercial interests of the business partners were being downplayed, social and political activists led a media campaign against the project, arguing that it was entirely driven by the interests of multinational corporations.

Community leaders argued that it was the lack of access to safe, affordable drinking water rather than the failure to wash hands with soap that led to the transmission of disease ... 'Give us drinking water first, instead of [brand name] soap', the president of a village governance committee in a region with high rates of coliform bacteria in the water supply told reporters ... Business leaders argued that the public–private partnership would destroy Kerala's indigenous soap manufacturers, including those small-scale and environmentally sustainable cottage industries that had been established by micro-credit and poverty-alleviation programmes in the state.

... In India the Health in Your Hands partnership misjudged the publics it hoped to educate. While consumers might not be put off by debates about the risks of triclosan use in the US, social activists, political representatives and local business people proved highly sensitive to the political economy of globalization ... [R]eferences to 'local' knowledge and industries pointed to the failure of the 'global partnership' to position itself as a spokesperson for local interests. Instead, opposition to the partnership as an external imposition mobilized powerful distinctions between 'local' versus 'foreign' and 'public' versus 'commercial' interests. Protests by social movements and opposition parties led to the Government of Kerala pulling out of the partnership and the World Bank withdrawing support. As a result the initiative came to a standstill.

Complete Disclosure

In the aftermath of their public–private partnership in Kerala, Hindustan Unilever altered its approach to health and hygiene in India ... In relationships with public partners and consumers the company now made a complete disclosure of its commercial objectives and presented this as evidence of trustworthiness. The launch of two pilot projects in the state of Andhra Pradesh exemplified this approach. While these projects continued to draw on scientific evidence and research to legitimize their aims, the company had learnt from the Kerala experience that broader alliances were crucial if it was to market Lifebuoy soap successfully as a health commodity without drawing public criticism. These new initiatives addressed the failure to gain popular support in Kerala by making its commercial interest explicit and by incorporating 'local' consumers as active participants in the marketing and distribution process.

The first project, Swasthya Chetna, was an educational campaign that aimed to prevent the spread of diarrhoeal disease by teaching schoolchildren about the need to wash their hands with soap, and in doing so forge new associations with Lifebuoy soap. The project involved classroom workshops that created direct associations between hand-washing, hygiene and their brand. Unilever envisaged schools as 'entry points into communities' and schoolchildren as 'change initiators' who would convey the Lifebuoy message to adult consumers in their homes.

... The second project, Project Shakti, was a direct distribution scheme that used existing funding for micro-enterprise to reshape Unilever's regional distribution system and expand the company's sales coverage into 'media-dark' regions that they had been unable to reach. Unilever's initiative was to provide members of micro-credit schemes run by the state and community-based NGOs with business opportunities, by recruiting them as saleswomen or direct distributors. Project Shakti women are not Hindustan Lever employees, but the company helps train them, provides local marketing support, and offers incentives, bonuses, prizes, 'Amma of the Month' award schemes, and web profiles.

... The Shakti Ammalu – or Shakti Mothers – have emerged as rural India's equivalent to the Avon Ladies of 1950s Britain: by 2004 they had covered 50,000 villages across 12 states, selling to some 70 million consumers. Unilever's promotional materials describe Project Shakti as empowering women 'in ways that are much more profound than the income they earn selling soap and shampoos, it has brought them self esteem, self empowerment and a place in society' ...

Consumers and Co-production

As corporate players in the Indian soap market have sought to extend or consolidate their market position among poor, rural consumers, they have cooperated with government and international organizations to fund public health messages, sponsored drama groups and artists to promote brand awareness, trained nurses and midwives to propagate behaviour change, and supported local conferences or campaigns organized by local professional associations in order to establish tacit endorsement for their products ... Hindustan Unilever's involvement in the Health in your Hands partnership fits into this broader pattern.

What made Swasthya Chetna and Project Shakti different, however, was their use of lay consumers rather than scientific or expert actors and institutions to bring legitimacy and credibility to the brand. The active participation of children and women in Swasthya Chetna and Project Shakti has been essential to the production of Lifebuoy soap as a 'social good'. Each initiative incorporates the practices and relationships of end users or consumers in ways that create specifically 'social' outcomes. When schoolchildren who have been taught to wash their hands with soap in Hindustan Unilever's classroom-based educational campaigns return home to their parents, or when rural women on low incomes use small loans to sell soap to neighbours, friends and kin, they produce the very relationships through which Lifebuoy soap acts as a prophylactic against water-borne disease and a driver of social and economic development.

In the business literature on initiatives at the bottom of the pyramid, this interaction between the corporation and the consumer is understood as one of mutual benefit ... [H]owever, Lifebuoy soap is primarily a 'brand', a corporate asset that remains the legally protected intellectual property of Unilever. If we are to look at the social practices and relationships created by the consumer as forms of labour that add a specific value to this 'brand' then the interaction between corporation and consumer demands to be understood in different terms. Anthropologists are familiar with the way that micro-enterprise interventions like Project Shakti do not just create the capacity to consume among families but also shape entrepreneurial subjectivities ... and incorporate the social practices of the poor into the market ... [M]icroenterprise initiatives appropriate those relationships, networks and forms of cooperation with which people survive without the state and subsume them into projects of market development. The alliance between micro-enterprise and market expansion in Project Shakti takes this work of appropriation further, by activating relations of kinship, community and indebtedness in which the women recruited as salespeople are immersed in order to create attachments to specific products. When the Shakti Amma sells soap to village women in rural Andhra Pradesh, her existing network is appropriated by a project of market development, and the work of building and maintaining these relationships is the creative labour that Hindustan Unilever extracts to add value to the Lifebuoy soap brand. In both initiatives

Hindustan Unilever enlists children and women consumers as producers of value, and it is their active involvement which enables Unilever to differentiate Lifebuoy soap from other brands as simultaneously public health commodity, development project and viable commercial venture.

Enterprise Evangelism

India's postal department has traditionally used stamps to honour political leaders and commemorative events. On World Health Day 2006 Lifebuoy soap became the first commercial product to appear on an Indian postage stamp, symbolizing the immense political power that projects combining public service with market expansion now have. India's Chief Postmaster General launched the stamp by congratulating Hindustan Unilever on initiating a 'socially beneficial movement' for good health and said: 'I urge all my brothers and sisters to take personal hygiene habits like washing hands with soap extremely seriously'.

The international development industry and global business are tightly interlocked. Development paradigms and policies are largely premised on the role of the market as a mechanism for improving access to health care or reducing poverty and, where existing markets have been found to be flawed or imperfect, interventions have sought to strengthen its institutions and actors. The surge of interest in markets at the 'bottom of the pyramid', however, suggests that relationships between business and development are now more dynamic than ever before. While public–private partnerships and corporate social responsibility ventures repeatedly fail to surmount a moral opposition between 'market' and 'society', bottom-of-the-pyramid strategies which make their self-interest explicit and which incorporate scientific knowledge and poor consumers into the marketing, production and distribution process appear to gain acceptance as successful composites of both social and commercial interest.

The assemblage of logistical innovations involved in the production of a social good sees transnational capital forging fresh alliances with scientific communities, public-sector bodies and civil-society organizations, and building new relationships with poor people not as passive consumers but as co-producers. Enterprise and the entrepreneurial spirit are today asserted as solutions to diseases of poverty and rural livelihoods with evangelical zeal. The corporate search for value at the 'bottom of the pyramid' is transforming the landscapes in which many anthropologists work. What will the pyramid look like when anthropologists look up?

Reference

Prahalad, C.K. *The Fortune at the Bottom of the Pyramid* (Philadelphia: Wharton School Publishing, 2006).

Edited extract from: Jamie Cross and Alice Street, 'Anthropology at the Bottom of the Pyramid', *Anthropology Today* 25/4 (2009), pp.4–9.

43   Japanese Hip-Hop and the Globalization of Popular Culture
Ian Condry

In this extract from an article first published in 2002, Ian Condry looks at the globalization of popular culture in the case of Japanese hip-hop. Condry is one of a growing number of contemporary social anthropologists whose research is carried out in a 'field site' that is sometimes extended, multiple or even virtual. He points out the tension between 'being there' as a key feature of ethnographic research, and the fact that 'there' may stretch across the world in the shape of a musical genre or a consumer fashion. Yet the significance of the local and the concrete shines through his narrative, and he shows vividly how a global popular culture is reflected and experienced through distinctively Japanese values and practices.

Introduction

Japanese hip-hop, which began in the 1980s and continues to develop today, is an intriguing case study for exploring the globalization of popular culture. Hip-hop is but one example among many of the transnational cultural styles pushed by entertainment and fashion industries, pulled by youth eager for the latest happening thing, and circulated by a wide range of media outlets eager to draw readers and to sell advertising. In Tokyo, a particular combination of local performance sites, artists, and fans points to ways that urban areas are crucibles of new, hybrid cultural forms. Hip-hop was born in the late 1970s in New York City as a form of street art: rapping on sidewalk stoops, outdoor block parties with enormous sound systems, graffiti on public trains, and breakdancing in public parks. In its voyage to Japan, the street ethic of hip-hop remains, but it is performed most intensely in all-night clubs peppered around Tokyo. This paper examines these nightclubs as an urban setting that helps us grasp the cultural dynamics of Japanese hip-hop. In particular, the interaction between artist-entrepreneurs and fans in live shows demonstrates how 'global' popular culture is still subject to important processes of localization.

Anthropologists have a special role in analyzing such transnational forms because of their commitment to extended fieldwork in local settings. Ethnography aims to capture the cultural practices and social organization of a people. This offers a useful way of seeing how popular culture is interwoven with everyday life. Yet there is a tension between ethnography and globalization, because in many ways they seem antithetical to each other. While ethnography attempts to evoke the distinctive texture of local experience, globalization is often seen as erasing local differences. An important analytical challenge for today's media-saturated world is finding a way to understand how local culture interacts with such global media flows.

On one hand, it seems as if locales far removed from each other are becoming increasingly the same. It is more than a little eerie to fly from New York to Tokyo and see teenagers in both places wearing the same kinds of fashion characteristic of rap fans: baggy pants with boxers on display, floppy hats or baseball caps, and immaculate space-age Nike sneakers. In Tokyo stores for youth, rap music is the background sound of choice. Graffiti styled after the New York City aerosol artists adorns numerous walls, and breakdancers can be found in public parks practising in the afternoon or late at night. In all-night dance clubs throughout Tokyo, Japanese rappers and DJs take to the stage and declare that they have some 'extremely bad shit' (*geld yaba shitto*) – meaning 'good music' – to share with the audience. For many urban youth, hip-hop is the defining style of their era. In 1970s Japan, the paradigm of high school cool was long hair and a blistering solo on lead guitar. Today, trendsetters are more likely to sport 'dread' hair and show off their scratch techniques with two turntables and a mixer. In the last few years, rap music has become one of the best-selling genres of music in the United States and around the world as diverse youth are adapting the style to their own messages and contexts.

But at the same time, there are reasons to think that such surface appearances of sameness disguise differences at some deeper level. Clearly, cultural setting and social organization have an impact on how movies and television shows are viewed. Yet if we are to understand the shape of cultural forms in a world that is increasingly connected by global media and commodity flows, we must situate Japanese rappers in the context of contemporary Japan. When thinking about how hip-hop is appropriated, we must consider, for example, that most Japanese rappers and fans speak only Japanese. Many of them live at home with their parents, and they all went through the Japanese education system. Moreover, even if the origin of their beloved music genre is overseas, they are caught up in social relations that are ultimately quite local, animated primarily by face-to-face interactions and telephone calls. So while these youth see themselves as 'hip-hoppers' and 'B-Boys' and 'B-Girls', and associate themselves with what they call a 'global hip-hop culture', they also live in a day-to-day world that is distinctly Japanese.

For those interested in studying the power of popular culture, there is also a more practical question of research methods. How does a lone researcher go about studying something as broad and unwieldy as the globalization of mass culture? One of the tenets of anthropological fieldwork is that you cannot understand a people without being there, but in the case of a music genre, where is 'there'? In the fall of 1995, I began a year-and-a-half of fieldwork in Tokyo, and the number of potential sites was daunting. There were places where the music was produced: record companies, recording studios, home studios, and even on commuter trains with hand-held synthesizers. There were places where the music was promoted: music magazines, fashion magazines, TV and radio shows, nightclubs, and record stores. There was the interaction between musicians and fans at live shows, or in mediated form on cassettes, CDs, and 12-inch LPs. To make matters worse, rap music is part of the larger category of 'hip-hop'. Hip-hop encompasses not only rap, but also breakdance, DJ, graffiti, and fashion. The challenge was to understand the current fascination among Japanese youth with hip-hop music and style, while also considering the role of money-making organizations. How does one situate the experiential pleasures within the broader structures of profit that produce mass culture?

As I began interviewing rappers, magazine writers, and record-company people, I found a recurring theme that provided a partial answer. Everyone agreed that you cannot understand Japanese rap music without going regularly to the clubs. Clubs were called the 'actual site' (*genba*) of the Japanese rap scene ... It was there that rappers performed, DJs learned which songs elicit excitement in the crowd, and breakdancers practiced and competed for attention. In what follows, I would like to suggest that an effective tool for understanding the globalization of popular culture is to consider places like Japanese hip-hop nightclubs in terms of what might be called 'genba globalism'. By using participant-observation methods to explore key sites that are a kind of media crossroads, we can observe how globalized images and sounds are performed, consumed, and then transformed in an ongoing process. I use the Japanese term 'genba' to emphasize that the processing of such global forms happens through the local language and in places where local hip-hop culture is produced. In Japanese hip-hop, these clubs are important not only as places where fans can see live shows and hear the latest releases from American and Japanese groups, but also as places for networking among artists, writers, and record company people ... To get a sense of what clubs are about, let's visit one.

Going to Harlem on the Yamanote Line

A visit to Tokyo's Harlem is the best place to begin a discussion of Japanese hip-hop. Opened in the summer of 1997, Harlem is one of many all-night dance clubs, but as the largest club solely devoted to hip-hop and R&B, it has become the flagship for the Japanese scene (at least, at the time of this writing in February 2001). Nestled in the love-hotel area of the Shibuya section of Tokyo, Harlem is representative of the otherworldliness of clubs as well as their location within the rhythms and spaces of mainstream Japan.

If we were visiting the club, we would most likely meet at Shibuya train station around midnight because the main action seldom gets started before 1 AM. Most all-night revelers commute by train, a practice that links Tokyo residents in a highly punctual dance. The night is divided between the last train (all lines stop by 1 AM at the latest) and the first train of the morning (between 4.30 and 5 AM). The intervening period is when clubs (*kurabu*) are most active ... Shortly after midnight, Shibuya station is the scene for the changing of the guard: those heading home, running to make their connections for the last train, and those like us heading out, dressed up, and walking leisurely because we will be spending all night on the town. The magazine stands are closing. Homeless men are spread out on cardboard boxes on the steps leading down to the subways. The police observe the masses moving past each other in the station square towards their respective worlds. Three billboard-size TVs looming overhead, normally spouting pop-music videos and snowboard ads during the day, are now dark and silent. The throngs of teenagers, many in their school uniforms, that mob Shibuya during afternoons and all weekend have been replaced by a more balanced mix of college students, 'salarymen' and 'career women', and of course more than a few B-Boys and B-Girls – the hip-hop enthusiasts in baggy pants and headphones. The sidewalks are splashed with light from vending machines – cigarettes, soda, CDs, beer (off for the night), and 'valentine call' phone cards. A few drunken men are being carried by friends or lie in their suits unconscious on the sidewalk.

...

Traveling to a club instills a sense of moving against the mainstream in time and space. Others are going home to bed as the clubber heads out. When the clubber returns home in the morning, reeking of smoke and alcohol, the train cars hold early-bird workers as well. So the movement to and from the club, often from the distant suburbs, gives clubbers a sense of themselves as separate, flaunting their leisure, their costumes, and their consumer habits. During the course of my year-and-a-half of fieldwork, between the fall of 1995 and the spring of 1997, I went to over a hundred club events around Tokyo and I began to see that clubs help one understand not only the pleasures of rap in Japan, but also the social organization of the scene and the different styles that have emerged. This becomes clear as you spend time inside the clubs.

...

Inside the club, the air is warm and thick, humid with the breath and sweat of dancing bodies. Bone-thudding bass lines thump out of enormous speakers. There is the scratch-scratch of a DJ doing his turntable tricks, and the hum of friends talking, yelling really, over the sound of the music. The lighting is subdued, much of it coming from a mirrored ball slowly rotating on the ceiling. The fraternity-house smell of stale beer is mostly covered up by the choking cigarette haze, but it is best not to look too closely at what is making the floor alternately slippery and sticky. The darkness, low ceiling, black walls, and smoky murk create a space both intimate and claustrophobic. Almost everyone heads for the bar as soon as they come in. An important aspect of clubbing is the physical experience of the music and crowded setting ... Much of the time is spent milling around, talking, drinking, and dancing. The live show often produces a welcome rise in the excitement level of the clubbers. Some events feature several live acts, often followed by a freestyle session.

...

The year 1996 was ... a time of a 'freestyle boom', when most shows were closed with an open-ended passing of the microphone. Anyone could step on stage and try his or her hand at rapping for a few minutes. This has been an important way for younger performers to get the attention of more established acts. There is a back-and-forth aspect of performance in the clubs that shows how styles are developed, honed, and reworked in a context where the audience is knowledgeable, discriminating, and at times participates in the show itself.

It is important to understand that over the years, this kind of feedback loop has helped determine the shape of current Japanese rap styles. One of my main sites was a weekly Thursday-night event that featured another collection of rap groups called Kitchens. Hip-hop collectives such as Kitchens, Little Bird Nation, Funky Grammar Unit, and Rock Steady Crew Japan are called 'families' (*famirii*, in Japanese). The different groups often met at clubs or parties, at times getting acquainted after particularly noteworthy freestyle sessions. Over time some would become friends, as well as artistic collaborators, who performed together live or in the studio for each others' albums. Such families define the social organization of the 'scene'. What is interesting is how they also characterize different aesthetic takes on what Japanese hip-hop should be. Kitchens, for example, aim to combine a pop music sensibility with their love for rap music, and, like many such 'party rap' groups, they appeal to a largely female audience. The Funky Grammar Unit aims for a more underground sound that is nonetheless accessible, and they tend to have a more even mix of men and women in the audience. Other families like Urbarian Gym (UBG) are less concerned with being accessible to audiences than with conveying a confrontational, hard-core stance. The lion's share of their audiences are young males, though as UBG's leader, Zeebra, breaks into the pop spotlight, their audiences are becoming more diverse.

The lull that precedes and follows the onstage performance is a key time for networking to build these families. In all, the live show is at most an hour long, at times closer to twenty minutes, and yet there is nowhere for the clubbers to go until the trains start running again around 5 AM. It is not unusual for music magazine writers to do interviews during club events, and record company representatives often come to shows as well, not only as talent scouts but also to discuss upcoming projects. I found that 3.00 to 4 AM was the most productive time for fieldwork because by then the clubbers had mostly exhausted their supply of stories and gossip to tell friends, and were then open to finding out what this strange foreigner jotting things in his notebook was doing in their midst.

Japanese cultural practices do not disappear just because everyone is wearing their hip-hop outfits and listening to the latest rap tunes. To give one example, at the first Kitchens event after the New Year, I was surprised to see all the clubbers who knew each other going around and saying the traditional New Year's greeting in very formal Japanese: 'Congratulations on the dawn of the New Year. I humbly request your benevolence this year as well'. There was no irony, no joking atmosphere in these statements. This is a good example of the way that globalization may appear to overshadow Japanese culture, but one needs to spend time in clubs with the people to see how surface appearances can be deceiving.

...

... [G]oing to a club involves a strange mix of the extraordinary and the routine. On one hand, you visit a place with bizarre interior design, listen to music at exceedingly high volume, stay out all night and, often, get drunk. It is a sharp contrast to an ordinary day of school or work. We must also recognize, however, that while a club may strive to be a fantastic microcosm, it is still embedded in Japan's political-economic structures, characteristic social relations, and the contemporary range of cultural forms. It is not by chance that clubs tend to attract people of specific class, age, sexuality, and to some extent locale. Moreover, if you go regularly to clubs, after a while it becomes just another routine. It is largely predictable what kind of pleasures can be expected, and also the generally unpleasant consequences for work or school after a night without sleep. Clubbing offers freedom and constraints. This tension is the key to understanding how clubs socialize the club-goers by structuring pleasure in characteristic ways.

I have only suggested some of the ways that clubs offer insight into the ways that global hip-hop becomes transformed into a local form of Japanese hip-hop, but we can see how an idea of 'genba globalism' can help us understand the process of localization. Globalism is refracted and transformed in important ways through the actual site of urban hip-hop clubs. Japanese rappers perform for local audiences in the Japanese language and use Japanese subjects to build their base of fans. In contrast to club events with techno or house music, hip-hop events emphasize lyrics in the shows and the freestyle sessions. There is a wide range of topics addressed in Japanese hip-hop, but they all speak in some way to the local audience.

...

Understanding Globalization in Local Terms

Rap music in Japan offers an interesting case study of the way popular culture is becoming increasingly global in scope, while at the same time becoming domesticated to fit with local ideas and desires. At the dawn of the twenty-first century, entertainment industries are reaching wider markets and larger audiences ... [T]he transnational market for hip-hop is still growing, and most major rap stars do promotional tours in Japan.

An important feature of pop-culture commodities is that they tend to be expensive to produce initially, but then relatively cheap to reproduce and distribute. Compact disks are one of the most striking examples. Although studio time is expensive ... the CDs themselves cost about eighty cents to produce, including the packaging. Obviously, the more one can sell, the higher the return, and this helps explain the eagerness of entertainment businesses to develop new markets around the world.

Less clear are the kinds of effects such globalized pop-culture forms might have. The fluidity of culture in the contemporary world raises new questions about how we are linked together, what we share and what divides us. The spread of popular culture seems in some ways linked with a spread in values, but we must be cautious in our assessment of how and to what extent this transfer takes place. It is safe to say that the conventional understanding of globalization is that it is producing a homogenization of cultural forms. From this perspective, we are witnessing the McDonaldization and the Coca-Cola colonization of the periphery by powerful economic centers of the world system. The term 'cultural imperialism' captures this idea, that political and economic power is being used 'to exalt and spread the values and habits of a foreign culture at the expense of the native culture' ... In some ways, anthropology as a discipline emerged at a time when there was a similar concern that the forces of modernity (especially missionaries and colonial officials) were wiping out 'traditional cultures', and thus one role for ethnographers was to salvage, at least in the form of written documents, the cultures of so-called 'primitive peoples'. Many people view globalization, and particularly the spread of American pop culture, as a similar kind of invasion, but the idea that watching a Disney movie automatically instills certain values must be examined and not simply assumed. In some ways the goals of anthropology – combating simplistic and potentially dangerous forms of ethnocentrism – remain as important today as when the discipline was born.

...

It is important to recognize, however, that globalization involves much more than Hollywood movies and pop music. [A recent author analyses] three aspects of globalization, namely, economic, political, and cultural. He contends that globalization processes go back five hundred years, and that the relative importance of economic, political, and cultural exchanges has varied over that time ... From the sixteenth to nineteenth centuries, economics was key. In particular, the growth of the capitalist world system was the driving force in linking diverse regions. During the nineteenth and twentieth centuries, politics moved to the fore. Nation-states produced a system of international relations that characterized global linkages with multinational corporations and integrated national traditions. Now, at the dawn of the twenty-first century, cultural forms are leading global changes in both politics and economics. [This author] argues that a 'global idealization' is producing politics based on worldwide values (e.g., human rights, the environment, anti-sweatshop movement) and economic exchanges centered on lifestyle consumerism. The key point is that while economics and then politics were the driving forces in globalization of previous centuries, it is cultural flows that are increasingly important today ... [T]his points to the importance of studying the kinds of ideals that are spread around the globe.

What ideals are spread by hip-hop in Japan? Clubbing certainly promotes an attitude that stresses leisure, fashion, and consumer knowledge of music over other kinds of status in work and school. Although it is important to recognize that the effects of lyrics are somewhat complicated, it is worth considering, to some extent, the messages carried by the music. Although rappers deal with a wide variety of subjects, one theme appears again and again, namely, that youth need to speak out for themselves. As rapper MC Shiro of Rhymester puts it, 'If I were to say what hip-hop is, it would be a "culture of the first person singular". In hip-hop ... rappers are always yelling, "I'm this". Such a message may seem rather innocuous compared to some of the hard-edged lyrics one is likely to hear in the United States, but it is also a reflection of the kind of lives these Japanese youth are leading. In Japan, the education system tends to emphasize rote memorization and to track students according to exams. Sharply age-graded hierarchies are the norm, and may be especially irksome in a situation where the youth are likely to live with their parents until they get married. Moreover, the dominant ideology that harmony of the group should come before individual expression ('the nail that sticks up gets hammered down') makes for a social context in which the hip-hop idea that one should be speaking for oneself is, in some limited sense, revolutionary. At the very least, it shows how global pop-culture forms are leading not to some simple homogenization, but rather adding to a complex mix that in many ways can only be studied ethnographically through extended research in local sites.

...

Conclusion: Global Pop and Cultural Change

In the end, the globalization of popular culture needs to be understood as two related yet opposing trends of greater massification and deeper compartmentalization. On one hand, the recording industry is reaching larger and larger markets, both within Japan and around the world, as mega-hits continue to set sales records. On the other hand, there is an equally profound if less visible process by which niche scenes are becoming deeper and more widely connected than before, and in the process, new forms of heterogeneity are born. Although I have only been able to touch on a few of its aspects here, Japanese rap music is a revealing case study of the social location, cultural role, and capitalist logic of such micro-mass cultures. It is important to recognize, however, that these micro-mass cultures also have the potential to move into the mainstream.

...

Walking to a hip-hop club in Tokyo, one is confronted with a tremendous range of consumer options, and it is this heightened sense of 'you are what you buy' that has in many ways become the defining feature of identity in advanced capitalist nations, at least among those people with the money to consume their preferred lifestyle. At the same time, it is important to be sensitive to the ways that, outward appearances notwithstanding, the consumers of things like hip-hop are embedded in a quite different range of social relations and cultural meanings. It makes a difference that B-Boys and B-Girls, listening to American hip-hop records, still feel it is important to go around to their friends and associates with the traditional New Year's greeting of deference and obligation. This is an example of the ways social relations within the Japanese rap scene continue to carry the weight of uniquely Japanese practices and understandings.

...

Edited extract from: Ian Condry, 'Japanese Hip-hop and the Globalization of Popular Culture', reprinted in J. Spradley and D.W. McCurdy (eds), *Conformity and Conflict: Readings in Cultural Anthropology* (Boston: Pearson, 2008) pp.370–85.

III.2 Local and Global Processes: Ethnographic Perspectives

44	**Helping or Hindering? Controversies around the International Second-hand Clothing Trade** *Karen T. Hansen*

Karen T. Hansen is another social anthropologist who has directed attention to the local impacts of macro-level economic practices – in this case, the international trade in second-hand clothing. In this edited extract, she contrasts the generally negative views prevalent in the West about the harmful effects of this trade on local economies, with the creativity in clothing styles, and the vitality of micro-economic activities, made possible by the second-hand clothing market in locations such as the Philippines and Zambia. Her analysis, like that of Cross and Street above in relation to the marketing of soap in India, demonstrates how detailed ethnographic research can comment on – and in some cases challenge – received views and taken-for-granted assumptions, and reveal new facets to 'what is going on'.

The international second-hand clothing trade has a long history, yet it is only very recently that its changing cultural and economic nexus has become the focus of substantive work, at the point of either collection or consumption. … [It] is a commodity trade subject to the fluctuations of supply and demand in domestic and foreign markets. Yet the news stories about this trade that I came across rarely changed. Shrouding the export of second-hand clothing in a rhetoric of giving and helping, news accounts hide the economic process, including the cultural construction of demand, from view. Above all, the news story tends to hand down moral judgment about everyone involved: people in the West who donate clothing to charitable groups, the not-for-profit organizations which resell the major part of their huge donated clothing stock, and the commercial textile recyclers, graders, exporters and importers who earn their living from marketing clothing that was initially donated. And at the receiving end, ordinary people in poor countries like Zambia are chided for buying imported second-hand clothing instead of supporting domestic textile and garment industries.

International and local concerns about second-hand clothing imports to the Third World cannot be ignored. They matter, but perhaps not in the way that has been most vocally argued. This article briefly examines some of the

Unravelling
Journey of the Western world's unwanted clothes.

Filmstill from *Unravel* by Meghna Gupta, 2012. Distributed by the Royal Anthropological Institute.

arguments about the negative effects of such imports. I describe the organization of the global trade, discuss some recent anthropological studies, and turn to Zambia for an account of the trade's impact on local livelihoods.

The Second-hand Clothing Trade

In the West today, the second-hand clothing trade in both domestic and foreign markets is dominated by not-for-profit organizations and textile recycling/grading firms. Charitable organizations are the largest single source of the garments that fuel the international trade in second-hand clothing, through sales of a large proportion, between 40 and 75 per cent, depending on whom you talk to, of their clothing donations. The textile recyclers and graders purchase used clothing in bulk from the enormous volumes gathered by the charitable organizations, and they also buy surplus clothing from resale stores. The bulk of this clothing is destined for a new life in the second-hand clothing export market. Poor-quality, worn and damaged garments are processed into fibres or wiping rags for industrial use. At their warehouses and sorting plants, the clothing recyclers sort clothing by garment type, fabric and quality. Special period clothing is set aside to be purchased by domestic and foreign buyers on the lookout for stylish garments for the changing vintage market. The remainder is usually compressed into standard 50 kg bales, although some firms compress bales of much greater weight, usually containing unsorted clothing. The lowest-quality clothing goes to Africa and medium-quality to Latin America, while Japan receives a large proportion of top-quality items.

The economic power and global scope of the second-hand clothing trade have increased enormously since the early 1990s, in the wake of the liberalization of many Third World economies, and following the sudden rise in demand from former Eastern bloc countries ... Many large importers of second-hand clothing in South and South-east Asia, such as Pakistan and Hong Kong, are also textile and garment exporters, putting an interesting spin on arguments about the negative effects of used clothing imports on domestic textile and garment industries. This is also the case with some African countries, for example Kenya and Uganda, which are large importers of second-hand clothing but also have textile and garment manufacturing firms that export to the United States under the duty-/quota-free provisions of the African Growth and Opportunity Act ...

Second-hand Clothing in the News

Ministries of trade and commerce, customs departments, textile and garment workers, unions and manufacturer associations from Poland through Pakistan to the Philippines take issue with second-hand clothing imports. Some of their objections involve hygiene and public health issues – for example, the Latvian ban, in 2001, on imports of second-hand clothing and footwear from countries in Europe affected by foot-and-mouth disease ... The government of Tanzania recently banned the import of used underwear, in order to prevent skin problems and even venereal diseases ... insisting that it would check consignments to ensure that the 'offending garments' were not imported ...

By far the most frequently raised issue is the adverse effect of used clothing imports on domestic textile and garment industries. Second-hand clothing imports are banned in Indonesia because of the threat they pose to local garment production ... Poland's growing demand for, and re-export of, second-hand clothes to the former Soviet republics led clothing manufacturers to attribute their industry's decline to this trade ... Second-hand clothing disrupts the retail, clothing and garment industry according to the Clothing and Allied Workers Union in Lesotho ... where many South-east Asian-owned factories manufacture garments for export ... Philippine law forbids the import of used clothing that the Ministry of Industry and Trade views as a threat to textile industries ...

Most strikingly, allegations about the dumping effects of imported used clothing demonstrate widespread ignorance about the economic dynamics of the trade. And even in the absence of medical evidence, popular suspicion in some countries, especially in this time of HIV/AIDS, that used clothing spreads disease feeds into discourses about clothing and bodies. I heard many poorly informed economic arguments about this trade in Zambia during the time when second-hand clothing imports were growing rapidly in the early 1990s. One clothing manufacturer, for instance, complained that the import was 'killing local industry'. Like many others, he pleaded with the government to 'create a level playing field', either by banning or increasing tariffs on a commodity entering the country as 'donated' clothing. A union representative from Lesotho expressed a similar misconception when he explained that, in most cases, this clothing leaves its overseas destinies [sic] to be donated to the poor and destitute in the developing countries, but ends up in market stalls ...

Many countries forbid the import of second-hand clothing, while others restrict the volume or limit it to charitable purposes rather than resale. Regardless of import rules, and because borders are porous, smuggling and other illegal practices accompany the trade. Illegal imports of second-hand clothing and shoes into the Philippines are alleged to hide drugs ... In Pakistan, where used clothing imports are legal, under-invoicing and imports of new clothes from South-east Asia make it impossible for local garment manufacturers to compete, as brand-new goods enter the country with customs declarations as second-hand clothes ... The Nigerian customs service has seized containers of prohibited goods, including second-hand clothes, entering with false customs declarations ...

Journalists in the West string such news into a largely negative story. But these accounts can be qualified with reference to aggregate worldwide trade figures as well as to specific country situations. A recent study questioned the claim that imported second-hand garments flood the clothing markets in developing countries, highlighting the very small proportion of total world trade in textiles and garments made up by second-hand clothing, and pointing out that ... imports are not targeted solely at the Third World ... Such observations do not by themselves tell us much, but they do invite closer investigation at continental, regional and national levels. The salient questions become empirical, hinging on the relationship of domestic textile and garment industries and informal-sector tailoring to permitted and illegal imports of textiles, new garments and used clothing. Widely varying customs and tariff regulations affect supply of these commodities, which is ultimately shaped by local cultural issues around demand.

...

Imported Second-hand Clothing in Local Contexts

Anthropologists have made passing reference to the recent flourishing of second-hand clothing markets. In the Andes, for example, second-hand garments are among the many styles of 'ethnic cross-dressing' exhibited by distinct local groups today on different occasions ... A favourite pastime of young Tonga Islanders in the Pacific is attending Saturday-morning flea markets to buy clothes, shoes and cosmetics. Most of the clothes are second-hand, shipped to the islands in containers by relatives who live in Britain and the United States. The flea market creates business enterprise and offers young shoppers the excitement of developing their own style, distinct from the dominant Christian-influenced dress conventions ...

While anthropologists have noted the presence of imported second-hand clothing, they have mostly stopped short of examining it in the larger context of its sourcing, distribution and consumption. Recent works begin to do just that, casting a new light on the process which contrasts with the repeated negative accounts in the popular media. The Philippines forbid the import of second-hand clothing, yet the trade has grown in the wake of the shift to democratic government in 1986. Second-hand clothing from North America, Europe, Australia and Japan is shipped in containers to Manila and Cebu, where the bales are retailed illegally. Some used clothing is shipped via Hong Kong, which sources used clothing both internationally and from local charitable organizations. Much of this clothing reaches the Philippines in individually addressed boxes, known as *balikbhayn* (a term used for returning contract workers), of standard size for airline check-in, each of which contains the duty-free allowance of personal effects contract workers may bring with them on their return.

The number of second-hand clothing stores in northern Luzon grew dramatically between the mid and late 1990s ... As a collection and distribution hub, Banguio City in northern Luzon is an important retail centre. The second-hand clothing trade is largely in women's hands, and ... provides women with new opportunities for self-employment. The traders organize their enterprises through personalized relations, often based on kin, social networks and associations that they draw on locally, and similarly personalized contacts with wholesalers and importers. The women's active work, harnessing economic capital from this international trade to support the household, offers a stark contrast to the image of the powerless Filipina woman as foreign contract worker in domestic service across Southeast Asia and beyond, her overseas employment a major source of revenue for the Philippines' declining economy.

Controlling an important part of the dress market, women traders in second-hand clothing offer customers an attractive alternative to new factory-produced garments.

Combining second-hand garments into dress styles that display knowledge of wider clothing practice or alter their meanings, traders and consumers refashion this imported commodity to express their personal and community identities ... The trade resonates widely with popular culture.

...

'Killing' Local Industry in Zambia?

In a couple of recent media accounts about Zambia, second-hand clothing imports are used as an example of the negative effects of the neo-liberal market, alleged to be killing the local textile and garment industry ... or as a metaphor for the adverse effects of the policies of the World Bank, the International Monetary Fund and 'America' on the lives of the country's many poor people ... [S]uch accounts fail to take into account local perceptions about the availability of second-hand clothing as an improvement of livelihoods. A real exception to such accounts from small-town Zambia highlights local views on second-hand clothing: because 'no two items look alike', it enables people to dress smartly ... Zambia has permitted the import of second-hand clothing since the mid to late 1980s, when the centrally controlled economy began to open up. The term *salaula* (meaning, in the Bemba language, to select from a pile in the manner of rummaging) came into use at that time.

Imports grew rapidly in the early 1990s, and came to form the largest share of both urban and rural markets. According to a clothing consumption survey I conducted in 1995 in the capital, Lusaka, three-quarters of the urban population bought the vast majority of garments for their households from second-hand clothing markets ...

It is easy, but too facile, to blame *salaula* for the dismal performance of Zambia's textile and clothing industry. Numerous textile and garment manufacturers closed down in the early 1990s, not because of *salaula* imports but because they were already moribund. When government protection gave way to free-market principles in the transition to multi-party politics in 1991, the industry was in a precarious state. Its heavy dependence on imported raw materials, its capital intensity, inappropriate technology, poor management and lack of skilled labour, especially in textile printing, resulted in gross under-utilization of capacity. The new government was slow to improve circumstances for the industry.

...

With the open economy offering readily available, affordable, high-quality, good-looking printed textiles imported from South and South-east Asia, the textile plants ceased printing *chitenge* (colourful cloth widely used for wraps and women's dresses) for the local market, concentrating instead on production of loom-state cloth for export mainly to the European market ... While the growing import of *salaula* in the first half of the 1990s served as an easy scapegoat for the decline of Zambia's textile and garment factories, the experience of other industries in recent years reveals general problems facing the manufacturing sector in the era of economic liberalization.

Zambia is one of the world's least developed countries, in United Nations terms. Development economists would be inclined to view the growth of the second-hand clothing market in Zambia as a response to economic decline. While this observation is accurate, there is much more involved here than cheap clothing. Such an account fails to do justice to the opportunities this vast import trade offers for income generation in distribution, retail and associated activities, as well as for consumers to construct identity through dress.

My research in Lusaka's large markets, in some provincial towns and at rural sites where people are wage employed, clearly demonstrates the economic importance of *salaula* retailing in Zambia's declining economy ... The reduction in public- and private-sector employment and the decline in manufacturing jobs have drawn old and young job-seekers of both sexes to second-hand clothing distribution and allied activities. Urban *salaula* traders employ workers or pay for the upkeep of young relatives to help them run their business. When constructing market stalls, they purchase timber and plastic sheeting from other traders. They buy metal clothes hangers from small-scale entrepreneurs, and snacks, water and beverages from itinerant vendors. Young men carrying *salaula* bales on their heads or hauling them in 'Zam-cabs' (wheelbarrows) move goods from wholesale outlets to markets or bus stations for transport to peri-urban townships and more distant locations.

... While *salaula* has put some small-scale tailors out of work, it has kept many others busy with repairs and alterations, including the transformation of *salaula* into differently styled garments. Above all, the growth of the *salaula* market has challenged tailors to move into specialized production of garments and styles not readily found in *salaula*: women's *chitenge* cloth ensembles, two-piece office outfits, large sizes, inexpensive trousers, girls' party dresses, and many more styles that they find it easy to produce because of the ready availability of a wide range of fabrics whose import was restricted in the days of the centralized economy.

When I completed this research in 1998, the *salaula* trade appeared to have settled in Zambia. Imports had stabilized, no longer increasing from year to year. Government efforts to create a level playing field for industry had led to increased import tariffs rather than prohibition. The textile plants began to print *chitenge* cloth again. Efforts were being made to improve the collection of daily stall fees in established markets, including from *salaula* traders who comprise the single largest market segment across the country. *Salaula* was rarely a subject of debate in the local media.

Conducting research in Lusaka on an unrelated subject every year since 2000, I still take time to follow developments in the second-hand clothing trade. In retailing and distribution in 2003, stallholders at Soweto market, Lusaka's largest, employed proportionately more workers than in the 1990s. In a snap survey of every tenth stallholder, my assistant and I found workers and helpers everywhere, with some traders employing several workers. Some stallholders, especially men, have consolidated, combining numerous stalls where they sell different types of garments, displayed in the manner of a department store floor. And while Zambian consumers today have access to many more imported garments, especially inexpensive new clothes from South-east Asia, than when I began my study in 1992, they all go to *salaula* markets for value for money, everyday fashions and more. In the view of consumers, garments from *salaula* are 'incomparable' and not 'common'.

Clearly, much more is involved in the growth of second-hand clothing imports in a country like Zambia, and probably elsewhere, than the purchase of inexpensive garments to cover basic clothing needs. Clothing is central to the sense of well-being among all sectors of the population. Zambia's rural areas, where basic necessities were scarce throughout the 1980s, were described in 1992 with some enthusiasm: 'there is even *salaula* now' ...

People in Zambia approach second-hand clothing as a highly desirable consumer good, and incorporate the garments they carefully select into their dress universe on the basis of local norms of judgment and style. In short, second-hand clothing practices involve clothing-conscious consumers in efforts to change their lives for the better.

...

The revision to the popular media's account of the dangers used clothing imports pose to local industries that I offer here suggests that, by and large, domestic textile and garment manufacturing firms and second-hand clothing imports do not target the same consumers. The single most striking point about accounts of the negative effects of the second-hand clothing trade appearing in local and Western news media is their lack of curiosity about the clothes themselves and how consumers deal with them. In effect, in these accounts the clothes are entirely incidental. Aside from their utilitarian value for money, what in fact accounts for the attractions of imported second-hand clothing? The points of view of local consumers command our attention, if we are to understand why clothing, in particular, is central to discussions about democratization and liberalization.

Edited extract from: Karen Tranberg Hansen, 'Helping or Hindering? Controversies around the International Second-hand Clothing Trade', *Anthropology Today* 20/4 (2004), pp.3–9.

45 The Kayapo Resistance
Terence Turner

As Eriksen points out in the extract from his work included above, global influences can create victims but they can also place power in the hands of peoples who are otherwise relatively weak and powerless. Terence Turner is an American anthropologist who has specialised in the study of peoples of the Amazon basin. Most readers will be aware that this is a region under heavy threat from the environmental degradation and social disruptions resulting from large-scale extractive industries such as mining and logging, as well as industrial changes to the river systems on which subsistence fishing depends. In this extract from an article originally published in 1993, and recounting events that took place mainly in the 1980s, Turner describes for us how the Kayapo see the environment and subsistence as integral to the creation of the human person and human community. He goes on to show how the Kayapo, faced with multiple threats to their physical and human world from global economic interests, were able to draw on other aspects of the globalised world – environmental activists, the international media and public opinion, celebrities, politicians in many countries, and the leadership of other Amazonian peoples – to mount a resistance that was effective (at that time at least).

As increasing numbers of people have become aware of the imminence of the destruction of the world's tropical forests and the probable consequences for the atmosphere and climate of the planet, voices have increasingly been heard drawing attention to the need for concern for human populations of forest dwellers, as well as the floral and faunal components of the ecosystem. This has been motivated in part by humanitarian concerns, in part by more specific concerns for indigenous political and legal rights, in part by an awareness that native forest peoples may possess valuable knowledge of their environments, and also, at times, by a realization that the traditional adaptive activities of such peoples may make important functional contributions to the ecosystems in which they live. Whatever their specific point of departure, however, advocates of native forest peoples have tended to assume that recognition of the rights and contributions of the native inhabitants of the forests, as well as their physical and cultural survival, would depend, like the salvation of the forests themselves, upon them. That native forest peoples themselves, many of whom number among the most ... remote human societies on earth, should come to play an important role as allies and even leaders in the world struggle to save the forests, is a prospect so apparently remote as to seem only a little less improbable than Martians arriving to lend a hand. Yet this is precisely what has been happening in the last few years, nowhere with more impressive scope and success than in the case of the Kayapo Indians of the Brazilian Amazon.

...

The Kayapo are a nation of Ge-speaking Indians who inhabit the middle and lower reaches of the valley of the Xingu River, one of the major southern tributaries of the Amazon. Their total population is currently around 2,500, divided among fourteen mutually independent communities. The largest of these communities, Gorotire, has about 800 inhabitants, but several others are little more than hamlets. Kayapo country is a mixture of forest and savannah land, with rather more forest than open country around most of the villages. The total area covered by Kayapo communities and their associated land-use patterns is about the size of Scotland.

The massive destruction of the Amazonian environment represented by the cutting and burning of the forest, the cutting of roads, and the soil erosion and river pollution caused by mining and the building of giant hydroelectric dams, have had a shattering impact on the environment and way of life of many forest Indians of the Amazon. Even groups whose lands have not yet been reached by these activities, or are just beginning to be affected by them, now live in the permanent shadow of the threat. To

Kayapo Resistance
Early in 1989 the Kayapo rallied other Brazilian Indians to attend a reunification of the tribes at Altamira, the proposed site of a massive hydro-electric dam that would flood large parts of the Xingu valley. The gathering also served as an international media event.

Production Still: The Kayapo. Out of the Forest Disappearing World series, 1989; Distributed by the Royal Anthropological Institute. Published in A. Singer and L. Woodhead 1988 *Disappearing World: Television and Anthropology.* Granada Television Ltd.

understand the meaning of this threat for indigenous peoples like the Kayapo, one must stand in a Kayapo village under the dense clouds of smoke that now darken the sky over Kayapo country at the end of every dry season, as Brazilian squatters and ranchers burn off vast stretches of previously forested land to the east and south, rapidly approaching the traditional borders of Kayapo territory along a 700-mile front. It is to feel one's world burning, with the ring of fire drawing even tighter.

For members of modern industrial societies, one of the most difficult points to grasp about the relation of native tropical forest peoples to their environment, as articulated through their modes of subsistence production, is that the relationship is not felt or conceived to comprise a separate 'economic' sphere in our sense. Rather, it forms an integral part of the total social process of producing human beings and social life. The threatened annihilation of such a society's environmental base of subsistence is therefore not felt merely as an 'economic' threat, nor one that can be located and confined in an external, 'environmental' sphere. It is a threat to the continuity and meaning of social life. Understanding this point is essential, not only to appreciate the traumatic effects of wholesale ecological devastation on traditional societies of subsistence producers like the Kayapo, but also to understand the nature of their political response and resistance to such threats.

...

For the Kayapo, like most other contemporary Amazonian native peoples, traditional patterns of subsistence adaptation are still the basic way of life. The Kayapo produce their means of subsistence by a combination of slash-and-burn horticulture, hunting, fishing, and foraging. According to the division of labor by gender and generation, men engage in all productive pursuits incompatible with the care of young children, while women perform those which can be carried out while caring for children. This means that men hunt, fish, do the heavy and dangerous work of clearing gardens, and gather certain wild forest products that grow at great distances, requiring overnight journeys. Women do the planting, weeding, and harvesting of gardens; cut firewood; cook the food; build traditional shelters (now done almost exclusively in trekking camps); forage for such wild products as can be found within a day's round-trip walk from the village or camp; and care for children. Girls begin to help their mothers with household and garden chores while still children, but boys do little productive labor until they are inducted into the men's house, a bachelors' dormitory and men's club which stands apart from the family houses in the middle of the round village plaza.

...

Kayapo patterns of environmental adaptation and subsistence production are intricately interwoven with their ways of producing human individuals. This process of human production includes what we call 'socializing' children, but continues through the life cycle and the final rites of death. This individual process, in turn, is treated by the Kayapo as an integral part of the process of reproducing collective social units like extended-family households, age-sets, and ceremonial organizations, and thus of society as a whole ... [T]he division of labor in the production of material subsistence is defined in relation to the division of labor in the production of social persons and relations, with women specializing in the socialization of children. It must be clearly understood that this is not simply a natural result but a culturally imposed social pattern. Women who do not happen to be raising young children nevertheless do not go hunting and fishing. At a higher level of organization, the nuclear family forms the social unit of cooperation in the production and consumption of material subsistence, but as a social unit it owes its form primarily to its role in producing new social persons, not its functions in expediting subsistence activities. Subsistence production thus finds its place as an integral part of the global process of social production, which also includes the socialization of children, the recruitment and reconstitution of families and collective groups, and the celebration of the great communal ceremonies.

...

The Kayapo attitude toward the nonhuman natural environment must be understood as a part of this same global pattern. The Kayapo do not oppose 'nature' to human society as mutually exclusive, externally related domains; nor can they be said to possess a single, uniform concept of 'nature' in our sense. They recognize that the forest and savannah beyond their village clearings are products of forces that are independent of humans and not under social control. They further recognize that they depend upon these natural forces and products for their own social existence, and that social persons are in fact largely 'natural' beings, whose physical bodies, senses, and libidinal energies are as extra-social in origin as any forest tree or wild animal. Disease, death, shamanic trance, insanity, and periods of transition in [life]-crisis ritual are seen as moments when the continuity between the internal natural core of human social actors and the external natural environment of the forest and animal world asserts itself, short-circuiting and blacking out the interposed, insulating social veneer.

...

Society and its members ... are essentially seen as appropriating and channeling natural energy, and are thus dependent on the ability of the natural world (meaning the forest, animals, birds, rivers, and fish) to reproduce itself and continue as a great reservoir and source of the energy society must continually draw upon to live. The destruction of the forest, the killing or driving away of its animals, or the pollution of the rivers and killing of their fish, therefore, are not seen by the Kayapo simply as an attack on 'the natural environment' in our sense, but as a direct assault upon them as a society and as individuals.

...

Since the 1960s there has been constant pressure from small squatters and large ranchers attempting to infiltrate Kayapo areas and clear small farms by burning off patches of forest. Land speculators have attempted to build illegal airstrips and to survey and sell off large chunks of Kayapo land to which they did not even hold legal title. In 1971, the Brazilian government built a major road of the Trans-Amazonica highway system through Kayapo country, secretly altering the route so as to amputate the Kayapo area of the Xingu National Park ... The road brought heavy truck and bus traffic carrying settlers and supplies to the new settlements farther west, bringing with them the perils of infectious disease and the potential for conflict with the Indians. Timber companies interested in the large stands of virgin mahogany within the boundaries of the remaining officially delimited Kayapo reserve ... sought and obtained logging concessions for large tracts from Kayapo leaders in exchange for sizable money payments and the construction of modern housing and other facilities in Kayapo villages.

...

The discovery of gold at the huge mine of Serra Pelada near the eastern border of the Kayapo Indigenous Area led to intense prospecting and exploratory gold-mining activity within the eastern borders of the Kayapo Indigenous Area. This culminated in 1983 with the opening of two large illegal gold mines only ten kilometers from Gorotire village ...

As if all this were not enough, the Kayapo began to hear rumors that the Brazilian government was planning to build a series of hydroelectric dams along the Xingu and its tributaries, which would result in the flooding of large areas of Kayapo land and end the value of most of the river system as a fishery. The scheme was to be funded by loans from the World Bank. Repeated attempts to learn the truth about the government's plans were met with stonewalling and denials that any such plan existed. The rumors persisted, however, and construction sites began to be cleared at certain points along the river. The Kayapo were outraged by the government's disregard for their political and legal rights to be consulted about a project which would so heavily affect their lands and livelihood. They were equally concerned about the ecological effects.

...

This daunting array of threats to the Kayapo environment, communal lands and resource base, political and civil rights, is a representative sample of the human face of the environmental crisis in the Amazon. The Kayapo confronted this apparently overwhelming onslaught beginning in the early 1970s as a still largely monolingual people of Ge speakers scattered over a vast area in fourteen mutually autonomous and politically uncoordinated settlements. In most of the villages, some of the men (but almost no women) spoke Portuguese, and a handful had learned to read, write, and do simple arithmetic. A few leaders had obtained some experience of Brazilian administrative and political ways through working in the Indian Service or as members of Brazilian expeditions to contact other tribes. They had a few contacts with the outside world through anthropologists and indigenous advocacy groups, and the Brazilian Indian Service (FUNAI) offered some support, although it could not be counted upon to represent the Indians' interests against the more threatening forms of economic development mounted by government or powerful private interests. Aside from this slender array of assets, the Kayapo had no political resources with which to defend themselves and their forest beyond their own largely intact tribal institutions and culture. These, however, were to serve them well in the trials that lay ahead.

...

This is what they did. The two western communities whose land had been severed by the road began an unrelenting campaign of armed attacks on all Brazilian intruders who attempted to open ranches or settle in the separated area. After fifteen years and perhaps fifty Brazilian dead, with no Kayapo casualties, no Brazilian settler remained in the entire area. The leaders of the two Kayapo groups meanwhile carried out a campaign of diplomacy, making repeated trips to Brasilia to pressure the government to return the stolen land and thus end the violent standoff in the area. The government capitulated in 1985, returning the area to the Kayapo and ceding an additional area immediately to the north of the old area ... The two communities of the region joined again into a single large village and have resolutely banned all Brazilian mining, timber and agricultural interests and settlers from their reclaimed areas.

Also in 1985, the two illegally opened gold mines were assaulted and captured by 200 Kayapo, armed with a mixture of firearms and traditional weapons. The larger mine was accessible only by air, so the Kayapo seized and blockaded the landing strip, confronting the Brazilian government with a choice: either cede title and administrative authority over the mines to the Kayapo, together with a significant percentage of the proceeds ... or the Kayapo would allow no more planes to land or take off, either to supply or evacuate the three thousand miners at the site. After a tense ten-day standoff, the government gave in to the Kayapo demands.

The leaders of Gorotire, the nearest and largest Kayapo village, used the first income from the mine to purchase a light plane and hire a Brazilian pilot. They put the plane to use to patrol their borders from the air to spot intruders and would-be squatters. If any were seen, patrols were dispatched to expel or eliminate the invaders. Within a year, invasions effectively ceased. They have also used the plane to fly to other Kayapo villages and to Brazilian cities to purchase goods and bring people out for medical assistance ...

All timber concessions on Kayapo land were suspended by the Indian Service (FUNAI) at the end of 1987, at the urging of the most influential Kayapo leaders ... Some concessions, however, were surreptitiously continued by a few other leaders who have lined their own pockets with the fees paid by the companies ... Meanwhile, resistance to any new concessions continues to be strong, and one community ... has declared its part of the Kayapo Indigenous Area an 'extractive reserve' closed to all ecologically destructive forms of timber and mineral exploitation.

...

Most of the other threats posed by the enveloping national society proved less divisive, and the Kayapo were able to mount concerted, well-organized responses to them without internal dissension or conflict. When the government's plan to dump ... radioactive waste on traditional Kayapo land was announced, the Kayapo sent a hundred men to Brasilia to demonstrate against the plan. Suitably painted and feathered, they staged a sit-in in the president's palace. Nothing like this had happened in Brazil in the twenty years since the *coup d'état* that established the military regime that was then in the process of relinquishing power. The initial incredulity and indignation of the authorities, however, gave way to acquiescence to the Kayapo's demands, and the dumping plan was abandoned ...

...

In 1988, two Kayapo leaders were invited to the United States to participate in a conference on tropical forest ecology. From there, they traveled to Washington, met with members of Congress, and spoke with World Bank officials about the effects of the proposed Xingu dam scheme on the peoples and environment of the area. They were able to obtain copies of the entire dam project, the very existence of which the Brazilian government had continued to deny, from the Bank. Shortly after the Kayapos' visit, the World Bank announced that it was deferring action on the Brazilian loan request. Enraged, elements of the Brazilian national security and political establishment had criminal charges brought against them and their American interpreter under a law prohibiting participation in political activity in Brazil by foreigners. The charges were ridiculous in strictly legal terms; since the actions in question had taken place in the United States, the American had been acting in his own country, and the Kayapo were not in any case foreigners. The transparent attempt at legal terrorism boomeranged, as nongovernment organizations (NGOs), anthropologists, and the congressmen whom the Kayapo had met on their tour organized an international outcry.

When one of the Kayapo leaders came to Belém, the capital of the state of Pará, where the charges had been brought, to be arraigned, the Kayapo organized a massive protest demonstration. More than five hundred Kayapo men and women danced through the streets and massed in the square before the Palace of Justice to support their kinsman and denounce Brazilian political repression. The defiance turned to ridicule when the judge refused to allow the Kayapo leader to enter the courthouse for arraignment until he changed his paint and feathers for 'civilized' (Brazilian) clothes. The Kayapo refused and told the judge he would have to come to the Kayapo village of Gorotire if he wanted another chance to arraign him on the charges. Meanwhile, Kayapo orators unrolled the map of the Xingu dam scheme obtained from the World Bank in Washington on an easel erected in the square and explained the entire secret project in Kayapo and Portuguese for the benefit of the many Brazilian onlookers, who included reporters and TV crews. The government never again dared to try to arraign the Kayapo leader, and eventually dropped all the charges.

With the World Bank still actively considering the Brazilian government's request for a loan to enable the building of the Xingu dams, the proposed multi-dam hydroelectric scheme in the Xingu River valley now appeared to the Kayapo as the greatest threat, not only to their environment, but to their political and legal control over their lands and resources. Since the government still refused to disclose its plans to build the dams, the Kayapo resolved to force it to reveal its intentions and to receive, before an audience of national and world news media, their criticisms of the human and environmental effects of the dams ... To accomplish this, they decided to convene a great congress of Amazonian peoples at the site of the first of the dams the government hoped to build: Altamira, near the mouth of the Xingu. To the meeting would be invited representatives of the Brazilian governments; representatives of the World Bank; representatives of the national and world news media; nongovernmental organizations active in the environmentalist, human rights, and indigenous peoples' support fields; delegates from as many indigenous nations of Amazonia as possible; and as many Kayapo as could be transported and accommodated. At the meeting, the government representatives would be asked to present their plans, to give an account of their probable effects on the environment and the human inhabitants of the region (Brazilian as well as native), and to explain why they had tried for so long to keep their plans secret from those who would be most affected by them.

...

The event took on the aspect of an international media circus. The Pope sent a telegram of support. The rock star Sting flew in for a day and gave a press conference at the Kayapo encampment, denouncing the destruction of the forest and promoting his own project for the creation of a new Kayapo reserve ... A British Member of Parliament, a Belgian Member of the European Parliament, and a half-dozen Brazilian deputies of the National Congress ... mounted the platform and gave unreserved support. A final communiqué was issued, on behalf of all native peoples of Amazonia, condemning the dam project. By the time the conference closed with a dance from the Kayapo New Corn ceremony (joined in by assorted Indians of other tribes, European and Brazilian activists and media personnel, momentarily giving it the air of a 1960s hippie love-in), the Altamira gathering had become an international media success of such proportions as to generate serious political pressure against any international funding of the dam scheme, or indeed any attempt to go on with the plan by the Brazilian government. Within two weeks after the end of the meeting, the World Bank announced that it would not grant the Brazilian loan earmarked for the dam project, and the Brazilian National Congress had announced plans for a formal investigation and debate on the whole plan.

...

The success of the Kayapo in furthering their own cause ... has had an important effect upon the politics of the developed world, and in particular, of the environmentalist movement. The support of environmentalist groups and public opinion has been essential to the Kayapo victories, but it is equally true that the Kayapo have won important victories for the environmentalist movement, and partly as a result have exercised an important influence upon its thinking, strategies, and organizational tactics. Perhaps most importantly, in a few short years they have revolutionized the consciousness of many activists and ordinary persons concerned with the fate of the world's tropical forests, teaching them that indigenous forest-dwelling peoples are not just a passive part of the problem, but an active part of the solution. By their own example, they have demonstrated that native forest peoples, no matter how apparently primitive, remote, or numerically insignificant, can become potent combatants and allies in the struggle to avert ecological disaster. In addition, they have helped bring about working relations of mutual trust and collaboration between members of a number of important organizations, scientific specialists, and politicians, who had previously never considered working together, and in many cases mistrusted one another's politics and policies.

Before the advent of the Kayapo on the international stage, many environmentalists had realized that there could be no solution to the problem of saving the forests that did not include the human inhabitants of the forests. Many who had arrived at this relatively enlightened opinion, however, continued to think of aboriginal forest peoples, and even forest-dwelling members of national societies like the Brazilian rubber-tappers, as historical basket cases, with all the capacity for political action in their own behalf of endangered animal species like the black cayman or the Amazonian giant otter. It has been a humbling, disconcerting, but delightful surprise to many of these same good people suddenly to discover that some of these supposedly hapless victims of progress have assumed a leading role in the struggle environmentalists had thought (perhaps a tad condescendingly) they were leading, and that these same native peoples have even succeeded in bringing to the effort a degree of unity and effectiveness that had previously eluded its familiar leadership …

Edited extract from: Terence Turner, 'The Kayapo Resistance', reprinted in J. Spradley D.W. McCurdy (eds), *Conformity and Conflict: Readings in Cultural Anthropology* (Boston: Pearson, 2008), pp.391–409.

46 Tourism
Thomas Hylland Eriksen

The mass movement of people, whether voluntary or enforced, is very much part of the contemporary globalised world, although it has its historical antecedents (think of the slave trade between Europe, Africa and the Caribbean two centuries ago). Both kinds of mobility are of great interest to contemporary anthropologists. The anthropology of tourism has grown into a major field of specialist research in recent years, as has the anthropological study of refugees, migration and diasporas, displacement and resettlement. In this second extract from Thomas Hylland Eriksen's book Globalisation: The Key Concepts, *the author (who is Norwegian) draws a general comparison between the situations of the (voluntary) tourist and the (involuntary) refugee. The two extracts which follow give examples of how anthropologists have approached these two sharply contrasting situations.*

The inhabitants of Norway in 1850 never went on holiday. Some of the very rich went on once-in-a-lifetime tours of Europe, some from the privileged classes studied in Copenhagen or Berlin, and thousands of sailors travelled abroad because it was their job. Half a century later, this began to change. The imported idea of the seaside resort materialized, and mountain trips dear to the emerging middle-class nationalism began to resemble tourism in the modern sense, featuring the exotic (local peasants) and the magnificent (the mountains). Half a century later again, the package trip to the Mediterranean was introduced, but most Norwegians still spent their holidays (which they were now entitled to) at home or in another Scandinavian country.

Similar developments took place earlier in a few other countries, notably Britain, where forty-eight London coaches a day served the seaside in

'Want a Camel, Yes?'
Interactions between camel drivers and tourists visiting the Giza pyramids in Egypt.

Filmstill from *Want a Camel, Yes?* by Christian Suhr and Mette Bahnsen (Royal Anthropological Institute Film Festival 2009).

Brighton as early as the summer months of the 1830s, and the package trip was invented by Thomas Cook as early as 1844. Nevertheless, the emergence of mass tourism has happened, and has unfolded, fairly synchronically, in the rich countries. Whereas my parents spent their summer holidays in the family cottage when they were young, I went to southern Europe with my friends on an Interrail ticket, and those who are twenty years younger than me would travel to South America or Thailand. This illustrates the evolution of tourism, from local to regional to global, as it has unfolded in most parts of the rich world.

The word 'tourist' was still a recent invention in the mid twentieth century. Due to economic growth and technological changes (including, notably, cheap flights), the tourist industry has grown steadily since the 1950s, making it the possibly largest economic sector in the world. By the mid 1990s, 7 per cent of the global workforce, around 230 million persons, were employed in tourism ... Tourist organizations predict that in the year 2020, 1.6 billion people will make a trip abroad. The Mediterranean area, the most popular foreign destination for north Europeans, received about six million tourists annually in 1955. In 2005, the number was 220 million, expected by the World Tourist Organization to grow to 350 million by 2020 (unless something unexpected happens, such as paleness becoming fashionable again, or rapid climate change making the heat unbearable in summer). Most tourists in the Mediterranean area ... 'have to get used to vacationing in an eternal construction site'.

Global tourism can be interpreted along several lines. One is homogenization, industrialization and mass production ... Leafing through the free catalogues distributed by the large tour operators, it is difficult to notice where the Spanish section ends and the Brazilian section begins. There is a global grammar of package tourism which entails that tourist destinations have to conform to a minimal set of requirements. If the destination is of the sun-and-sand type, nightclubs, snorkelling trips, swimming pools, playgrounds and charming, open-air markets are *de rigueur*. Food is either 'international' or modified local. Tennis courts and mini-golf are ubiquitous. If the destination is a city, standardized 'sights' (the Rijksmuseum, the Sacre Coeur, the Tower of London) are featured along with advice on shopping opportunities. Hotels are classified according to an international ranking system.

Another perspective on global tourism would emphasize its *glocal* dimension, blending local culture, food and music with the common denominators required by the global grammar of tourism. Toilets and bathrooms, the tourist staff's language skills and food preparation, to mention a few dimensions, cannot be tampered with too much within this grammar, which ensures that any tourist destination should in principle be accessible to middle-class travellers from anywhere. However, local flavour is sometimes considerable and is indeed often a main attraction. Along the lush and picturesque Gudbrandsdal valley of central southern Norway, numerous converted farms and newly built guesthouses in an old-fashioned style are calibrated to attract tourists (many of them Norwegian-Americans) in search of 'the authentic'. So staff are paid to wear traditionalist clothes, to serve dishes rarely seen on Norwegian dinner tables, and to play fiddle music. In general, the cultural dimension of tourism has become more and more pronounced as the number of tourists grows and their interests diversify. The folklore show has become a staple in many 'exotic' tourist locations, and in some areas (such as South Africa and Indonesia) tourists' group tours to real villages or real townships have become an important source of income to people living there.

Tourist destinations are at least two places at one and the same time: a holiday destination and a local community. People from Benidorm live in a Spanish town, whereas tourists are on holiday in southern Europe, a place with totally different connotations. In many popular tourist destinations, not least in the Mediterranean, locals are shocked and outraged at what they see as a hedonistic culture of permissiveness, especially among the young vacationers, coming from northern Europe. A colleague in Cyprus was visibly relieved, but also expressed concern, when I told him that the young Scandinavians who engage routinely in casual sex and take recreational drugs in the clubs dotting the island's south coast would never dare to behave in the same way at home.

As always, there are exceptions to this rule. Cancun, on the Caribbean coast of Mexico, was non-existent as late as the mid 1970s. By early 2007 it had about half a million inhabitants, virtually all of whom are employed directly or indirectly in the tourism industry. It is a place with no history and no collective identity, established because of the need among US tour operators to find a new appropriate destination – Florida was filling up – four hours or less by plane from the main US cities. (Slightly south of Cancun, a town apparently designed for European tourists was developed, namely Playa del Carmen, with smaller hotels, less traffic and pedestrian streets with quaint shops and bars.)

The tourist ... is a skilled vacationer who knows the cultural codes and rules regulating the role of the tourist. However, tourism has diversified, and today it would probably be correct to speak of a plurality of tourisms. 'Anti-tourism' of the generic backpacker kind, for example, has been institutionalized and standardized for decades, so that popular 'alternative' travel guidebooks like the Lonely Planet and Rough Guide series can be bought in every airport or bookshop, giving sound advice as to which local bus to take to see temples off the beaten track and which guesthouses to avoid because staff tend to steal from the guests.

...

The Tourist and the Refugee

... Although most people in the world continue to lead most of their lives near the place where they grew up, some are free to travel on vacation (or business), whereas others are forced to leave their homes as refugees or economic migrants. According to figures from the United Nations High Commission for Refugees (UNHCR), there were 185 million international migrants in 2005. To this may be added tens of millions of internal migrants, not least in populous countries like China and India. The number of international refugees grew from 2 million in 1975 to 15 million in 1995, but decreased to less than 10 million in 2004. However, the number of internally displaced persons, more difficult to count, is estimated to be tens of millions.

The contrast between the tourist and the refugee is stark. The tourist can travel anywhere or almost anywhere with a minimum of friction; the refugee is interrogated at every international border and is likely to be turned away. The tourist moves in a 'third culture' where everybody has a smattering of English, and can easily buy everything he needs. The refugee is usually penniless and dependent on charity, and often encounters serious problems of understanding with the locals due to lack of a shared language. The tourist, of course, is free to leave any moment, while the refugee is ordered to and fro. Tellingly, the tourist, always short of time at home, makes a virtue of reducing his or her speed and limiting the daily activities while on vacation, and the refugee's life is full of slow, empty time where nothing happens. Both exemplify the predominance of movement in the contemporary world, and between them, the refugee and the tourist give an accurate depiction of the uneven distribution of resources in the globalized world.

Edited extract from: T.H. Eriksen, *Globalization: The Key Concepts* (Oxford: Berg, 2007), pp.97–101.

47 'Foreword' to *Thinking through Tourism*
Margaret E. Kenna

In this extract from the Foreword to a volume of anthropological studies of tourism, Margaret Kenna deals with the relationship between being a tourist and being an anthropologist. Readers have probably had some experience of the encounters Kenna describes between 'tourists' and 'locals', and might use this vivid account of her experience on a Greek island to reflect on their own, drawing upon similar anthropological concepts. For example, can the relationships and social practices involved be described as 'friendship', 'tourism', 'observer/ participant', 'socially appropriate behaviour', 'performance', 'authenticity', 'traditional island behaviour'? Kenna explores these interpretations in her attempts to 'anthropologise' her own experience on the Greek island of Anafi.

The Anthropologist as Tourist, Traveller and Theoretician

When I first went to carry out research in Greece in the spring of 1966, I was careful to differentiate myself from tourists and travellers in a way I now recognize to be a reaction to the threat of 'contamination' to my mission, which I saw as in some way morally superior to the search for pleasure and recreation which I assumed characterized these others. From what I have read ... this attempt to mark difference of essence and intent has been common among other researchers, as well as among academics in other disciplines ('you've come to whale-watch, but I'm a cetologist').

I was not in Greece, I told myself, to sunbathe, to read Fowles's *The Magus* or translations of Kazantzakis's *Zorba* on the beach or on the decks of inter-island ferries; I was there to become a real anthropologist, to carry out participant observation, to live with local people all year round, winter as well as summer. I might look like a typical backpacker but I felt that I was different. I became aware that some of these other visitors to Greece, like myself, also saw themselves as different, but my interpretation then was that this was a rationalization of their economic position (usually coupled with age). Backpackers claimed that they were there to experience the 'real Greece', and that those who travelled in air-conditioned coaches, or had cabins with bunks rather than sleeping on deck, were missing some kind of authenticity in their encounter with places and people. The question of what constituted 'the "real" Greece', and how best to find it, gained salience for me much later; at that time I assumed that I would have access to it through long-term participant-observation fieldwork.

I was not confident enough then, however, to anthropologize the situation I found myself in and to problematize the different kinds of tourists and travellers I met and in contrast to whom I tried to assert a different identity. Even if I had done this, I think I would have felt that the focus of my studies should be the local people not the visitors.

... I was then completely unaware of any anthropological studies of, or thinking about, tourism.

...

... During this first fieldwork (1966–67), fewer than ten people came to Anafi [the Greek Cycladic island which was the author's fieldwork site] who could be classified as tourists or travellers. Not surprisingly, they were nearly all backpackers, carrying sleeping bags and basic supplies, in case they could not find a place to sleep or anything to eat. And the islanders were certainly not set up to receive, nor did they seem even to welcome, the arrival of these visitors ... The topic of tourism hardly featured in the material written up from this period.

However, the anthropology of tourism forced itself on my consciousness in 1974 when electrification, coupled with some repairs and improvements to the harbour which allowed steamers to dock directly at the jetty, brought tourism to the island. Anafiot migrants returned from Athens to open restaurants and cafés, while locals began to convert storehouses to offer to the increasing numbers of foreign and domestic tourists as rooms to rent, and then began to purpose-build such rooms. From 1989, lorries and refrigerated trucks could reach the outskirts or the village on a newly constructed road, which replaced the donkey-track, up which scooters, but not cars, had bumped their way since 1974. Village houses now had piped water and were connected to a sewerage system. Tourism-related enterprises took another quantum leap forward: now rooms to rent had en-suite bathrooms, and there were apartments with kitchenettes. Tavernas and restaurants now began to differentiate their menus and to offer 'specialities'. The road provided further opportunities for locals too, as its route opened up areas of land on the way to, and around, the village which had been previously impossible to reach. Some of these newly accessible building-sites, particularly those on steep hillsides, were developed into multi-storey apartment blocks, with panoramic views, and new village neighbourhoods were thus established. In each cluster, one apartment would provide a daughter's dowry, and the rest would bring her in an income when rented during the summer season. Outside the season, the large number of schoolteachers appointed to teach at the newly created secondary school and sixth-form college ... provided a smaller but steady income. Within another decade, a network of unpaved 'agricultural' roads, constructed with money from European Union grants for the development of peripheral areas, contributed not only to the resurgence of agriculture, but also to the repair and renovation of country cottages, and to the building of new holiday retreats for migrants who found the village too noisy during the tourist season. As a result, new neighbourhoods were emerging outside the village as well as in it, and new kinds of social relationships were being established. Reading material on 'locals' and 'outsiders' in tourism-related enterprises elsewhere, it seemed to me that those who had written on this topic could not have had long-term in-depth knowledge of local communities and the relationships between people. Otherwise they might have asked the question how these outsiders had found out about the opportunities to set up tourist enterprises, and thus the researchers would have discovered that there were many kinds of already established ties between these 'outsiders' and people in the local community ... In the material I had collected, these ties were predominantly based on having a common place of origin. Migrants whose parents or grandparents had gone to the city to find work now brought their urban-acquired capital with them to take advantage of each decade's improvements on the island. But they had urban contacts (friends, neighbours, employers, fellow employees) who also recognized the economic opportunities of a newly developing tourism-oriented summer seasonal economy. So even those who could indeed be classified as 'outsiders', turned out to have some kind of link with islanders or migrants which explained their presence running a bar in the village or a mini-market at the harbour, in a building rented from a local contact. Knowledge of long-running enmities between village families, of local schisms and factions, also helped to explain why some of these outsiders' enterprises were actively promoted by some islanders – as a way of taking custom away from those with whom they were on bad terms as much as of supporting someone whom they felt they had 'sponsored' to come to the island.

Before the road was finished in 1989, most villagers were able to provide roughly the same 'product' to tourists (a room to rent, meals composed of similar ingredients). The creation of a personal relationship between a room renter or taverna owner and customers attempted to ensure that the tourist returned to them next time, and not to any other provider of the same service. I had witnessed this in Athens in the streets where shop after shop offered exactly the same stock, whether electrical cable, plastic pipe, or zips, buttons and ribbons. Men went to particular electrical supply shops, and women to specific haberdashers, as a result of familiarity and of long-term relationships, often established in previous generations. Prices were adjusted, or additional services provided, to ensure that these relationships continued. Just so, on Anafi, new relationships (in island terms) were being built up between service providers, based on an urban pattern (which itself was based on patterns brought from the places of origin of migrants to the city).

Seeing Oneself (and One's Environment) as Seen by Others

Starting off in a similar fashion (trying to create a repeat-customer relationship), another kind of relationship was also being established, and that was between villagers with rooms to rent and domestic and international holidaymakers who were becoming 'regulars', booking for the same week or fortnight every year (almost a kind of timeshare). Some of these had a much more detailed knowledge than I did of the changes which had taken place over the years between my visits to the island, and some of them knew much more than me about the family from whom they regularly rented accommodation. I became aware that I could no longer make claims to possessing encyclopaedic authoritative information about the island – this was worse than the unease that I had experienced twenty years earlier with the backpackers!

But this time I was able to diffuse the sense of threat by speculating about these relationships. Were these 'friendships'? Or were they defined and regarded in different terms by the two sets of participant? For example, a Dutch couple who had been coming every Easter for a decade said that they had a warm personal friendship with the owners of the rooms they rented; one year they had brought with them and left behind a coffee-maker, which was now ceremoniously unpacked and put in 'their room' each year before their annual visit. They were always invited to the family's Easter celebrations and given fresh vegetables and fruit from their garden, gifts which were reciprocated with specialities from Holland, and, of course, colour photographs of the couple and their children and of picturesque views of the island. But was this perceived as a friendship by the room-renters?

These ponderings overlapped with thoughts arising out of changes I had noticed in the celebrations of the island patron saint's festival day. The improvements in facilities that had led to the return of migrants and the development of tourism had also resulted in larger numbers of people attending this festival (usually regarded as important in demonstrating the power of the saint in attracting devotees ... After the morning service on the day of the festival, the patron saint's icon (miracle-working holy picture) was carried in procession three times anticlockwise around the church where it was housed. Over the years I noticed that there was an increase in the number of people wanting to take photographs, and later, video-recordings of this event. Some were islanders, and some were migrants, both feeling that they had superior claims over others to do this because of their special relationship with their patron saint. These concerns began to clash with the desire of foreign tourists (and with domestic tourists from other parts of Greece, who seemed to regard themselves as observers rather than as participants) to capture images of what they seemed to regard as a particularly authentic example of traditional island custom ... They jostled with each other, and with Anafiots, for positions from which to film. Comments were made that the festival was turning into a tourist attraction and the procession into a 'photo-opportunity' rather than retaining its character (exactly what this character was provided an issue for debate, with islanders and migrants split into a number of factions).

Outside-in and Inside-out

These thoughts about what constituted authenticity also overlapped with a particular understanding I was reaching about Greek Orthodoxy, which seemed to me (and, I later discovered, to other scholars who worked in Greece) not to be particularly concerned with the internalized conscience and with guilt, but rather with avoiding public shame and with comporting oneself in accordance with public expectations (which on the island usually lagged behind urban mores) ... What was important to the islanders was a socially acceptable performance, whatever one's personal feelings were. There were, of course, occasions when what I considered to be 'real emotions' were openly displayed (the happy glow of a young woman finally engaged to the young man of her choice; the uncontrollable grief of the female relatives of a teenage girl, who had been killed in a fall from a donkey and then down a rocky ravine), but proper behaviour by the protagonists seemed to be the key aspect of positively evaluating others' actions and words, and therefore became a guiding principle of the main actors' behaviour. So if the islanders themselves were not particularly concerned with sincerity and authenticity but rather in a reasonable representation of socially appropriate behaviour, how could these notions of evaluation from the anthropology of tourism be applicable? If most behaviour was 'performed authenticity', what counted as 'genuine' and 'sincere'?

I found myself returning to texts which I had studied as an undergraduate, including articles by Meyer Fortes based on his research among the Tallensi of West Africa ... In one [Fortes] muses on two religious and ethical conceptions, mutually opposed, 'different cosmological doctrines about the universe, and different conceptions of the nature of man and his relations with spiritual powers' ... The story of Oedipus deals with the notion of fixed and inescapable fate, in the face of which questions of responsibility and guilt are irrelevant. The story of Job ends with Job accepting God's authority without resentment, seeing it as benevolent in intention even when used punitively – just as the Tallensi accept without question that ancestors are just and that men have no choice but to submit to them ... 'This is the essence of filial piety' ...

In the other article, clearly linked to these thoughts on Job, Fortes considers the notion of pietas (filial piety – 'faithfulness to duties naturally owed to parents and relatives', what he elsewhere calls 'the axiom of amity' in kinship relationships) and the role of conformity to custom in overriding personal feelings and even ethically grounded behaviour: 'Morality in the sense of righteous conduct does not count. All that matters is service and obedience ... [not good deeds, but] conformity with the basic moral axioms in fulfilling the requirements of all social relationships' ...

These ideas relating to unquestioned axioms of customary behaviour illuminated for me the islanders' carrying out of an expensive cycle of rituals for the souls of their parents and other deceased relatives, regardless of the quality and content of the relationship when the person was alive. Here, I felt it could be argued, the focus was on performance ('fulfilling requirements' in Fortes's terms) in front of an audience – or, more strictly, viewers – of members of their own community. These ideas were equally suggestive in coming to some kind of understanding of the new kinds of relations which were being created on Anafi with short-term and long-term tourists, the attempt to forge a link to ensure a return visit to a cafe or taverna during the tourists' stay, or to rented rooms the next time they came to the island.

Further insights came from writers who interpreted local hosts' behaviour in terms of seeing themselves through tourists' eyes. The Anafiot villagers were now looking at the island landscape, and areas of the village, as if they were themselves tourists, evaluating their own surroundings in ways that they had not done before, as an 'object of consumption rather than merely production' ... Cafés and bars that had views facing the west were now being promoted as places to sit and have an early evening drink while watching the sunset (this had been the case for decades on the neighbouring island of Santorini); rooms with views over the south coast were recognized to be more desirable for summer visitors than those facing inward (much less cold and windy than in the island winter). Beaches, and even the action of the sea itself, were evaluated in terms of potential for tourist activities – from the more usual swimming and sunbathing to wind-surfing and kayaking. Springtime bookings from birdwatchers and wildflower enthusiasts (an area of the island had been given a special status under a European 'Natura 2000' programme) were encouraging active responses to develop ecotourism.

Just as the Anafiot environment now meant something different to Anafiots because it had a different meaning to visitors, so, in a similar fashion, islanders presented themselves differently. They behaved towards visitors as 'traditional island people' still practising the traditional Greek defining characteristic of hospitality (*filoksenia*) – a word which in Greek literally means 'love of strangers/foreigners/guests' ... Whether tourists were or are now regarded on Anafi as constituting a different category from either strangers or guests, the newly emerging type of 'customer oriented' behaviour, as described above, attempts to create good-humoured relationships, which might even be defined as 'friendships', and which would engender feelings of personal obligation. Each party in this relationship, or in the interaction of an encounter, might well have culturally different notions of what was constituted, and yet enough common ground to make it work ...

Authenticity and Performance

...

With respect to the Anafi material, I would argue that because most non-locals, whether Greek domestic tourists or foreigners, do not (usually) know who among the other people in cafés and tavernas are island migrants (some running the enterprise, others there as customers), they interpret the conviviality, singing and dancing there as 'traditional island behaviour' which they have been able to witness, and have been lucky enough to take part in – an 'authentic experience' of 'the real Anafi' (what they imagine was 'traditional' behaviour – note the conflation of authenticity and tradition) ... [S]uch jollification is not characteristic of islanders' behaviour out of season, except on festival days or at weddings. It is, however, typical summer holiday behaviour during the tourist season, and, in the past, occurred occasionally during the summer visits of Anafiot migrants. So ... I would argue that what is happening is as 'authentic' as it needs to be to satisfy both the tourists and other visitors, who are 'performing' as much as the locals are. Indeed, if one accepts that 'authenticity' is an essentially Western notion, grounded in a historical context relating to ideas of the individual; and that the label 'sincerity' depends on ideas of acting outwardly in conformity with inner feelings and selfknowledge ... then these are inappropriate concepts to make sense of behaviour in a context like that on Anafi (or indeed among the Tallensi) where public performance is evaluated without reference to its relationship in expressing private feelings.

On this basis, it could be argued that societies and cultures which place a high value on appropriate behaviour rather than inner truth, on what might be called the performance of outward forms ('going through the motions'), have no initial problem with 'performing' for tourists. Authenticity, and sincerity, only become problematic as they become more Westernized. And thus, notions of 'being true to the 'essential nature' of something, be it a dance form or an architectural style, began to creep in. People cannot help but equate 'authenticity' in their cultural forms with the past, and with notions of 'tradition'. They also take on board Western notions of being true to themselves, of the hypocritical nature of acting in one way while believing or thinking something else. In other words, authenticity, however it may be defined as an analytical category, at an 'emic' level is socially constructed ...
[Editors' note: In anthropology, the term 'emic' refers to social situations or processes as seen from the inside – that is, from the perspective of the participants – in contrast to the 'etic' or observer's perspective.]

Conclusion

This brings the discussion back to the situation with which it began: the assertion of a specific identity in the face of ambiguity and category confusion. The material presented here suggests that questions of authenticity and clear category membership arise in conditions of change and uncertainty. Just as in 1966 I could not feel confident about my identity as an anthropologist when it had not yet been established, nor sure of how to define 'the real Greece' when I had so little experience of the country and its people, so the Anafiots are beginning to question who 'counts' as a 'real islander', and what is 'authentically Anafiot'. While the legal appellation 'permanent resident', to establish voting rights, can include various degrees of residence on the island, the question of who counts locally as an islander, so as to have a recognized, legitimate, voice in discussions and local decision-making, whatever their legal status, is problematic. Does it include those migrants who come only in the summer to run tourism-related enterprises? Or is it restricted to those people who live on the island outside the tourism season (even if they go to Athens for the winter months), or should it be confined to those who live on the island all year round? Who defines what is, or was, an island custom? Not surprisingly, the majority of those who want a more encompassing definition are those who would be excluded if a narrower one was introduced. And, ironically, my own status as an anthropologist is legitimized by having fieldnotes and photographs dating back over the past forty years which could be used to validate certain definitions of local customs and behaviour.

Edited extract from: Margaret E. Kenna, 'Foreword', in J. Scott and T. Selwyn (eds), *Thinking Through Tourism* (Oxford: Berg, 2010), pp.xiii–xxi.

48 The Road to Refugee Resettlement
Dianna Shandy

Refugees are often seen as helpless victims, and rightly so, but as US anthropologist Dianna Shandy shows in this edited extract from a longer article, this is far from a complete picture; nor are refugees necessarily altogether passive in the face of violent displacement and insensitive bureaucracy. Anthropologists commonly use a detailed individual case history as a way of revealing more general social patterns. Here, the story of 'Thok Ding' shows him as an active agent, making positive use of opportunities provided by friendship, knowledge of the expectations of authorities, and luck, to get to where he wants to be. While the references throughout are to the refugee situation in the US, readers will readily find points of similarity and difference with the treatment of refugees and asylum seekers in other countries.

... When I began ethnographic work among Nuer refugees living in Minnesota, Iowa, and several other regions of the United States in 1997, I immediately was struck by the incongruity of their lives. The Nuer are a famous people in anthropology. They were the subject of three books by ... Sir E.E. Evans-Pritchard, who described their pastoralist mode of subsistence, complex segmented kinship system, and religion. Evans-Pritchard conducted research among the Nuer in the 1930s. He described the Nuer as a tall, independent, confident people whose existence revolved around the needs of their cattle, especially the requirement to move the animals from high to low ground and back again each year. During the dry season from September to April, the cattle were herded to lower ground where there was still water and grass. During the rainy season, the lowlands became a swampy lagoon and the herds had to be moved to the highlands where rain had restored the range. This transhumant lifestyle and the need to guard cattle against raiders from nearby tribes had shaped Nuer society ...

So when I first met Nuer people in Minnesota in the mid 1990s, these Northeast African pastoralists seemed out of place. Tall (most men are well over six feet in height) and still displaying the (for men) prominent forehead scars received at their initiations, the Nuer had come to live in one of the coldest parts of the United States. Why had they left their ancestral home? What did their status as refugees mean and how did they get it? How had they managed to come to the United States? ... How would a people raised as cattle herders adapt to US urban settings? ... How would they maintain a relationship with the families they left behind? And finally in a broader sense, what does all this tell us about the interconnectedness of a globalizing world and about anthropology's role in it?

...

Over the last 50 years ... refugees have come to occupy a formal status. ... Officially ... a refugee group is one that shares a 'well-founded fear of persecution' based on any of five factors such as race, religion, nationality, membership of a particular social group, or political opinion, and who has left their home country. How the United States or national governments apply this definition when they seek to certify individuals as refugees varies. But the number of people that claim to fit this description and who seek asylum skyrocketed at the end of the Cold War in 1989 to an estimated 12 million in 2003.

Bureaucracies control who can be classified as a refugee. In 1950 the United Nations established a formal agency to help with the refugee 'problem', headed by the United Nations Commissioner for Refugees (UNHCR). The agency recognises three options, or what it calls 'durable solutions', to address the situation of refugees around the world: voluntary repatriation to the country of origin, integration into a country of asylum, or, more rarely, third country resettlement, meaning a move from one country of asylum to one that offers possibilities for a more permanent home. Initially housed in refugee camps, displaced people can apply for official refugee status with the hope of resettlement in another country, or that conditions will stabilize in their own country, allowing them to return home.

... Over the past decade, the United States has resettled an average of 87,000 refugees here each year, with a sharp dip in numbers in the wake of September 11, 2001. The process is complicated by the fact that the criteria for admission can change, different government officials interpret the criteria dissimilarly, and resettlement policy can shift from one year to the next. It is also complicated by cross-cultural misunderstanding. The US bureaucracy works differently from the way governments operate in the refugee's country of origin. Languages are a major barrier. Categories of meaning are not shared. The screening process is intended to determine 'real' refugees, or those who cannot be protected by their home governments, and 'economic' migrants who leave their home voluntarily to seek a better life. In practice the distinction is often difficult to establish.

The Nuer living in Minnesota and other regions of the United States have managed to come through this process successfully. They have made it to camps that process refugees, discovered how to enter the bureaucratic process designed to certify them as refugees, learned how to tell a sufficiently convincing refugee story to gain certification and found a way to get on the list to be resettled in the United States.

Thok Ding's life illustrates this process. Thok was born in southern Sudan and lived in a small village. As in most Nuer households, Thok lived with his mother, father, siblings, and his father's extended family. Thok had family members who lived in a nearby town and attended school, but there was no school in his village. His first memory is of going to the forest to take care of his calves when he was seven or eight. He would leave home in the early morning with other boys his age, taking food with him to eat while he was grazing the cattle and protecting the calves from wild animals. Girls, on the other hand, would stay closer to home and were charged with milking the cows.

When he was in his early teens, he, along with other boys who were the same age, he underwent the ritual scarification *gaar* ceremony ushering him into manhood. After undergoing this painful ritual, Thok said that now that he was a man, he could be 'free'. 'You can do whatever you like. You can have a woman. You can have a home by yourself. You can live away from your parents'.

Shortly after his initiation, the civil war that wracked the southern Sudan caught up with him. Fueled by events that extend back much further in time, civil war has engulfed the Sudan since just before it gained independence from joint English-Egyptian colonial rule until the present, with just a brief interlude of peace from the early 1970s until 1983 ...

...

In the late 1980s, government troops attacked Thok's village, killing many people including his father. Although many of the survivors elected to stay and to keep herding cattle, with his father dead Thok felt it was wisest to leave Sudan after this tragedy. He traveled on foot for three days with his mother and siblings and their cattle to an Ethiopian refugee camp called Itang.

One feature of camp life was the presence of a Christian mission school, which provided Thok with his first taste of formal education, something that would prove useful later as he sought refugee status. He advanced quickly in school, skipping several grades ... As a result, he was transferred to Gambela, another Ethiopian camp, to attend school, leaving his mother and siblings behind. Food scarcity made life in Gambela very difficult. Thok recalls that students were given only a small amount of corn each month. They would grind the grain into flour, cook the mixture with water, and eat it plain without a stew.

His education at Gambela progressed nicely, but was ended when war broke out in Ethiopia. Threatened by the dangers it posed, Thok rejoined his mother and siblings. Together they returned to Sudan where the United Nations had established a temporary camp to care for the Sudanese refugees who were streaming back across the border from Ethiopia. Thok weighed his options and decided to return to Ethiopia on his own. He went to the capital of Ethiopia, Addis Ababa, where he encountered some friends from school who shared information on how to get to refugee camps in Kenya.

[Thok] travelled to Kenya by bus, negotiating his way past border and police checkpoints along the way ... Once in the camp, he filled out a form that documented his background, and requested that he be considered for resettlement in another country. Because Thok had no relatives who had been resettled to other countries, he applied for resettlement anywhere that would accept refugees from the Sudan. These included Australia, Canada and Sweden as well as the United States, the country that finally admitted him.

Two years elapsed from the time Thok arrived in the camp until he was sent to the United States. Life in the Kenyan camp was much more difficult than the one he had stayed at in Ethiopia. There was nothing to do, no river, no place to keep cattle, and no garden plots. Thok did, however, meet some friends he had made earlier in school, and together they cooked food and found ways to pass the long days in the camp. He and his friends also listened to the stories other Nuer told of their encounters with the refugee officials who interviewed people requesting resettlement. In a tragic commentary on how devastation can seem 'normal', they learned that the biggest mistake people made was to invent dramatic stories to make themselves eligible for resettlement. For example, one Nuer man said, 'People feel they need a reason, so they tell the person interviewing them that they killed someone and if they return to Sudan they will be put in jail. But the story didn't work because the interviewer thought the refugee must be a violent man'. The Nuer men who worked as interpreters in the camps believed there was a better approach. 'We told the community, we need to tell them the reality. Don't say you killed someone, just say you were caught in the crossfire'. They had learned that the refugee officials were looking for certain kinds of experiences to determine who fit the criteria for refugee resettlement.

...

There were about thirty refugees from Sudan and Somalia on Thok's flight from Nairobi, Kenya to New York's JFK International Airport. When Thok boarded the plane, he knew no one. By the time he arrived in New York many hours later, he felt like the eight Sudanese men he had travelled with were his new best friends. In a wrenching sort of dispersal, the eight men were all directed by airline staff to different gates at the airport to await the next leg of their journey to far-flung destinations, like San Diego, California; Nashville, Tennessee; Dallas, Texas; and Minneapolis, Minnesota.

...

When they finished with the paperwork, the case manager ... took [Thok] to what was to be his apartment. Thok found the place to be very dirty, particularly the carpeting that had not been cleaned after the last tenants departed. There was a strong smell of cigarette smoke, cockroaches in the kitchen, and a very leaky [tap] in the bathroom. Despite these problems, Thok would have his own place that would be affordable when he got a job ...

... Where refugees work and the kinds of jobs they can get depend somewhat on the level of education and training they received prior to arrival in the United States. Upon arrival, most Nuer have little formal education and can, unfortunately, only find jobs that most people born in the United States do not want, such as unskilled factory worker, security guard, parking lot attendant, fast food server, and nursing home assistant. Or, if they do have a degree when they arrive, like many immigrants, they are 'underemployed', or work in jobs below their level of credentials. Many of the Nuer who have settled in the upper Midwest have found work in meat-packing plants. Thok first got a job filling beverage trays for airplanes at the airport after he arrived in the United States. His back and arms ached from the lifting he was required to do, and he did not like his boss.

Several weeks later, Thok spotted another Nuer man while he was shopping ... Thok did not know him personally, but after they started talking he discovered that he knew the village where the man was from in the Sudan. It was good to see someone from 'home', and Thok invited him back to his apartment to cook a meal and eat together. This man had moved to Minnesota from Iowa and was able to tell Thok the names and even the phone numbers of some Nuer who were living in Des Moines. Thok knew some of these people from the refugee camps in Ethiopia, and the next day he bought a phone card to get in touch. Thok could hardly believe his ears when he heard his friend John Wal answer the phone. After a conversation that lasted until the phone card expired, Thok decided to board a bus and leave Minnesota to move to Iowa. John had talked about the sizable Nuer community living in Des Moines and the well-paying jobs offered by a meat-packing company. Thok called his case manager and left a message saying he was going. He packed his personal items ... and boarded a Greyhound bus.

In Des Moines, Thok moved in with John and another Nuer man. Thok worked in a packing plant for a while, but found it very difficult. At first his job was to kill pigs as they entered the processing line. He found it so hard to sleep at night after doing this over and over again all day that he asked to be transferred to some other part of the line. He still found the work exceedingly hard.

One motivation to find a job quickly is to make it possible to bring over his family members to join him, but Thok has not managed to do this yet. In addition to his mother and siblings, Thok would also like to bring over a wife. There are roughly three Nuer men for every Nuer woman in the United States, and most of the women are already married or engaged to be married. Thok and other Nuer men struggle with what they perceive as 'the unreasonable levels of freedom' afforded to women in US society. One way to marry a wife with more 'traditional' Nuer values, or so men think, is to let their family facilitate a marriage in the Sudan or in Ethiopia and try to bring the wife over as a spouse or a refugee.

...

Staying in contact is very important to many Nuer refugees. They are adept at devising strategies for remaining in contact with other Nuer dispersed across the United States and those whom they left behind in Africa. The process of incorporation into the United States as a refugee is also about maintaining ties to Africa. One aspect of Nuer life that sets them apart from the experience of previous waves of immigrants to the United States is the means by which they keep in contact with those who remain at home in the Sudan, in refugee camps in neighbouring African states, and around the world.

Immigrants have always retained some ties with the homes they left. But, in a 21ˢᵗ century context the possibilities for frequent, affordable, and rapid contact are greatly expanded. Anthropologists refer to these cross-cutting social ties that span the borders of nation-states as transnationalism. For instance, Thok, who wants to marry, could phone his brother in Gambela, Ethiopia, to arrange the event. He can use Western Union to send money to his brother to buy cows to give to the prospective bride's father. In Nuer eyes, the groom does not even have to be present for the marriage to be legitimate, but this is not true in the eyes of immigration authorities. Even though the groom can do his part to sponsor the marriage from the United States, he still must travel to Ethiopia for the marriage to be recognized officially for immigration purposes. The bride can apply as a refugee herself but increases her chance of resettlement by also applying as a spouse joining her husband.

...

... Often seen as victims of tragic circumstances, refugees are also amazingly adept at finding ways to survive these same circumstances. Refugees' lives depend on an international and national bureaucracy, and those who pass through the process represent a very small percentage of people who are displaced. Starting a life in a vastly different cultural environment than the one they were raised in presents a number of hardships. Refugees cope with these challenges by trying to maintain their original ethnic group identity. Transnational communication is one way to do this. So is moving to find people they know from their homelands.

Anthropologists, such as Evans-Pritchard, used to journey to faraway places to study distant 'others'. Nowadays it is often the objects of study that make the journey to the land of the anthropologists. Refugees such as the Nuer are among the latest newcomers to urban and suburban areas in the United States, and anthropologists can play a role in the adaptation process of Nuer in the United States. For example, some anthropologists work for voluntary agencies where what they learn about refugees through their ability to conduct ethnographic research helps to ease refugee adjustment to unfamiliar surroundings. Other anthropologists work at the federal and state levels to advise about the efficacy of the social programs designed to meet the needs of recently arrived populations and suggest changes if they are needed. Sometimes these roles also take the form of advocacy.

But through it all, anthropologists still do the fieldwork in much the same way. They learn the language of refugee populations, ask open-ended questions in interviews, conduct participant observation at such events as weddings, funerals, graduation ceremonies, and political meetings, and try to understand life from their informants' perspective.

Although he now knows an anthropologist, Thok Ding goes about his new life in the United States with the same independent determination that got him [t]here in the first place. He will continue to move his residence if he thinks it will help him, increase his level of education, find better paying jobs, and eventually if all works out, marry a woman from the Sudan, bring his whole family to the United States and in the end, become a new American.

Edited extract from: Dianna Shandy, 'The Road to Refugee Resettlement', in J. Spradley and D.W. McCurdy (eds), *Conformity and Conflict: Readings in Cultural Anthropology* (Philadelphia: Pearson, 2008), pp.345–54.

49   Cults: The Persistence of Religious Movements
Joy Hendry

The global spread of the major world religions, through conversion, conquest or other means, is a form of globalisation that has taken many twists and turns over the centuries – and continues. Anthropologists have taken a particular interest in local transformations of 'mainstream' religious ideas in the context of people's own experience and living conditions. In this extract from her book An Introduction to Social Anthropology: Sharing Our Worlds, *Joy Hendry outlines some of the connections between the rise of new religious movements – or new interpretations of established religious ideas – and various forms of social stress and upheaval. She describes in particular the widespread phenomenon of millenarian movements (termed 'cargo cults' in Melanesia because of the belief spread by local prophets that spiritual regeneration would bring the people 'cargo', or white men's goods).*

... [D]espite the predictions of sociologists and others that modernisation would bring with it secularisation in the world at large, religion does not seem to be giving way to more 'rational' ways of explaining the world. Indeed, new religious sects are appearing abundantly around the world – and there is quite a variety to choose from. In Japan, some people turn from one to another, seeking solutions to problems they may be experiencing, and in several countries around the world Japanese new religious groups are quite active ...

New religious movements have often appeared in times of great social change and upheaval, according to another variety of anthropological explanation, and some special cults demonstrate an interesting expression of cultural confusion. Typically where the lives of one people have been profoundly affected by the invasion, however peaceful, of another, religious reactions can be shown to express efforts to adjust in one way or another to the new situation. In North America, for example, there was widespread practice of a 'ghost dance' among the Plains Indians whose land and livelihood had been devastated by the arrival of Europeans. The aim of the dance was to rid the ancestral land of these cruel and destructive invaders and bring about a return of the native bison they had hunted. The medium was prayer to the ancestors through dance.

Native Americans, called First Nations in Canada, have in fact made some considerable progress in renewing their association with their lands and their ancestors, though they may not have succeeded in expelling the 'invaders', and there are now even new herds of bison being bred. The Red Power movement of the 1960s was perhaps the turning point, with the occupation of the island of Alcatraz and the site of their massacre at Wounded Knee. A first-hand description of this period, and its religious associations, is graphically portrayed in the book *Lakota Woman* by Mary Crow Dog ... who gave birth to her first son during their siege at Wounded Knee. Local activities of a spiritual or 'religious' nature are practised all over the Americas, but there is an interesting pan-Indian movement that has emerged, and the annual Sundance gathering that takes place at Pipestone, Minnesota is one event that expresses this new form of identity.

Even more spectacular examples of religious reaction to the arrival of outsiders sometimes took place at considerable distance from the new settlement so that knowledge of the invaders was largely second-hand. Cults would grow up whose aim was to achieve the greater standard of living which had been observed, possibly only by one or a few prophet-like figures, and the aim was again a kind of moral regeneration of society. Usually, there would be a charismatic leader, and the results were sometimes devastating. In one part of South America, for example, a whole congregation of indigenous people jumped off a cliff, believing that they would subsequently be reborn white, with all the advantages they had heard that would bring.

In Melanesia, cults arose which have become known as 'cargo cults', for their practices were aimed at attracting the goods to which they saw white people had access. Some of these have been brought to the attention of the public in film and on stage. A Jacques Tati film showed a group of people building an airport in the hope that they could attract the enormous birds they saw delivering all manner of good things to the white people who had settled nearby. A stage play entitled *Sergeant Ola and His Followers* illustrated even in its title the role of the charismatic leader. In this production, local people dressed up as whites and spent their time trying to replicate their activities, reading newspapers and tapping away at a typewriter, although they were in fact still illiterate.

Peter Worsley's book *The Trumpet Shall Sound* (1970) includes a comprehensive survey of these cults, which were found in various parts of New Guinea as well as in Fiji, the Solomon Islands and the New Hebrides.

Koriam's Law
The Pomio Kivung movement founded in 1964 by a local spiritual leader in Papua New Guinea.

Film still: *Koriam's Law and the dead who govern*. Film by Gary Kildea, 2005
Distributed by the Royal Anthropological Institute.

He also calls them millenarian movements because of their similarity to movements found all over the world that are characterised by a belief in the imminence of the end of the world, some of which occurred in Europe in the run up to the year 1000. The expectation is that a cataclysm will destroy everything, but that the ancestors, or some prior god, will return and liberate the people from their new oppressors, incidentally making available all the goods these same oppressors seem to own. Hence the preparations.

These movements are, of course, not peculiar to Melanesia, as Worsley himself points out, nor are they only to be discovered in the anthropological fieldnotes of the past, especially as another new millennium has now been entered. The shocking release of poisonous gas in the Tokyo underground in 1995, and the mass suicide/murder of members of the Branch Dravidian cult in Waco, Texas, two years before that, may both be seen as examples of the continuing power of people preaching about the end of the world. The tale of the Japanese group Aum Shinrikyo, which has been blamed for the deaths and injuries in Tokyo, is a textbook example of a millennium cult. In a well-informed study of the group, Ian Reader writes of its leader, Asahara Shōko:

> He … achieved prominence because of his frequent, drastic prophecies, which stated that an apocalypse would occur before the end of the century to engulf the vast majority of humanity and sweep away the corrupt material world and destroy Japanese society. He proclaimed that he was a messiah who had come

to save his followers from the apocalypse and lead them forward to form a new, ideal spiritual universe that would emerge from the ruins of the old. (1996: 2)

Worsley's survey concludes by putting the Melanesian material in a broader anthropological and historical context, where he identifies common features in a wide range of different movements. Resistance to oppression is a common theme, as is the drawing together of a new, and possibly powerful amalgamation of smaller groups. The promise of a better life is of course another powerful characteristic, and the charismatic leader is a virtual sine qua non. These cults allow a kind of generalisation, which is rare in anthropological literature, and Worsley's book is an accessible example of how this may be done.

References

Reader, Ian. *A Poisonous Cocktail: Aum Shinrikyo's Path to Violence* (Copenhagen: Nordic Institute for Asian Studies, 1996).
Worsley, Peter. *The Trumpet Shall Sound: A Study of 'Cargo Cults' in Melanesia* (London: Paladin, 1970).

Edited extract from: Joy Hendry, *An Introduction to Social Anthropology: Sharing Our Worlds*, 2nd edn. (London: Palgrave, 2008), pp.144–46.

50   The Power of Mary in Papua New Guinea
Anna-Karina Hermkens

In this extract from her ethnographic account of devotion to the Virgin Mary in Papua New Guinea, Anna-Karina Hermkens illustrates many of the general principles outlined by Joy Hendry in the previous text. As she shows, the figure of Mary, and the powers ascribed to her, have taken many forms at different times and in different places, and they have occasioned controversy within the Roman Catholic Church. Hermkens' analysis powerfully shows how Mary in Papua New Guinea becomes a figure of on-the-spot protection, especially for women, in the face of their specific experience of domestic violence, rape, HIV/AIDS and war. She also points to contradictions inherent in this global–local axis: how, for example, Mary's local powers as a protector of women are in tension with her globally emphasised qualities of submission and acceptance.

At the beginning of the 21st century, the mother of Jesus has re-emerged as a popular icon. She appears to people all over the world, while Marian sites such as Lourdes are attracting thousands of pilgrims. Yearly processions in which the statue of Mary is borne through the streets flourish in Europe and beyond. The rosary, a prayer meditating on the life of Jesus and Mary and considered a powerful instrument for devotion to God through devotion to Mary, is still recited every day all over the world. This popularity of Mary was acknowledged by Pope John Paul II, who announced 2003 as the Year of the Rosary. However, Mary's position within and outside the Catholic Church has not always been so pre-eminent, nor has it been uncontroversial.

Through time and place, Mary has taken on different appearances and significances ... In early Christianity she was portrayed as 'God-bearer' (*Theotokus*) and her privileges – her immaculate conception, her assumption and the power of her intercession – were honoured from the 11th century on ... From this time onwards, Marian devotion in the form of hymns, pilgrimages, processions, shrines, icons and statues multiplied, while Marian art became instrumental in spreading Marian devotion and establishing her status as great intercessor with God ... In 1962, repeated efforts to contain the influence of Mary culminated in the Second Vatican Council which ... dethroned Mary as the symbolic Queen of Heaven. By refusing to grant Mary her own document, and confining her role to that of helper of Christ, the Vatican Council tried to 'overcome theological and devotional excesses and deviations which resulted from unduly isolating Mary from the mystery of Christ and the Church' ... This decision sparked criticism both within and outside the Catholic Church ...

So what is the place of Mary in Papua New Guinea, where Roman Catholicism is the dominant Christian denomination, accounting for 27 per cent of all those who professed a faith ... [In recent times,] Christianity in Papua New Guinea has become a burgeoning field of study. Nevertheless, there are virtually no anthropological studies dealing with Marian devotion in this part of the world ... Responses from members of the Association for Social Anthropology in Oceania to a question on ASAONET, the organization's electronic bulletin board, show clearly that Mary is honoured all over Papua New Guinea. As in other parts of the world, men and women of various ages, classes and ethnicity have erected shrines to Mary, perform annual processions with statues of the Virgin, and both devotion to Mary and adherence to the rosary are strong. Moreover, Papua New Guinea hosts several Marian pilgrimage sites. This seems to indicate that Marian devotion shows similar features all over the world, suggesting a transnational 'Marian cult'.

However, in Papua New Guinea (as elsewhere) the rituals promoted by global institutions are locally configured and do not always adhere to official doctrine. As I experienced during my research, faith healing, exorcism, speaking in tongues, dream visions and other ecstatic practices, which the Western Catholic Church has often decried, are basic to Marian devotion in Papua New Guinea.

In addition, people ascribe powers to Mary that go beyond her official status as mere helper. Mary's official titles in Papua New Guinea, such as 'Mary Help of Christians' and 'Our Lady of Peace' ... reflect people's strong belief in her power to provide assistance and comfort, and to empower those who pray to her.

Mary in Papua New Guinea

Santu Maria, Mama bilong God, pre bilong helpim mipela manmeri bilong sin, nau na long taim mipela i dai. Amen ('Holy Mary, Mother of God, pray for us sinners, now and at the hour of our death. Amen'), echoes through the forest, as almost 2,000 men, women and children pray the rosary and sing Marian hymns, while slowly making their way to the isolated site of Maria Helpim ... Each year, people coming from Madang and more distant areas make the two-hour muddy, uphill and difficult trek to the top of a wooded hill in the surroundings of Madang. At the site, a picture of Our Lady of Perpetual Help is attached to a wooden-roofed wall, together with a plaque honouring the missionaries who died in World War II. A statue of the Pietà is carried up to the site and placed in front of the wall under a makeshift shelter. Seated around this shelter, the pilgrims hear a two-hour Mass. Afterwards, many hurry forward to touch the figures of Jesus and Mary while murmuring their individual requests and pledges.

This scene is illustrative of how Mary is venerated in Papua New Guinea. While supplicants engage in a personal relationship with her, she is asked to address both personal and communal affairs. As spiritual mother, 'Mama Maria' is believed to care for people and guide them through their lives. As mother of God and hence a human woman with great divine power and alliances, Mary is expected to answer all prayers made to her and to overcome evil. As Mediatrix, she is approached as gateway to heaven. Embodying the human, the sacred and the mystery, Mary is believed to transcend the boundaries between heaven and earth, thereby having both the power and the compassion to bring about people's admission to heaven, and thus their salvation.

Mary's reputation is largely self-confirming. It is embodied and fostered in personal experiences and idealist narratives that stress her power to bestow help and peace. These narratives are shared with others to affirm Mary's powers as well as individuals' relationship with her. Through these experiences and narratives, Mary has a demonstrated history of fulfilling requests varying from catching the bus, protecting devotees against sorcery (*sanguma*) and illness, evicting bush spirits (*masalai*) and helping children pass their exams to bringing peace in the family, changing violent partners into good Christian husbands and ending the violence in Bougainville.

In Papua New Guinea, Marian pilgrimages, processions, healing sessions and other religious practices take place against a backdrop of a general decline in government services and structures, and the disintegration of social cohesion, law and order. Scandals involving corrupt government officials, rising criminality and violence and the looming threat of a HIV/AIDS epidemic are some of the issues communities in Papua New Guinea are dealing with. In Bougainville these are augmented by the collapse of infrastructure and traumas due to a secessionist war that was recently brought to an end by an intensive peace process. It is in this climate that an upsurge of religious activities, especially of charismatic movements is emerging ... Like the Protestant charismatic movements, Marian devotion addresses personal and cultural anxieties engendered by contemporary socio-political and economic problems. In particular, it seems that a general fear of declining morality draws people closer to Mary, and to Christianity in general. Below I examine this power of Mary to save not only the individual but also the moral community in the context of the looming threat of HIV/AIDS infection, domestic violence and the war in Bougainville.

The Power of Mary: AIDS and Domestic Violence

> My husband did not use condoms when having sex with me. I did not either. I do not think he used condoms when sleeping with other women. So I say: 'Thanks Lord! You protected me!' God also protected my daughter from getting AIDS when she was raped ...

One of the major problems communities in Papua New Guinea are facing today is the threat of an HIV/AIDS epidemic. The reasons for this crisis include gender-based violence ... and increasing impoverishment, which combine to create a high degree of vulnerability to the virus ... Moreover, because women's general health is poor, women and girls face a higher risk of HIV infection ... This risk is increased by the fact that women have hardly any means of protection against the virus. While the government advocates the use of condoms, it appears that because women are unable to negotiate for safer sex, many cannot use them ... Moreover, especially among Catholics there is a strong belief that condoms interfere with God and are in fact actually helping to spread AIDS by encouraging sexual promiscuity.

In order to deal with and change the immoral behaviour that is believed to result in illnesses such as AIDS, many people look for spiritual help. Certain Catholic healing ministries make use of statues of Mary and other saints, holy water, prayer and the rosary to free people from demonic possessions and illness. This faith in divine healing is grounded in both Catholic doctrine and locally (customary) established concepts about the nature and purpose of healing as well as of sickness in general. The two streams of knowledge reinforce the belief that illness is not a medical but a social and moral phenomenon. As ... [the above quoted] statement shows, people strongly believe in God's power to safeguard them against HIV infection. This indicates a belief in God as protector of those who have strong faith and lead a good Christian life. At the same time, it reflects a belief that those who have AIDS have called down misfortune on themselves through immoral behaviour. In some areas, AIDS is seen not only as evidence of moral decay, but as a sign marking the period approaching the end of the world; AIDS is thus interpreted within a framework of apocalyptic Christianity ... Among Catholics in Port Moresby and Madang, Mary is promoted as a role model who can help believers to stay on the right path, thereby both preventing infection and enabling salvation. For example, an article by medical doctor Thomas Vinit, of Madang hospital, in the *Post*

Courier in December 2004, urges: 'Let us use good models that portray chastity and purity, such as the devotion of the Virgin Mary' in order to address the root of the HIV/AIDS problem in Papua New Guinea, which is 'moral and socio-economical problems'.

This emphasis on using Mary as a role model in order to solve moral and social problems is also instrumental in how Catholic women deal and cope with domestic violence ... Confronted with such dilemmas as divorce in an environment where the practice is seen as sinful, many Catholic women seek spiritual guidance, finding solace in prayers directed to Mary and gaining strength by following her example. Thus Mary enables women to endure their suffering, and her example helps to give them confidence in the process of transforming themselves into good and strong Christian wives. Many see this transformation as empowerment, a case of being able to change themselves and, eventually, their husbands.

At the same time, Mary's submissive image falls in line with pre-existing gender relations and gender hierarchies, in which women are constituted as submissive to their husbands, their primary role being that of caretakers of the families, as mothers. In fact, as has also been noted in other parts of the world, the virtues ascribed to Mary in the teachings of the Church and Marian movements, such as silence, obedience and modesty, 'constitute the very quintessence of passive, female submission' ... From this perspective, the veneration of Mary is actually a form of normative violence, or a state of violence, that is crucial to 'cultural processes of routinization and legitimation' ... In this respect Mary is both part of the solution and the problem women face. In an entirely different setting, as I show below, a similar ambiguity of Marian devotion becomes visible.

The Power of Mary: War and Peace

In 1901 the Catholic faith was introduced in Bougainville by missionaries of the Society of Mary (MSSM), known as Marists ... Thanks to the zealous efforts of these missionaries, the Marist spirit spread all over Bougainville. Today the majority (69 per cent) of the circa 180,000 Bougainvilleans are Catholic, followed by adherents of the United Church (UC, 15 per cent), Seventh Day Adventists (SDA, 7 per cent) and Pentecostalists (6 per cent) ... It is therefore no surprise that Mary is well-known all over Bougainville, her image displayed in peoples' houses and printed on clothes, her statue being paraded all over the island. Although Marian devotion was widespread before the crisis, it assumed great importance during a vicious secessionist war that devastated most communities on the island.

From 1989 until the late 1990s, the people of Bougainville were immersed in a vicious war that resulted in immense human suffering and destroyed nearly all infrastructure and social services. The number of people who died as a result of the conflict is estimated at around 15,000 ... Besides numerous losses, 'no one has escaped the twists and turns of fighting zones, having families trapped in opposite camps' ... On top of this, many people lost loved ones through the denial of basic services, medicines and access to help ... In addition to grief, traumas resulting from rape and torture are widespread.

...

During the conflict Marian movements flourished and many people devoted themselves to Mary and received revelations from her. Some of this belief resonates in particular with the matrilineal kinship system of many Bougainville communities and traditional ideas about life-force and rights vested in women ... Others combined ideas about tradition (*kastom*) with Christianity and appropriated both God and Mary into an ideology of resistance. Francis Ona, the main figure behind the BRA [Bougainville Revolutionary Army, one of the actors in the conflict], personifies this ideology in which devotion to Mary is central. Every day, Ona addressed Mary's statue and as a token of his devotion, he created the 'Marian Mercy Mission' movement. As explained by a number of his followers, Ona's idea was that through devotion to Mary, Bougainville would get faithful leaders who are connected with the land and lore of the island. Since Bougainville was perceived as *Me'ekamui* (holy land) the people, and especially the leaders, would have to become holy as well. Ex- BRA combatant and BRA prayer leader, Albert, explained:

> Francis Ona said this land must become holy again, *Me'ekamui*. We prayed to God and He gave us the strength. This directed us to make a clean fight, a holy fight. We were fighting for our rights, to get rid of all these bad companies and their effects. All BRA and all Bougainvilleans, everybody practised this holiness. Our spirits must be holy so God would get rid of Satan [the mining companies]. And God helped us. How? His power worked through the rosary.

Mary's holiness was appropriated and expressed in a variety of ways by both men and women. The rosary became an important tool to achieve holiness and to obtain protection. Before going on patrol, Catholic BRA soldiers would pray and ask Mary for protection. With the rosary in their pockets or around their necks, the BRA would then venture into enemy-controlled areas. People were still killed, but both ex-BRA soldiers and villagers describing Mary's role in the crisis often blame these deaths on the victims' immoral behaviour.

It was not only the BRA who sought help from Mary; local villagers also appealed to her by praying the rosary. As Lucy and Raphael, from Penko village in Koromira, recalled: 'During the crisis, the rosary was special because we looked to Mama Maria as someone who could help us'. Many survivors claim that Mary provided food and protected people from getting sick or killed. Marian movements such as 'Our Lady of the Sacred Heart', 'Our Lady of Mercy' and 'The Immaculate Conception' were all established during the crisis as people searched for new spiritual guidance in order to deal with the hardships they encountered.

Both during and after the crisis, many people claim to have had apparitions of Mary. Just as she interceded in ethnic conflicts elsewhere in the world, such as those in Medjugorje and Rwanda, Mary appeared to Bougainvilleans to appease suffering and to transmit political messages. In fact, those who witnessed the pilgrimage of the international Pilgrim Virgin Statue of Our Lady of Fatima to Ona's hideout in Panguna in 1997 claim that Ona was persuaded by Mary to end the fighting. Captured on an unreleased film by Catholic missionaries, Ona is seen and heard praying in front of this statue, making a promise to Our Lady to work towards peace. One year later, on 30 April 1998, a ceasefire agreement was signed by all parties, officially ending the crisis …

In addition to her perceived role in persuading Ona to stop fighting, Mary is believed to have given courage and strength to Bougainville women to help them fight for peace. Bougainville women's active involvement in ending the violence has been widely documented … but it is less commonly known that Marian devotion played an important role in women's actions. As narrated by Catholic women involved in the peace process, mothers were standing in the frontline, praying and clasping the rosary in their hands in an attempt to stop the shooting. According to these women's experiences, it was Mary and the rosary that gave them strength to intervene, thereby enabling them to facilitate the ending of the crisis. Seen from this perspective, Mary has indeed succeeded in bringing peace.

Conclusion

This article has described some of the ways in which Marian devotion is perceived and lived, at the same time elucidating Christianity's role in the fields of crisis and conflict. It shows that Marian devotion can be regarded as not just an individual, but also a collective practice – a societal solution to the ills of contemporary society. It becomes clear that Marian devotion provides people with strength, hope and optimism. Moreover, it gives them a sense of control while at the same time allowing them to give up control to a beneficent Mary. This ambiguity is also apparent in the role Mary plays in humanitarian crises, thereby elucidating the ambiguity of religion in general, as it is used to support both empowerment and disempowerment, both violence and peace.

Within a context of AIDS and domestic violence it is clear that Marian devotion, and Christianity in general, may contain groups of people within the normative constraints of Church doctrine and gender relations, thereby actually facilitating violence. The Bougainville example shows how religion, and in particular the veneration of Mary, is grounded within a context of both warfare and reconciliation. In this case, religion legitimizes power and violence, supports charismatic leadership, and inspires people to fight against oppression and for peace at the same time.

A more detailed analysis of the cultural meanings of Mary would show that her capacity to both empower and disempower her adherents, and to both facilitate and end violence, lies in local perceptions of her personal history of violence and suffering, as well as of her identity as both warrior against evil and mother of peace. People project their feelings and experiences onto these complex meanings of Mary and take on roles as good Christian wives and husbands, mothers and fathers, sufferers, legionaries, warriors, peacemakers, etc. In conclusion, it is clear that Mary teaches people not how to live in a world without violence, but how to live with and despite violence.

Edited extract from: Anna-Karina Hermkens, 'The Power of Mary in Papua New Guinea', *Anthropology Today* 23/2 (2007), pp.4–8.

51 Arsenal in Bugamba: The Rise of English Premier League Football in Uganda
Richard Vokes

Our final extract in this Section is drawn from anthropologists' growing interest in the ethnography of sport. In this piece, Richard Vokes sets the scene by tracing the history of football in Uganda within the tapestry of the nation's political development. The advent of global media, as he recounts, enabled Ugandans to become fans of international, especially English, clubs, and to follow their fortunes via radio and (later) live satellite transmission. Based on his research at his own village field site, Vokes argues convincingly that the popularity of English Premier League football in rural Uganda is no mere ephemeral effect of globalisation, but is having far-reaching and long-lasting economic and social impacts, going as deep (he suggests) as to affect public perceptions of time and space. The apparent gains of such global interconnectedness can, however, be vulnerable to tragic reversals when the economy or technology of the wider world shift, as in the sad end to the story of the would-be entrepreneur 'Mugisha'.

Over the last few years, a growing number of residents of my long-term field site in Bugamba sub-county, in rural south-western Uganda, have become committed fans of English Premier League (EPL) football. As one might expect, this trend has been particularly marked among Bugamba's young people, but it has also included many of the village's older residents. As a result, when moving around the various shops and bars that constitute the main hub of social activity in these parts, one today hears not only the more usual talk of crop yields, school fees and the like, but also conversations about the past week's EPL results, movements in its transfer market, and its various teams' chances over the months ahead.

The interiors of these same shops and bars are now decorated not just with random pages of newsprint, drinks adverts, or out-of-date political posters – as would have generally been the case until a few years ago – but also with the glossy images of EPL match schedules, team photos, and portraits of players. A sizable number of Bugamba's young people are also now attired in EPL-branded clothing. Thus most residents under the age of about thirty are able to sport at least one T-shirt, headscarf or baseball cap emblazoned with the logo of some or other team, either Liverpool, Manchester United or – the team that appears to be particularly popular – Arsenal.

However, the scale of the development was not impressed on me until a visit I made to the village in early 2009. A few days into this stay, the head of 'my' household in Bugamba, Mr Grace Bwire, informed me that a dinner we were due to attend that evening had been postponed, because 'everyone [would] be watching the game'. At the time, this statement struck me as a little odd: although Grace and I had on occasion watched football in a hotel on the main road to town – some five miles or so from our present location – it was difficult to imagine how 'everyone' in the village (*abantu bona*) might possibly have access to a screen. As far as I was aware, there were only two small, black-and-white televisions in the whole village, and one of these – the one belonging to Grace himself – was perennially out of action.

Such was my surprise, then, to discover that a year or so beforehand a young neighbour (I shall call him Mugisha) had not only purchased a brand-

Mugisha's place, in the world.

© Richard Vokes (Royal Anthropological Institute Sport Photo Contest 2011).

new satellite system, but had also converted his homestead's entire compound into a large viewing hall. Moreover, for each EPL game, Mugisha's place became packed to the rafters, as young people came in from miles around on foot, by bicycle and on the backs of the several dozen or more motorcycle taxis, or *boda-bodas*, that now operate in these parts, many of them further elaborately decorated with various EPL teams' colours. Indeed, so popular had these broadcasts become that on the occasion of my own first visit to Mugisha's place – on that same Sunday evening – I found at least 150 patrons there (in a village of just 86 households), for a game between Chelsea and Manchester United. Moreover, I later discovered that at the height of the EPL season this scene might be repeated up to three or four times per week.

The History of Football in Uganda

Football itself is not new in Uganda. On the contrary, its history can be traced back to the early days of colonial rule in the country, when it was reputedly introduced by the Church Missionary Society's Robert Henry Walker and Alexander (Alek) Fraser. From the time of his arrival in Uganda in 1900, Fraser organized nightly matches for his servant boys at their home on Mengo Hill, in the belief that the sport's key elements – in particular its requirement for constant teamwork – represented a perfect metaphor for the Christian faith ... Later, when selecting a location for the CMS's first secondary school in Uganda, (what became) King's College Budo, Fraser showed a particular concern for finding a site with a playing field big enough for a football pitch. From the time the school opened in 1906, football was a key part of the curriculum, and the football club quickly became one of the college's most prestigious organizations.

Such was the esteem in which the game came to be held that already by 1910, the *Kabaka* (king) of Buganda himself, Daudi Chwa, had created his own team – in which he played as captain – to rival the King's College boys. This was followed, over the next decade or so, by the formation of various other teams, most of them associated with various new institutions of learning ... and in 1924 all of these clubs joined up to create the Uganda Football Association, with Daudi Chwa as its first president.

From the beginning, therefore, football was marked as a key symbol of modernity in Uganda, and moreover, one particularly associated (the *Kabaka*'s team aside) with the modern institutions of the colonial state. This also helps to explain why the sport later became such an important symbol for political mobilization in the country, as different constituencies sought to use the game as a means through which to project their own ideas about how those same institutions (and therefore the Ugandan state as a whole) should be organized. The very first instance of football being used in this way occurred in 1942, at King's College itself.

In the context of the infamous 'College revolution' of that year, during which the school's teachers first claimed ownership of the college, and the authorities subsequently closed the school for a period, loyalty to the college football club became a key mark of students' allegiance to the 'traditionalist' agenda of the then *Kabaka*, Muteesa II ... However, the association of football with political activity was particularly strong in the period immediately pre- and post-independence when, in the context of increasingly intense jockeying for power in Uganda, football clubs also became key forums through which the newly formed political parties engaged their popular bases.

Perhaps the best known example is that of Express FC (Kampala), which from the time of its creation in 1957 was used as a vehicle by the leadership of the Baganda nationalist party *Kabaka Yekka* (literally 'kabaka only'; even today, Express remains synonymous with the Baganda nationalist cause) ... The last years of the colonial period also saw the elevation of the Uganda national team, the Cranes, by a colonial administration concerned with promoting a popular symbol of national unity on the eve of the country's independence. This began with a state-sponsored tour of Britain by the Cranes in 1956, making them the first African team to visit the country, and culminated in their participating in the World Cup in England in 1966 (which remains the only time that Uganda has ever qualified for the tournament) ...

Finally, following independence in October 1962, the administration of 'Obote I' again sought to patronize football, this time with a view to extending the influence of the various organs of state throughout the new nation. Thus over the course of the 1960s, practically every state enterprise – from the army and the prison service to the district administrations, commercial marketing boards and so on – was encouraged to create a team of its own, with the result that by the early 1970s the Uganda league had expanded to include several divisions, with teams spread across all of the country's urban centres and beyond. Many of these clubs have continued to operate on and off, sometimes under changed names, ever since.

However, the current popularity of specifically English football is a more recent development, and stems from the media reforms that were introduced by the current government, the National Resistance Movement (NRM), following their accession to power in 1986. As part of the wider 'structural adjustment' programmes that were brought in by the NRM during their early years in power, both print and broadcast media were 'opened up' to commercial competition, with the result that by the late 1990s Uganda had as many as twenty-five privately-owned FM radio stations and half a dozen or more TV providers.

Prior to this, the main way in which Ugandans would have had access to any sort of European football was via an international radio broadcaster, such as the BBC World Service – which has broadcast to the country via shortwave relay stations since the 1940s. However in practice, few people appear ever to have followed football in this way, especially during the years of political turbulence in Uganda, and especially during 'Obote II', when the very act of tuning in to an international station could be interpreted as political subversion ... But in the context of the newly liberalized media markets of the 1990s, most Ugandans (in the main urban areas, at least) quickly gained access to a quite startling array of European football content, which ranged from results services and commentary/analysis shows to actual games.

However, primary among this new content, from 1995 onwards, were the live EPL matches that were put out by the country's first satellite TV provider, the South African-based Digital Satellite Television (DStv) ... From early on, these were broadcast regularly in hotels and bars throughout Kampala, and even in some of the larger regional hotels ... Indeed, already by the time of my own first visit to Uganda in 1997, these DStv matches had become major public events and appeared to have galvanized not only Uganda's existing, and already sizable, football fan base, but also wider sections of the country's viewing public.

Football in the Villages

This national history of football is mirrored at the local level, in villages such as Bugamba (and doubtless hundreds, if not thousands, of others like it). Thus, just as the sport was introduced to the country as a whole through school teams, so too the very first match to be played in this village involved Bugamba School, following its opening in the 1960s. Bugamba School then went on to lay the area's first dedicated football pitch ... And just as football clubs became a vehicle for political aspirations at the national level, so they later came to serve this function at the village level. For example, since at least the 1980s it has been common practice for local officials to patronize school teams by buying them kit, by organizing their transport to matches and their refreshments and entertainments after the game (including discos), and even by laying on entire tournaments for their benefit. These easily double as political functions for the officials themselves ...

It is also quite common for these patrons to try to strengthen 'their' teams by bringing in talented players from further afield, and they will often pay the young men's school fees and even put them up in their own homes in order to do so (the logic here is presumably that by bringing in a player from distance, a patron demonstrates the extent of his connections; or perhaps it is simply that a more successful team is seen as a more effective display of one's political prowess?). Thus over the course of my own decade-long research living in the home of Grace Bwire, who is also Local Council (LC) 3 Chairman for this sub-county, I have, on occasion, shared quarters with several of these young men, who are known locally as *bacuba* in reference to the Cuban workers who first came to Uganda in the 1970s. Indeed in Grace's particular case, some of these players have been brought in from as far away as Buganda, and even in one case from eastern Uganda. Finally, if the newly liberalized media environment of the 1990s resulted in the general popularity of football in Uganda becoming refocused onto the

English game, it appears to have now had the same effect in villages like Bugamba.

In Bugamba's case, the current widespread interest in the EPL began not with satellite television, but with a number of the new regional radio stations which had also begun to proliferate from the late 1990s onwards. In particular, sometime around 2006 a station called Greater African Radio, which has for long played up its cosmopolitan credentials ... began to put out live commentaries of EPL games from its studio in Mbarara Town, in which a presenter would describe a game on air as he himself watched it on a DStv system. Broadcast in a variety of local languages, including Runyankore/Rukiga, the main vernacular of south-western Uganda, the format soon proved popular and was quickly taken up by a number of other Mbarara-based stations. However, within a short space of time one of these, Vision Radio, came to dominate the field, something that most of my respondents put down to the excitable style of that station's main commentator, DJ Nestor. Nestor's patter, which has since been copied by his successor DJ Nana, mirrors that of the impassioned 'South American' commentator, complete with shouts of 'GOOAALL!!' whenever a team scores, and makes quite compelling listening.

However, it was not until the establishment of the village's first satellite TV venue that the EPL became quite as popular as it is today. But DStv has always been, and remains today, prohibitively expensive for anyone in rural Uganda. Thus the very fact that someone like Mugisha has been able to purchase a satellite TV system at all reflects a further development in that market. Specifically, from mid 2007 onwards a British-based company, Gateway TV (GTV) ... began to expand aggressively into Africa, with a business model that included a US $200 million investment into the continent – the biggest ever single investment in African media. A large proportion of this money was used to wrest the African broadcasting rights for 80 per cent of EPL games away from DStv ... while another portion was used to subsidize the sale of the physical TV equipment to consumers like Mugisha. The combined result was that within barely a year of its creation, GTV already had over 100,000 subscribers across more than twenty African countries ... Thus it is likely that the scenes I witnessed during that first live match at Mugisha's place were at that very moment being repeated in similar venues across urban and rural Kenya, Rwanda, DR Congo and beyond.

New Media and the Rise of the English Game

Thus in Bugamba, reflecting the wider Ugandan experience, the initial appeal of football may be traced to the sport's association with the institutions and political processes of the colonial and later postcolonial state, and its more recent growth in popularity to the advent of a new, more 'globally' inflected, media environment over the past decade or so. A key question nevertheless remains here as to what has made these new media sources in general, and the new satellite TV broadcasts in particular, quite so compelling over such a short period of time (to the extent that one hundred or more people are now willing to gather to watch these broadcasts several times a week, many of them newly committed EPL fans)?

At least part of the answer here may lie in a longer history of media in this part of the world, and, in particular, in the local story of radio. Specifically, from the early 1940s onwards, in the period before the advent of cheap, portable transistor radios, early experiments in radio broadcasting were conducted in rural Uganda by the colonial government through communal listening posts. Crucially, in the southwest at least, these posts were invariably sited at various public administration buildings, themselves often located at the heads of valleys (which are generally marked as places of heightened symbolic significance in local cosmologies) ... [T]his resulted in radio broadcasts becoming coded as essentially public goods, and as especially powerful, and these aspects have continued to shape patterns of consumption ever since.

Thus the very fact that the new satellite television mirrors that earlier history of radio, especially in its production of a communal viewing environment, might itself be significant here. Or to put it another way, in attempting to explain the inherent power of these broadcasts, at least part of the answer might lie in the operation of the physical technology itself ...

However, as the DJ Nestor case indicates, the content of the media output is clearly also a factor here. Indeed this probably explains why it is English football, in particular, that has become the obsession (on satellite systems which also relay live German, Spanish and other European football). Certainly, it is tempting to explain this EPL connection with reference only to Uganda's colonial past, and to the fact that it is it therefore to the UK that most Ugandans now travel when, for example, undertaking *kyeyo* (literally 'broom'; the term evokes the menial work of sweeping, and is today used to describe almost all forms of international economic migration). However, perhaps more important here is the fast-paced, and generally exciting, nature of English football, and the fact that EPL teams tend to have more African and other black players than do their European counterparts ... These were the two main reasons given by my respondents as to why they especially liked the English game. (The identification with African players may also explain why, as of early 2009, Arsenal had become the most widely supported club in Bugamba, given that at that time the Arsenal team included a number of key African 'superstars' – including the then African Footballer of the Year, Togolese captain Emmanuel Adebayor.)

However, the popularity of specifically English football must also be seen as an outcome of the EPL's, and EPL clubs', own advertising and marketing strategies, which have always had a more global focus than those of their European counterparts, such that the EPL is today broadcast to 202 countries, by far the most of any European league. Moreover, in recent years these strategies have been increasingly targeted at African audiences, in the run-up to this summer's [2010] World Cup in South Africa. Thus, for example, increased subsidies have been provided to African media outlets – such as the Ugandan national newspapers The *New Vision* and The *Monitor* – to print the kind of glossy EPL posters that now adorn so many of Bugamba's shops and bars. At the same time, African imagery has become increasingly prominent in the league's own promotional materials. Thus the EPL's current introductory sequence – a forty-second segment that is played before all EPL match broadcasts, worldwide – now includes a simulation of an African village viewing-hall similar to the one I have described.

Football and Social Change

Yet even if the current popularity of EPL football is (at least partly) explicable with reference to projected symbols of Africa and to international marketing strategies, this does not necessarily mean that the phenomenon is therefore best viewed through a lens of 'crude globalization'. In particular, such a view might lead to a mistaken perception that the new fandom is a largely ephemeral phenomenon, one soon to be replaced by the next media-endorsed fad, and therefore lacking in any wider social significance. The initial evidence I have collected from this one field site, at least, suggests that on the contrary, the current enthusiasm for English football is already having significant, in some aspects profound, social effects.

Most obvious among these has been the emergence of a new, and already quite influential, network around the figure of Mugisha himself as a result of the huge revenues his operation generates. From the beginning Mugisha has charged each of his patrons UgSh 500 per match (a significant sum, in a context in which a day's labouring typically earns around UgSh 2000), with the result that each game generates earnings of up to UgSh 75,000 – about the cost of a calf. And it is worth repeating here that at the peak of the EPL season, three or four significant matches take place each week …

As a result, Mugisha himself has quickly become one of the major employers in the village, as he engages large numbers of his extended kin, friends and neighbours to work on match days. These individuals act as ticket collectors, bouncers (to police the rowdier sections of the crowd), barmen (to keep patrons stocked with either commercial bottled beer or the locally produced banana spirit, *waragi* – and I would note that Mugisha's viewing hall has also now become the most popular drinking spot in the area, even outside of 'footballing hours'), as technical operators (one of whom seems to be constantly fiddling with the television equipment throughout each match), and/or as ushers (in a particularly nice touch, these characters move through the crowd during each game, providing patrons with free groundnuts) …

Indeed, during that first evening at Mugisha's place I observed at least nineteen people working, and I have since estimated that as many as eighty may be in Mugisha's regular employ. Yet even more significant than this, Mugisha and his associates have also used their vast new revenues to patronize all sorts of other ongoing exchange relationships throughout the village. Thus, although it wasn't possible for me to collect in-depth data on such matters during this recent short period of fieldwork, I did record one instance in which the group had funded an entire wedding ceremony, including the bride-price. In addition, respondents spoke of the ways in which Mugisha's network had also provided various sorts of grants and loans to at least two local shops, to several *boda-boda* operators, and to a village tannery venture.

Thus the current interest in English football has created new lines of power and influence in the village. Yet it also has bolstered the authority of existing office holders, including the LC chairmen. While these individuals have long used local football as a vehicle for their own political advancement, the current popularity of the sport has amplified these efforts by increasing the general profile of the school teams, and the matches, that they sponsor. Take, for example, the case of one LC2 Chairman, Mzee Mugyenyi, who is a long-standing supporter of, and a conspicuous presence at any event involving, one nearby school team. At the time of my first visit to the Bugamba area, in 2000, Mugyenyi's association with this side was of somewhat limited utility, in that the team only played friendlies about once a month, to a crowd of perhaps sixty or so people ... Compare this with the current situation, in which the association currently provides the Chairman with a regular constituency, as his team now plays in a regular league which – mirroring the EPL – runs for several months, and involves two games a week, each of which draws a crowd of up to 400 ... In addition, the team has even begun to hold nightly 'training sessions' in a public space behind their school, which also draw a regular crowd as people stop to watch the boys on the way back from their day's work in the fields. Indeed, some team sponsors have capitalized even further on the EPL's current popularity. For example, one government official had recently become the talk of all of the bars in the surrounding areas by buying the school team he sponsors a complete set of replica Arsenal kit, in which they now play all of their matches.

However, it is not only amongst the new media owners and team sponsors that the social effects of the new fandom can be observed. Ordinary supporters, and their social worlds, also appear to have been significantly influenced by the phenomenon. In this regard, I would disagree with the views of one Ugandan development professional I spoke to later, who suggested that the new popularity of the EPL had led to a general increase in 'idleness' in villages throughout Uganda, as people now preferred to watch football than to engage in productive activities. Nevertheless, I did note that as a result of their engagement with the EPL, people's descriptions of time had become more specific than ever before. Thus, for example, in a context in which everyday idioms of time rarely discriminate beyond 'morning' (*akasheeshe*), 'afternoon' (*omwabazyo*) and 'night' (*ekiro*), I was somewhat surprised by one occasion on which I was told – in response to a question I had asked – that a particular broadcast was due 'to start at a quarter past eight' (*kutandika shaaha ibiri n'edakiika ikumi n'itaano*, emphasis mine). Not only had I never heard this particular phrase 'a quarter past' before, but I can't recall ever having heard any phrase which discriminates units smaller than half an hour. However, I later learned that under the influence of EPL start times, such talk has now become quite common in everyday speech …

Perhaps more significantly, the arrival of the EPL has also altered perceptions of space. In particular here, in a context in which most people previously knew the world outside of Central Africa only through the inchoate category of *buraeya*, a term which is best glossed as 'the global domain' … the particular style of English football commentators, who have for long demonstrated an obsession with stating the country of origin for each EPL player, has forged a much more specific understanding of the geography of European nations in particular. Indeed, this may be the new football's most profound impact in villages such as this, given the particular power, even cosmological significance, that the category of *buraeya* previously conveyed …

Yet with English commentators constantly peppering viewers with such observations as 'the Frenchman Clichy passes to the Spanish playmaker Fabregas, who lays it off to the Czech international Rosicky', and so on, the very notion of a generalized 'global domain' has today become largely redundant among young people, at least. Instead, it has become increasingly common for one to overhear conversations of the sort that I caught during that first evening at Mugisha's place, in which three young men argued over whether a particular player was from Slovenia, Croatia or the Ukraine. More generally, I also got a sense during this trip that people were more aware than ever before that I am from the UK specifically, although now living in New Zealand, (and the fact that I was born a short distance from the Arsenal stadium elicited even greater interest, of course).

Yet the changes which have been brought by the new interest in EPL football are not only conceptual in nature: the new fandom has also altered the flow of existing social practices and relations. For example, in addition to the arrival of the new practices of supporting EPL teams that I have already identified, the establishment of Mugisha's place has also created a new interest in gambling in the village. Thus, mirroring the long-established practices of urban television halls, large numbers of Mugisha's patrons now regularly bet on the results of EPL matches, which player will score a game's first goal, and so on. Moreover, some of the more committed chancers have now extended these activities beyond the television hall, to form informal gaming groups which also meet outside of EPL hours. Indeed, the emergence of these new groups – who are often seen playing dominoes, draughts or some other board game, in their members' compounds – is one of the most visible social changes to have occurred in Bugamba in recent years. In addition, patterns of visiting have also been altered. Thus on one occasion during my recent visit, an old associate of mine arrived at our home and waited several hours for me to return, yet then left within minutes of my arrival because a match was 'about to start'. And anecdotal evidence suggests that such incidents are becoming increasingly common. Moreover, if the dinner to which I have already referred was postponed because of an EPL game, it transpires that such rescheduling is now a regular feature of village life. Indeed, within barely a fortnight of arrival in the field, I had already recorded one church service, one baptism ceremony and one wedding function that had been similarly rescheduled.

Postscript

Unfortunately, this particular story does not have a happy ending. In early February 2009 it was announced that GTV had gone into liquidation, as a result of the global 'credit crunch'. It turned out that the company's massive $200 million expansion into Africa had been funded entirely through loans, and that in the context of the economic crisis, these were no longer sustainable. As a result, the GTV signal was turned off, and the television systems of people like Mugisha, and the 7,000 other GTV subscribers in Uganda, and the tens of thousands of others across the continent, were rendered useless ...

However, for Mugisha himself, the situation was more dire still. Following the GTV switch-off, it further transpired that Mugisha had raised the initial UgSh 650,000 needed to buy his own system through the mortgage of not only his land, but also that of his brother (who was at the time working in Rwanda as a schoolteacher). Thus the collapse of the broadcaster raised the spectre that both men might now lose their properties. When I left Uganda a short time later, it still remained unclear how Mugisha was going to solve this problem (and whether, for example, he would be able to 'call in' some of the loans that his network had made over the previous year). Yet it seemed almost certain that his brother was about to bring a court case against him, something that could potentially land Mugisha in prison.

Thus, if over the past few years the arrival of EPL football has demonstrated to the people of Bugamba the speed at which the 'new' globalization can produce a range of social effects, then so too it has also shown them just how toxic these consequences can sometimes be.

Edited extract from: Richard Vokes, 'Arsenal in Bugamba: The Rise of English Premier League Football in Uganda', *Anthropology Today* 26/3 (2010), pp.10–15.

SECTION IV

PRACTISING ANTHROPOLOGY
METHODS AND INVESTIGATIONS

Introduction to Section IV

Hilary Callan, Brian Street and Simon Underdown

In Section IV, we look at key features of the practice of anthropology, including the production and communication of anthropological knowledge, the place of the observer in the process of observation and description, and the ethics of anthropological research. A core concept running through the extracts in this Section is that of 'reflexivity'. This refers to a radical shift that has taken place within social anthropology over the past few decades in the way anthropologists as observers place themselves in relation to what is being studied. Previously, the dominant approach had been one derived from natural science, in which the observer stood outside the process of observation and recorded what was going on in a manner assumed to be 'objective'. More recently it has come to be recognised that ethnographic reports need to include the observer's presence in the processes of observation and description, and that anthropologists need to reflect on how their research questions are selected and framed.

IV.1 The Production, Communication and Use of Anthropological Knowledge

This group of extracts deal, in different ways, with what is involved in ethnographic research and writing. A. Lareau and J. Schultz address the process of learning and experimentation through which one becomes an ethnographer. They suggest that while ethnographic research does involve distinctive methods within a particular academic tradition, this learning is not in essence different from other ways in which we all learn and grow. Much like life itself, social life is often unpredictable, and ethnographic fieldwork calls for flexibility and imagination. The aim is to detect meaning through the complex flow of events: to understand 'what is going on'. In the next extract, Jeremy MacClancy discusses three contrasting works of anthropological writing – by Laura Bohannan, Nigel Barley and Katy Gardner – addressed to non-specialist readers. These works date from different periods of anthropological practice, and we can see in MacClancy's account of the most recent (Gardner's *Songs at the River's Edge*) how the debate over reflexivity has influenced anthropologists' work. Where Bohannan's book is autobiographical but set within a fictional frame, and Barley's books draw MacClancy's criticism for presenting the author as a humorous but essentially superior outsider, in Gardner's work the ethnographer is fully present and visible within the ethnography itself.

The anthropological study of gender was briefly touched on in Section I of the Reader. The next extract is taken from a longer paper by Edwin Ardener, first delivered in 1968 and republished several times since. It marks a significant moment in the 'bringing to consciousness' among anthropologists of the significance of gender at a theoretical as well as a descriptive level, and of the imbalances and distortions in anthropologists' accounts of a society that could result from speaking primarily 'to' men and 'about' women. Why should it be more difficult for ethnographers, whether male or female, trained in the dominant theories of the half century up to the 1960s, to address women's experiences? Rejecting what he terms the simplistic 'hot stove argument', Ardener offers cogent reasons why men might have been more ready than women to provide 'models' of their society that in turn appealed to ethnographers. This extract brings home to us that the production and communication of anthropological knowledge, like most knowledge, exists in time and has its own contextuality. Ardener's theoretical arguments did not of themselves invent feminist anthropology, but they had a strong influence on it, as did the rise of the broader feminist movement happening at around the same time, which led to fundamental re-theorising in a number of human disciplines including anthropology. Underlying Ardener's argument is the issue of 'articulacy', in the sense that within a society some groups may find it harder than others to get a hearing and recognition for their particular experiences and viewpoints. This insight can usefully be tried out in other contexts. For example, it has been argued that educational disadvantage among children from some minorities in the UK and US is linked less to limited command of English than to their styles of communication not being easily recognisable to teachers from more dominant cultural backgrounds. What is your opinion on this?

James Clifford was involved in one of the key texts that challenged dominant views of ethnography in the 1980s (Clifford and Marcus 1986) which focused on the personal involvement of fieldworkers in the writing of their accounts. As noted above, such 'reflexivity' has become a key component of anthropology, challenging the previous emphasis on a more neutral or positivist attempt to describe things in a supposedly 'natural' way. Following this work, fieldworkers became more conscious of the need to situate themselves in their accounts, as we have seen. Our extract from Clifford's article 'Notes on (Field) Notes' looks directly at the operation of writing things down in the field: the raw material from which the more polished ethnographic account is later constructed. Using illustrations drawn from classic images of ethnographers at work, he breaks this operation down into 'moments' of what he terms inscription, transcription and description. Each of these moments, as the images show, is interactive and social; but the fieldworker also needs space for private reflection and contemplation.

Along with writing and the production of ethnographic material, goes reading and understanding. The analysis and interpretation of how anthropological texts are produced and read is a key feature of ethnography. The selection from the work of D. Jacobson included here specifically addresses the reader and how we might read anthropological texts, at the same time relating this closely to the issue of how those texts are written. Researchers, whether full-time anthropologists or students doing projects, need to take account of both writing and reading, and the ideas they bring to bear on their subjects as they do so. Jacobson's work alerts us to the processes of framing, selection and filtering that go into observing, writing and reading, both in anthropology and in many departments of 'normal' life as well. The continuity of ethnography with normal life is taken forward in the brief extract from the work of Del Hymes that follows. Hymes suggests that the kinds of sensitivity and social competence that ethnographers need to cultivate professionally are also the qualities that contribute to citizenship of a democratic society. We conclude this group with the Buddhist fable of 'the Turtle and the Fish', which highlights the challenge facing the ethnographer in an unfamiliar place who must learn to step back from his or her mindset in order to see what is there instead of missing what is not.

IV.2 Studying 'Others' and Studying 'Ourselves'

Under this heading, we bring together two very different pieces of writing. Edmund Leach was one of the most eminent social anthropologists of his time, and one of the few to be recognised in Britain as a public intellectual. In this extract from his introductory book *Social Anthropology*, he addresses an inherent tension within anthropology between understanding other, unfamiliar, ways of life, and understanding the society to which one belongs and experiences in which one shares. Leach's primary emphasis, in common with most anthropologists at that time, is on what one can learn by studying cultures other than one's own – both about the other cultures in question, and about the common human experiences we all share. In the years since he wrote, increasing numbers of anthropologists have turned their attention to 'ethnography at home' – that is, anthropological study of aspects of one's own society, in which personal knowledge and experience contribute directly to the analysis. This different focus is illustrated in the extract which follows, from an account from the Mass Observation project in the UK. This project, now based at the University of Sussex, was founded in 1937 and, following a break, has continued since 1981. The material is based on the writing of correspondents – 'ordinary people' – recording their daily experience according to their own judgment of what is interesting. The archive has produced a wealth of rich material, much of which has been analysed and published. One correspondent's wartime diary, that of Nella Last, has recently become famous through the TV adaptation *Housewife, 49*, starring Victoria Wood. As the extract included here makes clear, Mass Observation raises questions that are deeply pertinent for anthropology. It explores what it is to 'study ourselves' as anthropologists, and it also challenges us to consider who is entitled to write and record, and who is excluded from giving voice to their experience.

IV.3 Ethics in Anthropology

All anthropological work has an ethical dimension, whether it concerns (for example) biological research involving human remains or nonhuman primates, or participant fieldwork among living human communities. For most scientific disciplines in the Western world there are now well-established protocols and institutions such as Ethics Committees for granting approval to particular research projects – although there is still much controversy in areas such as medical research and research using animals. Because anthropology deals with complex human experience in very specific contexts, it is difficult to lay down hard-and-fast ethical rules to cover all situations. Yet ethical questions enter into the planning, conduct, communication and interpretation of all anthropological research, whether it be at a professional level or that of small-scale projects carried out by students. To illustrate this, we include here, with permission, edited extracts from the ethical guidelines published by two representative bodies in anthropology: the American Association of Physical Anthropologists in the USA (AAPA), and the Association of Social Anthropologists of the UK and Commonwealth (ASA). Both these documents are primarily addressed to professional anthropologists and so include issues such as relations with funding agencies and Governments, but they also cover questions which should concern anyone carrying out research in a human environment, however small-scale the project may be.

In Section I of the Reader we encountered some of the ethical issues surrounding research on the bodily remains or artefacts of historical humans, some of which are (or were until recently) held in museums and research collections. Included here is a brief example, drawn from the debates surrounding the repatriation of human remains to their communities of origin. This case illustrates the complexity of the issues involved, where the materials may originally have been acquired by morally dubious means and where there is conflict between the claims of descendant groups to the remains of their ancestors and those of science to derive knowledge that might be of benefit to all in understanding our human past. As the extract shows, there are typically many voices, and diverse interests, involved in such disputes, claims and counter-claims, and there are seldom easy answers.

Reference
Clifford, James, and George Marcus (eds). 1986 *Writing Culture: The Poetics and Politics of Ethnography* (Berkley: University of California Press,).

IV.1 The Production, Communication and Use of Anthropological Knowledge

52	**Journeys through Ethnography** *Annette Lareau and Jeffrey Schultz*

*The book edited by Lareau and Shultz, from the Introduction to which
we have taken the following extract, sees doing ethnography as a
'journey', which they compare to other journeys we may engage in
during our lives, some romantic, some academic, but all involving
discovery, making mistakes, learning through practice. Doing
ethnography, like these other activities, is not something you can
determine beforehand and then just carry out; rather, we learn by
doing: 'research methodology can only be mastered through
experience'. They are, then, critical of methodology books that claim
you can know beforehand – such accounts are full of 'platitudes' they
believe. In the case of ethnography, the researcher is led into varied and
unpredictable situations, which may not always work out as expected.
The difficulties encountered in the field should be admitted and made
explicit, rather than remain 'private' as in previous accounts of 'how to
do fieldwork'. Like James Clifford (see his piece on fieldnotes included in
this Reader), the contributors to Lareau and Schultz's volume recognise
the importance of 'reflexivity' in fieldwork, of being open about the
problems and about one's own role as the researcher as you engage
with a variety of subjects – as they put it, 'revelations of the unevenness
of the process are helpful'. Lareau and Schultz then helpfully set out to
define, or at least describe, what is involved in ethnographic
methodology, a concept used across a number of disciplines not just
anthropology, though this is where it was originally developed. In
particular they see participant observation as a key element along with
in-depth interviews with key informants. They distinguish this
approach from work in experimental research and surveys, and in the
use of 'sampling'. In contrast, 'in participant-observation the researcher
is interested in 'meaning', in particular the meanings held by their
subjects and, rather than using independent tools, they see the person
as the "instrument". These are key issues for students of anthropology to
discuss as they read and try to make sense of accounts of ethnography
by previous researchers and as they set out themselves to do any*

*participant observation of their own. How will they find out 'what is
going on here?' Will they also want to use surveys or questionnaires,
and if so how reflexive can they be about their own continuing role in
both designing the project and in taking it directly to their subjects? As
Lareau and Shultz put it, 'How a researcher acts in the field shapes the
contours of the results'.*

The longest journey begins with one step.

At one point or another in our lives, we are all beginners. We begin college,
a first job, a first love affair, and a first research project. We bring a great deal
to these new situations, including our temperament, previous education,
and family situations. Yet, as adults, we also learn. In romantic relationships,
couples report having to learn how to interact successfully with their
partners. College students report being better at reading, studying, paper
writing, and test taking as seniors than as freshmen. They have learned how
to be students while they were students. Now close to graduating, some
view they have finally mastered the role. Ideally, of course, we would have
the necessary information in hand before we needed it. We would already
know, without being told, what makes a loved one angry or frustrated. All
students would be spared the frustration of working hard on a paper and
having it not be well received. Especially, researchers would never make
mistakes.

Indeed, some individuals go through life believing that they should know
how to do something ahead of time. In this view, mistakes are aberrations.
After making a mistake, individuals can torture themselves with repeated
accusations and self-blame. They see their foibles as an indication of their
own lack of capability as a person. Some plunge into despair and conclude
they will never sustain a romantic relationship, succeed in college, or
complete a valuable research project.

Nevertheless, the reality is that learning is a process and that mistakes,
including costly ones, are integral to that process. Although reading, teaching,
and guidance are helpful, there are key aspects – for example, of romantic
relationships, college course work, and research methodology – that are
mastered through experience. Usually, although not always, humans get
better at something through practice. This learning process can be exhilarating,
difficult, boring, uplifting, lonely, exciting, frustrating, and scary.

This book is about learning to do research variously called 'ethnography',
'naturalistic studies', 'qualitative research', and 'case studies'. This
methodological approach is used by anthropologists, sociologists, and
folklorists as well as students of cultural studies, educational studies, and
religious studies. We are dissatisfied with the state of the current
methodological books in this genre. With few exceptions, we find the books
on qualitative research to be overly general in their expositions; many are

filled with platitudes. Standard methodological texts extol a set of virtues: Researchers using participant-observation should build rapport, gain the trust of the people in the study, provide detailed and accurate field notes, interpret the results in a theoretically informed manner, and write it up in a vivid and engaging style. We agree with these standards.

Yet, participant-observation necessarily brings the researcher into varied and unpredictable situations. In an effort to be with people and to understand their lives, researchers sometimes react in ways that they are pleased about; other times they say or do things that they regret. There is always a gap between instruction and implementation, but this pattern of success and regret has been traditionally private. Though often acknowledging briefly that there were some aspects of the project that did not proceed as anticipated, researchers – including those who use field research techniques – often skimmed across and minimized the inevitable difficulties in the field.

In part, these omissions in the presentation of self are driven by fear. Researchers correctly fear that revelations of weaknesses in the collection and analysis of data will be seized upon by readers and reviewers as weaknesses in the project. Because researchers want their results to be well

Fieldwork in Vanuatu.

Filmstill from *The Poet's Salary* directed by anthropologist and filmmaker Eric Wittersheim, (Royal Anthropological Institute Film Festival 2011); Distributed by the RAI.

received, the norm has been to reveal a minimum of difficulty. In addition, accepted social science practice is to introduce problems in the study and then attempt to explain to the reader how these problems were overcome and do not threaten the integrity of the results.

This collection provides a different vantage point. All of the authors write of being beginners in one fashion or another; most were beginning a senior thesis or doctoral dissertation. They show us how individuals learned to be researchers in the process of carrying out their projects. The chapters are 'confessional' … in the sense they reveal foibles. More to the point, they show how research actually gets done. We believe that revelations of the unevenness of the process are helpful. They provide comfort to beginners who know that even distinguished scholars … sometimes made foolish mistakes as they learned how to do research. They provide clarity of how methodological goals such as building rapport are translated into action. They provide insight into the kinds of factors other researchers considered when they stumbled into difficulty and the strategies – for example, of reflection and data analysis – that researchers used to extract themselves from their temporary woes. More to the point, they highlight the uncertainty and confusion that inevitably accompany field research. It is, as we explain in more detail further on, appropriate to be confused at various points of the project.

What Do We Mean by Ethnographic Methods?

Reasonable people disagree about the definition of ethnography. Traditionally, in anthropology, ethnographic studies had a host of characteristics including the use of participant-observation to study a community for an extended period of time, a holistic approach, the portrayal of the community from the perspective of the participants, a focus on culture (particularly the lived culture of the setting), and a focus on context … In other fields – including sociology, religious studies, and education – ethnography has been defined more loosely. Almost all definitions, however, include the use of participant-observation as well as in-depth interviews with key informants. There is an effort to understand the view of the participants; researchers seek to be in the setting long enough to acquire some notion of acceptance and understanding.

In this collection, we have taken a broader rather than narrower definition of ethnography. We include works from both perspectives … ethnographic methods can be distinguished from other approaches such as survey or experimental research. There is, clearly, a difference in scale. Whereas a survey researcher might give a standardized questionnaire to one thousand students, a researcher using participant-observation might 'hang out' with a few individuals. There are also differences in how the research is carried out and the data are analyzed. Survey researchers seek to control almost all aspects of their study. They 'select' in a sample who they study, and they ensure that the 'respondents' are asked the exact same question. They also standardize the answer categories in an effort to improve comparability among respondents ('Do you strongly agree, somewhat agree, neither agree nor disagree, somewhat disagree, or strongly disagree with the following statement'). In particular, survey researchers seek to assess the frequency of behavior in a population. They report, for example, the proportion of individuals who voted in the last election, used drugs in high school, graduated from college, and are employed.

Researchers who use participant-observation have a different set of goals. Rather than being interested in how frequent a behavior is, they wonder about the meaning of a behavior. They seek, generally, to understand the character of the day-to-day life of the people in the study. Ethnographers often ask, 'What is going on here?' The research is labor intensive; most studies cover a few individuals, one or two classrooms, or one tribe. Sometimes decisions are made, but once in the setting researchers end up collecting more data on some aspects of life than others. This 'sample' often is the result of serendipity. Participant-observers do not center their work on fixed-answer questions. They generally try to get to know respondents and to spend time with them over and over again. Thus they are interested in the character of social life. Rather than a survey showing X percentage of high school students smoked marijuana once in the last month, they explore what it is like to be a drug peddler and how it shapes the contours of one's life ... Instead of reporting by race, gender, and family background the number of students who stayed in college, they describe the day-to-day character of what it is like to be a student ... Unlike survey research, where a large number of persons review and adjust the research 'instrument', in participant-observation the person is the 'instrument'. How a researcher acts in the field shapes the contours of the results.

Edited extract from: A. Lareau and J. Shultz, 'Introduction', in A. Lareau and J. Shultz (eds), *Journeys through Ethnography: Realistic Accounts of Fieldwork* (Boulder, CO: Westview Press, 1996), pp.1–4.

53 Fieldwork Styles: Bohannan, Barley and Gardner
Jeremy MacClancy

This extract is taken from a chapter by Jeremy MacClancy in a collection he also co-edited, addressing the 'popularisation' of anthropology – that is, various styles and strategies that could be adopted by anthropologists to make their ideas accessible to a wider, non-specialised, readership. Such 'popularisations' have sometimes been regarded with suspicion by scholars within the discipline, on the grounds that to write about anthropology for the general public is inevitably to simplify and distort the complexity of the subject matter. However, it is increasingly recognised that (as is happening in other disciplines ranging from biology to physics, cosmology, history and classics) anthropologists need to convey the importance of their knowledge and insights to audiences outside academia. There is nonetheless a strong sense that this needs to be done with due care and sensitivity, as shown in MacClancy's critical comments on the 'sins' of Nigel Barley, one of the authors he cites. In this extract, MacClancy describes and compares three contrasting ways of constructing and communicating anthropological knowledge.

Every generation has its anthropologists, every epoch its ethnographers. Whether self-promoted or picked up by the public, candidates emerge in every period as the popular representatives of our discipline …

While the more dated of popular works have now been buried within the history of the discipline, the words of those who have tried to touch more enduring themes hold the promise of living a little longer. Among fieldwork accounts intended for a non-academic readership, Laura Bohannan's *Return to Laughter* was an early contribution to the genre, and it remains the definitive example. Nigel Barley's *The Innocent Anthropologist*, though perhaps too novel to be yet regarded as an established classic, continues to sell well and has helped to make its author the most well-known anthropologist in British non-anthropological circles.

In this chapter I wish to speak of both these works and of a more recent account, Katy Gardner's *Songs at the River's Edge: Stories from a Bangladeshi Village* … All three works speak of the rigours of a prolonged stay among exotic peoples. All three reveal to us something about both the anthropologist and the anthropologized. But beyond these basic similarities, this trio of books, published in 1954, 1983, and 1991 respectively, are popular for very different reasons.

Laura Bohannan's *Return to Laughter*, the fictional account of her time among the Tiv of Nigeria, is one of the best-selling descriptions of fieldwork ever written. Since its publication in 1954 it has been reprinted over twenty times and has now become a permanent part of introductory courses in anthropology. In the United States especially, students first learn about the subject via Bohannan. The question, of course, is why her book?

It is not merely that *Return* was one of the first introspective accounts of life in the field. Rather, it is because she deals in a straightforward yet engaging manner with the central moral problems of sharing a protracted length of time with people apparently very different to Westerners. For the primary focus of her novel is not the Nigerians she lived with but, as she states, 'the sea change in oneself that comes from immersion in another and savage culture'.

The protagonist (let us call her 'Elenore', after the pseudonym Bohannan used for her novel) is a well-read American brought up in an urban Catholic household. A highly disciplined and determined neophyte, she regards her

Black Mountain
Filming during fieldwork.

Filmstill from *Black Mountain* by Charlotte Whitby-Coles, 2008. Distributed by the Royal Anthropological Institute.

fieldwork as an uncomplicated means towards a fixed end: getting a doctorate from Oxford. However, despite her academic training in anthropology, she remains innocent about the lived reality of other cultures. Prefiguring the Tiv as whites in black skins, she imagines that they 'would differ only in externals of dress and custom, that their basic reactions to the same basic situation would be the same as mine' ... Since she, presumably, knows how to cope with Westerners, there should be no problem dealing with the Tiv.

In the field, Elenore does not want to get involved, merely to be accepted. She does not wish to be caught in a web of social obligations, but to be free to go her own way with their full confidence. Instead of letting untidy emotions mess her work, she intends to maintain a neat, scientific detachment ...

In her first weeks, all goes reasonably well. She assiduously compiles genealogies, lists of botanical terms, and other vocabularies; she maps the homesteads within her patron's influence; she names a child, jots down recipes, and joins women's weeding parties. She is learning. But Elenore is discontented:

> My dissatisfaction lay wholly in the part I was being assigned. I was rapidly being absorbed in the life of the women and children. All the magic, all the law, all the politics – over half the things professionally important to me were in

the hands of the men, and so far not one man had been willing to discuss such matters with me ... I had been identified with the women: unless I could break that association, I would leave the field with copious information on domestic details and without any knowledge of anything else. (Bowen 1954: 78–79)

And so her real troubles begin.

In order to learn about politics, she becomes a politician; in order to be told the details of witchcraft, she is not scared to be thought a witch. At first manipulated, she becomes adroit at manipulation. Treated as a pawn by rival elders, she turns into a queen able to check them both. But this sort of manoeuvring is common the globe over. It does not question one's understanding of the world.

What does prove subversive is her increasing awareness of Tiv values and her deepening emotional involvement with some of them. She realizes she cannot pigeonhole her neighbours into Western stereotypes (the *grande dame*, the crusty old man, the giddy matron, the Mr Milquetoast, etc.) for their emotional reactions to events may be different to ours. The culturally constituted consequences of a couple's adultery show her she must judge local acts by local, not by Western, standards. On learning the details of polygamy, she is surprised to find herself sorry for a man henpecked by five wives. At a wedding she is forced to make a choice:

'You must make up your mind', Udama announced loudly, so that all could hear, 'whether you wish to be an important guest or one of the senior women of the homestead. If you are an important guest, we will again lead out the bride, so you may see her. If you are one of us, you may come inside, but then you must dance with us'... [M]y hesitations were gone almost before she stopped speaking. I went inside the hut. (Bowen 1954: 123)

Watching over a close but mortally ill friend, she tussles with the professional standard of detachment and then rejects it for the sake of possibly saving her companion. On this and other occasions Redwoman (as she is called) loses her coolness and waxes passionate. During a smallpox epidemic she at first resists being 'infected by their fears', and then succumbs. Scared of the consequences of assisting the ejected scapegoat blamed for the epidemic, she stays indoors and suffers her conscience instead.

There was no doubt in my mind – and there is none now – that by leaving him to his fate I denied the greatest of our moral values: one must not withhold help which it is in one's power to give. The dilemma was naked before me, and before it I shrank back in naked inadequacy ... Fear made us all cruel. (Bowen 1954: 273, 277)

In the early stages of her stay with the Tiv, Elenore had noted and appreciated their easy laughter, their proud bearing, and their grace of speech and movement. Later she had come to regard these cultural attributes as superficial, as cloaking an ugly harshness and cruelty. People prepared to laugh at the trials of a blind man lost in the jungle could not be admired. Now, on her return after fleeing the epidemic, she feels diminished and painfully aware of her own fallibility. It is her friends who show her the error of her self-judgement.

The disease gone, the homestead re-established, they stage an evening of story-telling. As a variety of participants act out a hilarious series of local fables, Elenore is forcibly reminded of the ethics underpinning their society. One trio play the roles of litigant, interpreter, and administrator. As the case becomes ever more involved, the colonial officer becomes ever more confused, so the final judgement he passes is an entirely irrelevant decision based on wholly erroneous grounds. The audience are laughing so much they cannot hear the speakers and the chief, almost choking on his chuckles, comments, 'That is the way it is ... They judge us, but they do not understand us, and what can we do?' (Bowen 1954: 293). The next skit is of a blind man stumbling about the bush. The impersonator plays his part so well that even Elenore, despite herself, starts to laugh. 'That is the way it is', remarks the chiefs' brother, himself partially blinded by the smallpox, 'Indeed it is so. What can one do?'

Now Redwoman's eyes have been opened. She sees that the Tiv are not, as she had earlier thought, callous and indifferent to suffering. Though tragedy, in their harsh environment, is genuine and frequent, they do not try to avoid their grim reality, but to face it – with laughter. This mirth is not a form of humour, but a lively, and often embittered, acceptance of their lot. 'It is the laughter of people who value love and friendship and plenty, who have lived with terror and death and hate'. If they could not look death in the face, and smile, they would go insane.

...

Elenore's training at the hands of the Tiv may help her to qualify as a professional academic, but her fieldwork is in fact more a process of spiritual, rather than of anthropological, education. For Elenore is concerned about the state of her soul – at that time still a current concept – while the central theme of Bohannan's book is the crooked progress of her protagonist as she painfully stumbles her way towards some sort of self-knowledge and spiritual realization. In this sense, *Return to Laughter* is... a kind of modern *Pilgrim's Progress*.

...

Bohannan's academic models may come from the world of Boas and Evans-Pritchard, but her stylistic ones derive from that of the Bible and Shakespeare – both the sacred text and the *Collected Works* are on Elenore's bookshelf. She is not an unschooled traveller, but an educated pilgrim steeped in the traditions of her tribe. Her quest for herself, though pursued in an exotic setting, proceeds down an already well beaten path.

...

Laura Bohannan seeks to understand the social role of laughter; Nigel Barley, in contrast, does not wish to investigate humour, but to produce it. The point of his fieldwork accounts is less to portray the anguish of the soul in an exquisitely wrought prose than to puncture the pretensions of sanctimonious anthropologists and to amuse the reader. Instead of the over-solemn books written by these serious characters, Barley wants to dwell on precisely those aspects of fieldwork usually regarded as 'irrelevant', 'unimportant', 'not anthropology'. He does not want to be part of a supposedly discipline-wide cover-up, but to lay the subject bare.

In *The Innocent Anthropologist* (1983) and *A Plague of Caterpillars* (1986), Barley gives us the low-down on his two field-trips to the Dowayo, mountain pagans of northern Cameroon. On neither excursion do things go well. He is, by turns, lonely, bored, depressed, diseased, injured, cheated, exhausted. The only time he experiences hysterical joy is the day of his departure from the village. Persistently pestered by goats, termites, mice, cicadas and scorpions, he has also to cope with the demands of locals thirsty for beer and hungry for money. He tries to ingratiate himself with the villagers but fails to make more than one or two Dowayo friends; most regard him as at worst a harmless idiot, and at best an entertaining curiosity, a 'jester in shorts'. Unsure of his command of their tonal language, he wonders whether he has ever done more than teach them his pidgin version of it. When he does try to do his job, Dowayo are vague and evasive about what they know and, despite his assiduity, he only learns the local lore in a haphazard, spasmodic manner. Rites are confusing, magical practices are secret, goats eat his notes, rivers wash his films, and mould patterns his lenses. Fieldwork is difficult and discouraging, and Barley chronicles the obstacle course well.

...

Barley's idea of writing up the parts other ethnographers leave out sounds an eminently laudable aim. It is also a highly marketable one. His five popular books are all still in print and the first one is now in its seventh impression. His literary ability and productivity have made him so well known that his popular fame has shunted Levi-Strauss and lesser figures into the academic shade. He is feted in the national press and has even been given his own television series. Yet, though social anthropology thrives on competing viewpoints and alternative approaches, and though all but the most dour practitioners of the subject enjoy a laugh at themselves, Barley is not liked by his peers ... What, exactly, has he done to annoy them so?

His detractors ... claim not to begrudge the fact that [Barley] was prepared to say what others were scared, or insufficiently talented, to write. These academics might be suspicious of the popular, but they do not regard that in itself as sufficient grounds for damning his books. Instead, what they complain about is the way he laughs at those who cannot answer back, and his apparent readiness to reinforce pejorative stereotypes.

It is true that Barley tends not to let professional ethics get in the way of his sense of fun. His portrayal of the Dowayo, while often sympathetic, is fundamentally unflattering: their way of life appears to be crude, their lived environment smelly and squalid, and their magician's technical equipment a joke. If I were the village chief who acted as Barley's host, I would not like to be remembered by many thousands of Britons as a beer-swilling sluggard who only took pains to avoid unwelcome visitors. Nor would I like to be the most powerful rainmaker of the area, a locally revered man whose impotence is now the laughing-stock of Barley's readers. Since this pair and most of the Dowayo are illiterate, they have no redress. They have been mocked and they have no possibility of offering alternative representations in the written medium that Barley was able to utilize ...

Barley's sins become blacker, however, when he moves from the particular to the general. For he regards some of his specific fieldwork difficulties as typical of those experienced by most anthropologists living with peoples low on some Western developmental scale. He opens, for instance, the section dealing with his attempt to elucidate kinship terms from villagers with a comment on how much has been written 'on primitive peoples' ability or inability to deal with hypothetical questions' ... Later, when discussing his efforts to learn remedies from local healers, he states that 'in primitive society knowledge is seldom freely available' ... When not comparing the Dowayo with other technologically underdeveloped peoples of the globe, he regards the villagers he lived with and the Cameroonians he met on the way as providing him with enough evidence to comment on a whole continent. He thinks, for example, that analysing data and pursuing the demands of abstract thought without interruption or distraction 'most un-African' ... His perhaps most insulting generalization is reserved for his page on copulatory customs: 'Sexual encounters in Africa are so unromantic and brutish in their nature that they serve rather to increase the alienation of the fieldworker, not to moderate it, and are best avoided' ...

...

One worry about Barley's typecasting is that his public may come to think his crass stereotyping and gross insensitivity are standard anthropological practices. In other words, this successful author, by consistently stereotyping others, aids the stereotyping of his own profession. And since he is so successful, the danger is that, with the decline ... in the authoritativeness of those anthropologists previously regarded as exemplars, his readers may begin to regard him as on a par with true masters of the discipline such as Evans-Pritchard and Levi-Strauss.

...

Defenders of Barley might claim that his mocking comments are tolerable because they are directed at everyone – including the author. Throughout his books he is, it is true, more than ready to laugh at himself and to underline the occasionally ridiculous nature of his fieldwork investigations. But, while the wisdom of the locals, the sanity of the expatriates, and the value of anthropology may sometimes be placed in doubt, the one thing that is never questioned in Barley's books is his intelligence. No matter what happens to him, no matter how horrific, squalid, or demeaning the situation, his prose style unfailingly displays his invincible IQ. He may at times make a fool of himself but, at the end of each volume, he always makes sure he comes out on top.

...

Gardner, compared to Barley, is not peahen-proud. In *Songs at the River's Edge: Stories from a Bangladeshi Village*, she does not place herself at centre-stage, nor does she confine the locals to bit-parts. Instead of using them as foils in amusing anecdotes, she lets stories of their lives take up the greater part of her text. The point of her literary production is not to deflate fellow academics, but to portray the cultural reality and the common humanity of the villagers she stayed with. Unlike Bohannan, however, Gardner is not concerned about depicting the lives of all the different sorts of people within her homestead. For, in contrast to the works of both Bohannan and Barley, Gardner's fieldwork account is most emphatically one by a woman about women, and the unstated aim of her book is to correct the androcentric bias of the genre.

Gardner opens and closes her *Stories* with chapters on the twin pains of arrival and departure. Otherwise she fills her text with the problems and predicament of the female villagers themselves. Different chapters describe the lot of a servant, the anguish of a bride who has yet to meet her groom, the labour of birth, the fears of a barren wife that her man will desert her, an impoverished woman's improvident purchase of a new sari and her subsequent beating by her husband, the devastation caused by the monsoon, and the ease with which death comes. It is, on the whole, an empathetic catalogue of female woes in a distant ... setting. Western women readers can contrast their own fate and count their blessings, or note their common damnation.

The men who appear in the episodes Gardner narrates are, almost without exception, wretched, insignificant, selfish, ugly, laughable or brutal. The titular heads of households, they can try to organize others, can batter their women, and may administer barbaric punishments. She curses men for the privileges they are granted, and only one man is ever commended in her text: a young savant of local lore, praised by her as being 'more mature and wiser than any of my university-educated men friends back in Britain' ... The point of her praise, however, is soon revealed, as it serves to highlight his downfall in the city where he is regarded as an illiterate bumpkin and is promptly duped by an unscrupulous middle-man ...

... Gardner lets ... [the local women's] down-to-earth virtues shine through her stories. Though they have to rear large families, prop up households, and submit to their husbands, they survive; some thrive and are, at times, exemplars of strength to their Western readers. Born 'stunningly beautiful', they may, despite decades of wearying hardship, remain radiant.

...

Gardner is uninterested in brotherhood. It is not that the village men are unfriendly, rather that she feels she does not, and never would, belong with them. What she wishes to nurture is a sense of sorority. And she tries to feed it in spite of her new-found friends' possible desires to the contrary. She insists on serving herself at mealtimes and, when in the first month of her fieldwork her dirty clothes are snatched from her, she cries, 'Aren't I a woman? Aren't I equal? Why shouldn't I wash my own clothes?' ... Her female hosts are prepared to accede to these demands, but even Gardner has to admit, from the very beginning, that her supposed equality with the local women-folk is but a polite form of play-acting they are courteous enough to perform.

In a setting of such poverty and destitution, the anthropologist is a rich interloper who has the power to accept, or reject, the local rules whenever it suits her. Though Gardner calls the daughters of the Muslim family she lives with 'my new sisters', and though she 'wanted more than anything to be one of them', she does not stall in resisting those aspects of the village culture which grate against her personality. She refuses to wear a veiled cape, does not dress smartly on important occasions, and is disrespectful to a young male student of the Qur'an ... As she confesses in the conclusion, 'my transformation into a Bangladeshi woman had never been more than a surface veneer of habits and appearances which for the most part had remained entirely within my control' ... Unlike Bohannan's Elenore, whose personality underwent a sea-change because of her time with the Tiv, Gardner is able to slough off what she has learned as easily as a snake shedding its skin ... All that stays with her at the end is an emotion – her love, reciprocated, for Sufia, her best Bengali friend.

...

In order to be professionally correct, the neophyte just back from the field has to submit to the literary laws of the discipline. If she, or he, wishes to be accepted by her superiors as a potential equal, she has to follow the already established ethnographic guidelines of her department. Until very recently, that entailed producing a text which was meant to appear objective, thorough, and dehumanized. In the process the locals under study were all too often transmuted into the two-dimensional victims of a social determinism, as though they were puppets whose movements are all culturally prescribed. Their describer was under no obligation to recount the way she carried out her fieldwork, the specific people she relied upon, the sorts of difficulties she faced, nor those aspects of local life she could not, or did not wish to, study. Instead of cataloguing her inadequacies, failures and omissions, she could make herself appear omniscient, omnipresent and omnicompetent. In these circumstances, it is not surprising that many ethnographies seem unbelievable, and are unbelievably boring.

Personal accounts of fieldwork were, and are not, confined by such constraints. Their authors can portray the locals as characters in the round. In these volumes the indigenes need not be depersonalized but may be described as individuals, each with his or her own strengths, idiosyncrasies and foibles. Unlike the stick-men of standard ethnographies, their particular personalities are not lost within some abstract and generalizing analysis. They can be shown as the emotionally complex and psychologically subtle characters they may well be. They can also be revealed as people with individual life-histories, ones whose sustained interaction with one another unfolds in an intricate manner over time. In personal accounts, the sequential narration of events is not forsaken for the synchronic analysis of structure.

Personal accounts are doubly personal, for they can expose the personalities both of the locals and of their scribe. Rather than confine herself to a confessional sketch in the introduction of her ethnography, the fieldworker can chronicle the crooked, uneven course of her investigation. Instead of appearing all-knowing, ever-resourceful and totally unflappable, she may detail her ignorance, blunders, and occasional inability to control her moods. Elenore loses her temper over the unsuccessful attempts of Tiv medical techniques to save the life of her friend; Barley rails at the swindling ways of local merchants; Gardner reacts to the condescending manner of a Bengali hotel-keeper by calling him a 'patronising git'. Since she delivers the epithet in English and accompanies it with a saccharine smile, the man does not even raise his eyebrows. In these accounts, the lofty academic can appear engagingly human, at times all too human.

Fieldwork is the distinctive method of social anthropology. It is thus surprising that it has remained, until relatively recently, a mysterious process whose secrets were not discussed in print by the initiated. The authors of personal accounts of the experience have chosen to buck this code of silence by revealing just how aleatory [gamble-like] fieldwork can in fact be. The ethnographer may have a well-organized, cleverly constructed schedule of work, but these plans are often shredded as the locals refuse to comply with their guest's expectations. Writers like Bohannan and Barley expose the central role of chance and of their own personalities in influencing the course of their research. By focusing on the personal, they emphasize the ethnographers' reliance on those locals who, for some reason, have come to enjoy the newcomer's company ... On the example of these writers, fieldworkers need to be as cunning as they are resourceful.

Personal accounts try to engage the public in a way staid ethnographies do not attempt to achieve. By itemizing their feelings and reactions, warts and all, writers in this genre can present themselves as mirrors for their readers to look into. Armchair travellers can play at identifying with the protagonist: how would they have responded to life in the bush, to the rigours of the Cameroonian highlands, or to the pervasive poverty of rural Bangladesh? Could they have coped with an over-affectionate primate, an accusation of witchcraft, or sharing a small house with fifteen others during the monsoon?

Sedentary voyagers can also reassure themselves that what they are reading is 'the real thing'. Barring missionaries and exceptional characters such as Charles Doughty, most literary travellers have neither the time nor the knowledge to make other than superficial comments. In contrast, an anthropologist is supposed to have spent sufficient time in one place to get to know the locals as well as she can. Her words are meant to be authoritative, and her literary product veridical. Her experience is so rich she has no need to pad her text with tales.

...

... [W]hat Bohannan and Gardner both reveal in their own ways is the inadequacy of any pre-established code of professional ethics, no matter how comprehensive it pretends to be. Each of them has to face unforeseen moral quandaries, and each has to resolve them in order to be able to remain in their field-community. Bohannan forsakes standards of detachment in order to help save a friend. Gardner loses her cool when a townsman tries to cheat a villager. Also, both of these writers reveal that, despite moral differences, a form of human solidarity may be attained, that a human bond, born of intimate contact, may unite fieldworker and field worked. Perhaps it is for these reasons that Barley is so disliked by his peers: by pointedly omitting any ethical dimension to his work, he underlines his determination to let nothing get in the way of a joke; by playing the solitary role of jester, he denies the possibility of a human bond which could bridge cultural divides – and so denigrates his hosts all the more. ...

...

Each of this literary trio does something different, each in its own way defines a variant of the genre, and each is very much a product of its time. Bohannan's phrasing of fieldwork as a spiritual quest for oneself was particularly appropriate for her postwar peers: in the Oxford of her days, the largest society in the University was the Christian Union, while existentialism provided succour for anguished undergraduates who were unattracted by established creeds. Barley's first book came out at a time when Lévi-Straussian structuralism had raised anthropology to a new level of public prestige and pomposity. Susan Sontag's much-quoted characterization of the anthropologist 'as hero' had become a pretentious trope waiting to be mocked, and Barley saw no reason to leash his tongue ... The publication of Gardner's book reflects, of course, the developing encounter between feminism and anthropology ... *Songs* ... is not a strident text penned by a termagant. Gardner does not rage constantly against the ills of a male-dominated world, nor, for that matter, does she wear her heart on her sleeve and let it bleed all the time. Instead, she has recounted some of the events she witnessed, in a sophisticated yet accessible manner which appeals to a broader audience than feminists tired by theoretical tomes and anthropologists bored by the anecdotes of their male colleagues. Her book is not a sermon but a seductively subversive text for the as yet unconverted.

The fieldworker as pilgrim, as peacock, as woman of her time – a successful trio of roles chosen by three different anthropologists of different generations. This triad of literary guises does not, however, exhaust the potential of the genre: there is a fecund variety of other parts for writers of fieldwork accounts to play; for example, the anthropologist as trickster, as advocate, as shaman, as detective, as victim, as cultural missionary, as spouse, or even as reconstructed male. Which role or roles will prove popular in the future is not something to be predicted by a commentator, but to be decided by the public.

References

Barley, Nigel. *The Innocent Anthropologist: Notes from a Mud Hut* (London: British Museum Press, 1983).

——— *A Plague of Caterpillars: A Return to the African Bush* (London: Viking, 1986).

Bowen, Elenore Smith [Laura Bohannan]. *Return to Laughter: An Anthropological Novel* (New York: Harper and Brothers, 1954).

Gardner, Katy. *Songs at the River's Edge: Stories from a Bangladeshi Village* (London: Virago, 1991).

Edited extract from: Jeremy MacClancy, 'Fieldwork Styles: Bohannan, Barley and Gardner', in J. MacClancy and C. McDonaugh (eds), *Popularizing Anthropology* (London: Routledge, 1996), pp.225–44.

54	## The 'Problem' of Women *Edwin Ardener*

As we saw in Jeremy MacClancy's description of Katy Gardner's work in the previous extract, it is no longer controversial or even unusual for anthropologists to focus attention directly on women's experience and on women's constructions of the social worlds they inhabit. But this has not always been the case in anthropology. The extract by Edwin Ardener reproduced here is taken from a longer theoretical article whose full title is 'Belief and the Problem of Women', originally written in 1968. Ardener addresses the paradox that, in the ethnographic writing that was conventional through the first half of the twentieth century, descriptive accounts based on observation of women's activities were routine, but women's views of society and the world were almost never represented in the theoretical models constructed by anthropologists of how a particular society worked.

The problem of women has not been solved by social anthropologists. Indeed the problem itself has been often examined only to be put aside again for want of a solution, for its intractability is genuine. The problem of women is not the problem of 'the position of women' ... [Rather] I refer to the problem that women present to social anthropologists ... Here is a human group that forms about half of any population and is even in a majority at certain ages: particularly at those which for so many societies are the 'ruling' ages – the years after forty. Yet however apparently competently the female population has been studied in any particular society, the results in understanding are surprisingly slight, and even tedious. With rare exceptions, women anthropologists, of whom so much was hoped, have been among the first to retire from the problem.

...

The methods of social anthropology as generally illustrated in the classical monographs of the last forty years have purported to 'crack the code' of a vast range of societies, without any direct reference to the female group. At the level of 'observation' in fieldwork, the behaviour of women has, of course, like that of men, been exhaustively plotted: their marriages, their economic activity, their rites and the rest. When we come to that second or 'meta' level of fieldwork, the vast body of debate, discussion, question and answer, that social anthropologists really depend upon to give conviction to their interpretations, there is a real imbalance. We are, for practical purposes, in a male world. The study of women is on a level little higher than the study of the ducks and fowls they commonly own – a mere bird-watching indeed ... [T]he truth is that women rarely speak in social anthropology ... [other than] in the sense of merely uttering or giving tongue ... Those trained in ethnography evidently have a bias towards the kind of model [of society] that men are ready to provide (or to concur in) rather than towards any that women might provide. If the men appear 'articulate' compared to the women, it is a case of like speaking to like ... [I]f ethnographers (male and female) want only what the men can give, I suggest it is because the men consistently tend, when pressed, to give a bounded model of society such as ethnographers are attracted to. But the awareness that women appear as lay figures in the men's drama (or like the photographic cut-outs in filmed crowd scenes) is always dimly present in the ethnographer's mind. Lévi-Strauss [1963: 61] ... thus expressed no more than the truth of all those models when he saw women as items of exchange inexplicably and inappropriately giving tongue.

    ... It is commonly said, with truth, that ethnographers with linguistic difficulties of any kind will find that the men of a society are generally more experienced in bridging this kind of gap than are the women. Thus, as a matter of ordinary experience, interpreters, partial bilinguals or speakers of a vehicular language are more likely to be found among men than among women. For an explanation of this we are referred to statements about the political dominance of men, and their greater mobility. These statements, in their turn, are referred ultimately to the different biological roles of the two sexes. The cumulative effect of these explanations is then: to the degree that communication between ethnographer and people is imperfect, that imperfection drives the ethnographer in greater measure towards men.

This argument … [however] … does not dispose of the problem even in its own terms … It is … a common experience that women still 'do not speak' even when linguistic aspects are constant. Ethnographers report that women cannot be reached so easily as men: they giggle when young, snort when old, reject the question, laugh at the topic and the like. The male members of a society frequently see the ethnographer's difficulties as simply a caricature of their own daily case … The 'articulateness' of men and of ethnographers is alike, it would appear, in more ways than one … Nor is it an answer to the problem to discuss what might happen if biological facts were different; arguments like 'women through concern with the realities of childbirth and child-rearing have less time for or less propensity towards the making of models of society, for each other, for men, or for ethnographers (the 'Hot Stove' argument)' are again only an expression of the situation they try to explain.

… [I]f the models of a society made by most ethnographers tend to be models derived from the male portion of that society, how does the symbolic weight of that other mass of persons – half or more of a normal human population … – express itself? … The fact is that no one could come back from an ethnographic study of 'the X' having talked only to women, and about men, without professional comment and some self-doubt. The reverse can and does happen constantly.

Reference

Lévi-Strauss, Claude. *Structural Anthropology* (New York: Basic Books, 1963).

Edited extract from: Edwin Ardener, 'Belief and the Problem of Women', reprinted in *The Voice of Prophecy*, ed. M. Chapman (Oxford: Basil Blackwell, 1989), pp.72–85 (extracts from pp.72–74).

55   Notes on (Field) Notes
James Clifford

Roger Sanjek's edited volume Fieldnotes, *in which James Clifford's article extracted below appears, provides multiple examples of ethnographic recording, with a particular emphasis on the social contexts in which such accounts were actually written down in the field. Clifford here describes three such 'scenes of writing', using photographs of well-known anthropologists in the field sitting with note books as they write up their fieldnotes. He then analyses these events as constituting three 'distinct moments' in the process of writing fieldnotes – 'inscription', 'transcription' and 'description'. Whilst the three of course overlap, he suggests that the categories provide a helpful way of breaking down the apparent unity of the fieldwork experience and unpacking the processes involved. Readers interested in doing some ethnography themselves might like to try out these ideas on their own field activities. To reflect on this process, recognising one's one involvement and how that might affect the subjects and, in Clifford's terms, to recognise what is involved in trying to write down their experience, can be a productive and revealing aspect of such investigation.*

This essay aims to complicate and decenter the activity of description in ethnography. It begins with three scenes of writing, photographs printed in George Stocking's *Observers Observed* [Stocking 1983]. The first, a recent photo by Anne Skinner-Jones, catches the ethnographer Joan Larcom glancing down at her notes while seated on a straw mat among women and children on the island of Malekula, Vanuatu. It is a moment of distraction. Larcom seems preoccupied with her notes. Two women look to the left,

Ethnographer Joan Larcom glancing down at her notes while seated on a straw mat among women and children on the island of Malekula, Vanuatu. Courtesy of Ann Skinner-Jones.

beyond the frame, at something that has caught their attention. Two boys stare straight into the camera. Another child's gaze seems riveted on the ethnographer's pen. The second image is a photograph from 1898 showing C.G. Seligman, Malinowski's teacher, in New Guinea. He is seated at a table surrounded by half a dozen Melanesian men. One of them sits rather tentatively on a chair drawn up to the table. Various ethnographic objects are scattered there. Seligman is intently writing in a notebook. The third scene, featured by Stocking on his volume's cover, finds Malinowski working at a table inside his famous tent in the Trobriands. He has posed himself in profile, turned away from a group of men who are looking on from just beyond the tent flaps.

These three remarkable photographs tell a lot about the orders and disorders of fieldwork. Each would repay close attention. But I am using them here merely to illustrate and to distinguish graphically three distinct moments in the constitution of fieldnotes. (I can only guess what was actually going on in any of the three scenes of writing.)

I use the first to represent a moment of inscription. I imagine that the photo of Joan Larcom glancing at her notes records a break (perhaps only for an instant) in the flow of social discourse, a moment of abstraction (or

Transcription: C.G. Seligman at work, Hula. Courtesy of the University Museum of Archaeology and Anthropology, Cambridge, England.

Malinowski working at a table inside his famous tent in the Trobriands. Courtesy of Mrs Helena Wayne-Malinowska.

distraction) when a participant-observer jots down a mnemonic word or phrase to fix an observation or to recall what someone has just said. The photo may also represent a moment when the ethnographer refers to some prior list of questions, traits, or hypotheses – a personal 'Notes and Queries'. But even if inscription is simply a matter of, as we say, 'making a mental note', the flow of action and discourse has been interrupted, turned to writing.

The second scene – Seligman seated at a table with his Melanesian informant – represents a moment of transcription. Perhaps the ethnographer has asked a question and is writing down the response: 'What do you call such and such?' 'We call it so and so.' 'Say that again, slowly.' Or the writer may be taking dictation, recording the myth or magical spell associated with one of the objects on the table-top. This kind of work was the sort Malinowski tried to dislodge from center stage in favor of participant-observation: getting away from the table on the verandah and hanging around the village instead, chatting, questioning, listening in, looking on – writing it all up later. But despite the success of the participant-observation method, transcription has remained crucial in fieldwork, especially when the research is linguistically or philologically oriented, or when it collects (I prefer 'produces') extended indigenous texts. Boas spent quite a few hours seated at a writing table with George Hunt. Indeed a large part of Malinowski's published ethnographies (their many myths, spells, legends) are the products of transcription. In

Return to Laughter, Laura Bohannan (Bowen 1954) advised prospective fieldworkers: 'You'll need more tables than you think.'

The writing evoked by the scene of Malinowski inside his tent may be called description, the making of a more or less coherent representation of an observed cultural reality. While still piecemeal and rough, such field descriptions are designed to serve as a data base for later writing and interpretation aimed at the production of a finished account. This moment of writing in the field generates what Geertz (1973) has called 'thick descriptions'. And it involves, as the Malinowski photo registers, a turning away from dialogue and observation toward a separate place of writing, a place for reflection, analysis, and interpretation. Stories of fieldwork often tell of a struggle to preserve such a place: a tent with the flaps closed, a private room in a house, a typewriter set up in the corner of a room, or, minimally, a dry, relatively quiet spot in which to spread out a few notebooks.

The three scenes of writing are, of course, artificially separated: they blend, or alternate rapidly, in the shifting series of encounters, perceptions, and interpretations called fieldwork. The term 'fieldwork' has a misleading unity, and breaking it up in this way may at least have a defamiliarizing effect. Moreover, it should be apparent that, as I am using them here, these 'scenes' are less representations of typical activities than images, or figures, standing for analytical abstractions. The abstractions refer to basic processes of recording and constructing cultural accounts in the field. I have found it useful to take these processes, rather than fieldnotes as such, as my topic. For it is clear ... from the diversity of observations contained in this volume, that there can be no rigorous definition of exactly what constitutes a fieldnote. The community of ethnographers agrees on no common boundaries: diaries and journals are included by some, excluded by others; letters to family, to colleagues, to thesis supervisors are diversely classified; some even rule out transcripts of interviews. The institution of fieldnotes does exist, of course, widely understood to be a discrete textual corpus in some way produced by fieldwork and constituting a raw, or partly cooked, descriptive database for later generalization, synthesis, and theoretical elaboration. But within this institution, or disciplinary convention, one finds an enormous diversity of experience and opinion regarding what kind of or how much note-taking is appropriate, as well as just how these notes are related to published ethnographies. A historical account of this diversity (linked to influential teachers, disciplinary exemplars, and national research traditions) would be revealing. There is, however, a problem of evidence: most of the actual practice and advice is unrecorded or inaccessible. Fieldnotes are surrounded by legend and often a certain secrecy. They are intimate records, fully meaningful – we are often told – only to their inscriber.

References

Bowen, Elenore Smith [Laura Bohannan]. *Return to Laughter* (New York: Anchor Books, 1954).

Clifford, James, and George Marcus (eds). *Writing Culture: The Poetics and Politics of Ethnography* (Berkley: University of California Press, 1986).

Geertz, Clifford. *The Interpretation of Cultures* (New York: Basic Books, 1973).

Stocking, George (ed.). *Observers Observed: Essays on Ethnographic Fieldwork* (Madison: University of Wisconsin Press, 1983).

Edited extract from: Clifford, James 'Notes on (Field) Notes', in R. Sanjek (ed.), *Fieldnotes: The Making of Anthropology* (Ithaca, NY: Cornell University Press, 1990), pp.47–52.

56 Interpretation and Analysis
David Jacobson

In this extract, D. Jacobson argues that ethnography is not just about describing what is going on but also involves ways of making sense of it. Indeed, a key argument here is that description on its own is not an innocent, 'natural' level of knowing, it is always rooted in ways of knowing, involving analysis and interpretation. Jacobson calls up a variety of classic anthropological authors to reinforce this point. Marcus and Cushman in the American Cultural Anthropology tradition, for instance, recognise that writing an ethnography is also a matter of representation: texts are not simply neutral description; their presentation 'is inseparably bound up with the systematic and vivid representation of a world that seems total and real to the reader'. Clifford Geertz, one of the best known names in American anthropology, coined the famous phrase 'thick description' to indicate that ethnographies are more than 'thin' descriptions of motions and physical behaviour – they also involve 'frames of interpretation' for making sense of such behaviour. Jacobson also invokes the British anthropologist Meyer Fortes to argue that anthropology involves 'a level of understanding that can go beyond that of the people whose behavior is in question', a view that, of course, raises interesting ethical issues also for the researcher, a point Jacobson raises later with respect to research by Edgerton and Langness in California, where the researchers were aware that 'The interests of the people among whom the anthropologist is doing research also shape what the anthropologist may observe'.

To make the point regarding the difference between description and analysis, Jacobson provides detailed accounts of anthropological analyses of marriage and bridewealth. In providing such accounts, 'anthropologists not only "break up" or analyze the reality of human action, they also attempt to provide a coherent representation of it'. It is not enough to try simply to describe what various surface levels of behaviour with regard to marriage mean in specific cultural contexts –

the anthropologist is also always engaging in some form of analysis, bringing to bear concepts such as 'rights' and 'duties' that lie beyond what can be physically observed. In relation to marriage and bridewealth, for instance, Fortes shows that bridewealth is not simply associated with the exchange of individuals, as might appear at a surface level of description; at a more analytic level it may also be about 'the transfer of rights or claims upon the services of individuals'. The rights of women and the expectations men may have of them, as wives and mothers, will vary, then, with the type of society – the rights and duties are different, for instance, in matrilineal and in patrilineal societies. We might also look at our own societies, with gender rights inscribed in law in some cases, to analyse what the rights and duties associated with marriage are.

We might also apply these ideas about description and analysis to other areas of social life such as, for instance, the distinctions offered in some contexts between 'science' and 'religion'. From an anthropological point of view, such a distinction may turn out to be a form of classification that will only work for particular social groups – newspapers in the UK are especially fond of such distinctions but they may not hold up against the more sophisticated interpretation involved in an anthropological theory of human nature and diversity. There is, then, an argument to be addressed, as Jacobson states: 'the observations in an ethnographic monograph are filtered. They are chosen in relation to the analytical interests of the ethnographer and to the interpretation he or she is presenting'. The same may be said about popular representations of such anthropological themes in public media, regarding, for instance, distinctions between science and religion, biological and social explanations, 'modern' and 'developing' societies, all of which appear differently from an anthropological point of view than they may appear in popular representations. And when doing fieldwork themselves, readers will find that reflexivity about the interpretations they bring to bear, consciously or unconsciously, can help them move beyond the account of peoples or cultures as simply objects and instead make explicit their own analysis and interpretations, as writers of ethnographic texts. From this point of view we may come to recognise, as Jacobson suggests, that 'an ethnography constitutes an argument'.

Understanding an ethnography begins with the recognition that it involves interpretation. Ethnographies do not merely depict the object of anthropological research, whether a people, a culture, or a society. Rather an ethnographic account constitutes the researcher's interpretation of what he or she has observed and/or heard. Fortes, in introducing what has become a classic ethnography, wrote:

> Writing an anthropological monograph is itself an instrument of research, and perhaps the most significant instrument of research in the anthropologist's armoury. It involves breaking up the vivid, kaleidoscopic reality of human action, thought, and emotion which lives in the anthropologist's note-books and memory, and creating out of the pieces a coherent representation of a society. (Fortes 1945: vii)

Marcus and Cushman, more recently, have made essentially the same point. They state that:

> Ethnographic description is by no means the straightforward, unproblematic task it is thought to be in the social sciences, but a complex effect, achieved through writing and dependent upon the strategic choice and construction of available detail. The presentation of interpretation and analysis is inseparably bound up with the systematic and vivid representation of a world that seems total and real to the reader. (Marcus and Cushman 1982: 29)

An ethnography presents the anthropologist's interpretation (of some aspect) of the 'reality of human action' and not merely a description of it.

The difference between description and interpretation is illuminated by considering ways in which anthropologists have distinguished between them. One well-known distinction is Geertz's differentiation between 'thin' and 'thick' description (Geertz 1973). Thin description depicts behavior in the sense of physical motions, as seen, for example, by the eye of a camera; in contrast, thick description reveals its significance. Geertz uses the example of 'twitches' and 'winks' to illustrate this point ... Both entail the same physical movement: the contraction of the muscles of the eyelid. A wink, however, conveys meaning: it may be a 'conspiratorial' signal or some other message possible within the framework of a 'socially established code'.

According to Geertz, the object of ethnography as thick description is to understand the 'frames of interpretation' within which behavior is classified and meaning is attributed to it. He argues (Geertz 1973: 10) that this involves apprehending and depicting the 'complex conceptual structures' in terms of which people behave and in terms of which that behavior is intelligible to them. Ethnography, then, is a matter of interpreting the meaning of behavior with reference to the cultural categories within which it is 'produced, perceived, and interpreted'. Winking exists, for example, 'when there is a public code in which so doing counts as a conspiratorial signal' (Geertz 1973: 6), and, as he adds, 'You can't wink ... without knowing what counts as winking' (Geertz 1973: 12).

Fortes (1970) argues for a level of understanding that can go beyond that of the people whose behavior is in question … and extends the possibilities of anthropological interpretation to include an understanding of behavior that might differ from that of the people involved and would permit comparison of behavior in different societies and cultures.

To advance his argument, Fortes draws a distinction between 'description' and 'analysis'. In a description, observations are grouped together as they actually happen. That is, they are included within an account in the order of their occurrence or because they occurred in the same place. Marriage, in an example used by Fortes, may be described as a sequence of customary activities succeeding one another in a set pattern, beginning with dating behavior, followed by courtship, betrothal, wedding ceremonies, and perhaps divorce as the event by which the relationship is terminated. The progression of these activities may be compressed, the periods between them condensed, but their relation to one another over time is preserved. The details of each activity may be presented more or less elaborately, but whatever attention is given to such particulars, the focus is on their sequence.

The procedure in analysis, in contrast to description, is to 'break up the empirical sequence and concomitance of custom and social relations and group [them] … in categories of general import' (Fortes 1970: 132). These categories are theoretically based. The task is to examine behavior in terms of these analytical categories and the relationships among them. 'Rights' and 'duties' are examples of such theoretical categories. They are aspects of a role, the culturally defined and socially sanctioned expectations or claims regarding the behavior of those who interact with one another. What people do, or fail to do, is interpreted in terms of such rights and duties.

The difference between description and analysis can be illustrated in the case of 'bridewealth', an event that occurs in marriages in many societies. Bridewealth entails the transfer of wealth from the group of the groom to that of the bride. From one perspective, bridewealth may be seen as compensation paid to one group for the loss of a woman, a view that seems to accord with the observation that such wealth is typically used by the group that receives it to acquire another woman, as a bride for one of its members. This sort of account is essentially descriptive. An alternative account follows from an analysis of bridewealth. It would assert that bridewealth is paid to acquire certain rights with respect to a woman's activities. Bridewealth, from this perspective, is not for the exchange of individuals, but for the transfer of rights or claims upon the services of individuals.

This way of viewing bridewealth helps to make sense of a wide range of observations. It brings out clearly the theoretical meaning of descriptive data. For example, Fortes suggests that if a woman is thought of in terms of the roles of wife and mother, then it is possible to identify several types of behavior expected of her. These include domestic and sexual activities associated with being a wife and childbearing associated with being a mother. In a patrilineal society, in which children are assigned membership in the group of their father, the groom acquires, with regard to his spouse, rights in her as both wife and mother, and, accordingly, the amount of bridewealth is typically large. By contrast, in a matrilineal society, in which children are assigned to the group of their mother, the husband has a claim on the woman only in her role as a wife, while rights to her in the role of a mother are retained by the group into which she was born. Accordingly, bridewealth payments in matrilineal societies are typically smaller than they are in patrilineal societies. Thus, an analytical account of bridewealth relates variations in its amount to the type of society in which it occurs (that is, patrilineal or matrilineal), rather than seeing it simply as one event in a sequence of events that constitute marriage.

Furthermore, interpreting bridewealth as the exchange of resources for claims on a woman with respect to different roles permits the analyst to make connections between observations that are not obviously or closely associated with one another temporally. For example, it not only implies relationships between types of society and amounts of bridewealth but also between those social facts and rates of divorce. Thus, in a patrilineal society it would be expected analytically that not only would bridewealth payments be relatively high but that divorce would be relatively low. This pattern would be expected because the husband's group would not want to relinquish claims over a woman who, in her role as mother, is or will become the producer of its new members. On the other hand, in a matrilineal society, a woman of the group (a mother, a sister, or a daughter) is the source of new members; an in-marrying wife does not contribute new members for her husband's group. Correspondingly, in a matrilineal society, bridewealth may be expected to be low and divorce rates relatively high.

From an analytical perspective, then, the meaning of bridewealth is to be understood in the context of the rights and duties associated with different roles and the ways in which they can be distributed and combined. Rights and duties are abstractions formulated by the analyst, although, as Fortes noted, they 'must have meaning in terms of the descriptive reality of social life' (Fortes 1970: 132). These categories or concepts are not necessarily those of the actors, and an analytical interpretation of behavior may not be the same as that held by the actors nor as an interpretation based solely upon an explication of the actors' categories … This is not to say that analysis does not consider cultural categories; rather, it typically takes them as a starting point for analysis, since what counts, for example, as a 'marriage' or as 'bridewealth' is to be understood in terms of the ways in which people classify such events and behaviors …

Ethnographies as Arguments

As Fortes noted, anthropologists not only 'break up' or analyze the reality of human action, they also attempt to provide a coherent representation of it. This representation is an interpretive conclusion, and the descriptive facts (for example, marriage customs and bridewealth payments) collected in the course of fieldwork and included within an ethnography constitute evidence in support of it. That is, the anthropologist's interpretation determines his or her selection of fieldwork observations for inclusion in an ethnographic account. The selection and presentation of facts in an ethnography is a result of analysis and interpretation and not simply a record of observations made during the anthropologist's fieldwork.

Edgerton and Langness (1974) address this issue in referring to the process by which the observations that constitute an ethnographic description are selected. These observations are selected 'twice'. First, observations are 'shaped' in terms of what anthropologists 'see' in the field, which is filtered through the 'personal equation' of the ethnographer. This includes, among other things, the anthropologist's personality, training, and theoretical interests. The interests of the people among whom the anthropologist is doing research also shape what the anthropologist may observe, since they can and do restrict the researcher's access to people and events. For example, male researchers may not be permitted to talk with women informants or to observe activities that are defined by informants as exclusively for women, and, of course, female anthropologists may be similarly constrained from doing fieldwork among male informants ...

Observations are also selected in terms of the anthropologist's representation of a people, culture, or society. This, in the language of Edgerton and Langness, is the second way in which the observations in an ethnographic monograph are filtered. They are chosen in relation to the analytical interests of the ethnographer and to the interpretation he or she is presenting. In other words, an ethnography constitutes an argument.

References

Edgerton, R., and L. Langness. *Methods and Styles in the Study of Culture* (San Francisco: Chandler and Sharp Publishers, 1974).

Fortes, Meyer. *The Dynamics of Clanship among the Tallensi* (London: Oxford University Press, 1945).

——— 'Analysis and Description in Social Anthropology', reprinted in *Time and Social Structure and Other Essays* (New York: Humanities Press, 1970).

Geertz, Clifford. 'Thick Description: Towards an Interpretive Theory of Culture', reprinted in *The Interpretation of Cultures* (New York: Basic Books, 1973).

Marcus, George, and Dick Cushman. 'Ethnographies as Texts', *Annual Review of Anthropology* Vol. 11, pp. 25-69.

Edited extract from: David Jacobson, *Reading Ethnography* (New York: State University of New York Press, 1990), pp. 3–7.

57	Ethnography as Democratic
	Del Hymes

This brief extract from the large and important work of Del Hymes in the field of the ethnography of communication brings home the immediate relevance of the subject of anthropology, beyond simply its academic role. Hymes points out that everyone, in fact, uses anthropological insights – in learning language and about language, in developing identity, in recognising difference. The use of ethnography as part of professional training is simply one end of a continuum, with its own particular features, including professional and disciplinary knowledge. He suggests that there are other professions that could gain from such understanding, notably those engaged in education. We might ask this question of our own contexts: What might teachers and pupils gain from applying ethnographic insights to their own context, beyond the formal qualification it leads to in educational contexts?

Ethnography is continuous with ordinary life. Much of what we seek to find out in ethnography is knowledge that others already have. Our ability to learn ethnographically is an extension of what every human being must do, that is learn the meanings, norms, patterns of a way of life.

...

The fact that good ethnography entails trust and confidence, that it requires some narrative accounting, and that it is an extension of a universal form of personal knowledge, makes me think that ethnography is peculiarly appropriate to a democratic society. Such a vision of a democratic society would see ethnography as a general possession, although differentially cultivated. At one pole would be a certain number of persons trained in ethnography as a profession. At the other pole would be the general population, respected (on this view of ethnography) as having a knowledge of their worlds, intricate and subtle in many ways (consider the intricacy and subtlety of any normal person's knowledge of language), and as having necessarily come to this knowledge by a process ethnographic in character. In between – and one would seek to make this middle group as nearly coextensive with the whole as possible – would be those able to combine some disciplined understanding of ethnographic inquiry with the pursuit of their vocation, whatever that might be. From the standpoint of education, obviously one wants to consider the possibility of adding ethnographic inquiry to the competencies of principals, teachers and others involved with schools. But on the one hand, there is no reason not to seek to extend a knowledge of ethnographic inquiry to everyone. And, on the other hand, there is no reason to think professional ethnographers privileged. In their own lives they are in the same situation as the rest – needing to make sense out of a family situation, a departmental situation or a community situation, as best they can.

Edited extract from: Del Hymes, 'Narrative Thinking and Storytelling Rights: A Folklorist's Clue to a Critique of Education', reprinted in *Ethnography, Linguistics, Narrative Inequality: Towards an Understanding of Voice* (London: Taylor and Francis, 1996), pp.13, 14.

58 The Turtle and the Fish
Anonymous

The following story has been chosen to illustrate the issue of ethnocentrism – that is, perceiving and evaluating other peoples' ways of living according to the standards and values of one's own society and culture. Buddhists relate this issue to the story of the turtle and the fish, and the story can help us understand what is involved in ethnography. If we go to another place, our first inclination is to describe it in terms of what it does not have that we are used to – waves for the fish; maybe science or Coca-Cola for Westerners travelling in the East; religion or rice for Easterners travelling in Europe, and so on. An ethnographic perspective shifts us out of this mind set and helps us firstly to 'imagine' things that do not exist in our own world and then to understand them in their own terms rather than to see them, in our terms, just as 'deficits'.

There was once a turtle who lived in a lake with a group of fish. One day the turtle went for a walk on dry land. He was away from the lake for a few weeks. When he returned he met some of the fish. The fish asked him, 'Mister turtle, hello! How are you? We have not seen you for a few weeks. Where have you been?' The turtle said, 'I was up on the land, I have been spending some time on dry land'. The fish were a little puzzled and they said, 'Up on dry land? What are you talking about? What is this dry land? Is it wet?' The turtle said, 'No, it is not'. 'Is it cool and refreshing?' 'No it is not'. 'Does it have waves and ripples?' 'No, it does not have waves and ripples'. 'Can you swim in it?' 'No you can't'. So the fish said, 'It is not wet, it is not cool, there are no waves, you can't swim in it. So this dry land of yours must be completely non-existent, just an imaginary thing, nothing real at all'. The turtle said that 'Well maybe so', and he left the fish and went for another walk on dry land.

In another version the fish said, 'Don't tell us what it isn't, tell us what it is'. 'I can't', said the turtle, 'I don't have any language to describe it'.

Extract from: http://www.beyondthenet.net/dhamma/nibbanaTurtle.htm

IV. 2 Studying 'Others' and Studying 'Ourselves'

59 My Kind of Anthropology
Edmund Leach

*Edmund Leach was one of the foremost anthropologists of his
generation, so his account of what it meant to do anthropology and
the methods associated with fieldwork pushes an important button for
anyone new to the discipline. He tells us of his own interest in 'moral
and cultural diversity' but then poses the question: 'But what does that
entail in terms of anthropological practice?' He addresses the classic
debates about exoticism and superiority, which were probably stronger
in his era than now, but then focuses on what he sees as key
epistemological as well as moral issues in the study of different peoples
– starting with introspection as the key way in and then claiming that
the local and specific findings of fieldwork are not to be taken as
'typical' but rather 'tell us more about the ordinary social behaviour of
mankind' than whole shelves of books claiming broader relevance.
Such a viewpoint can help directly in the study of methods and
investigations, and the opportunity this gives researchers to gain direct
experience – if on a small scale – of conditions of real research in
anthropology.*

What is it that social anthropologists actually do? What they are trying to
do is to arrive at insights which are generally true of all humanity (including
the anthropologists themselves) by observing very small-scale examples of
human life. But how do they go about it?

Malinowski ... puts stress on two outstanding characteristics of
anthropological field research: a central concern with kinship and marriage
and an emphasis on gaining understanding through participant observation
and the intimate, first-hand, use of vernacular concepts. This chapter is
intended to justify those priorities.

So far I have been arguing that the essential subject matter of all kinds of
anthropology is the diversity of mankind, both biological and cultural, while
my own particular concern, as a social anthropologist, is with moral
(cultural) diversity within a matrix of (approximate) species-wide biological
uniformity. But what does that entail in terms of anthropological practice?

Well first of all I must distance myself from the image that is presented
by nearly all introductory textbooks of cultural anthropology. These books,

suitably adorned with glossy illustrations of exotic customs and part-naked ladies, discourse at large upon a variety of supposedly universal characteristics of human culture which are then exemplified by thumbnail sketches of ethnographic miscellanea derived at third or fourth hand from a job lot of long ago anthropological monographs. The tribal peoples concerned are dotted around the map in quite arbitrary fashion; the arbitrariness being emphasized by dot references on a world map shown on the end covers of the book.

These samples of human oddity certainly exemplify cultural diversity but the choice of pictures immediately makes it obvious that the people who are to be discussed are 'primitives' who lack all the gadgetry of modern technology and modern sanitation. Whatever the authors' texts may say, the whole layout of such books implies that anthropology is essentially concerned with the lives of people who are in some way inferior and/or deprived. We need to escape from this traditional image of what anthropologists do, but it is not easy.

It is virtually dogma among social anthropologists of my sort that cultural otherness does not carry with it any necessary hierarchy of superiority/inferiority which can be appropriately labelled by such terms as 'primitive', 'backward', 'underdeveloped', 'childish', 'ignorant', 'simple', 'primeval', 'pre-literate', or whatever. My interest in the others arises because they are other, not because they are inferior. But in that case why study 'others' at all? If social anthropologists are sincere when they say that their subject is a kind of micro-sociology and when they proclaim that they no longer feel themselves to be members of a culture/society which is intrinsically 'superior' to that of the people they are studying, why don't they study themselves? Why suffer the discomforts of living in a longhouse near the headwaters of the Amazon when versions of what you want to know are available for observation just down the road?

This is a sensitive and difficult question. Social anthropologists can and do study members of their own society and they have been doing so for a long time, though mostly they do not do it very well. Certainly, field research of this kind of which you already have intimate first-hand experience seems to be much more difficult than fieldwork which is approached from the naive viewpoint of a total stranger. When anthropologists study facets of their own society their vision seems to become distorted by prejudices which derive from private rather than public experience.

...

[A]ll the best work by social anthropologists has at its core the very detailed study of the network of relationships operating within a single very small-scale community. Such studies do not, or should not, claim to be 'typical' of anything in particular. They are not intended to serve as illustrations of something more general. They are interesting in themselves. And yet the best of such monographs, despite the concentration upon a tiny range of human activity, will tell us more about the ordinary social behaviour of mankind than a whole shelf full of general textbooks labelled *Introduction to Cultural Anthropology.*

Despite my negative attitude towards the direct anthropological study of one's own society, I still hold that all the anthropologist's most important insights stem from introspection. The scholarly justification for studying 'others' rather than 'ourselves' is that, although we first perceive the others as exotic, we end up by recognizing in their 'peculiarities' a mirror of our own.

'We' – that is the readers of this book – conduct our daily affairs within a setting which most of us accept without question. Even a skeletal list of the fundamentally important matters which we thus take for granted would be very long. It would certainly include: the physical layout of the houses we live in and of the settlements of which they form a part; the general pattern of conventional procedures by which foodstuffs and other necessities of life are produced and distributed and finally consumed; the way children are brought up; the way tasks are allocated to different members of the household; the ideas we have about the nature of reality and of the cosmos, our sense of what is the proper way to behave towards kin and neighbours and persons in authority; the kinds of clothes and the styles of language which are appropriate to different occasions, etc. The catalogue might be extended almost indefinitely, but the point that I want to emphasize is that, for the most part, these distinctive features of our own way of life are not of our own making. We do not live exactly as our parents lived but whatever we do now is only a modification of what was done before. It could hardly be otherwise. Very little of our public behaviour is innate; most of us have only very limited creative originality. We act as we do because, one way or another, we have learned from others that that is the way we ought to behave.

The whole system of things and people which surrounds us coerces us to be conformist; even if you want to be a social rebel you will still have to go about things in a conventional way if you are to gain recognition and not be rated as insane.

...

This will still be true even if you have been trained as an anthropologist. It is always exceedingly difficult to look at oneself within a familiar social setting without falling into conventional cliches. But social anthropological fieldwork is ordinarily conducted in unfamiliar social settings and, because the fieldworker is initially a stranger, he is not preconditioned to interact with those he studies in any particular predetermined way. This is a salutary experience. The anthropological fieldworker who eventually returns to the social setting of his homeland usually finds that it has become quite a different place. The bondage of our own cultural conventions has somehow been loosened up.

But what do social anthropologists actually do? I dare say they do many different things. I can only speak from personal experience. Fieldwork in this style is a very small-scale, private affair. The research 'team' is usually just a single individual, or perhaps a married couple, with maybe a local assistant. The field of study is a local community; perhaps just a hundred or so individuals, seldom many more than 2,000. Initially the principal researchers must be strangers to the community; hopefully, before they depart, they will be just the reverse. They will themselves have become members of the community, at least by adoption. They will have come to understand the socio-cultural system from the inside through direct participation in the network of transactions which constitutes the daily life of those who are being studied.

To achieve this transformation from the status of unwelcome stranger to that of effective kinsman calls for great tact and patience. A high level of linguistic competence is obviously an advantage but a flair for friendship is more important than an impeccable accent or a perfect lexicon. But what is this paragon of a social anthropologist trying to find out? It is important here to distinguish between the short-term objectives of the fieldworker and the longer-term objectives of the anthropological theorist. Many of the best known theorists in social and cultural anthropology have themselves done very little practical field research and their writings often give a quite false impression of the normal tribulations of anthropological practice. This practice seems to be very much the same no matter whether the personal orientation of the research worker is materialist or idealist, Marxist or anti-Marxist, structuralist or functionalist, rationalist or empiricist.

Different practitioners would justify these common activities in many different ways. My own version goes something like this. I am trying to comprehend a totality which might be called the 'way of life' of the people under study; this 'way of life' consists of the acting out of an endlessly repeated social drama. The characters in the drama, the social roles, are more or less fixed, as are their mutual relationships which constitute the dramatic plot. But the way the roles are played varies from occasion to occasion according to which particular individual is playing which particular part at any particular time.

This distinction between the roles in a drama and the actors who play the roles corresponds to the fact that the data of field research must always be looked at in two dimensions. The observer must distinguish between what people actually do and what people say that they do; that is between normal custom as individually interpreted on the one hand and normative rules on the other.

When they come to write up the results of their research different anthropologists will, for doctrinal reasons, give very different weight to these two major aspects of the data, but, in the field, the anthropologist must always pay attention to both sides. He must not only distinguish behaviour from ideology, he must also take careful note of just how they are interrelated.

...

Anthropological textbooks, along with the arrangement of the university syllabus, usually give the impression that an alien way of life can always be analysed according to a more or less standard set of chapter headings which divide up the total field into sub-sections denoted by the English language words: economics, kinship, politics, law, religion, magic, myth, ritual. This is misleading for two quite separate reasons. First, most professional anthropologists use these words as if they were technical terms, but there is no general agreement about how this should be done. Secondly, this list of headings conveys a quite false impression of how field research is conducted. No experienced fieldworking anthropologist in his senses would try to subdivide his observations into categories of this sort.

It is true that there is always an all-pervasive 'economic' dimension which enters into every aspect of social life. The ethnographic data which Marxist anthropologists discuss under the headings 'modes of production' and 'relations of production' are of central importance in any kind of holistic, functionalist analysis. Every fieldworker needs to acquire some insight into the basic infrastructure of the society he is studying.

Edited extracts from: Edmund Leach, *Social Anthropology* (London: Fontana, 1982), pp.122–24 and 127–29.

60 Writing Ourselves: The Mass-Observation Project
Dorothy Sheridan, Brian Street and David Bloome

The writing of 'ordinary' people for the Mass Observation project provides a powerful 'telling case' of both the use of ethnographic methods and also of issues involved in reading and writing texts from an anthropological perspective. As the authors describe below, borrowing from the anthropologist Clyde Mitchell's account of cases that tell us something rather than just being 'representative' in a statistical sense, the writing of 'ordinary' people can tell us both about their everyday observations of British society at first hand but also about what is involved in such writing, how the writing of ordinary people relates to that of researchers and academics. The term 'ordinary' was coined by the founders of Mass Observation to describe the people who provided accounts of everyday life that might be different from those of more 'expert' writers, such as newspaper journalists or academics. Here the wider debate raised by anthropological studies of literacy as a social practice, rather than just a technical skill, brings to the fore the power issues involved in determining whose writing counts, whereby the writing of artists and academics is ranked above that of 'ordinary' people. This links well with a major move in the study of ethnography in recent years that recognises the importance of 'reflexivity' (see Clifford, this volume) – that ethnographic accounts do not simply provide 'scientific' empirical studies of the world out there, but that the authors in their writing about 'other' people's lives need also to reflect on how they selected what to observe and describe and how they put these observations into writing. Mass Observation, then, can be a helpful entry for other 'ordinary' people setting out to do some ethnographic study of the people and society around them, in raising such key methodological issues, about telling cases and reflexivity, and also in addressing the issues involved in writing up such accounts The book from which the selections below are taken may provide a helpful way into this but students and researchers might also be able to find on line, through the Mass Observation web site (http://www.massobs.org. uk/index.htm) examples of the writing of 'Observers' and these can be used to reflect upon students' own writing as they engage in 'the practice of anthropology' for themselves.

Started in 1937, and revived in 1981 after a break of two decades, Mass-Observation is a small but important social institution in Britain. From all over the United Kingdom, ordinary people observe and reflect on everyday life and then write to the Mass-Observation Project at the University of Sussex. Scholars and students, mostly in the humanities and social sciences, use the Mass-Observation Archive to research a broad range of topics about contemporary society and the past ... The Mass-Observation Archive contains over one million pieces of paper; over 2,500 people have written to Mass-Observation since 1981, not counting those who participated during its early phase. A visitor to the Mass-Observation Archive would see the staff at one end of the room recording material on cards and on computer databases, making lists and indexes, labeling and filing, as well as writing letters and notes of guidance to the people who write for Mass-Observation. At the other end of the room, researchers and students sit at tables reading the contributions, taking notes and drafting essays and articles.

The Mass-Observation Project is part history project, part anthropology, part autobiography and part social commentary, but it is not history, anthropology, life history, or social commentary done only by those authorised to do those things. It is also constituted by ordinary people throughout Britain. Most people in the United Kingdom have heard of the Mass-Observation Project, but few know what it is or how it works. Most Mass-Observation correspondents do not publicise their participation, although few keep it a secret. Thus, somewhat like community writing projects and worker writing projects (Mace 1995), the Mass-Observation Project provides a forum for those typically excluded from having a voice in writing history; but unlike those community and worker writing projects, the Mass-Observation Project relies on academics (and others in established institutions, such as the BBC) to pull together the diverse written contributions to Mass-Observation and make them public. It is this unusual institutional 'location' of Mass-Observation that makes it interesting to study as a case of writing. This alone would warrant interest. But there is more to the warrant for studying writing associated with Mass-Observation – the people who write for it.

The people who write for the Mass-Observation live throughout the United Kingdom, although primarily in England. Currently the majority of correspondents are over 45 years of age and 70 per cent of them are women. They come from a range of economic and work backgrounds. Many of the women have experienced what we call a 'de-railed education' ...

Educational opportunities that they could reasonably expect to have were denied or hindered. For example, the parents of one Mass-Observation correspondent would not let her take the entrance exam for grammar school because they did not believe she needed that kind of education, although her teachers encouraged her to go on to grammar school. Another ran into trouble with her school for no fault of her own other than being inquisitive, and was denied needed and earned recommendations. But these demographic descriptions and educational experiences alone are not what warrants the study. It is the correspondents' interest in and pursuit of writing. Simply put, they write, not only for the Mass-Observation – most use writing in many other aspects of their lives. Nonetheless, few consider themselves to be writers. As a group of people who write, they warrant study for what their experiences with writing can reveal to us about the nature, place and conditions of writing in contemporary British society.

Theorising Literacy: Mass-Observation Project as a Telling Case

... [T]he description of literacy practices and the Mass-Observation Project is useful in ways other than those claimed by traditional studies and theories of literacy. Traditionally, researchers built abstract models of reading and writing based on and tested through experimental studies. These theoretical models could then be used to guide practice-teaching, assessment, and so forth – and to generalise to reading and writing across situations and contexts. Underlying such an approach to theory building are assumptions about writing and reading as decontextualised processes and assumptions about knowledge as abstractable from the contexts of its production and use. From that point of view, descriptions and interpretations of writing and reading practices viewed as inseparable from the contexts in which they are used and defined are of little use. They do not lead to empirical generalisations, and they do not test abstract experimental models that can be applied across situations. Rather, we view the nature of theorising and the use of description differently.

We see the Mass-Observation Project as a 'telling case' that informs about the nature of writing and literacy in contemporary society, not through empirical generalisation, but by revealing the principles that underlie relationships between specific writing practices, the local events of which they are a part, and the institutional contexts in which they take place.

> A telling case shows how general principles deriving from some theoretical orientation manifest themselves in some given set of particular circumstances. A good case study therefore enables the analyst to establish theoretically valid connections between events and phenomena which previously were ineluctable. From this point of view, the search for a 'typical' case for analytic exposition is likely to be less fruitful than the search for a 'telling' case in which the particular circumstances surrounding a case serve to make previously obscure theoretical relationships suddenly apparent. Case studies used in this way are clearly more than 'apt illustrations'. Instead, they are means whereby general theory may be developed. (Mitchell 1984: 239)

...

Theorising literacy is not a process of abstracting or decontextualising reading and writing from social life, but just the opposite: it is a process of explicating reading and writing as part of social life. That is, the questions to ask about reading and writing are not, 'What is reading?' and 'What is writing?' but rather, 'How is reading?' and 'How is writing?' Such questions require describing, interpreting and explaining what particular people do with written language in particular situations and events.

By describing, interpreting and explaining, we mean a recursive and reflexive process in which a specific event or situation is described, interpreted for its social significance and social consequences for the people involved, and explained as part of a broader set of events and contexts. Each process – description, interpretation and explanation – employs a theoretical framework or set of theoretical constructs; but at the same time, the processes of description, interpretation and explanation are used to challenge those theoretical constructs. The challenge is inherent in this view of theorising. Social life continuously evolves as social, economic, political and cultural conditions evolve; theoretical constructs and frameworks that hover close enough to everyday life to be of use in addressing and understanding social life must also evolve to incorporate the changes in social life. The changes in social life are not just a matter of broad, anonymous social trends (such as the evolution of the nation-state, the development of fast capitalism), but also of reflected, conscious action of people acting at both micro and macro levels on the worlds in which they live.

We focus on the Mass-Observation project for two reasons ... [T]he everyday literacy practices of ordinary people are nearly invisible ... The mass media portrays an illiterate and aliterate population, and politicians, bordering on demagoguery, castigate schools for producing pupils who cannot read or write. Our research and that of others studying literacy practices in everyday life ... shows that there is a great deal of writing going on in everyday life, writing outside of school, work and 'established' publishing. Yet, very little is known about the scope, nature, use and social contexts of writing in everyday life. Little attention is paid to writing in everyday life – it is frequently not even considered to be writing – and the people who produce such writing are not usually considered writers. When ordinary people write, there are very few contexts in which their writing is acknowledged and in which they are acknowledged as writers. The example of Mass-Observation is one of the few contexts where they become visible.

... Our study of literacy practices and the Mass-Observation Project is part of a broader effort to make visible the writing and literacy practices of ordinary people in their everyday lives. For example, through our interviews with the people who write for the Mass-Observation Project we were able to record how people organised space and time for writing. Mrs Friend (F1373) ... has a dedication to letter writing. She may write upwards of a dozen long letters a day, encouraging others to write as well. She writes in her living room, yet there is very little overt evidence of so much writing happening there: just chairs, sofa, end tables, a television, a dining table. However, hidden in the end tables are her writing supplies, and hidden elsewhere are a platform for writing, files of letters and reference books. She takes these out in the evening when her husband and she sit down in front of the television, and the room becomes a letter-writing workshop. Her writing, except to a few who know her and those who receive her letters, is invisible, but it is very much a part of her life and the life of her family and friends. To not see the writing is to not see important parts of her life and to overlook ways in which she acts upon the world in which she lives ...

The invisibility of the writing of ordinary people in their everyday lives is not just a technical matter corrected by better research methods, more field studies, or more sensitive researchers. It is also a power issue. We live in a society that has reserved 'legitimate' writing for a select few. Novelists, journalists, academics, government officials, poets and a small number of others are viewed as legitimate writers; their writing carries authority. The power of their writing – its ability to define reality, to set before the public the questions for debate, to inscribe emotions and morality in narrative, to make law and order – derives in part from their connections with institutions of power (for example, mass media, universities, government, business) and in part from the small number of people who are allowed to claim the identity of writer.

A great deal of effort goes into making the writing of this small group visible and the writing of ordinary people invisible. The difficulties of getting a book published create an artistic hierarchy that restricts the label 'author' and 'writer' to a select few, and the awards, by-lines, bibliographies and reference books (for example, social science and humanities index, citation indexes, compendiums and anthologies of literature) identify whose writing is and is not worthy. A whole range of procedures and activities conducted by publishers, book distributors, shops and libraries perpetuate and promote the predominance of certain kinds of books (and authors). Schools play an important part in creating visibility and invisibility, defining long before adulthood who is and who is not a writer.

Schools have not always played the role of defining writing as something reserved for an elite. Howard's (1991) historical study of learning to write shows that many writing practices employed in the late nineteenth century in Britain eschew the dominant role of school in learning. Conversely, Street and Street (1991) analyse the 'schooling of literacy' in classroom practices to illustrate how a restricted model of what counts as literacy is constructed and woven into everyday schooling practices. Grammar lessons, composition studies and educational standards marginalise all but a few who can apply those lessons, studies and standards to their writing; but most importantly it is the structure of writing education itself that makes clear that writing and writers are graded. The result is that most people feel that they are not writers and that their writing is not legitimate or worthy of note.

It takes an extraordinarily strong character and perseverance to counter the structure of visibility and invisibility, to see oneself as a writer and one's writing as worthy when few of the social institutions in society support such a view (and indeed may actively support just the opposite). Although they are few in number, organisations and programmes such as community writing projects and worker writing projects are a direct challenge to elitist views of writers and writing, asserting and supporting the efforts of ordinary people as writers of their own histories and lives (Mace 1995). To make visible and legitimate the writing of ordinary people in their everyday lives would eradicate the privileged status given to the few, and open up another venue for people to exercise power over their own lives. And thus, the maintenance of invisibility is a matter of control and power. The data on writing in the Mass-Observation Project … challenges this invisibility and the control associated with it.

Literacy Practices and Mass-Observation

The invisibility of the everyday writing of which Mass-Observation is evidence derives to some extent from popular images of reading and writing, including the notions that reading is 'in decline', that 'people don't write anymore', that 'standards of literacy are falling', that there is more 'illiteracy' than before … This image is often set against a 'high culture' view of writing as 'literary' and 'accomplished' that sets the standard for what it means to be 'literate' – as in many cultures, the word for literate in English can mean both the practical skills of reading and writing and the cultural standards by which 'civilised' society is judged … However, between the 'high' literacy of literary or professional endeavour and the literacy 'difficulties' and 'illiteracy' that dominate media discourses, there is another level of activity – the everyday social practices of reading and writing that perhaps represent a key feature of literacy in contemporary society, despite the dominant images.

The study of literacy practices and the Mass-Observation Project can tell us a great deal about the 'social facts' of this everyday literacy in contemporary Britain. Many of the people who write for the Mass-Observation Project appear to write a great deal; the Mass-Observation Project gives a particular form and structure to writing processes that are already going on in other contexts. The data that we have collected in our research on literacy practices and the Mass-Observation Project do two things in relation to this phenomenon: first, they establish evidence for the social fact itself; in this sense they represent a 'factual' kind of ethnography, which we discuss in more detail in Chapter 3. Once we know more about both the practices and the conceptions of literacy evident in the Mass-Observation collection, we will be in a better position to develop further research that might address how general the phenomenon of 'everyday' writing is, whether the Mass-Observation cohorts are distinctive, and to ask questions about other bodies of writers in contemporary Britain who might be focused on other social institutions and procedures ...

But the Mass-Observation writing is also evidence of a different kind: it involves analytic commentary by the writers themselves on their own lives and is reflective about some of the characteristics of their own 'everyday' writing itself; it asks and seeks to answer questions about what are its purposes and what are the social processes involved in its construction. This is the second set of insights provided by our data on literacy practices and the Mass-Observation Project. The people who write for the Mass-Observation Project become researchers themselves by commenting on (and theorising) their own writing practices. This usage corresponds to ... [a] broad definition of research ... that recognises that research can be done by people other than professional academics. This is closer to the reflexive ethnography that has come to dominate the discipline of anthropology in recent years. Through their personal knowledge and experience, the Mass-Observation writers provide insights into the nature of literacy that are not apparent in either the dominant discourse or in much of the academic research literature. More locally, such an analysis might also help us to 'read' the Archive: if we know what kind of writing it is, then when we read responses to different directives, we might be able to interpret them in the light of what we now know about what the respondents themselves are trying to achieve through their writing.

... Mass-Observation at its inception was very like the anthropological enterprise in attempting to give voice to people who were otherwise invisible and marginalised in academic circles, as were the non-Western societies which anthropologists usually studied. But Mass-Observation was different from the anthropology of the day in that it not only treated ordinary people as its subjects but also collaborated with them as fellow researchers. Mass-Observers not only gave data about their own lives to the experts but [ordinary people] were themselves responsible for the collection and analysis of social data around them; they were both subjects of research and researchers themselves ...

While other disciplines have been important in the development of Mass-Observation ... the particular emphasis we place upon anthropology derives from this twofold history: that anthropology and anthropologists played an important part in the emergence of Mass-Observation; and that anthropology provides an important underpinning to our own perspective on both Mass-Observation and on literacy as we research and write this account.

The questions raised by exploring literacy practices and Mass-Observation from this perspective draw attention to a boundary line between establishment institutions, in this case academic disciplines, and ordinary people ... Ordinary people, including those who write for Mass-Observation, challenge the legitimacy of researchers to construct valid knowledge about lives and worlds from which they are so far removed. So too the language of academic research may be challenged as also far removed from the language of everyday life. Knowledge is contested.

These challenges to legitimate knowledge are also a challenge to writing. It is frequently the case that writing is viewed as a transparent vehicle for communicating knowledge. From that perspective, the only question that can be asked is whether the writing accurately represents the knowledge. Scientific writing is taken as the epitome of accuracy, while the writing of ordinary people is taken as contaminated by subjective views, personalising accounts, narrative structures and emotional commentary ... While these views have themselves been called into question by anthropologists and others who have treated academic practices as cultural practices ... it is still fair to say that academic institutions and other dominant institutions (such as the media) view with suspicion the writing and claims to knowledge of ordinary people.

Given its social 'location', the Mass-Observation Project is constantly negotiating among many different social domains, institutions, definitions of knowledge and agendas. Thus, the literacy practices employed are exactly at that point of creative development that we indicated above in critiquing static models of literacy; they are located among such domains, institutions, definitions, and so forth, and the study of them holds promise for revealing how people use writing to cross boundaries and how new literacy practices evolve. It is the uniqueness of the Mass-Observation Project that makes it an important site for the study of literacy practices, an important telling case.

Edited extract from: Dorothy Sheridan, Brian Street and David Bloome, *Writing Ourselves: Mass-Observation and Literacy Practices* (2000), Hampton Press, New Jersey pp. 6–11 and 12–15.

References

Howard, U. 'Self, Education, and Writing in Nineteenth-century English Communities' in D. Barton and R. Ivanic (eds), *Writing in the Community* (Newbury Park, CA: Sage, 1991): 78–108.

Mace, J. (ed.) *Literacy, Language and Community Publishing: Essays in Adult Education* (Clevedon: Multilingual Matters, 1995).

Mitchell, J. 'Typicality and the Case Study' in R.F. Ellen (ed.), *Ethnographic Research: A Guide to Conduct* (New York: Academic Press, 1984): 238–41.

Street, J. and B. Street. 1991 [now in] B. Street and J. Street "The Schooling of Literacy" in B. Street, *Social Literacies* (Longman: London, 1995).

IV.3 Ethics in Anthropology

61 Code of Ethics
American Association of Physical Anthropologists

The American Association of Physical Anthropologists (AAPA) – in the US the term 'physical' rather than 'biological' anthropology is generally used – was formed in 1930 and today is the largest organisation for Biological Anthropologists in the world. The following piece is an extract from the code of ethics that has been developed by the AAPA as a set of guidelines for biological anthropologists. One of the issues facing those carrying out research in biological anthropology is the very wide range of subjects that researchers explore and the even greater number of methods they employ. While we are all still 'doing bio-anth' we might expect to encounter issues surrounding the use of human skeletons, collecting genetic samples from living people, measuring the impact human activity has on other primates through to implementing measures to eradicate childhood diseases or vector-borne diseases such as malaria. Clearly any set of ethical guidelines is going to have to be both wide ranging and flexible in order to cover so much ground. In the same way that social anthropologists often find their research being shaped by the people they interact with, so biological anthropologists have to react to the effects of their research on a very wide group of people and places. The AAPA Code of Ethics allows us to reflect upon how what might appear to be a 'simple' research question can create a range of ethical issues that need to be addressed if the answer to the question is to be properly discovered, disseminated and implemented.

Preamble

Physical anthropologists are part of the anthropology community and members of many other different communities each with its own moral rules or codes of ethics. Physical anthropologists have obligations to their scholarly discipline, the wider society, and the environment. Furthermore, fieldworkers may develop close relationships with the people with whom they work, generating an additional level of ethical considerations.

In a field of such complex involvement and obligations, it is inevitable that misunderstanding, conflicts, and the need to make choices among apparently incompatible values will arise. Physical anthropologists are responsible for grappling with such difficulties and struggling to resolve them in ways compatible with the principles stated here ... The purpose of this Code is to foster discussion and education. The principles and guidelines in this Code provide physical anthropologists with the tools to engage in developing and maintaining an ethical framework, as they engage in their work ...

Introduction

Physical anthropology is a multidisciplinary field of science and scholarship, which includes the study of biological aspects of humankind and non-human primates. Physical anthropology has roots in the natural and social sciences, ranging in approach from basic to applied research and to scholarly interpretation. The Code holds the position that generating and appropriately utilizing knowledge (i.e., publishing, teaching, developing programs, and informing policy) of the peoples of the world, past and present, is a worthy goal; that general knowledge is a dynamic process using many different and ever-evolving approaches; and that for moral and practical reasons, the generation and utilization of knowledge should be achieved in an ethical manner.

...

Physical anthropologists have a duty to be informed about ethical codes relating to their work and ought periodically to receive training on ethical issues. In addition, departments offering anthropology degrees should include and require ethical training in their curriculums.

No code or set of guidelines can anticipate unique circumstances or direct actions required in any specific situation. The individual physical anthropologist must be willing to make carefully considered ethical choices and be prepared to make clear the assumptions, facts and issues on which those choices are based. These guidelines therefore address general contexts, priorities and relationships that should be considered in ethical decision making in physical anthropological work.

Research

In both proposing and carrying out research, anthropological researchers must be open about the purpose(s), potential impacts, and source(s) of support for research projects with funders, colleagues, persons studied or providing information, and with relevant parties affected by the research. Researchers must expect to utilize the results of their work in an appropriate fashion and disseminate the results through appropriate and timely activities. Research fulfilling these expectations is ethical, regardless of the source of funding (public or private) or purpose (i.e., 'applied', 'basic', 'pure', or 'proprietary').

Anthropological researchers should be alert to the danger of compromising anthropological ethics as a condition to engage in research, yet also be alert to proper demands of good citizenship or host–guest relations. Active contribution and leadership in seeking to shape public or private sector actions and policies may be as ethically justifiable as inaction, detachment, or non-cooperation, depending on circumstances. Similar principles hold for anthropological researchers employed or otherwise affiliated with non-anthropological institutions, public institutions, or private enterprises.

A. Responsibility to people and animals with whom anthropological researchers work and whose lives and cultures they study.

1. Anthropological researchers have primary ethical obligations to the people, species, and materials they study and to the people with whom they work. These obligations can supersede the goal of seeking new knowledge, and can lead to decisions not to undertake or to discontinue a research project when the primary obligation conflicts with other responsibilities, such as those owed to sponsors or clients. These ethical obligations include:
   To respect the well-being of humans and non-human primates
   To work for the long-term conservation of the archaeological, fossil, and historical records
   To consult actively with the affected individuals or group(s), with the goal of establishing a working relationship that can be beneficial to all parties involved

2. Anthropological researchers must do everything in their power to ensure that their research does not harm the safety, dignity, or privacy of the people with whom they work, conduct research, or perform other professional activities

3. Anthropological researchers must determine in advance whether their hosts/providers of information wish to remain anonymous or receive recognition, and make every effort to comply with those wishes. Researchers must present to their research participants the possible impacts of the choices, and make clear that despite their best efforts, anonymity may be compromised or recognition fail to materialize.

4. Anthropological researchers should obtain in advance the informed consent of persons being studied, providing information, owning or controlling access to material being studied, or otherwise identified as having interests which might be impacted by the research. It is understood that the degree and breadth of informed consent required will depend on the nature of the project and may be affected by requirements of other codes, laws, and ethics of the

country or community in which the research is pursued. Further, it is understood that the informed consent process is dynamic and continuous; the process should be initiated in the project design and continue through implementation by way of dialogue and negotiation with those studied. Researchers are responsible for identifying and complying with the various informed consent codes, laws and regulations affecting their projects. Informed consent, for the purposes of this code, does not necessarily imply or require a particular written or signed form. It is the quality of the consent, not the format, that is relevant.

5. Anthropological researchers who have developed close and enduring relationships (i.e., covenantal relationships) with either individual persons providing information or with hosts must adhere to the obligations of openness and informed consent, while carefully and respectfully negotiating the limits of the relationship.

6. While anthropologists may gain personally from their work, they must not exploit individuals, groups, animals, or cultural or biological materials. They should recognize their debt to the societies in which they work and their obligation to reciprocate with people studied in appropriate ways.

B. Responsibility to scholarship and science

1. Anthropological researchers must expect to encounter ethical dilemmas at every stage of their work, and must make good-faith efforts to identify potential ethical claims and conflicts in advance when preparing proposals and as projects proceed.

2. Anthropological researchers bear responsibility for the integrity and reputation of their discipline, of scholarship, and of science. Thus, anthropological researchers are subject to the general moral rules of scientific and scholarly conduct: they should not deceive or knowingly misrepresent (i.e., fabricate evidence, falsify, plagiarize), or attempt to prevent reporting of misconduct, or obstruct the scientific/scholarly research of others.

3. Anthropological researchers should do all they can to preserve opportunities for future fieldworkers to follow them to the field.

4. Anthropological researchers should utilize the results of their work in an appropriate fashion, and whenever possible disseminate their findings to the scientific and scholarly community.

5. Anthropological researchers should seriously consider all reasonable requests for access to their data and other research materials for purposes of research. They should also make every effort to ensure preservation of their fieldwork data for use by posterity.

C. Responsibility to the public

1. Anthropological researchers should make the results of their research appropriately available to sponsors, students, decision makers, and other non-anthropologists. In so doing, they must be truthful; they are not only responsible for the factual content of their statements but also must consider carefully the social and political implications of the information they disseminate. They must do everything in their power to insure that such information is well understood, properly contextualized, and responsibly utilized. They should make clear the empirical bases upon which their reports stand, be candid about their qualifications and philosophical or political biases, and recognize and make clear the limits of anthropological expertise. At the same time, they must be alert to possible harm their information may cause people with whom they work or colleagues.

2. Anthropologists may choose to move beyond disseminating research results to a position of advocacy. This is an individual decision, but not an ethical responsibility.

...

Epilogue

Anthropological research, teaching, and application, like any human actions, pose choices for which anthropologists individually and collectively bear ethical responsibility. Since anthropologists are members of a variety of groups and subject to a variety of ethical codes, choices must sometimes be made not only between the varied obligations presented in this code but also between those of this code and those incurred in other statuses or roles. This statement does not dictate choice or propose sanctions. Rather, it is designed to promote discussion and provide general guidelines for ethically responsible decisions.

...

Edited extract from: American Physical Anthropology Association, 'Code of Ethics'. Reproduced with permission. The full version of these are available at: http://physanth.org/.

62 The Story of Seventeen Tasmanians
Chris Davies and Kate Galloway

As we have seen earlier in the Reader, in the piece 'Dem Bones' by Simon Underdown, the use of human skeletal remains in anthropological research can often create tensions between researchers and indigenous peoples. However, while it would be easy to imagine that this would be a simple story of science versus traditional beliefs, the actual picture is far more complex and neatly illustrates why anthropologists should always be cautious of assuming that all people from a given place believe the same thing or will react in the same way that they might to a given issue. In the following extract from their paper, Chris Davies and Kate Galloway, lawyers who specialize in anthropological issues, describe a case involving the skeletons of seventeen Tasmanian Aborigines which were held by the Natural History Museum in London. They reveal a story that is far from clear cut – instead of two opposing voices we see that there is no single 'community voice' within the Tasmanian Aboriginal population, while the scientific community, although agreeing to return the skeletons, argue for the retention of DNA samples to allow future research (which in turn prompts us to question what is the essence of our humanity anyway: our bones or our genetic blueprint?). Just as anthropology allows us to understand our own behaviours and thoughts in the light of other peoples, so it reinforces the need to refrain from making lazy assumptions about what people think. Human remains are unquestionably special. Those of us who work with them are fully aware of how privileged we are to have access to human skeletons to unravel the story of humanity. But at the same time we must not be blinded to the feelings of those who view our work as denigrating the memory of their ancestors. This presents a veritable Gordian knot to unravel. Can one group of present day people prevent work that will inform and benefit those in the future? Conversely, can this motivation override the beliefs and wishes of the cultures from which human material is taken (and this is without even touching upon the outrageous way many nineteenth-century skeletal samples were collected with total imperial arrogance!)? Which group, if any, can claim to be 100 per cent right in their views? With so much at stake, both groups must clearly reflect on what they are doing and how it will influence both local and humanity-wide issues in order to find a workable solution.

The Tasmanian Aboriginal Centre (TAC) has been involved in a legal battle with the Natural History Museum in London in regard to possession of the remains of seventeen Tasmanian Aborigines which the Museum has had in its possession since the nineteenth Century. While the Museum has recently agreed to repatriate the remains, it still seeks to DNA test some samples taken from the remains. For present day Tasmanian Aborigines, this is viewed as representing a degrading violation of Aboriginal cultural and spiritual beliefs ... The TAC is therefore maintaining its stance to try and prevent the tests taking place. This has created opposition from even within the Aboriginal community, with some claiming that the money spent on this battle could be better spent on other needs of the Aboriginal community ...

Even though remains have been repatriated, the case has raised many issues: moral and ethical, as well as legal. Legal issues include what property rights may exist in the remains; the legal right to a burial; legal requirements in relation to the carrying out of tests on human tissue; legal requirements in regard to repatriation, and even in this case, the question of the administration of estates. Some would argue that there is a clear moral and ethical argument that the study of a unique people (like the Tasmanian Aborigines) enhances our understanding of humanity, and therefore must override the desires of a relatively few number of people. This is balanced by the counter-argument that such testing not only infringes cultural beliefs, but also smells of nineteenth-century imperialism that saw people like the Tasmanian Aborigines treated as little more than curiosities ...

Edited extract from: Chris Davies and Kate Galloway, 'The Story of Seventeen Tasmanians and the Question of Repatriation: The Tasmanian Aboriginal Centre and Repatriation from the Natural History Museum', *Newcastle Law Review* 11 (2009): 143–66.

63 Ethical Guidelines for Good Research Practice
Association of Social Anthropologists of the UK and the Commonwealth (ASA)

The following is an edited extract from the Ethical Guidelines published by the Association of Social Anthropologists of the UK and the Commonwealth (ASA). They clearly apply mainly to professional social anthropologists conducting research, especially involving fieldwork, over an extended period. We include the extract with the particular purpose of enabling students, and others undertaking small-scale ethnographic research projects, to see and (if applicable) to discuss the ethical issues debated in the discipline more generally. While many of these will not directly apply to small-scale investigations conducted in students' own environments, some may. For example, the points for attention signalled under 'Relations with and Responsibilities towards Research Participants' may well apply to projects students may undertake in an ethnographic manner. Thus sitting in on school classes, watching playground behaviour, hanging around local shops or community organisations, may all involve some of the responsibilities listed here. Likewise, the use of photographs and visual media may involve the kind of sensitivity to subjects to which the Guidelines draw attention. And responsibility to colleagues and to the discipline may well arise if others (for example in a school or study centre) are made to feel that anthropology – which they may not know very well – appears to be intrusive or insensitive. In other words, students of anthropology at any level have some responsibility for how the discipline is viewed and understood in their own location, just as professional anthropologists have with regard to the universities, NGOs or other organisations where they mostly work. Likewise, whilst 'Responsibilities to the Wider Society' may not at first sight appear directly relevant to students' research, in fact there may be contexts where the investigation does raise such responsibilities; for instance, being sensitive to possible conflicts of interest; and recognising that the very act of engaging in fieldwork may have unintended – even negative – effects on some respondents. Review of, and reflection on, the ethical issues raised is intrinsic to the process of conducting ethnographic research and reporting on it, whether at professional level or that of projects carried out by students on a small scale. Discussions can provide a positive environment for pursuing such questions and the ASA Guidelines can provide a helpful focus.

The editors wish to record grateful thanks to the ASA for permission to reproduce this edited version of the Guidelines. Readers are encouraged to access the full text at http://www.theasa.org/downloads/ASA%20ethics%20guidelines%202011.pdf

Preamble

Social anthropologists carry out their professional research in many places around the world; some where they are 'at home' and others where they are in some way 'foreign'. Anthropological scholarship occurs within a variety of economic, cultural, legal and political settings. As professionals and as citizens, they need to consider the effects of their involvement with, and consequences of their work for the following: the individuals and groups among whom they do their fieldwork (their research participants or 'subjects'); their colleagues and the discipline; collaborating researchers; sponsors, funders, employers and gatekeepers; their own and host governments; and other interest groups and the wider society in the countries in which they work.

Anthropologists, like other social researchers, are faced increasingly with competing duties, obligations and conflicts of interest, with the need to make implicit or explicit choices between their own values and between the interests of different individuals and groups. Ethical and legal dilemmas occur at all stages of research: in the selection of topic, area or population, choice of sponsor and source of funding, in negotiating access, making 'research bargains' and during the research itself while conducting fieldwork, including the interpretation and analysis of results, the publication of findings and the disposal of data. Anthropologists have a responsibility to anticipate problems and insofar as is possible to resolve them without

362   *Practicing Anthropology: Methods and Investigations*

harming either the research participants or the scholarly community. They should do their utmost to ensure that they leave a research field in a state which permits future access by other researchers. As members of a discipline committed to the pursuit of knowledge and the public disclosure of findings, they should strive to maintain integrity in the conduct of anthropological research. This ethics code applies to anthropological work whether studying 'up' and/or 'down', with persons and/or animals, within and outside the UK as well as in cyberspace.

The ethnographic method – the process through which theory is developed on the basis of empirical data collected – is the dominant mode through which anthropology is practised. Ethnographic methods cover a range of research practices and methods often including long/short-term/multi-sited/repeated fieldwork/visits. These ethical guidelines address the stages of preparation, the process of fieldwork and the writing procedure. Within fieldwork, participant observation has been considered by anthropologists as one of the core methods. This is a holistic method of research which is usually carried out over a period of time and can be conducted with a wide variety of communities and groups. The contexts for research can include economic, political, legal, medical settings and concerns as well as religious, gender, and kinship dimensions, among many others. The range of participants is also, as a result, varied. Participant observation is inductive and has the potential for uncovering unexpected links between different domains of social life. Accordingly, a degree of flexibility in research design that allows modification of topic focus – following the initial formulation of a research question – is required. Participant observation includes engagement with and observation of various forms of participatory activities specific to the group being studied, usually in both public and private settings. Fieldwork is also carried out by means of casual conversations (with a wide range of participants, some of whom are well known and seen regularly, others during fleeting encounters), interviews (usually open-ended, qualitative and in-depth), surveys, audio and video recording, sometimes supplemented by subsequent co-viewing with participants. The methods can vary from the informal and unstructured (such as participant observation, conversations) through to structured methods (such as interviews, surveys, audio-visual recordings).

Participant observation involves certain key ethical principles:

1. Participants should be made aware of the presence and purpose of the researcher whenever reasonably practicable. Researchers should inform participants of their research in the most appropriate way depending on the context of the research.

2. Fieldnotes (and other forms of personal data) are predominantly private barring legal exceptions. This is the most important way in which confidentiality and the anonymity of subjects is ensured. Anthropologists

have a duty to protect all original records of their research from unauthorised access. They also have a duty to ensure that nothing that they publish or otherwise make public, through textual or audio-visual media, would permit identification of individuals that would put their welfare or security at risk.

Advance consent:

1. Given the methods used during fieldwork, and depending on the nature of the project, the researcher may be able to provide only rough approximations in advance ... of some of the likely participants an anthropologist will observe or converse with during fieldwork and some of the likely scenarios in which consent will be sought ... Given the open-ended and often long-term nature of fieldwork, ethical decision-making has to be undertaken repeatedly throughout the research and in response to specific circumstances.

2. Many of those participating in public events observed by the anthropologist will not be known to him or her. This is particularly the case for strangers visiting the community ... being studied; or in research on mobile groups (which could involve pastoral and nomadic groups, refugees or expatriate and corporate elites) who move around for various reasons (such as subsistence, ritual celebrations, pilgrimage, corporate meetings, wartime displacements) to other places; or in studies of large institutions. In such situations, the anthropologist should take all practicable steps to be introduced by local participants and identify him/herself as a researcher. Not everyone observed or photographed, especially in large crowds, will be known. Large-scale events (such as religious festivals, political rallies or mass protests) are clearly legitimate and necessary foci of anthropological study, but should be subject to various ethical considerations. Hence due sensitivity to those involved in large-scale events and necessary observation of ethical standards with regard to the sensibilities and security of the participants needs to be kept in mind depending on the nature of the event.

3. Many of the communities studied by anthropologists are highly suspicious of formal bureaucratic procedures and often of their state or local forms of the state. Under these circumstances, requests for signatures on printed forms are liable to arouse suspicion and therefore standard procedures for obtaining written consent can be problematic. It is possible and appropriate, however, to obtain informed verbal consent. In working with informants with limited literacy or with learning difficulties that might render informed consent as commonly understood problematic, it may be appropriate to give people the chance to discuss their consent to an interview with friends, family or other trusted acquaintances. Repeated checking with informants during the research process, can ensure that the continuity of consent is maintained.

4. In some cases, consent will initially need to be sought from individual gatekeepers such as community leaders and officials: chiefs, local councillors, headmen, hospital consultants, trade union leaders, etc. or from collective decision-making bodies such as community or neighbourhood assemblies. In addition to needing to negotiate access to the field through such 'gatekeepers', it will often be desirable to supplement the informed consent of collective bodies with that of individuals, particularly where substantial sectors of the local society are excluded from collective decision-making but are also subjects of the research. By the same token, in all settings further consent may need to be negotiated as the research advances and new fields of inquiry open up.

5. Photography (both stills and film) is a very important tool of anthropological inquiry. Filming should always be overt. Moreover, in the case of large public events it is likely that not everyone photographed/ filmed will have the chance to give verbal consent. In such cases the researcher should do all that is possible in his/her powers to not compromise people's identities or security in public presentations of the material. In light of these considerations, the weight of responsibility for adherence to good ethical conduct is on the anthropological researcher ...

For anthropology, once the research is completed the ethics of representation are a major issue. The principles outlined below are intended to guide anthropologists not only in the way they conduct fieldwork but in the way they represent and publish their results to wider audiences. To these ends the Association [of Social Anthropologists] has adopted the following set of ethical guidelines to which individual members, other anthropologists should subscribe. They follow the educational model for professional codes, aiming to alert researchers to issues that raise ethical concerns or to potential problems and conflicts of interests that might arise in the research process. They are intended to provide a practical framework for anthropologists to make informed decisions about their own behaviour and involvement, and to help them communicate their professional positions more clearly to the other parties involved in or affected by their research activities ... Anthropological researchers should expect to encounter ethical dilemmas at every stage of their work, and should make good-faith efforts to identify potential ethical claims and conflicts in advance when preparing proposals and as projects proceed ...

I. Relations with and Responsibilities towards Research Participants
The close and often lengthy association of anthropologists with the communities/cultures/societies among whom they carry out research entails personal and moral relationships, trust and reciprocity between the

researcher and research participants; it also entails recognition of power differentials between them.

1) Protecting research participants and honouring trust: Anthropologists should endeavour to protect the physical, social and psychological well-being of those with whom they conduct their study and to respect their rights, interests, sensitivities and privacy, other than in the most exceptional of circumstances. It would also be important to keep in mind the ethical responsibilities to non-human research subjects.

   a) The ASA maintains that their paramount obligation is to their research participants and that when there is conflict, the interests and rights of those studied should come first. This means that anthropologists must reflect particularly deeply on the likely impacts on the communities/cultures/societies they are studying; of any research, consultancy or other services that they might offer or be asked to provide to national/supra-national or foreign states or to non-state entities (such as transnational corporations, law enforcement agencies, NGOs or charities) that intervene or are seeking to intervene in the lives of those communities/cultures/ societies. Work for state or non-state organisations that is covert, and therefore breaches relations of trust and openness, is especially problematic. Overt work that is only possible because the participants are subject to coercion is also likely to breach basic ethical standards.

   b) Under some research conditions, particularly those involving contracted research, it may not be possible to fully guarantee research participants' interests. In such cases anthropologists would be well-advised to consider in advance whether they should pursue such research.

2) Anticipating harms: Anthropologists should be sensitive to the possible consequences of their work and should endeavour to guard against predictably harmful effects. Consent from subjects does not absolve anthropologists from their obligation to protect research participants as far as possible against any potential harmful effects of research:

   a) The researcher should try to minimise disturbances both to subjects themselves and to the subjects' relationships with their environment. Even though research participants may be immediately protected by the device of anonymity, the researcher should try to anticipate the long-term effects on individuals or groups as a result of the research;

   b) Anthropologists may sometimes be better placed than (at the least, some of) their informants to anticipate the possible repercussions of their research both for the immediate participants and for other members of the research population or the wider society. In certain political contexts, some groups, for example, religious or ethnic minorities, may be particularly vulnerable and it may be necessary to withhold data from publication or even to refrain from studying them at all.

3) Avoiding undue intrusion: Anthropologists should be aware of the intrusive potential of some of their enquiries and methods:

   a) Like other social researchers, they have no special entitlement to study all phenomena; and the advancement of knowledge and the pursuit of information are not in themselves sufficient justifications for overriding the values and ignoring the interests of those studied;

   b) They should be aware that for research participants becoming the subject of anthropological description and interpretations can be a welcome experience, but it can also be a disturbing one. In many of the social scientific enquiries that have caused controversy, problems have not arisen because participants have suffered directly or indirectly any actual harm. Rather, concerns have resulted from participants' feelings of having suffered an intrusion into private and personal domains, or of having been wronged (for example, by acquiring self-knowledge which they did not seek or want). Where feasible, participants should also be made aware that they can withdraw from the research at any time.

4) Negotiating informed consent: Inquiries involving human subjects should be based on the freely given informed consent of subjects. The principle of informed consent expresses the belief in the need for truthful and respectful exchanges between social researchers and the people with whom they study.

   a) Negotiating consent entails communicating information likely to be material to a person's willingness to participate, such as: the purpose(s) of the study and the anticipated consequences of the research; the identity of funders and sponsors; the anticipated uses of the data; possible benefits of the study and harm or discomfort that might affect participants; issues relating to data storage and security; and including limits to the degree of anonymity and confidentiality which may be afforded to informants and subjects. These can be communicated verbally, particularly to those participants with whom the anthropologist has close and continuing relations.

   b) Conditions which constitute an absence of consent: consent made after the research is completed and publicly made available is not meaningful consent at all. Where subjects are legally compelled (e.g., by their employer or government) to participate in a piece of research, consent cannot be said to have been meaningfully given by subjects, and anthropologists are advised not to pursue that piece of work. However, as has been noted above, in the case of exceptional circumstances such as large public events – especially where photographs are taken – consent sometimes might be sought after the event as it is often not possible to seek advance consent. Although it will not always be possible to obtain formal consent, reasonably practicable steps to do so should be taken.

c) Consent in ethnographic research is a process, not a one-off event, due to its long-term and open-ended qualities. Consent may require renegotiation over time; it is an issue to which the anthropologist should return periodically. Depending on the research project, researchers may only be able to provide a rough approximation of some of the likely scenarios in which consent might be sought. Thus continuous reflection on ethical issues and conduct is necessary.

d) When audio-visual media is to be used, be it merely for data-gathering or for broader representational purposes such as producing ethnographic films or photographic essays, the principal research subjects should be made aware of the technical capacities of these media and should be free to reject their use. These conditions should generally apply in public spaces as well as in private spaces where there is a reasonable expectation of privacy. And anthropologists must take steps at the beginning of fieldwork to sensitise themselves to local norms that may embody different ideas about the private and public from those of the anthropologist's' own society.

e) Anthropologists engaged in cyber ethnography or other forms of research that involve the use of electronic texts, images and/or audio-recordings already in the public domain and/or available through fora such as blogs, chatrooms, social media sites etc., should remain sensitive to the possible implications of re-using those electronic texts, images and sounds, not only in terms of ethical responsibilities to the subjects but also in relation to the Intellectual Property Rights held either by the subjects themselves or by those who created the images or recordings in the first place …

…

g) The long period over which anthropologists make use of their data and the possibility that unforeseen uses or theoretical interests may arise in the future may need to be conveyed to participants, as should any likelihood that the data may be shared (in some form) with other colleagues or be made available to sponsors, funders or other interested parties, or deposited in archives.

5) Rights to confidentiality and anonymity: informants and other research participants should have the right to remain anonymous and to have their rights to privacy and confidentiality respected. However, privacy and confidentiality present anthropologists with particularly difficult problems given the cultural and legal variations between societies and the various ways in which the real interests or research role of the

ethnographer may not fully be realised by some or all of participants or may even become invisible over time.

a) Care should be taken not to infringe uninvited upon the 'private space' (as locally defined) of an individual or group;

b) As far as is possible researchers should anticipate potential threats to confidentiality and anonymity. They should consider whether it is necessary even as a matter of propriety to record certain information at all; take appropriate measures relating to the storage and security of records during and after fieldwork; and use where appropriate such means as the removal of identifiers, the use of pseudonyms and other technical solutions to the problems of privacy in field records and in oral and written forms of data dissemination (whether or not this is enjoined by law or administrative regulation);

c) Researchers should endeavour to anticipate problems likely to compromise anonymity; but they should make clear to participants that it may not be possible in field notes and other records or publications totally to conceal identities, and that the anonymity afforded or promised to individuals, families or other groups may also be unintentionally compromised. A particular configuration of attributes can frequently identify an individual beyond reasonable doubt; and it is particularly difficult to disguise, say, office-holders, organizations, public agencies, ethnic groups, religious denominations or other collectivities without so distorting the data as to compromise scholarly accuracy and integrity;

d) If guarantees of privacy and confidentiality are made, they should be honoured unless there are clear and overriding ethical reasons not to do so. Confidential information should be treated as such by the anthropologist even when it enjoys no legal protection or privilege, and other people who have access to the data should likewise be made aware of their obligations; but conversely participants should be made aware that it is rarely, if at all, legally possible to ensure total confidentiality or to completely protect the privacy of records. Fieldnotes and other data should not be archived in raw form if this infringes either the promise of confidentiality and anonymity made to participants, or the stated reasons for the research on which informed consent was agreed. Extended embargo periods may provide a way of securing the material for future researchers, including those from source communities, while honouring present commitments. In the longer term, it might be proper to make available fieldnotes and other research material for use by other researchers, e.g., by including them in relevant archives. Anthropologists should make this clear when securing informed consent. Anthropologists should be cognisant that they might not be able to protect their fieldnotes to the fullest extent and hence care must be taken as to how data is recorded.

e) Anthropologists should similarly respect the measures taken by other researchers to maintain the anonymity of their research field and participants.

6) Fair return for assistance: There should be no economic exploitation of individual informants, translators, groups, animals and research participants or cultural or biological materials; fair return should be made for their help and services.

7) Participants' intellectual property rights: It should be recognised that research participants have contractual and/or legal interests and rights in data, recordings and publications, although rights will vary according to agreements and legal jurisdiction.

a) It is the obligation of the interviewer to inform the interviewee of their rights under any copyright or data protection laws of the country where research takes place, and the interviewer should indicate beforehand any uses to which the anthropological use of interview methods is likely to be put (e.g., research, educational use, publication, broadcasting etc).

...

c) Interviewers should clarify before interviewing the extent to which subjects are allowed to see transcripts of interviews, and field notes and to alter the content, withdraw statements, provide additional information or to add glosses on interpretations.

d) Clarification should also be given to subjects regarding the degree to which they will be consulted prior to publication.

8) Participants' involvement in research: As far as is possible anthropologists should try and involve the people from the communities/cultures/societies being studied in the planning and execution of research projects. They should recognise that their obligations to the participants or the host community may not end (indeed should not end, many would argue) with the completion of their fieldwork or research project.

...

II. Relations with and Responsibilities towards Sponsors, Funders and Employers

Anthropologists should attempt to ensure that sponsors, funders and employers appreciate the obligations that they have not only to them, but also to research participants and to professional colleagues.

1) Clarifying roles, rights and obligations: Anthropologists should clarify in advance the respective roles, rights and obligations of sponsor, funder, employer and researcher:

   a) They should be careful not to promise or imply acceptance of conditions which would be contrary to professional ethics or competing commitments. Where conflicts seem likely, they should refer sponsors or other interested parties to the relevant portions of the professional guidelines;

   b) Anthropologists who work in non-academic settings should be particularly aware of likely constraints on research and publication and of the potentiality for conflict between the aims of the employer, funder or sponsor and the interests of the communities/cultures/societies studied;

   ...

III. Relations with, and Responsibilities towards, Colleagues and the Discipline

Anthropologists derive their status and certain privileges of access to research participants and to data not only by virtue of their personal standing but also by virtue of their professional citizenship. In acknowledging membership of a wider anthropological community anthropologists owe various obligations to that community and can expect consideration from it.

1) Individual responsibility: Anthropologists bear responsibility for the good reputation of the discipline and its practitioners. In considering the methods, procedures, content and reporting of their enquiries, their behaviour in the field and relations with research participants and field assistants, they should therefore try to ensure that their activities will not jeopardize future research. Thus, anthropological researchers are subject to the general moral rules of scientific and scholarly conduct: they should not deceive or knowingly misrepresent (e.g., fabricate evidence, falsify, or plagiarise), or attempt to prevent reporting of misconduct, or obstruct the scientific/scholarly research of others.

2) Conflicts of interest and consideration for colleagues: It should be recognised that there may be conflicts of interest (professional and political) between anthropologists, particularly between visiting and local researchers, and especially when cross-national research is involved:

   a) Consideration for and consultation with anthropologists who have already worked or are currently working in the proposed research setting is advisable and is also a professional courtesy. In particular, the vulnerability of long-term research projects to academic intrusion should be recognised;

b) In cross-national research, consideration should be given to the interests of local scholars and researchers, to the problems that may result from matters such as the disparities in resources available to visiting researchers, and to problems of equity in collaboration. As far as is possible and practicable, visiting anthropologists should try and involve local anthropologists and scholars in their research activities but should be alert to the potential for harm that such collaboration might entail in some contexts.

3) Sharing research materials: Anthropologists should give consideration to ways in which research data and findings can be shared with colleagues and with research participants. However, in certain instances this can prove to be difficult where political leaders, invading armies, military, multi-national corporations and the state are being criticised on various matters of injustice.

a) Research findings, publications and, where feasible, data should be made available in the country where the research took place. If necessary, it should be translated into the national or local language. Researchers should be alert, though, to the harm to research participants, collaborators and local colleagues that might arise from total or even partial disclosure of raw or processed data or from revelations of their involvement in the research project. Anthropologists should weigh up the intended and potential uses of their work and the impact of its distribution in determining whether limited availability of results is warranted and ethical in any given instance.

b) Where the sharing with colleagues of raw, or even processed data or their (voluntary or obligatory) deposition in data archives or libraries is envisaged, care should be taken not to breach privacy and guarantees of confidentiality and anonymity, and appropriate safeguards should be devised.

4) Collaborative and team research: In some cases anthropologists will need to collaborate with researchers in other disciplines, as well as with research and field assistants, clerical staff, students etc. In such cases they should make clear their own ethical and professional obligations and similarly take account of the ethical principles of their collaborators. Care should be taken to clarify roles, rights and obligations of team members in relation to matters such as the division of labour, responsibilities, access to and rights in data and fieldnotes, publication, co-authorship, professional liability, etc.

5) Responsibilities towards research students and field assistants: Academic supervisors and project directors should ensure that students and assistants are aware of the ethical guidelines and should discuss with them potential (as well as actual) problems which may arise

during the stages/periods of fieldwork or writing-up. Teachers/mentors should publicly acknowledge student/trainee assistance in research and preparation of their work; give appropriate credit for co-authorship to students/trainees; encourage publication of worthy student/trainee papers; and compensate students/trainees justly for their participation in all professional activities. It should also be a duty to acknowledge the support and intellectual input of colleagues in the field.

...

IV. Relations with Own and Host Governments
Anthropologists should be honest and candid in their relations with their own and host governments.

1) Conditions of access: Researchers should seek assurance that they will not be required to compromise their professional and scholarly responsibilities as a condition of being granted research access.

2) Cross-national research: Research conducted outside one's own country raises special ethical and political issues relating to personal and national disparities in wealth, power, the legal status of the researcher, political interest and his or her national political systems:

   a) Anthropologists should bear in mind the differences between the civil and legal, and often the financial position of national and foreign researchers and scholars;

   b) They should be aware that irresponsible actions by a researcher or research team may jeopardise access to a research setting or even to a whole country for other researchers, both anthropologist and non-anthropologist. Being cognisant of the consequence of one's research activities is particularly relevant when anthropologists consulting for governments, multi-national corporations, invading armies and the military do not prioritise the rights and interests of the local population and in cases where the ostensible aims of the intervention might reasonably be questioned by critical and reflective social scientists.

3) Open research: Anthropologists owe a responsibility to their colleagues around the world and to the discipline as a whole not to use their anthropological role as a cover for clandestine research or activities.

...

V. Responsibilities to the Wider Society
Anthropologists also have responsibilities towards other members of the public and wider society. They depend upon the confidence of the public and they should in their work attempt to promote and preserve such confidence without exaggerating the accuracy or explanatory power of their findings.

1) Widening the scope of social research: Anthropologists should use the possibilities open to them to extend the scope of social inquiry and to communicate their findings for the benefit of the widest possible community. Anthropologists are most likely to avoid restrictions being placed on their work when they are able to stipulate in advance the issues over which they should maintain control; the greatest problems seem to emerge when such issues remain unresolved until the data are collected or the findings emerge.

2) Considering conflicting interests: Social inquiry is predicated on the belief that greater access to well-founded information will serve rather than threaten the interests of society/ies:

   a) Nonetheless, in planning all phases of an inquiry, from design to presentation of findings, anthropologists should also consider the likely consequences for the wider society, groups within it, and possible future research, as well as for members of the research population not directly involved in the study as well as the immediate research participants;

   b) That information can be misconstrued or misused is not in itself a convincing argument against its collection and dissemination. All information is subject to misuse and no information is devoid of possible harm to one interest or another. Individuals may be harmed by their participation in social inquiries, or group interests may be harmed by certain findings. Researchers are usually not in a position to prevent action based on their findings; but they should attempt to pre-empt likely misinterpretations and to counteract them when they occur.

3) Maintaining professional and scholarly integrity: Research can never be entirely objective – the selection of topics may reflect a bias in favour of certain cultural or personal values, the employment base of the researcher, the source of funding and any of these other factors may impose certain priorities, obligations and prohibitions. But anthropologists should strive for impartiality and fair representation and be open about known barriers to its achievement:

   a) Anthropologists should not engage or collude in selecting methods designed to produce misleading results or in misrepresenting findings, either by commission or omission;

   b) When it is likely that research findings will bear upon public policy and opinion, anthropologists should be careful to state any significant limitations on their findings and interpretations.

SECTION V

ANTHROPOLOGY IN THE WORLD

Introduction to Section V

Hilary Callan, Brian Street and Simon Underdown

The writings included earlier in Section III, notably T.H. Eriksen's account of globalisation, have already given an indication of the part anthropology can play – together with other disciplines such as history, sociology and economics – in casting light on large-scale world movements and processes. In Section V, we turn attention to anthropology in the wider world.

V.1 Anthropological Perspectives on World Issues

In this group of extracts, we look first at nationalism and the construction of national identity. Eva Mackey has made use of anthropological methods to investigate how the values of multiculturalism and inclusiveness have moulded Canadian beliefs about the history and foundations of the Canadian state. In the extract included here, she raises critical questions about how far the Canadian 'national myth' of inclusiveness and tolerance corresponds to actual historical reality, and suggests that liberal and multicultural ideals may not in themselves be enough to prevent minorities from being marginalised and silenced by dominant cultural patterns seen as the unquestioned norm. Mackey's insights could suggest parallels in other places, and illuminate the roots of our own ideas of nationhood and identity whatever our particular national, ethnic or political affiliation.

We turn next to global finance, and the worldwide banking collapse of 2008. This is a continuing story, but a number of books and TV documentaries have attempted to explain what happened and why it was so unexpected. One of the most influential of these has been Gillian Tett's *Fools' Gold*. In the extract included here, from the Preface to the second edition, Tett draws on her academic background in social anthropology to write about 'social silences' and 'silos', both of which inhibit the spread of knowledge and can make it virtually impossible for people to see and talk about realities which (with the benefit of hindsight) lie in plain view. Tett spoke more expansively on these themes in a keynote address given in June 2012 at the Royal Anthropological Institute's international conference on 'Anthropology in the World'. You can see and hear her address by following this link: http://www.youtube.com/user/royalanthro .

Section I of the Reader included material on the notion of 'race': its biological significance and the limitations thereof; the part it has played in the history of anthropology; and contemporary transformations of the 'race' concept in a political context. The next extract returns to this theme in a different way. Ciara Kierans and Jessie Cooper address organ donation policy in the UK, and the publicly held assumptions about 'race' that enter into decisions and publicity campaigns for organ donation. They argue that an apparent 'problem' – that of allegedly low donation rates among 'black and ethnic minority' (BME) populations in the UK – arises in part from classificatory schemes that assume a one-to-one biological correspondence with ethnic categories that are based as much on skin tone, geographical origin, religion or language, as on gene frequencies.

The two final extracts in this group look in more general terms at the anthropological study of science. While they both relate to modern or Western science, it is important to bear in mind that this is only one – albeit a highly dominant – way of viewing the world. A large body of anthropological research is, in fact, concerned with forms of local or indigenous knowledge and classification which may complement, or be quite different from, 'science' as recognised in the Western tradition. Here, however, we are concerned with ways in which anthropologists have approached science within the Western frame. As Sarah Franklin argues, modern science is at one and the same time a 'way of knowing' the material world, and a cluster of social, economic and political relations and practices. All these facets of the scientific enterprise repay study by anthropologists. This is exemplified in the following extract from the research of Hugh Gusterson among nuclear-weapons scientists. In this piece, Gusterson offers reasons why it is only recently that contemporary warfare, military institutions and weapons proliferation have come to be seen as subjects for anthropological study. But, even in the post-Cold War era, the significance of various forms of militarism for the human future needs no emphasis. And the work of anthropologists such as Gusterson, in analysing the social and cultural dynamics of institutions and technologies of conflict, has a key role to play in understanding and controlling these dangerous forces.

V.2 The Public Presence of Anthropology

A number of writers in recent years have voiced concern about the lack of knowledge among the general public of the kind of work anthropologists do and the knowledge they produce. Others have complained about the tendency of the public media, such as TV documentaries and 'reality shows', to distort or misrepresent the subject matter of anthropology for the sake of sensation and entertainment. Readers will readily find examples of such distorted depictions either of supposedly 'stone-age peoples ruled by superstition' or of anthropologists supposedly concerned exclusively with the exotic and remote. We conclude the Reader by looking briefly at the 'public presence' of anthropology – that is, the ways in which anthropological knowledge is received and understood beyond the specialised worlds of universities and research foundations. This theme has already been touched on earlier, where we included writings on 'popularising' anthropology.

In the first extract here, we return to the themes of international development and international finance, which we also looked at earlier in the Reader. David Marsden here complements Tett's observations (above) on the value of an anthropological approach to understanding the workings of money and capital. He traces the recent history of involvement of social scientists (including anthropologists) in development policy, and argues that their contribution was initially a restricted one, owing to the domination of models and assumptions derived from engineering and economics. However, the complex impacts of events such as the world financial crisis call for a 'renegotiation' of what is of fundamental value. This reconsideration, in Marsden's view, 'reflects an evolving cross-disciplinary concern to transcend the nature/culture divide, to recognize and incorporate complexity thinking, and to rethink dominant modes of interpretation'. Marsden calls for recognition of the key contribution of 'anthropological thinking' to the success of this project.

There is a widespread feeling that anthropologists, whatever their specialist interests, need to find ways to convey the realities of what they do to the general public – which, after all, funds much of their research through its taxes. In our final extract, Thomas Hylland Eriksen (whose work we have met at several points in the Reader) addresses this issue head-on. He makes a forceful argument that anthropology, by reason of its capacity to make us aware of the reality of other people's experience and hence the specificity of our own, deserves to form a key part of our general education and world-view. We may also call to mind Gillian Tett's and David Marsden's arguments for the importance of anthropology in enabling us to think across the boundaries of institutions, and the 'silos' of self-confined knowledge and practice which dominate the modern world. So we conclude by posing this as a question to the reader: Have your own explorations in anthropology persuaded you that Eriksen, Tett, Marsden and the other authors whose work features here, are right?

V.1 Anthropological Perspectives on World Issues

64	**The House of Difference** *Eva Mackey*

The following account starts with a postcard of a red-coated Mountie shaking hands with Chief Sitting Eagle as a way of addressing the relationship of colonisers and Aboriginal people and how the nation state, in this case Canada, deals with minorities. The author introduces a book on this subject with a critique of the dominant model of Canada, as a 'tolerant nationhood', symbolised by this picture, also sometimes referred to as 'multicultural-Canadian'. Such pluralism, she suggests, is an ideology and mythology that actually intersects with the ongoing construction of dominant national identity and culture in Canada that continues to marginalise minorities such as the Indians of which Chief Sitting Eagle is such a powerful symbol. Nationalist narratives of tolerance such as the Mountie myth, she claims, 'misrepresent the encounter between cultures and the brutal history of conquest and cultural genocide that Canada is founded upon'. Mackey's critique raises key issues for how anthropology might help us understand and deal with a cultural politics seemingly based on inclusion and tolerance rather than on erasure and homogeneity. Mackey, then, critiques not only the obvious forms of Western dominance and power but the more hidden and maybe insidious liberal concepts and practices of pluralism, diversity and tolerance, which may also finish up being equally dominating and exclusionary. This powerful critique of the liberal values that many of us may hold and that may indeed underpin much anthropology, can provide a basis for applying such debates and tensions in other contexts than Canada – the UK included! Mackey also draws attention to the 'multi-sited' and 'event-centred' methodology that she adopted in order to explore these issues. She describes how her own ethnographic research moved from the idea of a single site and an 'event-centred' approach, and how instead she came to research the 'Canada 125' celebrations in 1992 though a variety of contexts; she documented contests in public culture, interviewed cultural workers and bureaucratic elites, and did participant observation and interviews at numerous local patriotic celebrations. This is an approach that readers might take up as they problematise their own engagement with ethnographic methods and reflect on nationalism and identity in their own cultural context.

Introduction

> Unsettling differences: origins, methods, frameworks. Imagine how you as writers from the dominant society might turn over some of the rocks in your own garden for examination. Imagine … courageously questioning and examining the values that allow the de-humanizing of peoples through domination … Imagine writing in honesty, free of the romantic bias about the courageous 'pioneering spirit' of colonialist practise and imperialist process. Imagine interpreting for us your own people's thinking towards us, instead of interpreting for us our thinking, our lives, our stories. We wish to know, and you need to understand, why it is that you want to own our stories, our art … our ceremonies.
>
> —Jeanette Armstrong (1990: 143–44)

On the postcard, the red-coated Mountie smiles warmly as he reaches out to shake hands with Chief Sitting Eagle who is dressed in a colourful feather headdress, buckskins and beads. The caption reads, 'Here indeed are the symbols of Canada's glorious past. A Mountie, resplendent in his famed scarlet greets Chief Sitting Eagle, one of Canada's most colourful Indians'. This image of reconciliation and equality, presented in such a picturesque manner, invokes an older mythology of Canadian identity which I call the 'Benevolent Mountie Myth', a myth based on the story of the westward expansion of the nation at the end of the nineteenth century. The Royal Canadian Mounted Police, representatives of British North American justice, are said to have managed the inevitable and glorious expansion of the nation (and the subjugation of Native peoples) with much less bloodshed and more benevolence and tolerance than the violent US expansion to the south. This benevolent gentleness, it was believed, was a result of naturally superior forms of British justice, and was an important element in the mythologies of Canadian national identity emerging at the turn of the century … The image of the Mountie and the 'Indian Chief' places a representative of the state and a representative of minority culture – coloniser and colonised – in a friendly, peaceful and collaborative pose. Aboriginal people and the state are represented as if they are equal: as if the Mountie did not have the force of the crown and the military behind him, shoring up his power. This image of collaborative cultural contact could be contrasted with a quintessential American frontier image: cowboys chasing and killing 'Indians'. In the American images, the cowboys are presented as rugged individuals. In contrast, the Mounties in the Canadian image are symbols and representatives of the kind and benevolent state – the state

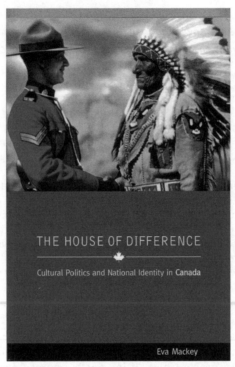

Cover for *The House of Difference* showing the Mountie and the 'Indian Chief'. Published by University of Toronto Press 2002.

that supposedly treated, and still treats, its minorities more compassionately than the USA.

The Mountie myth is one of many similar stories that utilises the idea of Canada's tolerance and justice towards its minorities to create national identity. From early versions of Canadian history through to the Quebec referendums of 1980 and 1995, and the Calgary pact made in September 1997, official definitions of English-Canadian history and identity present the past as a 'heritage' of tolerance. During the last three decades, the story of Canada's tolerant nationhood has often been framed in terms of its policy and mythology of 'multiculturalism', a policy defined in official government ideology as 'a fundamental characteristic of Canadian heritage and identity'. Canada is often described as a 'cultural mosaic' in order to differentiate it from the American cultural 'melting pot'. In the Canadian 'mosaic', it is said, all the hyphenated cultures – French-Canadian, Native-Canadian, and 'multicultural-Canadian' – are celebrated. One problem with this formulation, as many have pointed out, is that multiculturalism implicitly constructs the idea of a core English-Canadian culture, and that other cultures become 'multicultural' in relation to that unmarked, yet dominant, Anglo-Canadian core culture ...

This book explores the contradictory terrain wherein pluralism as an ideology and mythology intersects with the construction of dominant national identity and culture in Canada. A nation, Anderson stresses, is an imagined community, and nations are distinguished from each other by the stories they tell about themselves (Anderson 1991). Although it would be ridiculous to say that this particular 'invented tradition' (Hobsbawm 1983) is uncontested, the Canadian myth of tolerance has gained great authority throughout the nation's history. It offers a 'narrative of nationhood', and is one of the stories which is closely linked to the images, landscapes, scenarios, historical events, national symbols and rituals which, Stuart Hall argues, 'stand for, or represent, the shared experiences, sorrows, and triumphs and disasters which give meaning to the nation' (Hall 1992: 293). There is no doubt that nationalist narratives of tolerance such as the Mountie myth misrepresent the encounter between cultures and the brutal history of conquest and cultural genocide that Canada is founded upon. However, although the official stories misrepresent the messy and controversial reality of history, they do not, at least overtly, erase the presence of Aboriginal people or deny the existence of cultural differences within the nation. Aboriginal people are necessary players in nationalist myths: they are the colourful recipients of benevolence, the necessary 'others' who reflect back white Canada's self-image of tolerance. Pluralism and tolerance have a key place, and an institutionalised place, in the cultural politics of national identity in Canada.

This book examines the project of nation-building and the nationalism of dominant peoples within the context of pluralist mythology and 'multicultural' state policies. Nationalism has been the subject of a vast body of inquiry. However, analysts of the cultural politics of national identity often focus on extreme and exclusionary nationalisms, and studies of multiculturalism and cultural pluralism tend to examine the lives of minority groups and their processes of 'adaptation' or 'resistance' to mainstream cultures. In Canada, however, cultural pluralism is institutionalised as a key feature of the mythology of identity of the dominant white Anglophone majority. Multiculturalism, this book contends, has as much to do with the construction of identity for those Canadians who do not conceive of themselves as 'multicultural', as for those who do. It examines the cultural politics of pluralism as it is articulated in colonial and national projects, and in the subjectivities of people who conceive of themselves as 'mainstream' or simply 'Canadian-Canadians'. As such, it is a contribution to the burgeoning field of studies of 'whiteness' ...

This book maps the contradictions and ambiguities in the cultural politics of Canadian identity and raises a number of key questions. How can we critically understand a cultural politics seemingly based on inclusion and tolerance rather than erasure and homogeneity? How does 'tolerance' for 'others' work in the construction of an unmarked and yet dominant national identity? What are its effects? Do 'multiculturalism' and pluralism draw on and reinforce racial exclusions and hierarchies of difference? What kinds of conceptual continuities exist between colonial policies, multiculturalism, and the 'white backlash' of the 1990s?

The origins of *The House of Difference* are in the 'crisis' of anthropology that was in full flight when I began to study in the mid 1980s. At that time, feminist and postmodernist critiques of 'scientific objectivity' were shaking up the discipline and post-colonial critiques were inspiring anthropologists to grapple with historical and present-day issues of colonialism, imperialism and power. At the same time, work in feminist theory and cultural studies aimed to bring silenced and subordinated forms of knowledge into relief by exploring the worlds and lives of marginalised peoples. However, it became clear from the study of the politics of cultural differences that it was also necessary to examine the unmarked and yet normative categories such as 'whiteness', heterosexuality, masculinity and Western modernity that were often excluded from analysis.

Hazel Carby argues that preserving 'an analysis of gender only for texts about women ... or an analysis of racial domination for texts by or directly about black people will not by itself transform our understanding of dominant cultural forms' (Carby 1989: 40). It is only through problematising dominant categories – which are often invisible and yet powerfully normative – that we can begin to understand how they are invented and reproduced. The analysis offered here explores the construction of dominant forms of Canadian national identity, and does so as part of a broader goal: to understand how Western projects of identity function in terms of culture, difference and power. I engage in what Asad calls 'an historical anthropology which takes Western cultural hegemony as its object of inquiry' (Asad 1993: 24) and what Chakrabarty (1992) calls 'provincialising Europe' and the West. Such an anthropology interrogates the 'radically altered form and terrain of conflict' – the 'new political languages, new powers, new social groups, new desires and fears, [and] new subjectivities' – that characterise Western modernity (Asad 1991: 322–23). Nations have been described as a 'distinctly modern form' and even an 'engine of modernity' ...

Gellner argues that while 'having a nation is not an inherent attribute of humanity', it has now, in modernity, 'come to appear as such' (Gellner 1983: 6). Nations are the most universally legitimate, and seemingly natural, political units of our time. In modernity the nation-state 'has been granted universal recognition and validity as the authorised marker of the particular' (Ang and Stratton 1996: 26). Nation-building is a Western project – engendered by structures, narrative forms, desires, and classifying and differentiating practices which are essential to Western modernity – and national identity is 'modernity's fundamental identity' (Greenfeld 1996: 10–11). National identity, therefore, is a useful site through which to examine modern Western processes of identity construction.

Some radical critics of modernity, focusing on extreme forms of colonialism and nationalism, have presented modernity as nearly always destructive of cultural difference. Critics of Western cultural projects often suggest that the Western 'will to power' lies in its construction of a singular, universal, unified, and homogeneous modern subject. Homi Bhabha contends, for example, that dominant power and political supremacy seek to 'obliterate difference' (cited in Asad 1993: 262). Thus, resistance and liberation are found through 'resurrecting the virtues of the fragmentary, the local, and the subjugated' (Chatterjee 1993: xi) or in Bhabha's case, the critical 'Third Space' of cultural 'hybridity' (Bhabha 1994: 38).

In Canada, however, power and dominance function through more liberal, inclusionary, pluralistic, multiple and fragmented formulations and practices concerning culture and difference. This study of Canada's 'multi cultural' nation-building examines the subtle and less overt powers of liberalism and liberal pluralism. It explores how liberal 'tolerance' is mobilised to manage populations and also to create identities. As a result, this book questions and expands those formulations of the characteristics of Western power that oppose oppressive homogeneity with resistant fragmentation and hybridity. It develops an analysis of culture, identity, difference and power that accounts for liberal and apparently more inclusionary constructions of national identity. It explores how modern Western forms of power and identity have also been enacted through constructing forms of difference and heterogeneity, and through liberal concepts and practices of pluralism, diversity and tolerance. The powers of 'Western modernity', I argue, work not only through the erasure of difference and the construction of homogeneity, but are endlessly recuperative and mobile, flexible and ambiguous, 'hybrid' as well as totalising. As such, it should be stated at the outset that this analysis is one slice of a potentially immense topic. It is not a contribution to defining and delineating the authentic characteristics of Canadian nationalism or national identity. Neither is it an assessment of the policy of multiculturalism, or a detailed political and economic history of Canadian nation-building. It does not primarily seek to document many of the overtly racial and culturally genocidal state policies and practices applied to cultural minorities, nor the effects upon, or the resistance of, minorities to this process of nation-building. Instead, this book focuses on exploring the subtle and mobile powers of liberal inclusionary forms of national imagining and national culture. Rather than analyse power by examining the erasure of difference and the construction of homogeneity, it explores the cultural politics of the proliferation of difference and the construction of heterogeneity, including the links between discourses of tolerance and the emerging 'white backlash'.

In this mass-media age of *Dancing with Wolves*, of O.J. Simpson and Clarence Thomas, of affirmative action programmes, and of the 'multicultural marketing' seen in Benetton, Microsoft and Coca-Cola ads, taking apart multicultural tolerance is important not just in Canada, but on a broader scale. In the 'global marketplace', television screens, advertising, literature, popular culture and academia are now filled with complex and contradictory images of pluralism, images that do not simply erase difference, but often highlight and celebrate particular forms of diversity. Meanwhile the hegemony of the market becomes stronger, the 'white backlash' grows louder, and marginalised populations have fewer and fewer choices. The important question for me in this context is not 'How does dominant power erase difference?' but rather, 'How might we map the ways in which dominant powers maintain their grip despite the proliferation of cultural difference?' Further, it is important to ask how 'threatening' and 'dangerous' differences are contained, controlled, normalised, stereotyped, idealised, marginalised and reified.

A great deal of debate in recent decades on anthropological methods and objects of inquiry has circulated around the question of how the discipline can develop an 'anthropology of the present' (Fox 1991), which would account, both theoretically and methodologically, for the rapid transformations in social and cultural life at the end of the twentieth century ...

Since the closed and bounded localities anthropologists preferred to study in the past no longer exist – if they ever did exist – the issue of linking micro and macro levels of analysis, and of theorising and describing the relationship between global processes and local events and places, has been the subject of debate and argument ...

George Marcus argues for 'event-centred' and 'multi-locale' ethnographies that explore how 'any cultural identity or activity is constructed by multiple agents in varying contexts or places', and he suggests that ethnography must be 'strategically conceived' to represent such multiplicity 'in the network of complex connections within a system of places' (Marcus 1989). *The House of Difference* is a 'multi-site' or 'multi-locale' ethnography. Its methodology accounts for the fact that national identity is produced both in face-to-face encounters in multiple sites, as well as through representations, institutions, and policies. The study of national identity in modern media-saturated nation-states has often been problematic for anthropologists because they focus on single, localised field sites to the exclusion of the broader, multiple sites of national-identity production, reception and contest. As a multi-site ethnography, the book combines the use of traditional anthropological methods such as interviews and participant observation in numerous local sites, with an analysis of the construction of national identity in public culture and in state and business policies, both historically and in the present.

The analysis offered here is based on fieldwork carried out in 1992: a year in which highly contested debates about, and versions of, national identity and pluralism were ubiquitous in all forms of Canadian public culture. When I began fieldwork early in the year, my research plan was to examine conflicts over culture, race, nation and representation in Canada. I intended to start with an 'event-centred' approach, by documenting contested representations of history in the Columbus Quincentennial celebrations, an immense multinational cultural/historic event that was already promising to be controversial. I quickly discovered that while there were innumerable counter-Columbus activities, official government celebrations had been all but jettisoned. Some informants in government offices speculated that the Columbus celebrations were simply 'too controversial' largely because of the political activism of Native people and other minorities.

Instead of celebrating the Columbus Quincentenary in 1992, the federal government decided that Canada would celebrate the 125th anniversary of its formation as a nation – and began plans for the 'Canada 125' celebrations. The celebrations were part of a series of complex political manoeuvres by the federal Progressive Conservative government, including extensive debates on the constitution and, finally, a referendum. The very future of the nation – and the contested place of historically defined cultural, ethnic and racial groups within the nation – were the subject of immense political conflict and debate. Canadian citizens were also the objects and subjects of symbolic intervention by the federal government, in part through the 'Canada 125' celebrations and other 'pedagogies of patriotism' ...

The celebrations, designed to mobilise local people for patriotism and national unity, were excellent sites for ethnographic exploration of the construction of national and local identities. The broader political context provided intriguing and complex examples of contests over national identity in a public culture that is officially 'multicultural'. I documented the contests in public culture, interviewed cultural workers and bureaucratic elites, and did participant observation and interviews at numerous local patriotic celebrations. The 'multi-site' and 'event-centred' methodology allows for an in-depth analysis of the ways in which national political crises – often framed as 'identity crises' – become the conditions of possibility for the production, surveillance, and regulation of identities and difference at national and local levels. This book, therefore, shuttles between micro and macro, between public representations and local discourses, between past and present, and between the global, the national, and the local.

References

Anderson, B. *Imagined Communities: Reflections on the Origin and Spread of Nationalism* (London: Verso, 1991).

Ang, I., and J. Stratton. 'Assigning Australia: Notes Toward a Critical Transnationalism in Cultural Studies', *Cultural Studies* 10/1 (1996): 16-36.

Armstrong, J. 'The Disempowerment of First North American Native Peoples and Empowerment through their Writings', *Gatherings: The En'owkin Journal of First North American Peoples* 1/1 (1990): 143–45.

Asad, T. 'Afterword: From the History of Colonial Anthropology to the Anthropology of Western Hegemony', in G. Stocking (ed.), *Colonial Situations: Essays on the Contextualisation of Ethnographic Knowledge* (Madison: University of Wisconsin Press, 1991), pp.314–24.

Asad, T. '*Genealogies of Religion: Discipline and Reasons of Power in Christianity and Islam* (Baltimore: Johns Hopkins University Press, 1993).

Bhabha, H. *The Location of Culture* (London: Routledge, 1994).

Carby, H. 'The Canon: Civil War and Reconstruction', *Michigan Quarterly Review*, 28/1 (1989): 26–51.

Chakrabarty, D. 'Provincialising Europe: Postcoloniality and the Critique of History', *Cultural Studies* 6/3 (1992): 337–57.

Chatterjee, P. *National Thought and the Colonial World: A Derivative Discourse?* (London: Zed Press, 1986).

Fox, R. (ed.) *Recapturing Anthropology: Working in the Present* (Santa Fe, NM: School of American Research Press, 1991).

Gellner, E. *Nations and Nationalism* (London: Cornell University Press, 1983).

Greenfield, L. 'Nationalism and Modernity', *Social Research* 63/1 (1996): 3–40

Hall, S. 'The West and the Rest: Discourse and Power', in S. Hall and B. Gieben (eds), *Formations of Modernity* (Cambridge: Polity Press in Association with the Open University, 1992): 275–332.

Hobsbawm, E. 'Introduction: Inventing Traditions', in E. Hobsbawm and T. Ranger (eds), *The Invention of Tradition* (Cambridge: Cambridge University Press, 1983).

Mackey, E. 'The Cultural Politics of Populism: Celebrating Canadian National Identity', in C. Shore and S. Wright (eds) *Anthropology of Policy* (London: Routledge, 1997): 136–59.

Marcus, G. 'Imagining the Whole: Ethnography and Contemporary Efforts to Situate Itself', *Critique of Anthropology* 9/3 (1989): 7–30.

Edited extract from: Eva Mackey, *The House of Difference: Cultural Politics and National Identity in Canada* (Toronto: University of Toronto Press, 2002), pp.1–7.

65 Fool's Gold
Gillian Tett

Gillian Tett is a well-known British financial journalist and author, with a background in social anthropology. In this extract from the Preface to the paperback edition of her book Fool's Gold, *a probing analysis of the causes and consequences of the global financial crisis that erupted in 2008, Tett recounts how her readings in anthropology – specifically, the work of Pierre Bourdieu – helped her to understand the role of 'social silences', how they are created and sustained, and what interests they serve. She goes on to comment on the proliferation in the modern world of 'silos' – bounded spheres of knowledge and practice – which restrict and blinker the awareness of those inside them, and can make it hard to comprehend – or even to notice – other realities, even those in plain sight. One contribution anthropology can make to our understanding of the complex modern world is to encourage us to think and imagine 'outside our silos'. And, while few recent world-scale events have been more dramatic in their impacts than the financial crisis, Tett's use of Bourdieu's ideas can encourage us to think about other areas of 'social silence'. What, in public affairs or indeed in our everyday lives, do we not talk about, and why?*

... The first edition of [*Fool's Gold*] was published in the spring of 2009, as the financial world was still reeling from the bursting of the credit bubble. It would be quite wrong to claim that the credit derivatives sector – or, indeed, the world of financial innovation in general – was the *only* factor behind this terrible financial crisis, the worst seen for seventy years ... A key issue, however, one that exacerbated the credit bubble during the boom – and then vastly complicated the disaster when the bubble burst – was the presence of all those credit derivatives contracts.

...

I first crashed into this world back in early 2005, when I happened to spot – almost by chance – a frenzy of activity occurring in the credit sector that was being under-reported by the mainstream press. Between 2005 and 2007, I tried to penetrate this world, writing a string of articles for the *Financial Times* ... As I tried to piece together the tale of what the purveyors of derivatives were up to, I was startled by the scale of it. By 2005, the credit derivatives world, for example, was exploding, with more than $20 trillion contracts in the markets, most of which had been written in London or New York. The balance sheet of AIG alone was being stuffed with more than $400 billion worth of credit derivatives deals, which would later turn sour, producing that stupendous taxpayers' bailout bill.

Yet there was barely a whisper of this activity in public view. Men such as Gordon Brown, then UK Chancellor, for example, might sometimes have applauded the operations of the City of London – but they almost never discussed the workings of the derivatives sector at all ... Instead, when politicians, journalists or non-bankers discussed the financial world, it was almost always in terms of the stock market, or – on occasion – the type of mergers and acquisition work that banks were carrying out. Indeed, the difference was so stark that I sometimes likened the financial system to an iceberg: there was a small piece of activity, in particular the equity markets, poking above the surface, in plain sight, and then a vast chunk that was submerged from public view. Until, of course, late 2008.

As you read this book, one issue that I encourage you to reflect on is exactly *why* it took a crisis for those outside the credit derivatives sector to delve deeply into the way derivatives were structured and the risks they carried. Why had there been such a climate of silence? Why, for example, were so few people in the British parliament asking what was really driving the revenues of the City of London – barely two miles down the road. After all, if more people had asked hard questions at an earlier stage about what was happening in the credit derivatives world, and why credit was booming, there is every reason to think that the worst excesses might never have happened. Debate and scrutiny might have sparked concern and brought about more common sense, not just among the regulators but among the bankers too.

Of course, some journalists and politicians argue that the bankers were deliberately concealing the risks in credit derivatives. Personally, though, I suspect that the problem was more subtle than that – while at the same time more alarming, in terms of its implications for modern society, both inside and outside the financial world.

...

Many years ago, before I became a journalist, I earned a PhD in social anthropology, and one of the writers I studied who made a big impact on me was Pierre Bourdieu, an anthropologist-cum-sociologist who was part of a wave of creative intellectual thought that emerged in France in the 1970s. In his seminal work *Outline of a Theory of Practice*, Bourdieu observed that the way that elites tend to control a society is not simply by controlling the physical means of production (money and other resources) but also by influencing the cultural discourse, the way the society talks about itself, or its cognitive map. Moreover, when it comes to influencing a cognitive map, what matters is not merely what is publicly discussed, but also what is *not* mentioned in public – either because it is deemed impolite, taboo, boring or simply because it is taken completely for granted. Areas of social silence, in other words, are crucial to supporting a story that a society is telling itself, such as that about the credit boom.

Sometimes such a silence is maintained through overt strategies devised by members of a social group. They can consciously choose to hide facts, as part of a plot. But on many occasions, Bourdieu observed, social silences arise less deliberately, as a result of patterns of social conformity or shared ideology and assumptions – for example, about the ability of the market to regulate itself. And it is at this semi-conscious level that the most insidious types of social silence develop; insidious particularly when they serve the interest of one particular group. Or as Bourdieu wrote: 'The most successful ideological effects are those which have no need of words, and ask no more than a complicitous silence'. In many ways, the tale of the boom and bust of credit is exemplary.

Both inside and outside the banking world, a social silence developed about credit derivatives. This was in part because the topic was thought to be so technical, and therefore generally uninteresting to non-specialists, but it was also because this lack of scrutiny suited the banking industry so well. Opacity in the world of finance breeds fat margins. Another factor at play was the widely accepted presence of so-called silos – or self-contained realms of activity and knowledge that only the experts in those areas can truly understand. The banking system was producing fat profits as well as a stream of cheap credit for consumers. The boom had a strong allure.

...

These days, of course, it has become self-evident that this lack of questioning – the excessive laziness-cum-trust on the part of those who should have been probing more trenchantly – was a crucial reason why the banking system was able to spin so badly out of control. The real tragedy of this story, in other words, was that most of the folly was *not* due to a plot; instead, it was hidden in plain sight.

Therein lies a larger lesson of the financial crisis. The modern world is littered with pockets of specialist knowledge, where technical experts work in mental and structural silos. Indeed, these silos are proliferating, for as the pace of innovation speeds up, and spreads further and further around the globe, our world is becoming more technologically complex by the day ... In theory, as these innovations spread, we are all being connected more closely to one another. In practice, though, innovation is causing as much fragmentation as unity. After all, only a tiny pool of people today have the educational training or technological knowledge to truly understand the details of some of these silos; even fewer have the ability to hop between silos.

Alongside the need for technical experts, therefore, we also need generalists who can act as cultural watchdogs and translators. The world is critically short today of these cultural translators. Of course the media might appear to be charged with this role, but in practical terms, the media's resources are increasingly squeezed, limiting the time reporters have to do the kind of in-depth digging that is required. As for the politicians and regulators who are tasked with oversight, they are too often compromised by conflicts of interest and are at any rate spread dangerously thin.

...

As you read about how regulation failed and the activities of the bankers spun so desperately out of control, the nature of the reforms that are required will be clearly illuminated ... But the relevance of this tragic story reaches further, to this issue of the many other silos developing in our world that are potentially dangerous. The story of the 2008 financial crisis is a story not only of hubris, greed and regulatory failure, but one of these deeply troubling problems of social silence and technical silos. If we do not use the crisis as an occasion to seriously tackle these problems, then it is a crisis we may well be doomed to revisit, albeit in an innovative new form.

Reference
Bourdieu, Pierre, *Outline of a Theory of Practice* (Cambridge: Cambridge University Press, 1977).

Edited extract from: Gillian Tett, *Fool's Gold: How Unrestrained Greed Corrupted a Dream, Shattered Global Markets and Unleashed a Catastrophe* (London: Abacus, 2010), pp. ix–xv. See also the recording of Tett's plenary address to the Royal Anthropological Institute's conference on 'Anthropology in the World' (June 2012) accessible at http://www.youtube.com/user/royalanthro.

66 Organ Donation, Genetics, Race and Culture
Ciara Kierans and Jessie Cooper

A large body of present-day research in anthropology is concerned with the social and cultural dimensions of health and illness across the world. Equally, anthropologists are turning their attention to the institutions, practices and policies of medicine and healthcare. In this extract, Ciara Kierans and Jessie Cooper look at ways in which assumptions about 'race' and ethnic classification intersect with national policies on organ donation in the UK. They argue that the categories of ethnic classification in common use (think of the 'ethnic' boxes we are regularly asked to tick by public authorities) create artificial groupings that do not coincide with underlying genetic or biological realities. Furthermore, when it is assumed that such groupings correspond to 'communities', the effect can be to hold such assumed communities responsible for inequalities in access to scarce benefits such as (in this case) organ donations.

A recent BBC Radio 4 programme, *Blood for Blood* (2010), told the story of a young black man who died waiting for a bone marrow transplant. The programme emphasized the need for increased organ and blood donation from Britain's black and Asian populations, and looked at why these groups are far less likely to come forward as donors than their white counterparts. Is it because of fear and suspicion of the medical profession; is it because of culture or religion; is it simply a lack of awareness? The programme asked: 'Just what is behind the conundrum of Britain's black and Asian population's disinclination to volunteer as blood and organ donors?'

In this article we argue that this 'conundrum' acquires its force from a complex interweaving of biology/genetics and ethnicity/race within transplant medicine, an interweaving that both modifies and reinforces ideas of culture and responsibility. As we will show, low rates of organ donation among what are routinely referred to in healthcare domains as 'black and minority ethnic' (BME) 'communities' (here denoting people of African, Caribbean and South Asian backgrounds) are a problem that emerges within the professional matrix of UK transplant medicine and the organization of the health service to which it connects. At the same time, we show that, despite this, the problem is one that is increasingly viewed as the responsibility of those groups that transplant medicine collectively defines as being affected by it.

Our aim in what follows is to examine how ethnic populations have come to be problematized in relation to kidney donation. We will show that transplant medicine, in trying to work out a solution to this 'problem', has *culturalized* the issue by treating it as something that falls outside its own domain of practice and that, in doing so, it has entrenched *racialized* responsibility by mapping donor pools to cultural difference. We will also show how this problematic coupling of biology and ethnicity, two domains that have come to be treated as coextensive for the practical purposes of transplant medicine, works to deflect attempts to trace the complex genealogy of this 'problem'.

We chart the materialization of this problematic in three stages. First, we examine how inequalities in access to kidney transplantation are translated into social and cultural distinctions, as low organ-donation rates are viewed through the lens of ethnic and racial classifications; secondly, we trace the construction of ethnic difference through transplant practice and policy, with a particular focus on blood and tissue matching, and how these practices interplay with understandings of ethnicity. Finally, we discuss the work of the discursive technology of health-promotion campaigns in placing the moral imperative on specified ethnic groups to solve this problem for themselves.

Kidney Transplantation: Inequalities of Access and the 'Problem' of Organ Donation

In the UK, inequalities in access to renal-replacement therapies, in particular transplantation, are frequently broken down statistically in terms of ethnicity ... The problem is conventionally portrayed as follows:

BME groups are three to four times more likely than the white British population to develop End-Stage Renal Disease (ESRD) ... Despite constituting 8 per cent of the British population, BME groups make up around 28 per cent of the kidney transplant waiting list, and only 4 per cent of deceased organ donors ...

As blood and tissue matching requirements mean that transplant practices in the UK favour organ sharing within ethnic groupings, this translates into longer waits for suitable organs ... .

As a result, individuals from 'South Asian' and 'African Caribbean' 'communities' wait nearly twice as long for a kidney transplant than their white counterparts (1,368, 1,419 and 719 days respectively) ... and thus have a greatly reduced chance of receiving a transplant.

While responding effectively to health inequalities is of course important ... the relationship between low donation and ethnicity that is used to define this particular area of inequality is not, however, as straightforward as it might appear in light of the statistics. We might be tempted to conclude that low organ donation is a free-standing problem, that is, that BME groups simply donate less than their white British counterparts. However, we argue that this would be unwarranted: when we look at the matter in more detail, we see that low donation rates among certain populations have become a problem as a consequence of the specific ways in which transplant medicine in the UK has been configured so as to recognize and respond to genetic sameness and difference by translating biological markers into membership of social and cultural groups.

Organizing accounts of the problem according to classificatory schemas that distinguish the white population from BME populations has been central to this translation process ... In order to be able to explore how such schemas have been made to bridge clinical, policy and public domains in response to organ-donation issues, we need to examine where and how the donation-rates problem itself has been in large part forged (i.e., within transplant medicine itself), as much as where and in what terms it has been fixed in place (i.e., through linking to black and minority ethnic groups). ...

Marking the Boundaries of Race and Ethnicity within Transplant Policy and Practice

Anthropologists have tracked crucial developments in transplantation practices for much of the past twenty years, investigating the complex interplay among developments in transplant technology, a variety of social, cultural, political and economic arrangements, and the different kinds of relationships that link both the technologies and the arrangements at different moments in time ... Anthropological research has thus followed the ways in which different publics have been progressively implicated in the 'transplantation story' ... highlighting how transplant medicine has served to underwrite privilege and power by exposing already marginalized populations to new forms of biotechnical intervention grounded in new kinds of knowledge claim. Here, we want to explore such processes as they have played out in the context of British transplant medicine.

In the UK, organ-donation rates among BME populations became a focus of medical interest during the 1990s, as epidemiological research highlighted an increased prevalence of kidney disease among 'black' and 'South Asian' populations, due to higher instances of diabetes and hypertension among those groups ... Generally low donor rates meant that transplantation was not, at this stage, seen as a feasible solution, and efforts initially concentrated on prevention and management of renal failure and its associated conditions ... This changed with the introduction of the Organ Donor Register in 1994 and widespread acceptance of transplantation as the economically viable treatment option.

However, access to suitable organs for transplant in the UK has been restricted by an explicit orientation towards cadaveric donation and an 'opt-in' system of participation. For anyone classified as a 'BME' patient, these structural constraints on organ availability have been compounded by allocation policies that favour blood group and tissue, or HLA (human leukocyte antigen), matching ... Until relatively recently, kidney recipients and their donors were strictly matched by blood group. While Group O is the most common blood type in the UK, 38 per cent of 'Asian' people are Group B, compared with 24 per cent of 'black' people and 10 per cent of 'white' people ... Although it is possible to allocate Group O organs to patients of any blood group, Group O recipients can only receive O organs. With allocations organized in the context of a mainly white (and therefore mainly Group O) donor pool, standard practice was to only offer recipients exact organ-blood group matches. This put 'Asian' patients waiting for transplant at a disadvantage ... It was not until 2002 that the matching of O organs to recipients with blood group B was permitted, in recognition of the inequalities the previous policy had created ...

The practice of tissue matching, in which the HLA groups −A, −B and −DR are used as the basis for identifying suitable donors, carries similar implications. HLAs are present in all human bodies, and are essential to immune-system functioning and the maintenance of a healthy body. They work by recognizing foreign matter entering the body, and rejecting it through the production of antibodies. Foreign matter includes new organs – a central concern for transplantation. Because of this, the closer the HLA matches, the better the outcome. HLAs vary widely in humans and their distribution can be mapped to the geographic 'origins' of different populations, and to population 'mixing' ... However, in the transplant literature, what are highly complex variations are typically represented in simplified, analytically unstable racial terms ... with 'black' and 'Asian' populations routinely described as having different HLA distributions from 'white' groups.

Historically, adherence to HLA matching policies in the UK has meant a preference for transplanting organs between those from similar ethnic backgrounds – the effect being to divide donor pools not only along white/non-white lines, but also according to ascriptions of ethnic origin ... The instability of such translation practices aside, what is of greatest interest here ... is how this turns transplant medicine into an important contemporary site for the production of cultural difference.

From Society to Cell and Back Again: Grounding Organ Donation as a Moral Imperative

In its attempts to accommodate 'rare' HLA types, transplant medicine has fallen back on the same classificatory schemas that were implicated in the creation of the inequalities that recent policy shifts were intended to address – schemas that are based, primarily, on the assumption of a 'natural' basis for cultural differences. We suggest that this assumption has two reciprocal components: the claim that biological differences can be mapped to racial or ethnic categories; and the claim that these categories thus pick out real, sociobiologically distinct populations. We want to examine how these claims work in complementary ways to reinforce each other.

The idea that biological differences are conflated with race and ethnicity in this medical context has been the subject of much discussion. Writing specifically about the indexing of race to HLA matching in transplant medicine, [a recent author] highlights several issues. These include the largely arbitrary character of racial categorizations based on purportedly shared skin colour ('black', 'white'), shared geographic location ('Asian'), language ('Hispanic') or religion ('Jewish'); the scientific bias that sees 'white' HLA types as the standard against which 'rare' 'black' HLA types are identified; the failure to account for racial mixing in the indexing of HLA types, that is, the fact that people of mixed heritage are not represented in the standard schemas, which leads to the reification of racial difference; and the failure to acknowledge that developments in immunosuppressants make HLA (mis)matches increasingly irrelevant ...

... Empirical studies of the ways in which biomedical researchers construct, classify, standardize and analyse race and ethnicity suggest that these concepts are in increasingly wide use, despite the absence of any recognized way of defining, explaining or operationalizing them in accordance with such researchers' own criteria of objectivity ... Such racial and ethnic categorization is not simply an issue of ontological and epistemological (in)coherence, as this classificatory apparatus has serious real-life effects on those subject to it.

... [For example, in a comparable case from South Africa,] HLA types are used to define the boundaries between different populations → patients are more likely to find matches within the population they have been defined as 'belonging' to → patients from these groups don't donate → this generates unequal health outcomes for those affected, which are immediately cast in racial or ethnic terms → health-promotion campaigns are put in place to increase the number of 'black', 'coloured' and 'Asian' donors, even though it may make little sense in biological terms to divide populations in this way ...

...

In recent years, the UK has seen a stepping-up of health-promotion initiatives specifically aimed at members of 'black' and 'South Asian' 'communities'. These have been characterized by hard-hitting media campaigns that frame organ donation as a moral imperative. They also reflect an expanding research literature that traces the genealogy of low donation rates to cultural differences clustered around religious practices, beliefs, constructions of the body, knowledge, language and so on ...

Public-health initiatives in this area began with the ABLE project in 2001, which sought to 'raise the profile' of organ donation among 'South Asian' and 'African Caribbean' groups in Leicester and West London. With backing from the Department of Health, similar initiatives have since then been building momentum through poster campaigns, street plays and faith 'road shows' in cities with large ethnic populations ... Examples include the 2007 NHS Blood and Transplant service's 'Can We Count on You?' campaign, in which 'black' and 'South Asian' comedians such as Nina Wadia and Curtis Walker promoted the 'gift of life'. In 2009, the message of ethnic-group responsibility was reinforced by the targeting of 'black' and 'South Asian' populations as part of the 'Prove It' campaign. In a not-so-subtle reformulation of the campaign's general message, which was that individuals should 'prove' their belief in organ donation by joining the donor register, the BME campaigns focused on collectives first and individuals second, urging people to help their *communities* by registering as organ donors.

These and other campaigns have served to amplify the idea that donation is the collective responsibility of biologically, socially and culturally distinct and distinguishable communities. Taking their lead from transplant medicine's translation of the genetic bases of blood and tissue matching into ethnic classifications, these campaigns form part of the dynamic production of cultural difference within and across different domains of contemporary British social life.

Conclusion

What we hope emerges from this discussion is a recognition that the problem of 'low donation rates among BME groups' cannot be understood in isolation from the practices of transplant medicine itself. We must examine the various ways in which the categories of 'patient' and 'donor' have been worked up and refined in problematic ways over time, with conceptual connections being drawn between biological and cultural differences in response to circumstances such as changes in organ-donation targets and changes to the organization of the transplant services within which those targets are pursued; we must also carefully scrutinize the ways in which these categories and connections are presented to the various publics who are defined by them.

Most troublingly for us, these populations defined by these classificatory technologies may have no significance in cultural or even genetic terms, as individuals who have little in common are grouped into the same awkward biocultural space. Given this, it seems inequitable to treat such individuals as the solution to problems which have emerged from within transplant medicine itself. The question posed at the beginning of this article – 'Just what is behind the conundrum of Britain's black and Asian population's disinclination to volunteer as blood and organ donors?' – resonates very differently once we see the extent to which this ethnic responsibility is externally ascribed.

Whether or not one takes a particular stance on such issues, there can be little doubt that organ transplantation operates as a major contemporary site for the production of difference, and that in transplant medicine's own attempts to find a solution to the problems and inequalities that have arisen, we can discern a further entrenchment of such difference. This reflects a wider blurring of the boundaries between race, ethnicity and genetics that can be seen today at work across ever-expanding biopolitical terrains ... Given this, it is of critical importance that anthropologists continue to intervene in debates on these and related issues.

Edited extract from: Ciara Kierans and Jessie Cooper, 'Organ Donation, Genetics, Race and Culture: The Making of a Medical Problem', *Anthropology Today* 27/6 (2011), pp.11–14.

67   The Anthropology of Science
Sarah Franklin

As Sarah Franklin reports in this short extract from a longer article, social anthropologists are increasingly turning attention to contemporary science as a set of social relations and practices. She argues that despite the undoubted achievements and worldwide impacts of modern science, public attitudes to it are in some respects ambivalent. As she points out, science as a 'way of knowing' is neither as simple nor as straightforward as we might suppose. In general, the role of anthropology is not to reject or oppose science but to draw attention to the social and cultural factors that enter into the relationship between scientists and the world they seek to understand.

As anthropology has come to be more focused upon contemporary Western culture and society in the twenty-first century, one of the major new fields to emerge as an important ethnographic site has been the investigation of science and technology. This has taken a number of forms and has led to significant theoretical challenges for anthropology (itself also a science) including how to define what science is and does. While some anthropologists have worked alongside scientists in the laboratory as a means of conducting an ethnography of scientific practice, others have examined science as a cultural system, tracing its meanings and effects more widely. Still other anthropologists have examined science as a cross-cultural, or transnational, practice. In the process, anthropologists have asked how science emerges as a specific form of cultural activity, both in the West and elsewhere, and how it both shapes and is shaped by the broader currents of society. They have also asked what science is and how it may change in the future.

The production of scientific knowledge is a highly valued activity, and it has long been argued that Western scientific knowledge holds a privileged form of authority in modern industrial societies. Indeed the entire project of modernity is deeply rooted in a post-Enlightenment ethos of rationality, progress, and innovation epitomized by scientific, medical, and technological advances. At the same time, science has also been increasingly at odds with modernity in the second half of the twentieth century and at the turn of the new millennium. While modern, industrialized societies remain highly dependent on scientific and technological innovation, this is also seen to have potentially destructive effects, in the form of environmental damage, effects on human health, or disasters such as the one at Chernobyl. While scientific accomplishments are still held in high esteem, growing public distrust of science and increasing awareness of scientific uncertainty has created what some sociologists call the 'risk society' …

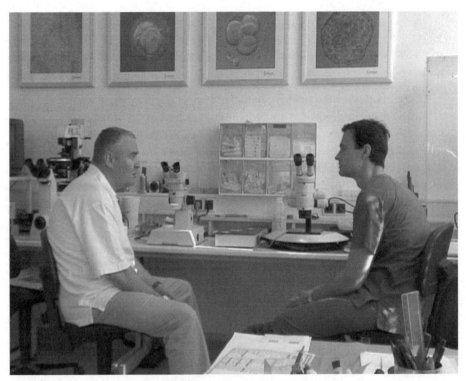

Biotechnology of human reproduction in a fertility clinic.

Filmstill from *Breeding Cells*, Anna Straube, 2009. Distributed by the Royal Anthropological Institute.

On the one hand, science is described as a means of objective description, based on the experimental method as a means of discovery and dedicated to improved and more accurate, rational understandings of the natural, chemical, and physical properties of the world around us. On the other hand, science is clearly a particular way of knowing, and while it is premised on an objective relationship to the phenomena it describes, this relationship is neither as fixed nor as straightforward as it might appear. Both in terms of how scientists who conduct scientific investigations understand their work, and in terms of how scientific ideas and imagery permeate other dimensions of social life, it is clear that science means many things to many people. From an anthropological perspective, this is neither surprising nor problematic, as science is in this respect no different from any other social activity. Indeed, it is the very diversity encompassed within the relations of science and society which has made it such a productive site of anthropological enquiry.

Edited extract from: Sarah Franklin, 'The Anthropology of Science', in J. MacClancy (ed.), *Exotic No More: Anthropology on the Front Lines* (Chicago: University of Chicago Press, 2002), pp.351–58 (extract taken from pp.350–51).

68 The Second Nuclear Age
Hugh Gusterson

In the previous extract, we highlighted in general terms the contribution anthropology can make to our understanding of science and scientific practice in the contemporary world. Hugh Gusterson's ethnographic work among nuclear weapons scientists, described in the following passage, illustrates this very well. Gusterson links his theme to anthropologists' expanding concerns with the global-scale transformations in the world, some of which were touched on earlier in the Reader. With regard to the practice of anthropology, he shows how important it is for anthropologists nowadays to trace the dispersed networks and channels of knowledge and communication that go beyond particular sites and nation-states.

... Anthropology largely missed the First Nuclear Age. Consequently there has been a big hole where there could have been a conversation between anthropologists and political scientists about international relations and the Cold War ... In the early years of the Cold War, European and American anthropologists were still predominantly focused on the description of the social and cultural dynamics of small-scale societies as they emerged from the colonial era. Any American anthropologists with an interest in larger political questions were ... given second thoughts in an atmosphere of McCarthyism that largely depoliticised the humanities and social sciences in the US for a generation.

From the late 1960s anthropologists did broach larger questions of international political economy but their interest was largely focused on the social dynamics of colonialism and decolonization, transnational migration, industrialization and, most recently, globalization. Those engaged in repatriated anthropology have tended to concentrate on issues of social stratification, gender politics, and cultural pluralism rather than militarism and science ... Insofar as anthropologists have taken an interest in war in recent years, it has been largely to debate whether war is a cultural universal and to write about some of the regional and civil wars generated by colonialism and decolonization. Given anthropologists' traditionally favoured research technique of participant observation in localized communities, the overarching global conflict, the Cold War itself, scarcely came into ethnographic focus; and in the days before the anthropology of science, the laboratories and expert communities at the heart of Cold War culture lay outside the analytic territory of anthropology departments.

Thus in the forty-five years of the First Nuclear Age, despite the huge social movements against the arms race in the 1950s and 1980s, we have only one major anthropological study of an anti-nuclear movement ... and only one major study of a Cold War military-industrial facility ... Although the Cold War brought about a substantial US military presence in many countries around the world, the ethnographic literature on Turkey and the Philippines, for example, barely mentions the huge US military bases in those countries. Meanwhile, anthropological writing on American culture during the Cold War scarcely references the fact that the US was engaged in a project as remarkable in its own way as the Egyptians' building of the Pyramids: the stockpiling, at a cumulative expense of $5.5 trillion ... rationalized by ideologies as bizarre as any we have ever discovered in rainforests and jungles, of enough nuclear weapons to end all life on earth many times over. Nor ... have histories of anthropology focused on the Cold War as an environment that shaped the practice and teaching of anthropology.

Many of the features that impeded anthropologists from attending to nuclear weapons issues in the past now seem to be less salient; recent years have seen the rise of an anthropology of the state and of globalism, of the anthropology of science, of repatriated anthropology and of a reinvigorated anthropology of elites, as well as a new openness to multi-sited fieldwork and other deviations from our traditionally canonical methods of small-scale participant observation. Anthropologists today are increasingly eager to understand global neo-liberalism, state bureaucracies, intra-state and inter-state wars, and ideologies of nationalism and modernity. This ensemble of interests, amounting to an emergent anthropological portrait of global society itself, will be incomplete without some attention to nuclear weapons and their place in human society. These weapons are important not only as material artefacts that might yet destroy global civilization as we know it but also as symbolic tokens the deployment of which regulated status hierarchies in the international system. Since the end of the Cold War there have been shifts in the international distribution of these weapons, in the treaty system that weakly regulates the rights and responsibilities of their owners, in the practices of their progenitors in the scientific community, and in our collective imagination of the threats the weapons embody and deter. These shifts, taken as a whole, define the transition from the First to the Second Nuclear Ages.

... I want to explore some of the properties of this emergent Second Nuclear Age and of the international system it defines, by way of a discussion of my fieldwork among American nuclear weapons scientists. I have been studying these scientists since 1987, when ... I embarked on an ethnographic study of the Lawrence Livermore National Laboratory, the Californian facility whose scientists designed the nuclear warheads for the Polaris, MX, and Ground-Launched Cruise missiles. Since the end of the Cold War I have continued fieldwork amongst the scientists of the Livermore Laboratory, but have expanded my research to other sites as well: the other American nuclear weapons laboratory at Los Alamos, where the bombs on

Hiroshima and Nagasaki were designed; the defence bureaucracy ... in Washington DC; and nuclear weapons networks in Russia ... This research aims to understand how American and Russian nuclear weapons scientists are adapting to the end of the Cold War and what sort of world order they and their counterparts elsewhere are creating in place of conflict ...

Such research requires methodological innovation. For example, while my first fieldwork ... did at least focus on a single localized site in the manner of classic ethnographies, it was a top secret site that was doubly inaccessible to me as a person lacking a security clearance and as a British citizen. In order to investigate the culture of the laboratory I was almost never allowed to visit, I developed a heterogeneous toolkit of approaches that I refer to as 'polymorphous engagement' ... These ranged from extensive reading of archival and journalistic sources to several dozen life-history interviews in weapons scientists' living rooms and participant observation in settings one step removed from the laboratory itself: housing ... Sunday church services ... offsite laboratory sports teams and so on.

My second fieldwork has decentred traditional fieldwork practices still further because I am investigating processes of negotiation that encompass the Congress and several different offices of the executive branch in Washington DC, one weapons laboratory in New Mexico and another in California, weapons scientists in Russia, and the diplomatic corps of several nations. George Marcus's (1995) celebrated notion of 'multi-sited fieldwork', intended to facilitate ethnographic study of global processes, is only partly adequate to charter research as it is still too tethered to concrete spatial locales rather than to radically decentred processes of decision-making. To really understand nuclearism, however, we need an anthropology that can trace connections and interfaces between spatially dispersed communities of scientists, politicians, military officers, defence intellectuals, diplomats, bureaucrats and journalists. These networked connections will by no means be contained within nation-states.

Reference
Marcus, G. 'Ethnography in/of the World System: The Emergence of Multi-sited Ethnography', *Annual Review of Anthropology* 24 (1995): 95–117.

Edited extract from: Hugh Gusterson, 'The Second Nuclear Age'. in J. Edwards, P. Harvey and P. Wade (eds), *Anthropology and Science* (Oxford: Berg, 2007), pp.114–32 (extract from pp.114–16).

V.2 The Public Presence of Anthropology

<table>
<tr><td>69</td><td>**W(h)ither Anthropology?**
David Marsden</td></tr>
</table>

*In this extract, David Marsden points to the importance of what he
terms 'anthropological thinking' to understanding the total
development landscape – and hence to the development of socially
inclusive, equitable theories and policies. Central to such
anthropological thinking, in his view, is the subject's capacity to
examine and sometimes transcend the intellectual framework and
modes of interpretation of more management-based approaches.
Marsden suggests that, in adding its voice to the total picture,
anthropology should draw on its strengths, such as a 'focus on
particular histories and contexts that can then be jointly crafted into
emergent paths'.*

My entire professional career has been associated with anthropology in and
of development. I have recently retired from nearly a decade and a half of
working in international financial institutions – first the World Bank and
more recently the European Investment Bank. Prior to that I worked as an
academic to promote an emerging Development Studies 'culture'. I have
struggled with the place of anthropology in both [international financial
institutions] and Development Studies contexts, and since formal retirement
have been putting more energy into enquiries about the place of an evolving
anthropology. I believe that anthropology will play a key role in our search
to overcome the monopoly over explanations currently exerted by the
'dubious sciences' that have emerged since the Enlightenment – particularly
economics. The recent financial crisis provides grist to that mill.

...

International financial institutions (IFIs) are still largely dominated by
engineers and economists who have employed linear and positivist ways of
thinking – with clear objectives, outputs and targets to be delivered. The
assumptions underpinning action are that the more one knows about an
object the easier it will be to manage and to achieve the predetermined goals
– targeting and destroying poverty, and promoting economic growth.

It was only in the mid 1990s that social scientists other than economists
began to be recruited to IFIs in significant numbers. This followed a growing

recognition that dominant approaches to development were deficient, that development efforts were enhancing inequality and that large development projects alienated and marginalized considerable sections of local populations. The social scientists recruited at that time had a vision of developing a sustainable agenda that would be much more holistic, participatory and inclusive. While not necessarily articulated in these terms, this vision challenged narrow nationalism and the new capitalism, and was supportive of a growing interest in environmental sustainability and in the role of non-governmental institutions in addressing such issues.

Unfortunately the role for, and contributions of, anthropologists were largely defined/confined by the linear assumptions of the still dominant engineers and economists. While the anthropologists wanted to open things up, the economists wanted to close things down. The focus was on constructing an agenda that could be quickly and simply understood by the generalist. The problem was, and still is, that the message from the non-economist social scientist emphasized context, culture, ambiguity, negotiation, trust and understanding risk in different ways ...

In the relatively short history of IFI involvement with the 'social' there have been a number of evolutionary changes. The Social Development Department in the World Bank was only given independent identity in 1997, with a five-year budget to bring its agenda into the mainstream of World Bank policy. It was absorbed back into a vice-presidency with responsibility for Sustainable Development dominated by environmental specialists in the early 2000s. The premises on which it was based remain fundamental to the achievement of sustainable development – social inclusion, cohesive societies and accountable institutions. The European Investment Bank employed its first social assessment specialist in 2005.

With the monopoly over explanations enjoyed by economics, the space for social development specialists was initially limited to dealing with the negative implications of involuntary resettlement, and to the rights and entitlements of 'indigenous' peoples. This initial approach focused on ensuring that 'social safeguard' policies were adhered to and that those obliged to relocate were not adversely affected. Nonetheless, in the wider development community a significant social development agenda was emerging following the Brundtland Report (1987) and the Copenhagen Declaration on Social Development (1995).

There emerged a larger recognition of the need to ensure widespread public consultation so that the views of 'affected peoples' were appropriately considered in project design and implementation, as well as the need for a comprehensive view of developments that incorporated economic, social and environmental concerns. An agenda for 'participation' emerged in 1995 in the World Bank, preceding the creation of the Social Development Department proper in 1997. This approach paralleled, and was often subordinated to, concerns with environmental conservation and sustainability, and developed separately from the safeguards agenda. The concern was to undertake projects with people rather than projects for people.

An emerging focus on 'poverty alleviation' as a development objective required that special attention be given to impoverishment risks for particular categories of people – women, and especially vulnerable groups. These wider concerns were articulated in the context of a consideration of the implications of involuntary resettlement and of disturbances to 'indigenous' communities, and the imprecisions and ambiguities that arose in drawing the line between those affected adversely and those not affected, as well as all the other actors touched by the development project in positive and negative ways. With hindsight, it is perhaps obvious that the negotiations surrounding the drawing of this line would be fraught and frequently challenged. For those with a job to do, the deployment of social development specialists was, to put it politely, a challenge. Here were specialists wanting to explore the ambiguities of engagement, rather than determining entitlements to compensation and giving managers concrete solutions.

Anthropologists tried to overcome these constraints by encouraging greater collaboration between IFIs and non-governmental organizations (NGOs) and/or by linking their work to the task of improving transparency and accountability to the public, and by contributing to quality enhancement through 'social audits' of one kind or another. This focus has been partially successful in linking 'social development' work to evolving concerns with sustainability, participation and accountability, and by increasing understanding of the complexities associated with the achievement of planned development objectives. These concerns have grown in importance despite rather than because of the contributions of anthropologists. Their evolution, however, has, been dominated by other 'disciplines', particularly economics and more recently 'organizational management', and the need to measure outcomes and results explicit in the audit cultures that were then developing.

The result has been the marginalization of anthropology's potential contributions to the achievement of a more sustainable and more participatory development agenda, and the place of anthropology in IFIs, as the reductionist principles associated with results-based management increasingly governed claims to relevance and appropriateness, and thus access to investment and research funds. The anthropologist has been identified with the cynic who raises additional problems rather than providing solutions.

And yet such a perception itself derives from the acceptance of particular ways of viewing the world, ones that engineers, economists, managers and many auditors tend to share. If, on the other hand, one's perspective on the world has always been from the margins (looking at the things that divide as well as connect) then this sort of marginality is to be sought after. It provides perspectives for looking at and through differences. While the positivist perspective adopted does not appear to have fundamentally shifted, increased attention is being given to issues of participation, sustainability and governance. The social scientists not trained as economists were brought into alliances with external relations departments attached to increasingly decentralized field offices. These alliances focused on building better relations with local NGOs and local specialists – in one sense a public relations exercise, in another a broadening of the networks of engagement and enhancement of citizen involvement, bringing IFIs closer to the field.

...

The dominant perspective posited a clear division between the 'hard', quantitative approaches adopted by economists and the 'soft' qualitative approaches adopted by non-economist social scientists. The former were perceived to be objective and scientific, the latter, subjective, derived from the 'humanities' and the 'moral sciences'.

Such a false set of dichotomies, coupled with the need for firm conclusions in the explanation of difference and the negotiation of change, took us away from a more robust and empathic engagement with a world in crisis. A world where the measures employed to achieve 'growth' are part of the problem, where development is increasingly associated with humanitarian crises, where the fundamental premises on which nature is separated from culture, and the individual defined and separated from the social, is being questioned, where the very Enlightenment principles on which the modernization project is based are being seriously revisited, as we reappraise, with a changed perspective, the work of such philosophers as Kant, Hume and Rousseau.

The shifts in viewpoint provided by such approaches as network theory, complexity theory and moral psychology are likely to be as important, if not more so, than the changed perspectives that emerged from the Enlightenment era itself. Here, I believe, anthropological thinking, rather than anthropology, can and will have a crucial role to play.

Anthropological studies that explore negative impacts and unintended consequences of development projects provide important pathways into the negotiation of new ways of moving forward. They are good to think with rather than useful for building an action agenda using the existing development premises. They provide different perspectives and thus enrich understanding of coping mechanisms – informal ways in which people negotiate with outsiders and/or sustain their livelihoods despite rather than because of development interventions in the name of the state ...

Similarly, there is the approach informed by the new cosmopolitan anthropology that involves the ethnographic analysis of banking institutions themselves as well as of development agencies – an investigation of the 'tribal' cultures within financial institutions ... or the history of the development and deployment of 'social development specialists' in the World Bank [or] on the ethnography of international human rights ...

The role of such institutions as the World Bank, and of the bases on which the 'dismal science' of economics has been promoted, have acquired greater prominence through the global banking crash, the failure of the 'development project' and the need to renegotiate what is seen as being of 'value'. More fundamentally, this reconsideration reflects an evolving cross-disciplinary concern to transcend the nature/culture divide, to recognize and incorporate complexity thinking, and to rethink dominant modes of interpretation. This involves crafting our ways through complex engagements and networks, weaving a tapestry that acknowledges and incorporates multiple threads that link the hand to the head, the mind to the body. Anthropology could be much more central to this new engagement because it has been able to negotiate between the lines drawn by other disciplines.

This requires the transcendence of the disciplinary boundaries that currently constrain us (and all the social sciences), and which have only emerged in the last hundred years. It also means a greater focus on particular histories and contexts that can then be jointly crafted into emergent paths. For me, that is what anthropology has always been about. I think we need to legitimize 'anecdotes' and 'value judgements' by foregrounding 'storytelling' and identifying the (often implicit) values in all e-value-ations.

These threads can be successfully woven together by telling one's own story – the inevitable compromises that have had to be made, the misrepresentation of messages, the negotiations with 'stakeholders', the developing encounters with different peoples and ideas, the personal contexts and compromises that rarely get included in the explicit record, but which inform one's own ramblings through an evolving set of landscapes. We need to develop the ability to read between the lines and create opportunities, to combine the personal with the political in the pursuit of more sustainable outcomes, and to recreate the bases for building trust and more empathic connections.

Edited extract from: David Marsden, 'W(h)ither Anthropology? Opening Up or Closing Down', *Anthropology Today* 26/5 (2010), pp.1–3.

70 Why Anthropology Matters
Thomas Hylland Eriksen

The past few years have seen a growing debate within anthropology over its public presence. Our final extract is taken from the closing chapter of Thomas Hylland Eriksen's Engaging Anthropology. *Eriksen addresses the issue of the public presence of anthropology, criticises the tendency of many academic anthropologists to retreat behind institutional walls, and makes an eloquent case for the subject's prime importance for everyone's understanding of the complex human world in which we all have to live.*

... A massive amount of high-quality, strictly academic research is continuously being produced in anthropology, and this is not merely wonderful, but is absolutely necessary. Yet much of this work fails to achieve the relevance it deserves, since it hardly enters into a wider ecology of ideas.

...

In this book, I have spoken about the possibility of presenting the intricacies of anthropological knowledge in straightforward, vivid language, our duty to make the world simpler and more complex at the same time, and the need for a greater awareness of form and style; but I have also stressed the importance of narrative throughout. The strange lack of good stories in most anthropological writing, and the general reluctance to make bold, surprising comparisons, makes these texts tough going most of the time. Moreover, the stories and comparisons that do exist are more often than not hidden in a labyrinth of academic claptrap and discussions internal to the subject. Equally important is the consciousness about there being a public sphere out there, that there are intelligent non-specialists who care about our knowledge and who are rightfully exasperated if we fail to get it through to them.

This argument is worthwhile only because anthropology has so much to offer. Apart from providing accurate knowledge about other places and societies, it gives an appreciation of other experiences and the equal value of all human life, and not least, it helps us to understand ourselves. In the contemporary, intertwined world, anthropology should be a central part of anybody's *bildung,* that is education in the widest sense. Anthropology can teach humility and empathy, and also the ability to listen, arguably one of the scarcest resources in the rich parts of the world these days. It can even be fun.

...

There is ... a real job to be done on anthropology's relationship to the societal circulation of ideas. Even when anthropologists go out of their way to write well, to tell stories and to confront the big issues – which they sometimes do, if far too rarely – they are not noticed. It sometimes feels as though one has been pigeon holed once and for all as a dated romantic writing impenetrable texts ... In this kind of situation, it is perhaps not surprising that most anthropologists retreat to their institutionalized university life. My view ... is that we should do the opposite, that anthropology needs a PR strategy, both for the sake of the enlightenment of the world and for the future of the discipline.

Seen from the perspective of the interested and enlightened layperson, scientific research can be likened to a space mission. One sends a probe into space, ceremoniously waving it off in the anticipation that it will return with new knowledge about the universe. Each time one such spaceship fails to return, but instead chooses to stay out there, pondering the calm darkness in silence, it becomes less likely that our enlightened citizen will contribute funds for another probe. If the world is our oyster, our job is to make it talk.

Edited extract from: Thomas Hylland Eriksen, *Engaging Anthropology: The Case for a Public Presence* (Oxford: Berg, 2006), pp.129–31.

Suggestions for Further Reading

Readers are encouraged to follow up the full versions of the books and articles of which extracts have been included here; and the references cited. The Royal Anthropological Institute's dedicated education website (www.discoveranthropology.org.uk) contains a range of useful learning and teaching resources. The Institute also has a large collection of anthropological films available for educational use. For details, contact: film@therai.org.uk

In addition, we suggest the following works as starting points for those wishing to explore anthropology in more depth. We emphasise that this short list is illustrative but not exhaustive; there are many directions in which you can pursue your interest in the subject.

General Texts

Eriksen, T.H. *What is Anthropology?* (London: Pluto Press, 2004).
Gosden, C. *Prehistory: A Very Short Introduction*, (Oxford: Oxford University Press, 2003).
Monaghan, J. and P. Just. *Social and Cultural Anthropology: A Very Short Introduction*, (Oxford: Oxford University Press, 2000).
Wood, B. *Human Evolution: A Very Short Introduction*, (Oxford: Oxford University Press, 2005).

Ethnographies

Brody, H. *The Other Side of Eden*, (London: Faber & Faber, 2001).
Okely, J. *The Traveller Gypsies*, (Cambridge, Cambridge University Press, 1983).

Section I. Being Human: Unity and Diversity

American Anthropological Association Statement on Race. http://www.aaanet.org/issues/policy-advocacy/AAA-Statement-on-Race.cfm
Basu, P. and S. Coleman. *Culture, Identity, Difference*, (a learning resource pack based on museum collections), (Brighton: Royal Pavilion and Museums, Brighton and Hove, 2009).
Bourque, N. 'Eating Your Words: Communicating with Food in the Ecuadorean Andes', in J. Hendry and C.W. Watson (eds), *An Anthropology of Indirect Communication*, (London: Routledge, 2011).
Dunbar, R. *The Human Story: A New History of Mankind's Evolution*, (London: Faber & Faber, 2004).
Fraser, M. and M. Greco (eds). *The Body: A Reader*, (London: Routledge, 2005).
Leach, E.R. 'Anthropological Aspects of Language: Animal Categories and Verbal Abuse', in E. Lenneberg (ed.), *New Directions in the Study of Language*, (Cambridge, Mass: MIT Press, 1964).
Miller, D. *The Comfort of Things*, (Cambridge: Polity, 2009).

Shaw, A. *Kinship and Continuity: Pakistani Families in Britain*, (London: Harwood Academic Publishers, 2000).

Strang, V. 'Negotiating the River', in Barbara Bender and Margot Winer (eds), *Contested Landscapes: Movement, Exile, Place*, (London: Berg Publishers, 2001).

Taylor, D.J. et al. (eds). *Biological Science* 1 & 2, (Cambridge: Cambridge University Press, 1997).

Section II. Becoming a Person: Identity and Belonging

Caplan, P. (ed). *The Cultural Construction of Sexuality*, (London: Routledge, 1987).

Cassidy, R. *Horse People*, (Baltimore: Johns Hopkins University Press, 2007).

Donnan, H. and T. Wilson. *Borders: Frontiers of Identity, Nation and State*, (London: Berg Publishers, 1999).

Eriksen, T.Hy. *Ethnicity and Nationalism*, (London: Pluto, 2002).

Johnston, A.M. *Is the Sacred for Sale? Tourism and Indigenous Peoples*, (London: Earthscan, 2006).

Knight, J. (ed). *Animals in Person: Cultural Perspectives on Human-Animal Intimacy*, (London: Routledge, 2005).

Overing, J. 'Today I Shall Call Him "Mummy": Multiple Worlds and Classificatory Confusion', in J. Overing (ed.), *Reason and Morality*, (London: Tavistock, 1985).

Taylor, L. and M. Hickey. *Tunnel Kids*, (Tucson: University of Arizona Press, 2001).

Weymiss, Georgie. *The Invisible Empire: White Discourse, Tolerance and Belonging*, (London: Ashgate Publishing, 2009).

Yates, P. 'Interpreting Life Texts and Negotiating Life Courses', in P. Spencer (ed.), *Anthropology and the Riddle of the Sphinx: Paradoxes of Change in the Life Course*, (London: Routledge, 1990).

Section III. Global and Local: Societies, Environments and Globalization

Greene, K. and T. Moore. *Archaeology: An Introduction*, 5th edn., (London: Routledge, 2010).

Hendry, J. *Reclaiming Culture: Indigenous People and Self-representation*, (New York: Palgrave, 2005).

Howe, G.M. *People, Environment, Disease and Death: A Medical Geography of Britain Throughout the Middle Ages*, (Cardiff: Cardiff University Press, 1997).

Inda, J.X. and R. Rosaldo (eds). *The Anthropology of Globalisation: A Reader*, (Oxford: Blackwell, 2002).

Iwabuchi, K. *Recentering Globalization: Popular Culture and Japanese Transnationalism*, (Durham, NC: Duke University Press, 2003).

Kiple, K.F. (ed.) *The Cambridge World History of Human Disease*, (Cambridge: Cambridge University Press, 1993).

Matthews, G. *Global Culture/Individual Identity: Searching for Home in the Global Supermarket*, (London: Routledge, 2000).

Mays, S. *The Archaeology of Human Bones*, (London: Routledge, 2010).

Roberts C.A. *Human Remains in Archaeology: A Handbook*, (York: Council for British Archaeology, 2009).

Roberts C.A. and M. Cox. *Health and Disease in Britain: From Prehistory to the Present Day*, (Stroud: Sutton Publishing, 2003).

Roberts C.A. and K. Manchester. *The Archaeology of Disease*, 3rd edn. (Stroud: History Press, 2010).

Street, B. (ed.). *Literacies across Educational Contexts*, (Philadelphia: Caslan Press, 2005).

Section IV. Practising Anthropology: Methods and Investigations

Agar, M. *The Professional Stranger: An Informal Introduction to Ethnography*, (London: Academic Press, 1980).

Gay y Blasco, P. and H. Wardle. *How to Read Ethnography*, (London: Routledge, 2007).

Brothwell, D. *Digging Up Bones*, (London: Museum of Natural History, 1981).

Davies, C.A. *Reflexive Ethnography: A Guide to Researching Selves and Others*, (London: Routledge, 2008).

Ellen, R.F. (ed.) *Ethnographic Research: A Guide to Conduct*, (New York: Academic Press, 1984).

Finnegan, R. *Oral Traditions and the Verbal Arts: A Guide to Research Practices*, (London: Routledge, 1992).

Heath, S.B. and B. Street. *On Ethnography: Approaches to Language and Literacy Research*, (National Conference on Research in Language and Literacy; Teachers College Columbia, 2007).

Hendry, J. *An Anthropologist in Japan*, (London: Routledge, 1999).

McElroy, A. and P.K. Townsend. *Medical Anthropology in Ecological Perspective*, (Boulder, CO: Westview Press, 2009).

Okely, J. and H. Callaway (eds). *Anthropology and Autobiography*, (London: Routledge, 1992).

Okely, J. *Anthropological Practice: Fieldwork and the Ethnographic Method*, (Oxford: Berg, 2012).

Roberts, C., M. Byram, A. Barro and B. Street. *Language Learners as Ethnographers*, (2000).

Sayer, D. *Ethics and Burial Archaeology*, (London: Duckworth, 2010).

Spencer, D. and J. Davies (eds). *Anthropological Fieldwork: A Relational Process*, (Newcastle upon Tyne: Cambridge Scholars Publishing, 2010).

Strang, V. *What Anthropologists Do*, (Oxford: Berg, 2009).

Section V. Anthropology in the World

Day, S. *On the Game: Women and Sex Work*, (London: Pluto Press, 2007).

Edwards, J., P. Harvey and P. Wade (eds). *Anthropology and Science: Epistemologies in Practice*, (Oxford: Berg, 2007).

Evans, G. *Educational Failure and Working-class White Children in Britain*, (London: Palgrave MacMillan, 2006).

Gee, J., G. Hull and C. Lankshear. *The New Work Order: Behind the Language of the New Capitalism*, (London: Allen and Unwin, 1996).

Giddens, A. *Modernity and Self-identity: Self and Society in the Late Modern Age*, (Cambridge: Polity Press, 2000).

Hannerz, U. *Transnational Connections: Culture, People, Places*, (London: Routledge, 1996).

Kapferer, B. (ed.). *The World Trade Center and Global Crisis: Critical Perspectives*, (Oxford: Berghahn, 2004).

Lock, M. *Twice Dead: Organ Transplants and the Reinvention of Death*, (Berkeley: University of California Press, 2002).

MacClancy, J. (ed.). *Exotic No More: Anthropology on the Front Lines*, (Chicago: University of Chicago Press, 2002).

Macdonald, S. (ed.). *Inside European Identities: Ethnography in Western Europe*, (Oxford: Berg, 1993).

Miller, D. and D. Slater. *The Internet: An Ethnographic Approach*, (Oxford: Berg, 2000).

Ribeiro, G.L. and A. Escobar. *World Anthropologies: Disciplinary Transformations within Systems of Power*, (Oxford: Berg, 2006).

Wilson, R. and J.P. Mitchell. *Human Rights in Global Perspective: Anthropological Studies of Rights, Claims and Entitlements*, (London: Routledge, 2003).

Wright, S. (ed.). *Anthropology of Organizations*, (London: Routledge, 1994).

Index